Monetary Policy, Fiscal Policies and Labour Markets
Macroeconomic Policymaking in the EMU

T0312113

A few years after the birth of the European Monetary Union (EMU) economists are still divided in their assessment of the ability of its key institutions to provide macroeconomic stability and foster the reforms necessary to stimulate economic growth. In this collection, experts focus on issues of fiscal policy, monetary policy and labour markets and ask: Can the stability and growth pact provide an adequate framework for the conduct of national fiscal policies? Is the ECB reacting with competence and flexibility to a rapidly changing macroeconomic environment? How will national labour markets react to the new macroeconomic institutions and what are the structural reforms needed in labour markets? Blending empirical and theoretical data, this book offers one of the most comprehensive surveys of recent research in macroeconomic policymaking within the EMU today.

ROEL BEETSMA is a Professor of Macroeconomics at the University of Amsterdam and a Research Affiliate of the Center for Economic Policy Research, London.

CARLO FAVERO is Professor of Economics at the Università Bocconi, Milan.

ALESSANDRO MISSALE is Professor of Economics at the Università degli Studi di Milano.

ANTON MUSCATELLI is the Daniel Jack Professor of Political Economy, Department of Economics, University of Glasgow.

PIERGIOVANNA NATALE is Professor of Economics at the Università degli Studi di Milano-Bicocca.

PATRIZIO TIRELLI is Professor of Economics at the Università degli Studi di Milano-Bicocca.

Monetary Policy, Fiscal Policies and Labour Markets

Macroeconomic Policymaking in the EMU

Edited by

R. Beetsma, C. Favero, A. Missale, V. A. Muscatelli,
P. Natale and P. Tirelli

CAMBRIDGE
UNIVERSITY PRESS

CAMBRIDGE UNIVERSITY PRESS
Cambridge, New York, Melbourne, Madrid, Cape Town, Singapore, São Paulo

Cambridge University Press
The Edinburgh Building, Cambridge CB2 8RU, UK

Published in the United States of America by Cambridge University Press, New York

www.cambridge.org
Information on this title: www.cambridge.org/9780521823081

© Cambridge University Press 2004

First published 2004
This digitally printed version 2007

A catalogue record for this publication is available from the British Library

Library of Congress Cataloguing in Publication data
Monetary policy, fiscal policies, and labour markets: macroeconomic policymaking
in the EMU / edited by R. Beetsma . . . [et al.].
    p.   cm.
Includes bibliographical references and index.
ISBN 0 521 82308 0
1. Monetary policy – European Union countries.   2. Fiscal policy – European Union
countries.   3. Monetary unions – European Union countries.
I. Beetsma, Roel M. W. J.
HG925.M6589   2003   339.5′094 – dc21   2003051535

ISBN 978-0-521-82308-1 hardback
ISBN 978-0-521-04183-6 paperback

Contents

Part III   Labour markets

Figures

Tables

Contributors

FABIO C. BAGLIANO is Professor of Economics at the Università di Torino. He received his Ph.D. from the London School of Economics. His research interests span the fields of theoretical and applied monetary economics; econometric analysis of the monetary policy transmission mechanism; time-series macroeconometrics and financial economics. He is the author of two books and several articles published in the *European Economic Review*, the *Journal of Banking and Finance*, the *Journal of Macroeconomics, Empirical Economics, Economics Letters* and *Applied Economics Letters*.

ROEL BEETSMA is Professor of Macroeconomics at the University of Amsterdam and a research affiliate of the Centre for Economic Policy Research, London. He obtained his Ph.D. from CentER, Tilburg University. He has been a visiting scholar for a long period at DELTA in Paris (on a fellowship from the European Commission), at the University of British Columbia (Vancouver) and at the University of California at Berkeley. His main areas of research are the macroeconomic aspects of central bank independence, fiscal and monetary policy interactions, monetary unification and public debt. His work has been published in various journals, including the *American Economic Review* and the *Economic Journal*.

PIERPAOLO BENIGNO is Assistant Professor of Economics at New York University. He is a graduate from Bocconi University and holds a Ph.D. from Princeton University. He is a research affiliate of the Centre for Economic Policy Research, London. His current research focuses on the optimal conduct of monetary policy in a currency area, on the relation between monetary policy rules and the exchange rate and on the conditions under which price stability is optimal in open economies.

LILIA CAVALLARI is Professor of Economics at the Università di Roma III, where she teaches international and labour economics. She also served as a visiting professor at the Centre for European Integration Studies at Bonn University. She holds a Ph.D. from the Università di Roma I. Her research interests are in the field of international macroeconomics and finance and focus on both theoretical and applied monetary policy issues. Her articles have been published in various books and journals, most recently in the *Journal of International Economics*, the *International Journal of Finance and Economics*, *Economic Notes*, the *Scottish Journal of Political Economy* and *Empirica*.

STEPHEN G. CECCHETTI is currently Professor of Economics at Ohio State University, where he has worked since 1987. He is also a research associate of the National Bureau of Economic Research. From August 1997 to September 1999 he was Executive Vice-President and Director of Research at the Federal Reserve Bank of New York, as well as Associate Economist of the Federal Open Market Committee. He also served as a visiting professor of economics at several institutions, including the University of Melbourne in 1996, Boston College in 1994 and 1995 and Princeton University in 1992 and 1993. In addition to his teaching at Ohio State University, Professor Cecchetti has edited the *Journal of Money, Credit and Banking* since 1992, and is on the editorial boards of the *American Economic Review*, the *Journal of Economic Literature*, the Ohio State University Press as well as the Economic Policy Review Board of the Federal Reserve Bank of New York. He has published over fifty articles in academic and policy journals on a variety of topics, including banking, securities markets and monetary policy.

ALEX CUKIERMAN holds the Amnon Ben-Nathan Chair in Economics at the University of Tel-Aviv. His research interests cover macro and monetary economics with particular emphasis on the economics and politics of central banking, European monetary unification, political economy and the positive theory of economic policy, government debt and deficits, imperfect information, inflation and relative prices, inflationary expectations, applied econometrics and business cycles. He is a research fellow at the Centre for Economic Policy Research and at CentER, Tilburg University. He is a former president of the Israel Economic Association.

GIUSEPPE DE ARCANGELIS is Professor of Economics and teaches international economics and econometrics at the University of Bari. He is the author of numerous articles in international economics and applied monetary economics. He holds a Ph.D. from the University of Michigan.

XAVIER DEBRUN is an economist at the International Monetary Fund, Research Department, World Economic Studies Division. He holds a Ph.D. in international relations (economics) from the Graduate Institute of International Studies in Geneva, where he worked as a research assistant between 1997 and 1999 under the supervision of Charles Wyplosz. His research interests include European monetary integration, regional currency areas, the design of macroeconomic institutions and political economics. His work has been published in the *Economic Journal, Open Economies Review* and *Swedish Economic Policy Review*, among others.

CARLO A. FAVERO has been Professor of Econometrics at Università Bocconi since 1994. He has published in scholarly journals on applied econometrics, monetary policy and time-series models for macroeconomics. He is associate editor of the *European Economic Review*, a member of the editorial board of *Giornale degli Economisti* and a research fellow of CEPR in the International Macroeconomics programme. He is advisor to the Italian Treasury for the construction of an econometric model of the Italian economy and has been a consultant to the European Commission on monetary policy and the monetary transmission mechanism in the euro area.

ROBERTO GOLINELLI is Assistant Professor of Applied Econometrics at the Università di Bologna. His recent research focuses on monetary rules for economies in transition; on money demand in the euro area and on price adjustment mechanisms.

ANDREW HUGHES HALLETT is Professor of Economics at Vanderbilt University and Cardiff University. He is a graduate of Warwick University and the London School of Economics and holds a Ph.D. from Oxford University. He is currently a research fellow at the Centre for Economic Policy Research in London, and an editor of the *Scottish Journal of Political Economy*. He has published 200 papers in international academic journals and acted as consultant to IMF, the World Bank, the European Commission and the European Central Bank. His main research interests are in the fields of international economic policy, economic and monetary integration, game theory and policy coordination, the theory of economic policy and econometric modelling.

SVEND ERIK HOUGAARD JENSEN is Director of Research at the Centre for Economic and Business Research in Copenhagen and research associate at the Economic Policy Research Unit, University of Copenhagen.

SERENA LAMARTINA works as an economist at the Fiscal Policies Division of the European Central Bank. She holds an M.Sc. in economics from Birkbeck College in London and a Ph.D. in applied economics from Università di Roma 'La Sapienza'.

LUCA LAMBERTINI is Professor of Economics at the Università di Bologna. He holds a Ph.D. from the Università di Bologna and a D.Phil. in Economics from Linacre College, University of Oxford. He is a well-known industrial economist.

CAMPBELL BLAIR LEITH is a lecturer in the Department of Economics at the University of Glasgow. He received his Ph.D. from the University of

Exeter. His work is based on applied and theoretical macroeconomics, with particular emphasis on the analysis of monetary and fiscal policy. He has published in several academic journals and contributed to books published by Cambridge University Press and the MIT Press. He is a member of the European Economic Association, the Royal Economic Society and sits on the executive board of the Scottish Economic Society.

DAVID LÓPEZ-SALIDO has been a researcher at the Bank of Spain since 1986. He holds a Ph.D. from the Centre for Monetary and Financial Studies in Madrid. His current research focuses on the business cycle implications of imperfect competition and nomial rigidities for the design of monetary policy, as well as in the empirical relevance of optimising models of sticky prices and sticky wages.

ALESSANDRO MISSALE gained his Ph.D. from the MIT. At present, he is Professor in Economics at the Università degli Studi di Milano. His main field of research is public debt management, a topic on which he has published a book and written several articles. In 1997 Alessandro Missale held a Houblon-Norman Fellowship at the Bank of England.

CLAUDIO MORANA lectures at the Università del Piemonte Orientale. He holds a Ph.D. from the University of Aberdeen.

ANTON MUSCATELLI has been a Professor of Economics at Glasgow University since 1992 and is currently Dean of the Faculty of Social Sciences. His current fields of interest are monetary economics (including central bank independence and EMU) and macroeconomics. He is a member of the Council of the Royal Economic Society and has also served on the Panel of Economic Advisors of the Secretary of State for Scotland (1998–2000) and been a consultant to the European Commission and the ESRC. In the recent past he has acted as a consultant to National Australia Bank/Clydesdale Bank. Recent journal publications include papers in the *Journal of Monetary Economics*, the *Journal of International Economics*, the *Review of Economics and Statistics*, the *Economic Journal*, the *Journal of the Royal Statistical Society*, and *Economica*. He is the co-author of the best-selling textbook *Macroeconomic Theory and Stabilisation Policy* (with Andrew Stevenson and Mary Gregory).

PIERGIOVANNA NATALE is Professor of Economics at Università degli Studi di Milano-Bicocca. She holds a Ph.D. from Exeter University. Her recent work addresses the issue of institutional design in monetary policy.

LUCA ONORANTE is a researcher at the European University Institute, Department of Economics, and an economist in the Fiscal Policy Division of the

European Central Bank. His fields of interests are monetary economics and Macroeconomics, with a particular focus on EMU and fiscal and monetary policy.

RICCARDO ROVELLI is Professor of European Economic Integration at the Università di Bologna. His research interests are in the fields of monetary economics and macroeconomics, with special emphasis on issues related to the European Union and to accession countries. His recent research has focused on models of the transmission mechanism and design of monetary policy rules; financial fragility in emerging and transition economies and the evaluation of the pre-conditions for accession to the EU.

PATRIZIO TIRELLI is Professor of Economics at the Università di Milano-Bicocca. His current research interests cover the economics and politics of central banking, the interdependence between monetary and fiscal policies, and EMU institutional design. He has written a book on simple policy rules in the open economy and is the author of articles published in *Oxford Economic Papers*, *Economics and Politics*, *The Manchester School* and *Applied Economics*.

CARMINE TRECROCI is a lecturer at the Università di Brescia. He received his B.Sc. in Economics from the University of Calabria, and then proceeded to further research at the University of Glasgow, where he took an M.Sc. (1997) and a Ph.D. (2000) in economics. Prior to joining Brescia, he has conducted research and teaching activities for the University of Glasgow (1999–2000) and the University of Naples 'Federico II' (1997–2000) and has participated in a research programme for the European Central Bank in Frankfurt (1999). His research focuses on macroeconomics and financial economics, with particular emphasis on econometric analysis, structural change and forecasting.

SIMON WREN-LEWIS has been Professor of Economics at the University of Exeter since 1995. He began his career as an economist in the UK Treasury. In 1981 he moved to the National Institute of Economic and Social Research, where as a senior research fellow he constructed the first versions of the world model NIGEM, and as Head of Macroeconomic Research he supervised development of this and the Institute's domestic model. In 1990 he became a professor at Strathclyde University, and built the UK econometric model COMPACT. He has published papers on macroeconomics in a wide range of academic journals including the *Economic Journal*, the *European Economic Review* and the *American Economic Review*. His current research focuses on interactions between monetary and fiscal policy, and equilibrium exchange.

Acknowledgements

The editors wish to thank Luisa Lambertini (UCLA) who enthusiastically contributed to the conference organising committee. A large number of papers were presented during the Conference and we wish to thank all the participants. (Some of these papers have been published in *Ifo Studien*, while others are available at http://dipeco.economia.unimib.it/workemu/)

The conference received financial support from MURST (contract no. 9913572993/003), CNR (contract no. 98.03700ST74) and the University of Milano-Bicocca.

Last, but not least, Silvia Pesenti and the secretarial staff of the Department of Economics of the University of Milano-Bicocca played a key role in the success of the conference.

Editors' introduction

A few years after the birth of the Economic and Monetary Union (EMU) in Europe, it is still uncertain whether EMU institutions can provide sufficient macroeconomic stability and foster the reforms necessary to stimulate economic growth. The debate among economists and policymakers has focused on three key issues:

(i) Does the Stability and Growth Pact (SGP) provide an adequate framework for the conduct of national fiscal policies or is stricter coordination of fiscal policies desirable? There are three aspects to this debate. First, whether the SGP gives national governments sufficient room for manoeuvre in stabilising domestic economies. Some economists point out that national governments still retain full discretion within the 3% deficit ceiling set in the SGP, whilst others regard the SGP as too rigid to allow for adequate stabilisation policies. As a result, suggestions to soften the SGP or discard it altogether are sometimes floated in the press. Second, whether the SGP approach, which is based on individual country fiscal discipline, will lead to uncoordinated fiscal policies which are detrimental to macroeconomic stability in Euroland. Third, whether discretionary fiscal policies may be insufficiently coordinated and inconsistent with the common monetary policy even if they are consistent with the SGP limits.

(ii) Can the ECB provide markets with adequate information about its intentions? Moreover, is the ECB reacting with sufficient competence and flexibility to a rapidly changing macroeconomic environment? The 'two pillars strategy' for the conduct of monetary policy, the secrecy surrounding ECB Council decisions and the apparent inertia in the decision-making process have been widely criticised. The ECB has reacted by pointing to the difficulties of implementing a monetary policy in a highly uncertain environment, where national financial markets are still adjusting to monetary union.

(iii) How will national labour markets react to the new macroeconomic institutions? How will trade unions react to ECB policies? Will the new macroeconomic environment induce wage restraint or will it lead to larger increases in wage inflation because trade unions internalise to a lesser

1

extent the macroeconomic consequences of their actions? Will monetary union lead to a more competitive environment for firms and hence lower inflationary pressure? Finally, can we expect further structural reforms of the labour markets now that EMU has been established?

These issues were the focus of a conference hosted by the University of Milano-Bicocca in September 2001. This book collects the key contributions to that conference. It is divided in three parts: Monetary policy, Fiscal policies and Labour markets. Each part contains an up-to-date survey of recent research in the area and a number of state-of-the-art contributions to the topics discussed above.

The theoretical contributions apply new modelling approaches to issues that will be crucial for the conduct of EMU macroeconomic policies in the years to come. The empirical papers on monetary policy deal with issues which are central to the conduct and assessment of ECB policies, while the empirical analyses of fiscal policies are part of a largely unexplored area of research.

Part I: Monetary policy

In chapter 1, Steven Cecchetti offers interesting insights on the institutional structure of the ECB and on the 'two pillars strategy' for the conduct of monetary policy. He also draws a comparison between the Federal Reserve System in the United States and the 'federal' structure of the ESCB where – he argues – the national central banks still play a predominant role.

In chapter 2, Carlo Favero examines the ECB's announced goals and apparent strategies. Favero also reviews the issues related to the choice of the optimal price index target. As the optimal index is related to the driving forces behind the dynamics of inflation, the chapter provides a framework for the analysis of the other empirical papers in this section.

In chapter 3, Pierpaolo Benigno and David Lópes-Salido build a micro-founded model of EMU, characterised by regional asymmetries in inflation dynamics. In one region the Phillips curve is purely forward looking, as in the standard New Keynesian models. By contrast, the rest of the Union is charac-terised by a hybrid Phillips curve. The authors show that the optimal price index target should give more weight to the sluggish component of EMU inflation. They conclude that, when there are important asymmetries in inflation dynam-ics across countries, the ECB's choice of a target for the Harmonised Index of Consumer Prices (HICP) is suboptimal.

In chapter 4, Fabio Bagliano, Roberto Golinelli and Claudio Morana provide econometric tools to analyse and forecast EMU inflation dynamics, starting from a small-scale cointegrated VAR system. In order to supply information on the long-run inflation trend, a forward-looking core inflation measure is estimated, based on long-run relations among major macroeconomic variables. The proposed measure could provide a suitable inflation forecast for the ECB's monetary policy strategy.

Part II: Fiscal policies

In chapter 5, Roel Beetsma and Xavier Debrun provide an overview of recent research on the interactions between monetary and fiscal policy in the EMU. The literature centres on two main issues: (i) how fiscal discipline affects the credibility of monetary policy in a monetary union and (ii) the role of fiscal policy in the stabilisation of (asymmetric) shocks, given that monetary policy can only be used to stabilise union-wide disturbances. The authors also discuss the institutional arrangements designed to deal with discipline and stabilisation problems, reviewing both existing arrangements and proposals for alternatives.

In chapter 6, Luca Lambertini and Riccardo Rovelli consider a model with three players: the ECB and two national fiscal authorities (FA). No player has incentives to engage in time-inconsistent behaviour. The model therefore focuses purely on stabilisation policies. The authors argue that fiscal coordination is welfare enhancing, provided that the FAs internalise the price stability objective. However, incentives exist for each FA to deviate from cooperative agreements. As a result, the authors envisage a role for a supranational fiscal institution that should discipline the behaviour of national FAs.

In chapter 7, Luca Onorante adopts a similar modelling strategy, where the ECB is assumed to be relatively more inflation averse than national FAs. His contribution explores the details of fiscal–monetary coordination when each FA is imperfectly informed about cyclical conditions abroad. Although the sharing of information is generally welcomed by economists, the author shows that this is not the case when the FAs act as a Stackelberg leader *vis-à-vis* a conservative ECB. He argues that a mix of informal coordination (i.e. exchange of information) and binding rules best preserves the objective of long-term price stability.

In chapter 8, Campbell Leith and Simon Wren-Lewis simulate a two-country dynamic model, where fiscal policies are decentralised and a single Central Bank controls monetary policy. The purpose is to examine how the speed of debt stabilisation of each member state affects the ECB's ability to control inflation. It is shown that the speed of fiscal adjustment, even when it is asymmetric across EMU members, has little impact on the ECB's ability to control inflation. Of far greater importance is the inflationary impact of shocks when the degree of price stickiness varies across EMU member states. Simulations suggest that incentives may exist for economies with little nominal inertia to require structural reforms in less flexible economies, whose slow adjustment can have adverse consequences for the rest of the Union.

The last two contributions in this part of the book are empirical and dwell on a largely unexplored area of research, offering interesting insights into the actual conduct of fiscal policies in the pre-EMU era. Both apply structural vector autoregression techniques.

In chapter 9, Giuseppe De Arcangelis and Serena Lamartina analyse the conduct of fiscal policies in a number of OECD countries. They identify the fiscal policy rule followed in each of these countries, that is, they test whether tax decisions have preceded (different types of) expenditure decisions or vice-versa. More specifically, they find that in France and Italy, unlike Germany and the USA, government expenditures on wages and transfers have been the driving force behind the tax increases which characterised these countries. Furthermore, they measure the impact of different fiscal shocks on national outputs, finding that an increase in government expenditure on wages and transfers has a positive, but small, effect on output; a decrease in the tax rate has a positive, but only short-lived, effect on economic activity.

In chapter 10, Anton Muscatelli, Patrizio Tirelli and Carmine Trecroci present an empirical analysis of the interaction between fiscal and monetary policies as well as their interactions with output and inflation. This provides a benchmark for assessing the empirical relevance of new theories of the interdependence between fiscal and monetary policies. There is almost no empirical evidence to date on fiscal–monetary interdependence, so this contribution fills an important information gap in the policy debate on EMU. In general, the authors find that the interaction between fiscal and monetary policy has varied considerably over time, with fiscal policy becoming less concerned with short-term stabilisation goals in the post-Maastricht era. In addition, monetary and fiscal policies seem to have become less divergent since the 1980s.

Part III: Labour markets

In chapter 11, Alex Cukierman surveys recent developments regarding the strategic interaction between trade unions and the central bank. An important message from this literature is that monetary regimes affect both nominal and real wages when unions have at least some market power. This issue is obviously relevant for EMU, where collective agreements cover a large fraction of wage settlements. In this regard the author discusses some recent attempts to identify the impact of monetary unification on national labour markets.

In chapter 12, Lilia Cavallari explores the impact of monetary unification on national labour markets. She finds that monetary union may discipline workers and reduce unemployment when wage setters have market power. She also shows that this leads to higher union-wide inflation, unless wage setting is coordinated across the union's members. A novel feature of her contribution is the use of explicit microfoundations for the macroeconomic model, following the new literature on open economy macroeconomics.

In chapter 13, Andrew Hughes Hallett and Svend Hougaard Jensen study the incentives to enlarge a monetary union under alternative assumptions about the extent of market reform conducted within the union and in candidate countries. It turns out that candidate countries that have a preference for greater labour market flexibility would prefer to join EMU only after more reforms have been undertaken within the pre-existing union. The opposite holds for candidates that are less reformed than the pre-existing union. The chapter has important implications for the future membership of EMU and for the incentives for labour market reform in the Union as issues such as EU enlargement are confronted, and countries such as Sweden, the UK and Denmark contemplate joining EMU.

Part I

Monetary policy

1   The European Central Bank: a view from across the ocean

Stephen G. Cecchetti

As I write, the European Central Bank approaches its third anniversary of operational responsibility for the monetary policy of the Eurosystem.[1] The thousands of people involved in coaxing this new institution into existence have done an extraordinary job. Against formidable odds and the dire predictions of numerous observers, their insights and hard work have manufactured an extraordinary product. I am in awe of the job that has been done in Frankfurt by the Executive Board and the staff of the ECB itself, and by the governors and staffs of what today are twelve national central banks (the NCBs) who have joined the European Monetary Union. The real measure of the success of the European System of Central Banks (ESCB) is how truly minor all of our criticisms are. I seriously doubt that any of us could have done better.

In this chapter I will comment on a number of aspects of the ESCB. Throughout I will try to provide comparisons with the structure of other central banks, especially the Federal Reserve System. I begin with a discussion of institutional structure, followed by a critical examination of the Eurosystem's 'two-pillar' policy strategy. I then discuss issues of communication and transparency, followed by a very brief examination of policy performance and a conclusion that describes some future challenges.

1   Institutional structure

Economists often ignore one of the central precepts of other social science disciplines: institutional structure is crucial for policy outcomes. The design of the ESCB embodies the received wisdom of a century of monetary policy-making. The lessons of history are numerous, and they have all been absorbed. For example, operational policy of the Eurosystem is centrally controlled – a lesson the Federal Reserve System did not learn until the 1930s. Care has been taken to ensure that the ECB is independent from political influence, thereby

This paper was prepared for the conference on EMU Macroeconomic Institutions at Università di Milano-Bicocca, 20–22 September 2001.
[1] I have adopted the nomenclature described in European Central Bank (2001).

avoiding problems that plagued the monetary policy of industrialised and emerging countries alike in the post-war period.

On its surface, the ESCB resembles the Federal Reserve System (FRS). There are twelve regional banks with a central board. But there are important differences. In the Federal Reserve System there is a sense in which the Board of Governors is in control. At the ECB, casual observation suggests that the reverse is true. While the Board of Governors supervises the regional Federal Reserve Banks, approving their budgets and overall management decisions, in the ESCB it is the NCB governors who supervise the ECB.

The Governing Council of the ECB resembles the Federal Open Market Committee (FOMC) on the surface as well. The former is composed of the six members of the Executive Board and the governors of the euro area NCBs, and the latter includes the seven governors of the Federal Reserve Board (the Governors) and the twelve regional Federal Reserve Bank presidents (the Presidents). Both formulate monetary policy.

But again, appearances can be deceiving. While decisions in both bodies appear to be taken by consensus, as a technical matter only five of the Reserve Bank presidents vote at any one time. This means that the Governors always comprise a substantial majority and can outvote the Presidents. In Europe, the claim is that the Governing Council does not take formal votes, but even so the NCB governors outnumber the Executive Board members by two to one.

In my view, the most important difference between the FRS and the Eurosystem policymaking procedures arises from the fact that all of the information provided to the FOMC comes from the staff of the Board of Governors. There is virtually no relevant information that either comes or is produced in consultation with the staffs of the regional Federal Reserve Banks that finds its way into the hands of all of the participants at an FOMC meeting. In my experience, the only information to be universally distributed was generated by the Board of Governors in Washington DC. The ESCB has an elaborate committee structure that was created to ensure that information from the NCBs had a natural and straightforward way to enter into the policymaking process. This means that economic forecasts, for example, are constructed with explicit input from the staffs of all of the central banks in the Eurosystem.

Beyond the frequency of the policy meetings (the Governing Council meets three times as often as the FOMC), they also differ substantially in attendance. As I understand it, the Governing Council meets alone (with the exception of someone charged with recording minutes). By contrast, FOMC meetings include between twenty and thirty staff members as well as the nineteen principals.[2] Each Reserve Bank President has one staff member present, and a number of members of the Federal Reserve Board staff are in attendance as well.

---

[2] For a description of the mechanics of FOMC meetings see Meyer (1998).

Furthermore, at FOMC meetings the staff participates actively. But again, it is primarily the staff of the Federal Reserve Board that does the talking. With the exception of the System Open Market Account Manager, who is an employee of the Federal Reserve Bank of New York, in my two years attending FOMC meetings I never heard any staff member of a Reserve Bank speak. Only Federal Reserve Board staff spoke.[3] This, along with the fact that the Governors speak among themselves about policy, serves to further increase the influence of the Board members over the policy outcomes.

There is one more important difference between the FRS and the ESCB: the ECB is a bank while the Board of Governors is not. As a consequence, the ECB itself is capable of operating in financial markets – and it has done so. Surely, the ESCB structure is set up to ensure that the bulk of operations take place at the NCBs. In many ways, this is the remaining role of these satellites of the ESCB system. But how long can a system be maintained that has (currently) thirteen separate operating locations, each with nearly the same capability?

The logic of having NCBs maintain regular financial operations is that these central banks have special knowledge of the mechanisms and participants in their local national markets. But since one of the major goals of monetary union is to accelerate the development of a pan-European financial system, it is just a matter of time before things are centralised. There will be an inexorable pull towards the centre, draining resources and power from the periphery.

A number of observers have noted the potential problems created by one country/one vote on the Governing Council.[4] This creates an inexorable pull toward the median country, and could compromise the objective of stabilising euro-area prices. Both von Hagen and Brückner (2003) and Alesina et al. (2001) suggest that, if this were the outcome, the Executive Board would not be doing its job. The majority of the evidence clearly suggests that the Governing Council is following its mandate, and not behaving in a nationalistic way.

2   Policy objectives and policy strategy

There are numerous detailed descriptions of ESCB policy strategy and the problems it has created.[5] As mandated in Article 105(1) of the Maastricht Treaty, 'the primary objective of the ESCB shall be to maintain price stability' and the

---

[3] Meyer (1998) confirms this.

[4] Allowing for each EMU country to have a vote on the ECB Governing Council will eventually create an additional problem as the number of countries participating in monetary union grows. With twelve countries in EMU there are eighteen voting members of the Governing Council. Without any change in the voting rules, and if countries joining the European Union become members of the Eurosystem, this number could potentially become much larger, thereby hampering the ability of the Council to arrive at consensus decisions.

[5] For a description of the strategy see European Central Bank (2001). The difficulties are discussed in von Hagen and Brückner (2003), among others.

ESCB shall 'without prejudice to the objective of price stability, . . . support the general economic policies in the Community with a view to contributing to the achievement of the objectives of the Community', including 'a high level of employment . . . substantial and non-inflationary growth, a high degree of competitiveness and convergence of economic performance'. This is what Federal Reserve Board Governor Laurence Meyer has called a *hierarchical objective* – price stability first, other things second.

Implementation of monetary policy required that the Governing Council define what is meant by the term *price stability*, and that it formulate a policy strategy. An 18 October 1998 press release entitled 'A stability-oriented monetary policy strategy for the ESCB' provided important operational details as to how this objective would be addressed. That press release (which is available on the ECB's website at http://www.ecb.int) stated that the policy strategy would have the following three components:

1. The operational definition of price stability would be inflation in the Harmonised Index of Consumer Prices (HICP) of less than 2% per year, in the medium term.[6]
2. Money would be assigned a prominent role in the evaluation of financial market conditions, and this role would be signalled by the announcement of a quantitative reference value for the growth rate of a broad monetary aggregate – they have chosen euro-area M3.
3. A broadly based assessment of the outlook for future price developments and the risks to price stability in the euro area would play a major role.

Let us take a look at each of these in turn. First, defining price stability in a clear quantitative manner is extremely difficult. Every inflation measure that we have available to us has its problems. They are all distorted by problems with weighting, with quality changes, with the introduction of new goods, with changes in expenditure patterns, and the like. The HICP has a particular problem in that it currently does not include owner-occupied housing. Given the high home-ownership rate in Europe, this is an unfortunate omission.

In looking at central bank strategies for achieving price stability objectives, the time horizon is often a subject of heated debate. Here, again, the ESCB has been criticised for its vague use of the phrase 'medium term'. My view is that this is not a serious issue. I agree with Mervyn King (1999), who argues that central banks with inflation objectives will ultimately be held accountable in such a way as to make the time horizon irrelevant. As King notes, if a central bank has a 2% target, then after ten years the question will be whether inflation averaged less than 2% over the entire period. The overriding issue is that longer

---

[6] The ESCB was criticised from various quarters for not stating that the operational definition was inflation in the HICP of between 0% and 2%. The suggestion was that somehow the current formulation left open the possibility of deflation. I view this criticism as inaccurate and generally unfair, as the term *inflation* clearly implies a positive value.

time horizons give somewhat more flexibility in responding to short-run real factors. Here, I believe the ESCB has done the right thing.

Let me digress briefly to note that, by comparison, the objectives of Federal Reserve System monetary policy are extremely unclear. The language contained in the Full Employment and Balanced Growth Act of 1978 currently guides monetary policy in the United States. It states there that the Board of Governors and the FOMC are required to 'maintain growth of money and credit aggregates commensurate with the economy's long-run potential to increase production, so as to promote effectively the goals of maximum employment, stable prices and moderate long-term interest rates'. This has been interpreted to mean that monetary policy should foster maximum sustainable growth and price stability.

Importantly, though, there are no numbers attached to what is meant by any of this. Federal Reserve Board chairman Alan Greenspan has said, 'We will be at price stability when households and businesses need not factor expectations of changes in the average price level into their decisions.'[7] But this statement seems very imprecise. What level of what price index constitutes price stability? Different people will have different interpretations.

The lack of clarity in the objectives of the FOMC creates an enormous problem for decisionmaking. How can a committee agree on policy actions if they do not agree on their objectives even privately among themselves? Surely it would be a step in the right direction to follow the suggestion of Governor Meyer (2001) that the FOMC adopt an explicit definition of price stability and make it publicly known.

We now move on to the second two components of the strategy, often referred to as the 'two pillars'. These are the prominent role for money and the use of a range of indicators for future price developments. The first of these has come under substantial attack, and I will now join the chorus. As Alesina et al. (2001) write, the ultimate goal of the ESCB is to keep inflation low. In fact, they have been doing something that closely resembles inflation-forecast targeting. It is difficult to see in this context why M3 is special.

What is the logic of this first pillar?[8] I think that the best explanation is based on politics and sociology, not economics. When creating a new institution, constructive ambiguity is often essential. In the case of the ECB, no one really knew what was going to work, and so the Governing Council hedged by saying they would look at money on the one hand, and everything on the other. Beyond this, the difficulties of reaching consensus in a group of people with diverse backgrounds who have not worked together before was surely difficult, at least initially.

---

[7] See Greenspan (1994).

[8] In chapter 5 of European Central Bank (2001) there is a lengthy attempt to justify the two-pillar strategy on economic grounds. I find the discussion unconvincing.

But we are now three years on, and the same arguments no longer apply. Instead, we can think of the ECB as just another central bank that controls interest rates in an effort to meet an inflation objective. Money is surely helpful in doing this, but then so are many other things. I agree with those who have said that this first pillar stands in the way of effective communication.

Beyond these conceptual issues, it is worth noting that the first pillar of the policy strategy has already caused some technical problems. The ECB defines M3 to include only currency, deposits and marketable financial instruments held by euro area residents (European Central Bank 2001: 32–3). Needless to say, it is difficult to discern the ultimate owner of deposit accounts or liquid financial instruments, and so estimating the size of euro-area M3 is not a trivial task. This difficulty created substantial problems in the spring of 2001. In his news conference on 10 May 2001 ECB President Duisenberg stated that 'there have been indications that the monetary growth figures are distorted upwards by non-euro area residents' purchases of negotiable paper included in M3. This has now been confirmed by clear evidence, and the magnitudes involved are significant.'

All of this suggests to me that the ECB should discard the first pillar of its policy strategy. There is precedent for throwing central bank articulated ranges for money growth overboard. In the Federal Reserve Board's 20 July 2000 *Monetary Policy Report to Congress* there is a footnote that reads:[9]

At its June meeting, the FOMC did not establish ranges for growth of money and debt in 2000 and 2001. The legal requirement to establish and to announce such ranges had expired, and owing to uncertainties about the behavior of the velocities of debt and money, these ranges for many years have not provided useful benchmarks for the conduct of monetary policy. Nevertheless, the FOMC believes that the behavior of money and credit will continue to have value for gauging economic and financial conditions, and this report discusses recent developments in money and credit in some detail.

This statement concisely summarises my own views, and leads me to the conclusion that the first pillar of the ESCB's monetary policy strategy should be jettisoned.[10]

Turning briefly to the second pillar, who can argue with the strategy of using a broadly based assessment of future price developments? Addressing uncertainties by bringing all possible information to bear – including that in broad monetary aggregates – is the obvious thing to do. Importantly, though, it leads to inflation-forecast targeting, and it would be helpful if the ESCB made it clear that this is what they are doing.

---

[9] This is footnote 2 in section 1 of the report. It is available on the Federal Reserve Board's website at http://www.federalreserve.gov/boarddocs/hh/2000/July/ReportSection1.htm:

[10] I would go even further and argue that the term 'monetary policy' should be changed to 'central bank policy' so as to change the impression that it has anything directly to do with money.

3   Communication and transparency

The next issue is communication and transparency. This is where the ESCB has, in my view, been at its worst. Let me give just one example from the spring of 2001. During March and April of that year there were numerous calls for policy easing. These came from places like the IMF, the OECB and the United States Treasury. Critics cited evidence of an impending slowdown in euro-area growth as the rationale for interest rate cuts. Initially, the ESCB responded that its objective was price stability, and inflation was in fact increasing. Its policy of maintaining relatively higher interest rates was consistent with this objective. As ECB President Wim Duisenberg famously said on 11 April 2001 'I hear, but I do not listen.'

On 10 May 2001 the Governing Council reduced the target-refinancing rate by 25 basis points, claiming that its long-term price stability objective was not in jeopardy. The stated reason for this policy reversal was that euro-area M3 had been mismeasured (see the previous quote). When the correction was made, and inflation forecasts were adjusted, the proper policy was to ease.

The ridicule was immediate and deafening. The *Financial Times* headline was the mildest: 'European central bank rate cut trips up markets.' Things only got worse, as one week later there was a report of a sharp rise in the euro-area inflation measure to a five-month high of 2.9% in April 2001, compared with 2.6% in March. The general reaction was that this surely wasn't consistent with HICP inflation of less than 2%.

What is it about the ESCB's communication strategy that has been such a failure? To understand, let us consider how an idealised central bank would communicate publicly. Blinder et al. (2001) argue that in creating transparent and clear communication a central bank must reveal

- what it is trying to achieve,
- the methods, data and models used for analysis,
- the substance of the policy deliberations, including which arguments have carried the day, how convincing they were and the degree of certainty surrounding current conditions.

I believe that on the first two of these, the ESCB has done well. It has been clear about what it is trying to do, and it has provided substantial insights into its data, models and forecasts. It is the third point, transparency of the substance of policy deliberations that is the source of the problems. Here, the Governing Council speaks in many voices, and they are occasionally at odds.

There are several possible solutions to this communication problem. Blinder et al. suggest shrinking the size of the Governing Council to reduce the likelihood of disgruntled members airing their disagreements in public. This is probably politically impossible. But why not issue minutes of meetings when they still matter?

4   Performance

Results are the real test of policy. Numerous people have examined the brief history of ECB policy in various ways. A decade ago John Taylor (1993) suggested the history of the US Federal Funds Rate could be adequately explained by a simple rule in which the policy rate depended on a long-run equilibrium interest rate, the deviation of inflation from a target level and the output gap. It has become very fashionable for academic researchers to compare actual interest rate paths to those implied by various version what are commonly called 'Taylor rules', and analysis of the ECB is no different.[11]

Such exercises conclude that interest rates were initially too low, and later were too high. I would ask whether it is possible to actually evaluate policy using such an exercise. If the rule had been followed at the beginning of the period, then inflation and growth would have been different later. This is obvious, and what it means is that you cannot look at the actual policy relative to a Taylor-style rule without embedding the rule in a fully articulated dynamic structural model of the euro area.

Originally, Taylor viewed this as a way of summarising policy history, not as a prescription for future action. In recent years, researchers and policymakers have taken this rule and examined its properties for policymaking. Such exercises must be done with great care, however. In particular, evaluation of the rule can only be done if it is embedded into a dynamic model of the economy as changes in the interest-rate instrument that deviate from historical experience will drive inflation and output away from their historical paths as well.

Rather than build such a model (or borrow one) I will simply look at the performance of the ESCB since its inception. Figures 1.1 and 1.2 plot GDP growth and inflation in the euro area. Growth data begin in 1992 and inflation data in 1996 – this is what is available from Eurostat and the ECB. It is surely difficult to tell from these data what the consequence of recent policy will be, but we can nevertheless make a preliminary evaluation. The results give the impression that policy has been more successful in fostering steady growth than in keeping inflation in check. The fact that HICP inflation has risen unabated since the ESCB started on 1 January 1999 is somewhat troubling, and provides support for the von Hagen and Brückner conclusion that policy was too loose early on. It is harder to argue that it became too contractionary, as inflation has continued its rise.

5   Future challenges

The report so far is of a new institution that has faced numerous challenges head on and emerged only mildly bruised. It is difficult to see how things could have

[11] See, for example, von Hagen and Brückner (2003).

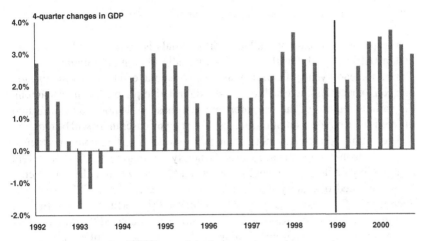

Figure 1.1 Real GDP growth in the euro area

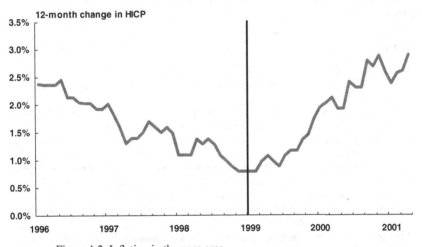

Figure 1.2 Inflation in the euro area

turned out any better than they have. But this is not the end of the story. The future challenges of the ESCB are nearly as daunting as those that have passed.

The biggest problem facing the ESCB is dealing with what is likely to be a constant conflict among national interests in policy setting. Recent reports have suggested that the right policy for Germany is more stimulus, while France might be better off if policy were tighter.[12] Inflation and growth differentials

---

[12] See 'The Right Rate for Europe?', *Wall Street Journal*, 17 May 2001, p. A18.

across the euro area will continue and create the need for a delicately balanced policy.[13]

The problem of national inflation differentials is compounded by the fact that, as Alesina et al. (2001) emphasise, not all inflation differentials are bad. During the early years of currency union and general economic harmonisation one can expect that there will be substantial relative price adjustments among the various regions of the euro area and that these will show up as measured differences in national inflation indices. But in many cases these will be required real economic adjustments, not inflation differentials creating policy problems.

In writing this chapter I have joined the nearly continuous stream of observers commenting on the performance of European Monetary Union. But in the end, I am reminded of a story that is told about a meeting in 1972 between US Secretary of State Henry Kissinger and Chinese Prime Minister Chou En Lai. According to the story, Kissinger asked Chou if he believed that when all its consequences were taken into account the 1789 French Revolution benefited humanity. Chou is reputed to have replied 'It is too early to tell.'[14] So too for the early years of the European System of Central Banks – it is still too early to tell.

REFERENCES

Alesina, A., O. Blanchard, J. Galí, F. Giavazzi and H. Uhlig, 2001, *Defining a Macroeconomic Framework for the Euro Area* (*Monitoring the European Central Bank*, vol. 3), London: CEPR.

Blinder, A., Charles Goodhart, Philipp Hildebrand, David Lipton and Charles Wyplosz, 2001, *How Do Central Banks Talk?*, Geneva Reports on the World Economy no. 3, International Center for Monetary and Banking Studies and Centre for Economic Policy Research.

Cecchetti, Stephen G., Nelson C. Mark and Robert Sonora, 2002, 'Price Level Convergence among United States Cities: Lessons for the European Central Bank', *International Economic Review* 43(4), 1081–99.

European Central Bank, 2001, *The Monetary Policy of the ECB*, Frankfurt am Main: European Central Bank.

Greenspan, Alan, 1994, 'Statement before the Subcommittee on Economic Growth and Credit Formulation of the Committee on Banking, Finance and Urban Affairs', US House of Representatives, 22 February.

King, Mervyn, 1999, 'Challenges for Monetary Policy: New and Old', in Federal Reserve Bank of Kansas City, *Challenges for Monetary Policy*, Proceedings of the Symposium, pp. 11–57.

Meyer, Laurence H., 1998, 'Come with Me to the FOMC', The Gills Lecture, Willamette University, Salem, OR, 2 April.

---

[13] See Cecchetti, Mark and Sonora (2002) for a discussion of how persistent inflation differentials are likely to be.

[14] Unfortunately, I have not been able to find any reliable source for this exchange, which may well be apocryphal. It is, however, a good story.

2001, 'Inflation Targets and Inflation Targeting', remarks at the University of California at San Diego Economics Roundtable, 17 July.

Taylor, John B., 1993, 'Discretion versus Policy Rules in Practice', *Carnegie-Rochester Conference on Public Policy* 39: pp. 195–214.

Taylor, John B. (ed.), 1999, *Monetary Policy Rules*, Chicago: University of Chicago Press for NBER.

von Hagen, Jürgen and M. M. Brückner, 2003, 'Monetary Policy in Unknown Territory: The European Central Bank in the Early Years', in D. Altig and B. Smith (eds.), *The Origins of Central Banking*, New York: Cambridge University Press.

2   Which measure of inflation should the ECB target?

C. A. Favero

1   Introduction

The ECB has intepreted its mandate for price stability as keeping the inflation of the Harmonised Index of Consumer Prices (HICP) between 0 and 2% per year, in the medium term. Price indexes such the HICP for the euro area are constructed to measure the cost of living and are not necessarily the best target for monetary policy. Two contributions in this part of the book deal with the measure of an appropriate inflation target for the ECB. I shall introduce the issue by first reviewing three years of ECB activity, as seen and judged by different groups of academic ECB watchers. The evidence shows that the uncertainty surrounding estimated econometric relationships is rather high, so high that it is very hard to extract from the data an assessment of the consistency between the deeds and the words of the European Central Bank. In fact, despite its apparently tight formulation, the mandate of the ECB, interpreted in the light of the uncertainty surrounding those relationships among the data relevant to the application of such a mandate, leaves plenty of room for flexibility. In other words, the fact that inflation has been above its target for more than twenty-four months since January 2000 does not lead to the rejection of the null hypothesis that the ECB has not violated its mandate. Some watchers have proposed to deal with uncertainty by choosing inflation of less volatile indexes. Others have proposed to use uncertainty and target aggregates other than the HCPI, with weights chosen optimally for monetary policy purposes rather than for statistical purposes.

The empirical evidence leads naturally to the question, 'Is there an optimal price index for monetary policy?' There are many things that the ECB can do. Given room for manoeuvre, it is important to establish a benchmark for the optimal price index for monetary policy and evaluate the difficulties in its empirical implementation. I would like to put the two other contributions of this section in this general framework. Therefore, I shall use a model by Mankiw and Reis (2002) to set the scenario within which discuss the proposals made by Benigno and López-Salido and by Bagliano, Golinelli and Morana in the two subsequent chapters.

2　Objective and strategies of the ECB: the mandate

Article 105(1) of the Maastricht Treaty states that the primary objective of the ESCB is to maintain price stability: 'without prejudice to the objective of price stability, the ESCB shall support the general economic policies in the Community with a view to contributing to the achievement of the objectives of the Community', including 'a high level of employment . . . substantial and non-inflationary growth, a high degree of competitiveness and convergence of economic performance'.

By definition, price stability means zero inflation. However, the Maastricht Treaty does not specify which price index is the relevant one for monetary policy. In a press release of October 1998 entitled 'A Stability-Oriented Monetary Policy Strategy for the ESCB' all the relevant operational details are provided. The ECB policy strategy has the following three main components:

- The operational definition of price stability is inflation of the Harmonised Index of Consumer Prices (HICP) between 0% and 2% per year, in the medium term.
- The first pillar of the ECB monetary policy strategy is money: a quantitative reference for the growth rate of M3 has been set at 4.5% and kept at that value until the time of writing this chapter.
- The second pillar of the monetary policy strategy would be a broad based assessment of the outlook for future price developments and the risks to price stability in the euro area would play a major role.

The target is then specified very strictly and the strategy is very tightly defined.

3　Objective and strategies of the ECB: the data

In spite of the interesting story about the 1972 meeting between Henry Kissinger and Chou En Lai mentioned by Stephen Cecchetti on page 18 above, I believe it is important to look at the actual data over the period 1999–2002 and evaluate them against the apparently strictly stated ECB mandate. Figure 2.1 shows the annual rate of growth of HICP, the annual rate of growth of M3, and the EONIA, the euro-denominated overnight interest rate, all data being measured at monthly frequency.

The facts are that over the period in which the ECB has been operating HICP inflation has been above target for well over two years after January 2000, the annual rate of growth of M3 has never been below the reference value, the correlation between money growth and inflation has been −0.26, while the correlation between the policy rate and inflation has been of 0.87.

These facts have been the focus of the work of ECB watchers during the ECB's first three years. The CEPR watchers in 2000 (Favero et al. 2000) looked

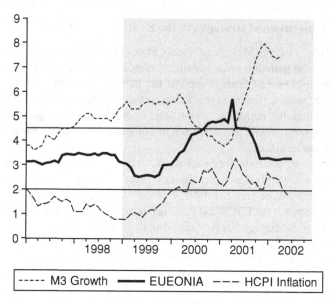

Figure 2.1 Annual rate of growth of HICP, M3, and the EONIA

at ECB behaviour in 1999 by simulating different Taylor rules and found that the reaction of the ECB to the Euro-wide one-year-ahead expected inflation and output gap was not statistically different from what the Fed or the Bundesbank would have done if faced with the same macroeconomic conditions. However, the data were also consistent with monetary targeting. Interestingly, the worst performing rule was one based on giving different weights to macroeconomic conditions in different countries. However, even the data counterfactually simulated from the worst performing rule were not outside the 95% confidence interval of the baseline simulation. The watchers concluded that '. . . on the basis of deeds and words to date, it is extremely hard to judge what kind of animal the ECB is . . .'

The ECB watchers of 2001 (Alesina et al. 2001), with one more year of available data, observed that a hybrid rule with the Central Bank responding quite aggressively to both core inflation and the inflation forecast (both expressed in deviation from a target of 2% and both receiving equal weights) could track closely ECB interest rate decisions. Neither the output gap nor money growth played any role in the preferred rule to explain ECB behaviour. In fact when discussing the M3 pillar the CEPR watchers did not lose the opportunity of quoting from Lars Svensson (Alesina et al. 2000, p. 97) 'the first pillar is actually a brick'.

The preferred rule of the ECB watchers of 2001 was quickly dismissed by the 2002 group (Begg et al. 2002), who reverted to a more traditional rule giving weights to both inflation and the output gap. The watchers also re-emphasised the importance of uncertainty showing that the confidence intervals on simulated rates when the simulation is started at the beginning of 2000 have a lower limit at 2.4% and an upper limit at 5% at the end of 2001 to reach a lower limit of 2% and an upper limit of 7% at the end of 2002. Again M3 played no role; in fact, the attack on the first pillar reached its strongest peak in this year. Leaving aside the label of 'poison pillar', the report convincingly shows that the correlation between money growth and inflation in the long run vanishes at low levels of inflation. In fact, such correlation ceases to exist when countries with inflation below 5% are considered.

Overall, three years of monitoring the ECB based on estimated Taylor rules shows that the uncertainty surrounding estimated econometric relationships is rather high, so high that it is very hard to extract from the data an assessment of the consistency between the deeds and the words of the European Central Bank, or indeed of any central bank. In fact, despite its apparently tight formulation, the mandate of the ECB, interpreted in light of the uncertainty surrounding the relevant relationships among the data relevant for the application of such a mandate, leaves plenty of room for flexibility. Interestingly, the information in the data is sufficiently powerful to reject the null that the ECB has been following a strict monetary targeting strategy. But, of course, the importance of the first pillar could be defended by stating that a reference value for money growth is not a target.

Three years of econometric evidence on European monetary policy show that the operational definition of price stability is inflation of the HICP of between 0% and 2% per year, with a rather wide confidence interval around the target in the medium term. This evidence leads to a rather traditional communication problem. In fact, the literal interpretation by the public of the wording of the mandate might lead to an underestimation of uncertainty surrounding inflation. The CEPS ECB watching group (see Gros et al., 2000, 2002) has been constantly worried about this issue and has proposed that the target be based not on HICP inflation but on core inflation, with an explicit confidence interval (target at 1.5% for core inflation with an upper limit at 2.5% and a lower limit of 0.5%. Core inflation is defined by the CEPS as the consumer price index excluding the most volatile components (food and energy).) Note that the CEPS proposal deals with uncertainty about economic data in two ways: first, data are smoothed by changing the relevant definition of inflation; second, uncertainty is explicitly recognised by specifying limits around the target.

A proper evaluation of the ECB monitors' proposals requires the explicit specification of an optimal price index for monetary policy and a careful discussion of the problems likely to be encountered in its empirical implementation.

4   Optimal price indexes for monetary policy

Price indexes, such the HICP for the euro area, are constructed to measure the cost of living. Within such a framework different goods are naturally weighted by the share of each of them in the budget of the typical consumer. Indeed the ECB has chosen to target the HICP but, as documented in the previous section, annual inflation has been above target for some considerable time.

A possible interpretation of such evidence is that price indexes designed to measure the cost of living are not necessarily the best target for monetary policy. In fact, there are plenty of historical example of monetary regimes targeting inflation with non-standard price indexes: the price of gold is the implicit target in a gold standard, the price of foreign currency is the implicit target in a fixed exchange rate system. There are also examples in which asset prices have been included along with the prices of goods and services in the relevant index for monetary policy (remember the several calls for Fed tightening to dampen 'asset price inflation' during the US stock-market boom in the 1990s), or of modifying the price index to measure core inflation rather than headline inflation and purge the data of the effects of the most volatile components of inflation.

I shall use a model recently proposed by Mankiw and Reis (2002) to frame the choice of the price index for monetary policy in the context of optimisation.

Consider a central bank committed to inflation targeting in the sense that the institution must choose a price index and commit itself to keeping that index on target, before shocks are realised (forecast inflation targeting). The model includes many sectoral prices which differ according to a number of features[1]:
- Sectors differ in their budget share and thus in the weights attributed to their prices in standard cost of living index.
- The degree of sensitivity to the business cycle varies across sectors.
- The size of sector specific, i.e. idiosyncratic, shocks varies across sectors.
- The degree of flexibility of prices varies across sectors.

The supply curve in each sector k can be written as

$$p_k = \lambda_k p_k^* + (1 - \lambda_k) E(p_k^*)$$

$$p_k^* = p + \alpha_k y + \varepsilon_k$$

$$p = \sum_{k=1}^{K} \theta_k p_k$$

---

[1] When applying the model to the euro area the sectoral dimension might be interpreted as a participating country dimension.

where all variables are expressed in logs, p_k^* is the equilibrium price in sector k, p is the conventional measure of the price level with θ_k being the share of the kth good in the budget of the typical consumer, y is a measure of economic activity, say output, ε_k is an idiosyncratic shock with zero mean and sectoral specific variance, and the parameters α_k and λ_k measure respectively the degree of sensitivity of prices to the business cycle and the degree of flexibility of prices. The central bank is committed to target inflation, i.e. to keep to a weighted average of sectoral prices at the given level. So we have

$$\sum_{k=1}^{K} \omega_k p_k = 0,$$

$$\sum_{k=1}^{K} \omega_k = 1.$$

Importantly, the target weights ω_k are to be chosen by the central bank taking sectoral characteristics as exogenous. Without prejudice to the objective of price stability, the central bank supports the general economic policy in the community with a view to contributing to the achievement of the objectives of the community, including a high level of employment, substantial and non-inflationary growth and a high degree of competitiveness and convergence of economic performance. In other words, its goal is to minimise $Var(y)$. If we abstract from the problem of monetary control by assuming away any uncertainty on the demand side of the model (the central bank can hit precisely whatever nominal target it chooses) the optimisation problem of the monetary policymaker can be stated as follows:

$$\min_{\{\omega_k\}} Var(y)$$

subject to

$$\sum_{k=1}^{K} \omega_k p_k = 0, \quad \sum_{k=1}^{K} \omega_k = 1,$$

$$p_k = \lambda_k p_k^* + (1 - \lambda_k) E(p_k^*),$$

$$p_k^* = p + \alpha_k y + \varepsilon_k,$$

$$p = \sum_{k=1}^{K} \theta_k p_k,$$

Mankiw and Reis (2002) work out a full solution to the problem in the two-sector case. In general they show that a CPI target is suboptimal. In particular they show that:

- the more responsive a sector is to the business cycle, the more weight that sector's price should receive in the optimal price index,
- the greater the magnitude of idiosyncratic shocks in a sector, the less weight that sector price should receive in the optimal price index,
- the more flexible a sector's price, the less weight that sector's price should receive in the stability price index,
- the more important a price is in the consumer price index, the less weight that sector price should receive in the optimal price index,
- if the two sectors are identical in all respects except price flexibility, then the monetary authority should target the price level of the sticky price sectors.

The two authors also apply their model to annual data for the US economy from 1957 to 2001. They examine four sectoral prices: food, energy, other goods and services and the level of nominal wages. They obtain two main results:

- The optimal price index gives most of its weight to the level of nominal wages.
- The gain in economic stability from targeting the optimal price index is rather large: moving the target from the consumer price index to the optimally weighted price index halves the variance of output.

These results are interesting but they probably give insufficient weight to the risk of targeting an optimal price index. Such risk crucially depends on the correct specification of the chosen model and on the uncertainty surrounding the relevant parameters in the definition of the optimal price index. The two authors do not run their exercise in real time, in fact they use data from the 1957–2001 period to estimate relevant parameters and then simulate the effect of choosing an optimal price index over the same period. This is not the situation with which central banks are usually confronted; rather, their decisions have to be taken in real time and only past data can be used to fit the parameters of interest. In fact, the procedure implemented by Mankiw and Reis minimises the risk associated with structural change of the relevant parameters. These considerations are particularly relevant to the ECB when the usual risk associated with structural breaks is heightened by the fact that past data come from a different regime. In fact, optimal weights might depend on parameters which are poorly identified or time-varying, in which case the index changes over time. Communicating to the public a modification in the price index due to a structural break in estimated parameters might prove a difficult task. However, it must be noted that in practice the Mankiw–Reis prescription for the optimal price index is very simple (giving most of the weight to wages) and if such a prescription is robust to some fluctuations in the key parameterisation of the model then the communication problem seems much less difficult to solve. After all, Taylor rules can be interpreted as an approximation to the solution of the optimisation problem for the monetary policymaker. Such rules are widely used, but only a tiny subset of the users are concerned with the parameters describing the preferences of central banks as opposed to those describing the structure of the economy. Similarly, if the optimality of targeting wages is robust to variations in the parameters describing the structure of different sectors, a central bank could very well target wages rather than prices and communicate this modification effectively to the public, leaving the academics to debate the range of deep parameters in which targeting wages is optimal.

5   Inflation persistence and optimal monetary policy in the euro area

The main message of chapter 3 below by Benigno and López-Salido is well understood in the general framework posed in the previous section. The empirical evidence on which their chapter is based suggests that European countries fall into two different groups in terms of their inflation dynamics. In Germany price-setters put more weight on their expectations about future economic conditions and revise their prices more frequently than price-setters do in other European countries. As a consequence there is an important asymmetry in the monetary transmission mechanism in Europe. When such an asymmetry is introduced in an optimising framework to determine monetary policy a natural conclusion arises: monetary policy should seek to stabilise an inflation target that gives more weight to the inflation rates in regions with a higher degree of rigidity. The intuition behind this result is rather simple: in a region with a high degree of flexibility a high inflation rate can be a symptom of efficient adjustment in prices in response to macroeconomic shocks, while in a region with a high degree of rigidity a high inflation rate might instead reflect an inefficient increase in prices. The existence of asymmetries in the mechanism of price-setting across Europe makes the optimal price index different from the HICP.

5.1   Issues for discussion

As illustrated in the previous section, while the theory of optimal price index is fairly clear cut, its practical implementability relies crucially on the robustness of the empirical results. The type of asymmetries in the monetary transmission crucial to the arguments proposed by Benigno and López-Salido are derived by obtaining different estimates across countries for the parameters in a hybrid New Phillips curve:

$$\pi_t = \omega^f E_t \pi_{t+1} + \omega^b \pi_{t-1} + \gamma x_t, \tag{2.1}$$

where π_t is some measure of inflation and x_t is some measure of excess demand. Identification of (2.1) is of crucial importance for the empirical application of the results. This is not a trivial issue. Rudd and Whelan (2001) have shown that the hybrid model is the observational equivalent of the following backward-looking model:

$$\pi_t = \beta\pi_{t-1} + \gamma x_t + \delta z_t + u_t, \tag{2.2}$$

where z_t is any variable that, although not directly included in equation (2.1), is used as an instrument for future inflation when estimating the parameters ω^f and ω^b. In practice, a high degree of estimated forward-looking behaviour might just be a reflection of mis-specification of a backward-looking model. In principle, as illustrated in Galí, Gertler and López-Salido (2001), the identification problem could be addressed more explicitly.

A second important issue for discussion is the possibility of non-linearity in the Phillips curve. Suppose that, as in Dolado, Dolores and Ruge-Murcia (2002), the correct specification for the Phillips curve is as follows

$$\pi_t = \beta\pi_{t-1} + f(x_t) + u_t,$$

where $f(x_t)$ is some non-linear function capturing, for example, the fact that the cost of not changing prices is lower at a low level of inflation. In this case, linear specifications estimated for data coming from two different inflationary regimes will deliver different parameters. European countries are grouped by Benigno and López-Salido into Germany and the others. As it is well known that there is a difference in mean and standard deviation of pre-EMU inflation in Germany and in the rest of Europe, the issue of non-linearity seems to be worth some further investigation. Moreover, the existence of two different regimes in the pre-EMU data is totally irrelevant if EMU causes the convergence to the low-mean, low-variance regime for inflation in all member countries.

Summing up, identification and specification seem to be two crucial issues in determining the robustness of the empirical evidence for the asymmetries used by Benigno and López-Salido to determine the difference between the optimal price index and the HICP.

6   Core inflation in the euro area

Bagliano, Golinelli and Morana (chapter 4 below) provide a measure of core inflation based on long-run relations among real money, real GDP, the nominal yield to maturity of long-term government bonds, the rate of capacity utilisation in the manufacturing sector, the short-term interest rate and HICP inflation. Their proposed measure of core inflation has the statistical interpretation of the long-run inflation forecast. Such a forecast is derived by specifying a VAR model for the six variables of interest, identifying the long-run cointegrating relationships among those variables, then identifying the two distinct sources of shocks having permanent effects on the system and hence two common trends.

Lastly, core inflation is measured by the estimated response of inflation to the common trends.

The identified long-run relations are a long-run money demand function, a term structure equation, a relation between the nominal long-term interest rate and inflation and capacity utilisation (which, being stationary, is subject to a degenerate cointegrating relationship). The two permanent shocks are identified as a real shock and a nominal shock. The nominal shock is differentiated from the real one by imposing the condition that it has no long-run effect on output.

The specification is not derived by theory; however, the choice of variables and the identification strategy for the long-run relationships are designed to be consistent with a two-pillar strategy, attributing a special informative role to money growth.

6.1   Issues for discussion

Bagliano, Golinelli and Morana have derived a statistical measure of core inflation which, by construction, is less volatile than HICP inflation. Is that measure useful for monetary policy? The question is left unanswered. In principle such a question could be answered empirically by running a counterfactual based on a baseline scenario in which the monetary policymaker follows a rule designed to target HICP inflation and in the alternative scenario follows a rule designed to target core inflation. Different effects on output and inflation could then be assessed.

However, thinking of this counterfactual, a number of problems emerge. First, the specification of the rule. In fact, in the model proposed the interest rate rule is derived by inverting money demand and, as we have seen, there is evidence that such a rule does not fit the behaviour of the ECB from 1999 onwards. This again raises the question of whether we can use data from the period 1980–99 unreservedly. The problem becomes more serious here. Core inflation, as measured by Bagliano, Golinelli and Morana, has a trend. The data for the period 1980–99 show a downward trend for inflation which stands at a level of about 10% at the beginning of the sample and ends up at a level just above 2% at the end of the sample. Now the ECB has a mandate for price stability, interpreted as fluctuations of HICP inflation between 0% and 2% in the medium term. So if the ECB fulfils its mandate, then HICP inflation in the medium term should fluctuate *without a trend* between 0% and 2%. So, does the ECB mandate change the identifying restrictions for core inflation from those (appropriately) chosen by the authors for the sample period to those restrictions implying that inflation is trendless ($\gamma_{31} = \gamma_{32} = 0$)? If the answer is yes and such conditions are imposed, then the volatility of core inflation becomes zero:

the long-run forecast for inflation is just the target of a credible central bank. There is no need to use econometrics to measure it.

REFERENCES

Alesina A., O. Blanchard, J. Galí, F. Giavazzi and H. Uhlig, 2001, *Defining a Macroeconomic Framework for the Euro Area* (*Monitoring the European Central Bank*, vol. 3), London: CEPR.

Bagliano F. C., R. Golinelli and C. Morana, 2003, 'Inflation Modelling in the Euro Area', chapter 4 in this volume.

Begg D., F. Canova, P. De Grauwe, A. Fatas and P. R. Lane, 2002, *Surviving the Slowdown* (*Monitoring the European Central Bank*, vol. 4), London: CEPR.

Benigno P. and J. D. López-Salido, 2003, 'An Evaluation of Alternative Targeting Rules for the ECB', chapter 3 in this volume.

Dolado J. J., R. M. Dolores and F. J. Ruge-Murcia, 2002, 'Non-linear Monetary Policy Rules: Some New Evidence for the US' CEPR Discussion Paper no. 3405

Favero C. A., X. Freixas, T. Persson and C. Wyplosz, 2000, *One Money, Many Countries* (Monitoring the *European Central Bank*, vol. 2), London: CEPR.

Galí J., M. Gertler and J. D. López-Salido, 2001, 'Notes on Estimating the Closed Form of the Hybrid New Phillips Curve', mimeo.

Gros D., O. Davanne, M. Emerson, T. Mayer, G. Tabellini and N. Thygesen, 2000, 'Quo Vadis Euro? The Cost of Muddling Through', 2nd annual report of the CEPS Macroeconomic Policy Group, Brussels: CEPS.

Gros D., K. Durrer, J. Jimeno, C. Monticelli and R. Perotti, 2002, 'Fiscal and Monetary Policy for a Low-Speed Europe', 4th annual report of the CEPS Macroeconomic Policy Group, Brussels: CEPS.

Mankiw N. G. and R. Reis, 2002, 'What Measure of Inflation Should a Central Bank Target?', paper presented at the International Seminar On Macroeconomics, Frankfurt

Rudd J. and K. Whelan, 2001, 'New Tests of the New-Keynesian Phillips Curve', Division of Research and Statistics, Federal Reserve Board

3   An evaluation of alternative targeting rules for the ECB

Pierpaolo Benigno and J. David López-Salido

1   Introduction

Macroeconomic indicators show that countries belonging to the European Monetary Union are at different points in the business cycle. In the month of September 2001, the average inflation rate in the EMU area was 2.6%, but there was a great deal of variance. Greece, Ireland, the Netherlands and Portugal had inflation rates above 4% while France had the lowest inflation rate, 2.2%. At the same time, the GDP of the area increased by 0.5% during the first quarter of 2001, but with a negative growth in Finland, the Netherlands and Portugal.

How should the European Central Bank (ECB) conduct overall monetary policy in this varied environment? The Maastricht Treaty is not silent on this issue. The primary objective of the ECB is that of maintaining price stability. Eventually, the monetary policymaker is permitted to stimulate the growth of the different regions, but only without jeopardising the goal of price stability.

The first bulletin of the ECB (January 1999) explicitly states that one of the main arguments for price stability is that it 'improves the transparency of the relative price mechanism thereby avoiding distortions and helping to ensure that the market will allocate real resources efficiently both across uses and across times. A more efficient allocation will raise the productive potential of the economy.'

The architects of the European Monetary Union specified a quantitative target to measure deviations from the price stability goal. This target is formulated in terms of a weighted average of the Harmonised Index of Consumer Prices (HICP) of the countries belonging to the union. Each country has a weight equal to the share of its consumption in total EMU consumption. The adopted target was that HICP inflation should not exceed 2%.

Is the HICP targeting process a good conveyor of the information relevant to the final goal of price stability?

In a recent study, Benigno and López-Salido (2001) analysed the inflation dynamics of five countries belonging to the European Union: France, Germany, Italy, the Netherlands and Spain. These countries represent 88% of the GDP of the euro area.

The first result that emerged from the study is that these countries fall into two groups in terms of the dynamics of their inflation rates. Germany is characterised by forward-looking price-setters' behaviour in which sellers, when setting prices, give more weight to their expectations of future economic conditions than to past performance. The other four countries – France, Italy, the Netherlands and Spain – are characterised by backward-looking price-setters' behaviour, where sellers give higher weight to past economic conditions.

The second finding is that the average duration of price contract, i.e. the average length of time during which prices remain fixed, is shorter in Germany than in the other four countries. In Germany, prices remain fixed on average for a period of five quarters, while in the other group they remain fixed for eight quarters.

This result brings out an important asymmetry in the transmission mechanism of monetary policy in Europe, notwithstanding the difference in the economic sizes of the countries. This asymmetry can be relevant in determining which target is a better indicator of efficiency in the allocation of resources.

In this chapter we address this issue in a dynamic general equilibrium model of a currency area following Benigno (2001), in which two regions are characterised by different price-setting mechanisms. In one region sellers evidence *forward-looking behaviour in setting prices* while in the other past inflation plays a crucial role in understanding inflation persistence, through what we call the *hybrid* model. We then exploit the micro-foundations of our framework in order to provide a welfare criterion for the central bank in terms of consumer utility. The policymaker seeks to stabilise the output gap as well as a weighted average of inflation rates in the area. Moreover, importance should be given to the deviation of the relative price between regions with respect to the natural level. Finally, given the role of past inflation in understanding inflation persistence in the area, monetary policymakers should also stabilise the change in inflation in the region characterised by the hybrid model. Within this framework we will analyse both the dynamic adjustment of regional and area-wide driving macroeconomic variables to terms-of-trade shocks, as well as the welfare implications of alternative monetary policy rules. We focus on four alternative policy rules: (i) *fully optimal policy*, (ii) *optimal inflation targeting policy*, (iii) *HICP targeting*, and (iv) *stabilisation of the area output gap*.

According to the criterion of efficiency followed by the ECB, we are able to show within our framework that, *in principle*, a quantitative target in terms of stabilisation of the *HICP* does not succeed in eliminating the distortions in the relative price mechanism. We have proposed two policies that may perform better: the *optimal inflation targeting* policy (the inflation rate in the region with the higher degree of rigidity should receive the greater weight), which generalises that outlined in Benigno (2001), and the *output-gap stabilisation* policy.

The chapter is structured as follows: section 2 presents the model; section 3 shows the log-linear approximation to the structural equilibrium conditions; section 4 analyses the welfare criterion; and section 5 compares the optimal monetary policy under commitment with the HICP targeting and other targeting rules.

2   The model

We develop a two-country optimising model with sticky prices as in Benigno (2001), incorporating elements from both the recent closed-economy literature on the effects of monetary policy and the recent open-economy literature on exchange rate determination.[1] In this section, we describe the main features of the framework. The analysis closely follows Benigno (2001). However, we depart in assuming a richer price-setting mechanism as in the model of Galí and Gertler (1999).

The simplest form of a currency area that is of interest for our analysis is a two-region area with a single central bank and two fiscal authorities. Each fiscal authority has sovereignty over only one region. The two regions are labelled H and F. The whole area is populated by a continuum of agents on the interval $[0, 1]$. The population on the segment $[0, n)$ belongs to region H, while the segment $[n, 1]$ belongs to F. There is no possibility of migration across regions. A generic agent, which belongs to the area, is both producer and consumer: a producer of a single differentiated product and a consumer of all the goods produced in both regions.

Each agent derives utility from consuming an index of consumption goods and from the liquidity services of holding money, and derives disutility from producing the differentiated product. The whole area is subjected to three region-specific sources of fluctuations: demand, supply and liquidity-preference shocks. Households maximise the expected discounted value of the utility flow.

Concerning the structure of financial markets, we assume that they are complete both within and across regions.

Money is important because households derive utility from its liquidity services. If real money balances and consumption are separable in utility and prices are flexible, money is neutral. In order to give a role to monetary policy, as it is common in the literature, we introduce both nominal rigidity and a market structure characterised by monopolistic competition. The latter assumption rationalises the existence of price stickiness, allowing producers not to violate any participation constraint. Nominal rigidity is introduced using a model *à la* Calvo

---

[1] Goodfriend and King (1997) summarise developments in the literature on monetary policy in a closed economy, while Lane (2001) surveys recent work on optimising sticky-price models in the open-economy context.

(1983), thus allowing fluctuations around the equilibrium for a longer period of time.[2] In particular, we are going to assume that region F is characterised by a pure forward-looking model in which during each period a seller faces a fixed probability $1 - \alpha^F$ of adjusting its price, irrespective on how long it has been since the seller had changed its price. In this event the price is chosen to maximise the expected discounted profits if the decision on the price is maintained. Thus $1/(1 - \alpha^F)$ represents the average duration of contracts within region F. In region H, we are going to assume that the price-setting mechanism behaves as in a hybrid model *à la* Galí and Gerlter (1999). In this model, it is still the case that a fraction $(1 - \alpha^H)$ of sellers can reset their prices in a certain period. However, only a fraction $(1 - \omega^H)$ behave in a forward-looking way as in Calvo's model. The remaining sellers, when adjusting their prices, follow a rule-of-thumb in which prices are linked to the past-period inflation rate.

Consumer problem   Preferences of the generic household j are given by

$$U_t^j = \mathrm{E}_t \left\{ \sum_{s=t}^{\infty} \beta^{s-t} \left[U\left(C_s^j, \xi_{D,s}^i\right) - L\left(\frac{M_s^j}{P_s^i}, \xi_{L,s}^i\right) - V\left(y_s^j, \xi_{S,s}^i\right) \right] \right\},$$

where the upper index j denotes a variable that is specific to agent j, while the upper index i denotes a variable that is specific to region i. We have that $i = H$ if $j \in [0, n)$, while $i = F$ if $j \in [n, 1]$. E_t denotes the expectation conditional on the information set at date t, while β is the intertemporal discount factor, with $0 < \beta < 1$.

Agents obtain utility from consumption and from the liquidity services of holding money, while they receive disutility from producing goods. The utility function is separable in these three factors. We have that U is an increasing concave function of the index C^j defined by

$$C^j \equiv \frac{\left(C_H^j\right)^n \left(C_F^j\right)^{1-n}}{n^n (1-n)^{1-n}} \tag{3.1}$$

and C_H^j and C_F^j are indexes of consumption across the continuum of differentiated goods produced respectively in region H and F. Specifically,

$$C_H^j \equiv \left[\left(\frac{1}{n}\right)^{\frac{1}{\sigma}} \int_0^n c^j(h)^{\frac{\sigma-1}{\sigma}} dh \right]^{\frac{\sigma}{\sigma-1}},$$

$$C_F^j \equiv \left[\left(\frac{1}{1-n}\right)^{\frac{1}{\sigma}} \int_n^1 c^j(f)^{\frac{\sigma-1}{\sigma}} df \right]^{\frac{\sigma}{\sigma-1}}. \tag{3.2}$$

---

[2] Yun (1996), in a closed-economy model, and Kollmann (2001), in an open-economy model, introduce Calvo's type of price-setting into dynamic general equilibrium monetary models.

We have that σ, which is assumed greater than one, is the elasticity of substitution across goods produced within a region, while the elasticity of substitution between the bundles C_H and C_F is 1. The parameter n denotes both the population size and the 'economic' size of region H, where the 'economic size' is the share of the bundle of goods produced within that region in the consumption index. ξ_D^i denotes a country-specific shock to the preferences towards consumption.

L is an increasing concave function of the real money balances, while ξ_L^i is a region-specific shock to the liquidity preference; we will interpret it as an exogenous disturbance to money demand. Agents derive utility from the real purchasing power of money, where M_t^j is the agent j's money balance at the end of date t, while P^i is the appropriate region-specific price index used to deflate M_t^j. Here P^i is defined as

$$P^i \equiv \left(P_H^i\right)^n \left(P_F^i\right)^{1-n},$$

$$P_H^i \equiv \left[\left(\frac{1}{n}\right)\int_0^n p^i(h)^{1-\sigma}dh\right]^{\frac{1}{1-\sigma}}, \quad P_F^i \equiv \left[\left(\frac{1}{1-n}\right)\int_n^1 p^i(f)^{1-\sigma}df\right]^{\frac{1}{1-\sigma}},$$

where $p^i(h)$ is the price of good h sold in the market of region i. The price index P^i is properly defined as the minimum expenditure in region i required to purchase goods resulting in the consumption index of C^j such that $C^j = 1$. Similar definitions are given for P_H^i and P_F^i. Here we assume that there are no transaction costs in transporting goods across regions; furthermore, prices are set considering the whole area as a common market. It follows that $p^H(h) = p^F(h)$ and $p^H(f) = p^F(f)$. Given these assumptions and given the structure of the preferences, it is also the case that purchasing power parity holds, i.e. $P^H = P^F$. We can then drop the index i from the consumption-based price indexes.

Here we define the terms of trade T of region F as the ratio of the price of the bundle of goods produced in region F relative to the price of the bundle imported from region H. We have then $T \equiv P_F/P_H$.

Finally, V is an increasing convex function of agent j's supply of its product y^j and ξ_S^i is a region-specific shock to the disutility of producing the goods.

Given a decision on C^j, household j allocates optimally the expenditure on C_H^j and C_F^j by minimising the total expenditure PC^j under the constraint given by (3.1). Then, given the decisions on C_H^j and C_F^j, household j allocates the expenditure among the differentiated goods by minimising $P_H C_H^j$ and $P_F C_F^j$ under the constraints given by (3.2). The demands of the generic good h, produced in region H, and of the generic good f, produced in region F are

$$c^j(h) = \left(\frac{p(h)}{P_H}\right)^{-\sigma} T^{1-n}C^j, \quad c^j(f) = \left(\frac{p(f)}{P_F}\right)^{-\sigma} T^{-n}C^j. \quad (3.3)$$

We can write total demand of good h and f as

$$y^d(h) = \left(\frac{p(h)}{P_H}\right)^{-\sigma} T^{1-n} C^W, \quad y^d(f) = \left(\frac{p(f)}{P_F}\right)^{-\sigma} T^{-n} C^W, \quad (3.4)$$

where the union aggregate consumption C^W is defined as

$$C^W \equiv \int_0^1 C^j dj.$$

We assume that markets are complete within and across regions. The budget constraint of household j in region i (expressed in real terms with respect to the price index) is for each state s_t at date t, and for each date t

$$E_t\{q_t B_t^j\} + \frac{M_t^j}{P_t} \leq W_{t-1}^j + (1 - \tau^i)\frac{p_t(j)y_t(j)}{P_t} - C_t^j + \frac{Q_t^{i,j}}{P_t},$$

with

$$W_{t-1}^j \equiv B_{t-1}^j + \frac{M_{t-1}^j + B_{t-1}^j}{P_t},$$

where B_t^j is the real value at time t of the portfolio held by agent j composed of contingent securities in units of the consumption-based price index with one-period maturity while q_t is the vector of the security prices.[3] $Q_t^{i,j}$ are nominal lump-sum transfers from the fiscal authority of region i in which j resides to the household j, while τ^i is a regional proportional tax on nominal income. The budget constraint at date t of the fiscal authority of region i for $i = H$ or F is

$$\tau^i \int_{j\in i} p_t(j)y_t(j)dj = \int_{j\in i} M_t^j - \int_{j\in i} M_{t-1}^j + \int_{j\in i} Q_t^{i,j},$$

where we have assumed that seignorage is returned to each region according to its source; M^U, the level of money supplied by the common central bank, is equal to the aggregate demand for money

$$M^U = \int_0^1 M_t^j dj.$$

Given the sequences of prices and incomes, and given the initial conditions, the problem of allocation of consumption is completely characterised by the utility function and the resource constraint. The latter is derived by combining an appropriate borrowing limit with the budget constraint of the households. As a first important equilibrium condition, the complete market assumption

---

[3] At each date t the economy faces one of finitely many states ($s_t = 1,2,3 \ldots S_t$). With h_t we denote the history of the states up to date t.

implies that the marginal utilities of consumption are equated across countries at each date t:

$$U\left(C_t^F, \xi_{D,t}^F\right) = U\left(C_t^H, \xi_{D,t}^H\right).$$

The exhaustion of the intertemporal resource constraint and the Euler equations (if we assume an interior optimum) describe the optimal allocation. We have the following optimality conditions: (i) that

$$\beta^{T-t} \frac{U_C\left(C_T^i(s_T), \xi_{D,T}^i\right)}{U_C\left(C_t^i, \xi_{D,t}^i\right)} = \Psi_{t,T}^i(s_T) \tag{3.5}$$

at each state $s_T \in S_T$, for each date t and every T, with $T > t$ and for $i = H$ or F; this is an optimality condition which equates the marginal rate of substitution, between future consumption in a particular state and present consumption, to the appropriate stochastic discount factor $\Psi_{t,T}^i$; (ii) that

$$L_{M/P}\left(\frac{M_t^i}{P_t}, \xi_L^i\right) = \frac{R_t}{1 + R_t} U_C\left(C_t^i, \xi_{D,t}^i\right) \tag{3.6}$$

at each date t and for each $i = H$ or F, where $L_{M/P}$ is the derivative of L with respect to the real money balance and R_t is the risk-free nominal interest rate, the instrument of the common central bank; here the marginal rate of substitution between real money balances and consumption is equated to the user cost in terms of the consumption good index of holding an extra unit of real money balances for one period; (iii) that the resource constraint holds with equality at each date t and in every history h_t. We can use the optimality conditions to price the risk-free nominal bond obtaining at each date t and for $i = H$ or F:

$$U_C\left(C_t^i, \xi_{D,t}^i\right) = (1 + R_t)\beta E_t \left\{ U_C\left(C_{t+1}^i, \xi_{D,t+1}^i\right) \frac{P_t}{P_{t+1}} \right\}. \tag{3.7}$$

In the equilibrium, the contingent securities are in zero net supply at the union level.

To complete the demand side of the economy we compute aggregate demand in both regions by using the appropriate Dixit–Stiglitz aggregators related to (3.2):

$$Y^H \equiv \left[\left(\frac{1}{n}\right) \int_0^n y^d(h)^{\frac{\sigma-1}{\sigma}} dh\right]^{\frac{\sigma}{\sigma-1}}, \quad Y^F \equiv \left[\left(\frac{1}{1-n}\right) \int_n^1 y^d(f)^{\frac{\sigma-1}{\sigma}} df\right]^{\frac{\sigma}{\sigma-1}}. \tag{3.8}$$

After applying (3.8) to (3.4) we obtain

$$Y^H = T^{1-n}C^W, \quad Y^F = T^{-n}C^W. \tag{3.9}$$

While consumption is completely ensured, aggregate production can vary between regions. From (3.9), it follows that changes in the terms of trade explain divergences in output.

Firms and price setting   Sellers are monopolists. Demand (3.4) is not taken as given, but it can be affected by different price decisions. On the other hand, sellers are small with respect to the overall market and they take as given the indexes P, P_H, P_F and C. Monopolistic competition does not imply price rigidity, but it creates the environment in which price rigidity can exist without violating any individual rationality participation constraint, assuming that the sequence of shocks is bounded. In region F, prices are subjected to changes at random intervals as in Calvo (1983). In each period a seller faces a fixed probability $1 - \alpha^F$ of adjusting its price, irrespective of how long it has been since the seller last changed its price. In this event the price is chosen to maximise the expected discounted profits if the decision on the price is maintained; in fact the seller also considers that the price chosen at a certain date t will apply in the future at date $t + k$ with probability $(\alpha^F)^k$. It is important to note that all sellers in the same region who can modify their price at a certain time will face the same discounted future demands and future marginal costs under the hypothesis that the new price is maintained. Thus they will set the same price. We denote by $\tilde{p}_t(f)$ the price of the good f chosen at date t and with $\tilde{y}_{t,t+k}(f)$ the total demand of good f at time $t + k$ if the price $\tilde{p}_t(f)$ still applies. The function to maximise is

$$E_t \sum_{k=0}^{\infty} (\alpha^F \beta)^k \left[\lambda_{t+k} (1 - \tau^F) \tilde{p}_t(f) \tilde{y}_{t,t+k}(f) - V \left(\tilde{y}_{t,t+k}(f), \xi^F_{S,t+k} \right) \right],$$

$$(3.10)$$

where revenues are evaluated using the marginal utility of nominal income $\lambda_{t+k} = U_C(C_{t+k})/P_{t+k}$, which is the same for all the consumers belonging to the union, because of the hypothesis of complete markets. The total demand is given by

$$\tilde{y}_{t,t+k}(f) = \left(\frac{\tilde{p}_t(f)}{P_{F,t+k}} \right)^{-\sigma} T_{t+k}^{-n} C_{t+k}.$$

The seller maximises (3.10) with respect to $\tilde{p}_t(f)$, taking as given the sequences $\{P_{H,t}, P_{F,t}, P_t, C_t\}$. The optimal choice of $\tilde{p}_t(f)$ is

$$\tilde{p}_t(f) = \frac{\sigma}{(\sigma - 1)(1 - \tau^F)} \frac{E_t \sum_{k=0}^{\infty} (\alpha^F \beta)^k V_y \left(\tilde{y}_{t,t+k}(f), \xi^F_{S,t+k} \right) \tilde{y}_{t,t+k}(f)}{E_t \sum_{k=0}^{\infty} (\alpha^F \beta)^k \lambda_{t+k} \tilde{y}_{t,t+k}(f)}.$$

$$(3.11)$$

The Calvo price-setting model implies the following state equation for $P_{F,t}$:

$$P_{F,t}^{1-\sigma} = \alpha^F P_{F,t-1}^{1-\sigma} + (1 - \alpha^F) \tilde{p}_t(f)^{1-\sigma}.$$

$$(3.12)$$

In region H, the price-setting mechanism involves a form of hybrid model as in Galí and Gertler (1999). As in Calvo's model, a fraction $1 - \alpha_H$ of firms are allowed to reset their prices. However, only a fraction ω^H of these firms will reoptimise in a forward-looking manner as in Calvo's model. They will set their price as it follows:

$$\tilde{p}_t(h) = \frac{\sigma}{(\sigma - 1)(1 - \tau^H)} \frac{E_t \sum_{k=0}^{\infty} (\alpha^H \beta)^k V_y(\tilde{y}_{t,t+k}(h), \xi_{S,t+k}^H) \tilde{y}_{t,t+k}(h)}{E_t \sum_{k=0}^{\infty} (\alpha^H \beta)^k \lambda_{t+k} \tilde{y}_{t,t+k}(h)}.$$

$$(3.13)$$

where

$$\tilde{y}_{t,t+k}(h) = \left(\frac{\tilde{p}_t(h)}{P_{H,t+k}} \right)^{-\sigma} T_{t+k}^{1-n} C_{t+k}.$$

The other fraction of firms that change their price, $1 - \omega^H$, follow instead a rule of thumb in which the chosen price is set as

$$\tilde{p}_t^b(h) = P_{H,t-1}^* \frac{P_{H,t-1}}{P_{H,t}}.$$

$P_{H,t}^*$ denotes the bundles of prices that are newly chosen in period t, which includes both the forward-looking price setters and the rule-of-thumb price setters, as

$$P_{H,t}^* = (\tilde{p}_t(h))^{\omega_h} (\tilde{p}_t^b(h))^{1-\omega_h}.$$

Finally, the law of motion of the price index $P_{H,t}$ is given at time t by

$$P_{H,t}^{1-\sigma} = \alpha^H (P_{H,t-1}^*)^{1-\sigma} + (1 - \alpha^H) \tilde{p}_t(h)^{1-\sigma}.$$

$$(3.14)$$

3   Log-linear approximations to the structural equilibrium conditions

With a cap ($\hat{\ }$), we denote the deviation of any variable from its steady state. Moreover, given generic variables X^H and X^F, we define $X^W \equiv nX^H + (1 - n)X^F$. In this section we present the log-linear approximation to the equilibrium conditions.

The log-linear version of the Euler equation and of the aggregate outputs in region H and F, respectively, are

$$E_t \hat{C}_{t+1}^W = \hat{C}_t^W + \rho^{-1} (\hat{R}_t - E_t \pi_{t+1}^W),$$

$$(3.15)$$

and

$$\hat{Y}_{H,t} = (1 - n)\hat{T}_t + \hat{C}_t^W, \qquad \hat{Y}_{F,t} = -n\hat{T}_t + \hat{C}_t^W,$$

$$(3.16)$$

where π is the inflation rate.[4] In (3.15) the expected growth of consumption depends positively on the real return. In (3.16), $\hat{Y}_{H,t}$ and $\hat{Y}_{F,t}$ are output in regions H and F, respectively.

The log-linear approximation to the aggregate supply equations in region F is

$$\pi_{F,t} = \lambda^F \widehat{mc}_t^F + \beta E_t\{\pi_{F,t+1}\}, \tag{3.17}$$

where the coefficient λ^F is defined as $\lambda^F \equiv (1 - \alpha^F)(1 - \beta \alpha^F)/(\alpha^F (1 + \eta\sigma))$ and where $\widehat{mc}_t^F$ represents the deviation of the real marginal costs with respect to the steady state. Under Calvo's style of price-setting behaviour, the current inflation rate should depend on real marginal costs and on expectations of the inflation rate one period ahead. Instead, consistent with Galí and Gertler (1999), we find that in the hybrid region past inflation is what matters and that the aggregate supply equation assumes the following form:

$$\pi_{H,t} = \gamma_b^H \pi_{H,t-1} + \lambda^H \widehat{mc}_t^H + \gamma_f^H E_t\{\pi_{H,t+1}\}, \tag{3.18}$$

where $\lambda^H \equiv (1 - \omega^H)\lambda^H \alpha^H/\phi$, $\gamma_b^H \equiv \omega^H \phi^{-1}$; $\gamma_f^H \equiv \beta\alpha^H\phi^{-1}$; and $\phi \equiv \alpha^H + \omega^H[1 - \alpha^H(1 - \beta)]$.

For each region, we can further decompose the real marginal costs by using the structure implied by the consumer's optimising behaviour. Indeed, real marginal costs coincide with the real wages in units of the price index of the produced good.

In region F we get

$$mc_t^F = \frac{V_y(C_t^W T_t^{-n}, \xi_{S,t}^F)}{U_C(C_t^F, \xi_{D,t}^F)} T_t^{-n}.$$

Taking a log-linear approximation of the above equation, we obtain that the deviations of the average real marginal costs from the steady state are

$$\widehat{mc}_t^F = (\rho + \eta)(\hat{Y}_t^W - \tilde{Y}_t^W) - n(1 + \eta)(\hat{T}_t - \tilde{T}_t),$$

in which we have defined the inverse of the elasticity of the disutility of supply goods and of the elasticity of substitution in consumption as $\eta \equiv V_{yy}\bar{Y}^F/V_y$ and $\rho = -U_{CC}\bar{C}^F/U_C$, respectively. Following the same steps, we get the log-linear approximation of the average marginal costs for the hybrid country H as

$$\widehat{mc}_t^H = (\rho + \eta)(\hat{Y}_t^W - \tilde{Y}_t^W) + (1 - n)(1 + \eta)(\hat{T}_t - \tilde{T}_t).$$

Finally, we can write the aggregate supply equation for the region F as

$$\pi_{F,t} = k_C^F(\hat{Y}_t^W - \tilde{Y}_t^W) - nk_T^F(\hat{T}_t - \tilde{T}) + \beta E_t\{\pi_{F,t+1}\}, \tag{3.19}$$

---

[4] Equation (3.15) represents a log-linear approximation of equation (3.7), while equations (3.16) are derived from (3.9).

where

$$k_C^F \equiv \frac{(1 - \alpha^F \beta)(1 - \alpha^F)}{\alpha^H} \frac{\rho + \eta}{1 + \sigma \eta} \quad \text{and} \quad k_T^F = k_C^F \frac{1 + \eta}{\rho + \eta}.$$

As in the corresponding closed-economy version, inflation depends on present and expected future values of the real marginal costs. However, in an open-economy framework, the real marginal costs are not proportional to the output gap, as a consequence of the interdependence induced by international relative prices. This result was first shown by Svensson (2000). The smaller and more open the country is, the more relative prices influence real marginal costs and thus inflation rates. In the same way, the aggregate supply equation for region H is

$$\pi_{H,t} = \gamma_b^H \pi_{H,t-1} + k_C^H (\hat{Y}_t^W - \tilde{Y}_t^W) + (1 - n)k_T^H (\hat{T}_t - \tilde{T}_t)$$
$$+ \gamma_f^H E_t \{\pi_{H,t+1}\}, \tag{3.20}$$

where

$$\gamma_b^H \equiv \frac{w^H}{w^H(1 - \alpha^H + \alpha^H \beta) + \alpha^H} \quad \text{and} \quad \gamma_f^H \equiv \frac{\gamma_b^H \alpha^H \beta}{w^H},$$

$$k_C^H \equiv \frac{\rho + \eta}{1 + \sigma \eta} \frac{(1 - \omega^H)(1 - \alpha^H)(1 - \alpha^H \beta)}{[w^H(1 - \alpha^H + \alpha^H \beta) + \alpha^H]} \quad \text{and} \quad k_T^H \equiv \frac{1 + \eta}{\rho + \eta} k_C^H.$$

The model is closed with the terms-of-trade identity, which in a log-linear approximation can be written as

$$\hat{T}_t = \hat{T}_{t-1} + \pi_t^F - \pi_t^H, \tag{3.21}$$

and with the policy rule followed by the common central bank.

4 Welfare criterion

As is common in the recent literature on monetary policy evaluation, we exploit the micro-foundations of our framework in order to provide a welfare criterion for the central bank based on consumer utility.[5] This criterion allows for a direct evaluation of the deadweight losses implied by the distortions included in the model. As the welfare criterion, we assume the discounted sum of the utility flows of the household belonging to the whole union. The average utility flow is defined as

$$w_t \equiv \int_0^1 [U(C_t^j, \xi_{D,t}^i) - \tilde{V}(y_t^j, \xi_{S,t}^i)]dj,$$

---

[5] See, for instance, Rotemberg and Woodford (1997), Woodford (1999b) and Erceg, Henderson and Levin (2000).

at each date t, where it has been implicitly assumed that each region has a weight equal to its economic and population size. We have further disregarded the utility derived from real money balances, as is common in the literature. The welfare criterion of the whole union is then defined as

$$W = E_0 \left\{ \sum_{t=0}^{+\infty} \beta^t w_t \right\}.$$

Following Rotemberg and Woodford (1997), Woodford (1999b), Amato and Laubach (2002), Benigno (2001) and Steinsson (2000), we compute a second-order Taylor series expansion of W around the deterministic steady state where all the shocks are zero. Our second-order approximation delivers an intuitive representation of the welfare function:

$$W = -\Omega E_0 \left\{ \sum_{t=0}^{+\infty} \beta^t L_t \right\}, \tag{3.22}$$

$$L_t = \Lambda \left[\hat{Y}_t^W - \tilde{Y}_t^W \right]^2 + n(1-n)\Gamma[\hat{T}_t - \tilde{T}_t]^2 + (1-\theta)\left(\pi_t^F\right)^2$$
$$+ \theta\left(\pi_t^H\right)^2 + \theta\psi\left(\Delta\pi_t^H\right)^2,$$

where $\Omega, \Lambda, \Gamma, \theta, \psi$ are functions of the structural parameters of the model.[6]

Note that a cap-variable ($\hat{\ }$) represents the deviations of that variable from the steady state under the sticky-price equilibrium, while a tilde-variable ($\sim$) represents its deviations from the steady state under the flexible-price equilibrium.

From (3.22) it follows that monetary policymakers should stabilise the output gap, $y_t^W = \hat{y}_t^W - \tilde{y}_t^W$, i.e. the deviations of area output from its natural rate, as well as the deviations of the terms of trade $\hat{T}_t$ from their natural rate $\tilde{T}_t$. Indeed, following an asymmetric shock, efficiency requires that relative prices should be moved in order to shift the burden of adjustment 'equally' across regions. Monetary policymakers should also stabilise a weighted average of the squares of the producer inflation rates in each region. However, there is a trade-off between stabilising inflation in both regions and stabilising relative prices to their natural level, in fact as prices are stable within a region, the terms of trade cannot be moved to offset asymmetric shocks. This trade-off is further amplified by the last term in the loss function. Given the importance of past inflation for understanding inflation persistence in the area, as in Amato and Laubach (2002) and Steinsson (2000), we find that monetary policymakers should also stabilise the growth of inflation in the hybrid region H. This term follows from the presence in this region of backward-looking agents who behave according to the rule of thumb. In the case in which the fraction of backward-looking agents

---

[6] Details are available in the appendix.

becomes zero, the last term disappears and the welfare criterion collapses to the one in Benigno (2001).

4.1   Calibration of the model

We calibrate the model to the euro area below following the empirical results of Benigno and López-Salido (2001) on the estimation of the AS equation across European countries. This study found evidence supporting the existence of two different zones inside the euro area. In one country (Germany) the forward-looking character of inflation could not be ignored. Germany represents around 35% of the GDP of the whole euro area. In another group of four countries (France, Italy, Spain and the Netherlands), inflation dynamics were found to have both forward and backward-looking components. These four countries represent around 53% of the GDP of the euro area. This empirical analysis suggests a possible partition of the countries analysed into two groups. Accordingly, the size of region H can be calibrated to $n = 0.6$ (53/88) while the size of region F is $(1 - n) = 0.4$ (35/88). This gives a value for α^F equal to 0.785. For the hybrid part of the area, α^H equals 0.75 and ω^H equals 0.48.

In the analysis that follows, we 'calibrate' the parameter σ equal to 6, which corresponds to a steady-state mark-up of 1.2. We set the inverse of the elasticity of substitution in consumption, ρ, equal to $1/6$ as in Rotemberg and Woodford (1997). The elasticity of the disutility of producing the differentiated goods is set equal to 0.6. Considering a reasonable value of the share of labour in total output to be 0.75, then the implied Frisch elasticity of labour supply is equal to 5.[7] Finally, we consider that the economy is subject to terms of trade shocks following a Markovian process of the kind

$$\tilde{T}_t = \tau \tilde{T}_{t-1} + \varepsilon_t,$$

where we set $\tau = 0.9$. As results from the micro-foundation of the model, these terms-of-trade shocks originate from asymmetric supply shocks. The value chosen for τ is consistent with the calibration used in the international business cycle literature (e.g. Backus, Kehoe and Kydland 1992; Kehoe and Perri 2000).

5   Terms-of-trade shocks and monetary policy

In this section, we compare the adjustment of the economies in responses to terms-of-trade shocks under different monetary policies from both positive and

---

[7] This value is in line with most of the authors in the RBC literature. Actually, our value of 5 is lower than the value used by Christiano and Eichenbaum (1992), and it is clearly lower than infinity, which is the value that corresponds to Hansen's model of indivisibilities (1985). Nevertheless, these values are higher than the ones emerging from the microeconometric estimates of the labour-supply literature (e.g. Killingsworth and Heckman, 1986).

Table 3.1. *Welfare and variability comparisons*

	$v(y^W)$	$v(\hat{T} - \bar{T})$	$v(\pi^H)$	$v(\pi^F)$	$v(\Delta\pi^H)$	δ
HICP targeting	2.1253	2.4923	0.0494	0.1112	0.0008	2.31
Optimal inflation targeting	1.0165	2.5210	0.0109	0.1884	0.0002	2.03
Output-gap stabilisation	0.0000	2.5119	0.0840	0.0800	0.0007	1.52
Optimal policy	0.0221	2.5094	0.0566	0.1041	0.0005	1.48

Note: σ_ε^2 has been normalised to 1%.

normative viewpoints. In particular, we focus on four alternative policy rules. The first policy under consideration is the *fully optimal policy*. Formally, this implies that monetary policymakers are committed to maximising the welfare function (3.22) under the constraints given by the structural equations (3.19), (3.20) and (3.21). The second class is the *optimal inflation targeting policy* in which policymakers are committed to the class of policies given by

$$p\pi_{H,t} + (1 - p)\pi_{F,t} = 0$$

and they choose optimally p. In particular under our calibration, it turns out that the optimal choice of p is 0.8. The third class is *HICP targeting*, which is similar to the previous class but, unlike the previous case, the parameter p is set equal to the size of the H country, say n.[8] It is always the case that optimal policy performs at least as well as the optimal inflation targeting policy, while the latter is always at least as good as HICP targeting. Finally, we further analyse a policy aimed at *stabilising the output gap* of the area, i.e. setting $y_t^W = 0$ at all dates t.

5.1   *Welfare comparisons*

A numerical quantification appears in table 3.1, where we present the welfare comparisons among all the above-mentioned policies. We summarise the comparisons in terms of the variability of the variables that are relevant for the computation of welfare, using the statistic $v(.)$. This operator, $v(.)$, applied to the generic variable x, is defined as follows:

$$v(x) = \mathrm{E}\left[\mathrm{E}_0(1 - \beta)\sum_{t=0}^{+\infty} \beta^t x_t^2 \right],$$

---

[8] A kind of HICP targeting can be seen as the policy followed by the European Central Bank (Alesina et al. 2001). The HICP inflation of the whole euro area is constructed as a weighted average of the HICP of the single countries belonging to the union, with weights equal to the share of each country's consumption in the consumption of the area.

where, as in Woodford (1999a), the unconditional expectations E are taken over the possible initial states of the economy $\tilde{T}_0$. By using this operator, it is possible to analyse welfare, W, as a composite of the operator $v(.)$ applied to the relevant variables. Thus, we are able to understand the contribution of the relative volatilities of inflation and output to welfare under alternative policy rules. In particular, we can decompose welfare into five components: first, the output gap of the area $v(y^W)$; second, the output-gap differential or the terms-of-trade gap $v(\tilde{T} - \tilde{T})^9$; third and fourth, the contributions of inflation in both areas, i.e. $v(\pi^F)$ and $v(\pi^H)$, respectively; and finally the changes in inflation in the sticky inflation area (i.e. the area where the hybrid model applies) $v(\Delta\pi^H)$. In table 3.1 we have ranked welfare starting from the worst policy, HICP targeting, and ending with the fully optimal one. In particular, we provide a measure of the losses in terms of permanent percentage shift in steady-state consumption. To this end, we define the index δ as

$$\delta^j \equiv -(1 - \beta) \cdot \left[\frac{W^j - W^E}{U_C \bar{C}} \right],$$

where W^E is welfare under the efficient policy, which is not feasible; W^j is welfare indexed by the four policies that are considered in this experiment, while U_C is the marginal utility of consumption and $\bar{C}$ is the steady-state level of consumption. Thus δ^j measures the permanent percentage shift in steady-state consumption that is lost under the policy j with respect to the efficient level.

Table 3.1 summarises the comparisons, where the variance of the shock ε has been normalized to one. However, the variance of ε is crucial for evaluating the magnitude of the costs in terms of a permanent shift in steady-state consumption. In keeping with the international real business cycle literature, we calibrate the variance of ε to be 0.01^2. Using the measure δ, we have then evaluated the costs of the fully optimal policy to be around 0.0148% of a permanent shift in steady-state consumption.[10] Output-gap stabilisation approximates the welfare that would be achieved under the optimal policy. The optimal inflation-targeting policy performs considerably better than HICP-targeting but less than the optimal policy and output-gap stabilisation policy. Indeed, the costs of the HICP targeting and the optimal inflation targeting policies are of the order of 0.023% and 0.020%, respectively. The output stabilisation policy is quite close to the fully optimal one since many of the welfare gains in the fully optimal

---

[9] Notice that the output-gap differential is proportional to the terms-of-trade gap, i.e. formally the following relationship holds:

$$y_t^H - y_t^F = \hat{T}_t - \tilde{T}_t.$$

[10] Lucas (1987) has evaluated the costs of the business cycle to be around 0.05% of a permanent shift in steady-state consumption.

policy arise from the fact that the output gap is almost fully stabilised in the area. Notice also that in the fully optimal policy the output gap of the area is not fully stabilised but the relative output gaps or the terms of trade are much more stabilised than in the case of the output-gap stabilisation policy. Inflation-targeting policies are far enough from the previous two policies, because they imply that the output gap of the area is far from stabilised.

An interesting observation is that all the policies under consideration perform equally in terms of the variance of the terms-of-trade gap. Given the high degree of price rigidity, and the persistence of the relative price shock, the terms of trade can adjust only slowly. Hence, monetary policy cannot efficiently shift the unfavourable shocks in region H to region F. In terms of the welfare function (3.22), it can only control the area output gap and, marginally, the inflation rates in each region. However, for this calibrated example, the weights on the inflation rates are of an order of magnitude *100 times* larger than the weights on the output gap, thus they matter far more for the maximisation of welfare. Interestingly, in our case, the output-gap policy also does not destabilise the inflation rate.

5.2   Dynamic adjustments

To illustrate graphically the previous results, in figures 3.1 and 3.2 we plot the impulse response functions of the variables that are relevant for the computation of welfare following a negative shock to the terms of trade, namely an unexpected transitory drop in $\tilde{T}$.

This shock can be interpreted as a decrease in productivity in region H relative to region F. Efficiency would require that terms-of-trade changes offset completely terms-of-trade shocks, without any movements in domestic inflation rates and output gaps. However, in a currency area, such efficient equilibrium is not feasible. After the unfavourable terms-of-trade shocks, inflation in region H increases, while it decreases in region F. Under the HICP targeting regime, inflation increases more in region H and decreases less in region F than under the optimal plan. In fact, HICP targeting does not adjust for the differences in the degrees of rigidity across countries. On the other hand, the optimal inflation-targeting policy gives a higher weight to the inflation rate in region H, which has a higher degree of rigidity. Hence, it succeeds better in stabilising inflation in that region. However, it fails to stabilise the area output gap. HICP targeting further exacerbates fluctuations in the area output gap. It so happens that, in our calibrated-estimated economy, the fully optimal plan requires quasi-stabilisation of the output gap at the area-wide level. In this case, the policy of stabilising the area output gap completely can approximate the optimal plan well. By stabilising the area output gap it is also possible to reach the right

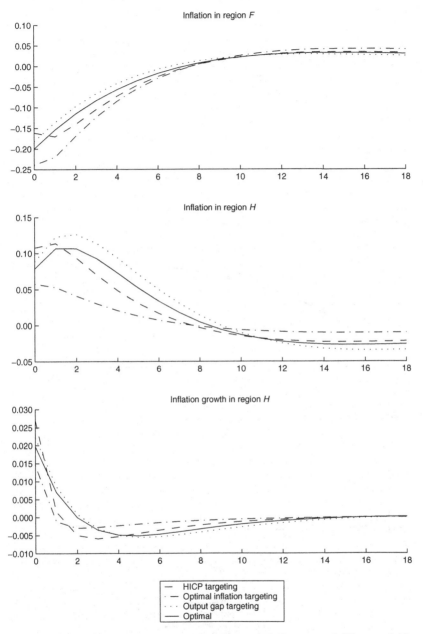

Figure 3.1 Impulse response functions – inflation, $\alpha_H = 0.75$, $\omega_H = 0.48$, $\alpha_F = 0.785$

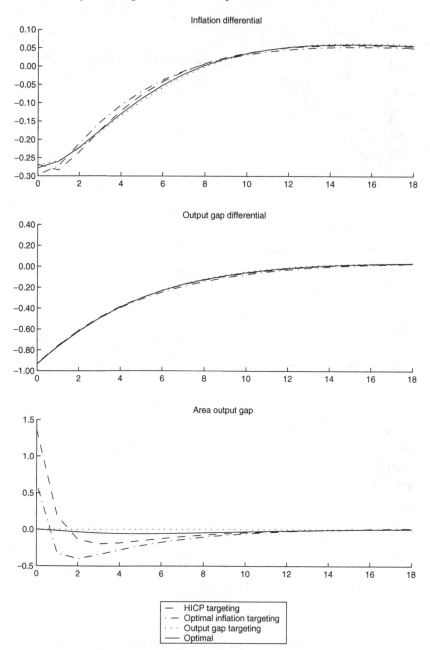

Figure 3.2 Impulse response functions – differentials, $\alpha_H = 0.75$, $\omega_H = 0.48$, $\alpha_F = 0.785$

inertia in inflation rates that the commitment to the optimal policy requires, so the path of inflation rates is also stabilised.

6   Conclusions: should the ECB abandon HICP targeting?

We have shown that when there are sizeable differences in rigidities across the countries belonging to the European Monetary Union, the monetary policy strategy followed by the ECB is not 'optimal' in our context. In particular, as a criterion for evaluation, we rely on a microfounded welfare function which, in the spirit of King and Wolman (1998) and Woodford (1999b), allows for an evaluation of the deadweight losses existing in the model.

We have proposed two policies that may perform better: the *optimal inflation targeting* policy, which generalises that outlined in Benigno (2001), and the *output-gap stabilisation* policy. In the previous section we have already described the *pros*, here we will focus on the *cons*. First, it may seem that an inflation targeting policy that assigns higher weight to countries with higher degrees of nominal rigidity penalises those countries further. Not only are they suffering from a higher degree of rigidity in their goods and labour markets, but also the common central bank is giving more weight to their inflation rate! Instead, this policy actually benefits those countries since, once the policy of the central bank is credible, it produces lower inflation rates for them simply because it cares more about those inflation rates. On the other side, when there are asymmetric shocks across countries that require an adjustment of relative prices across regions, movements in the prices of the more flexible regions should bring about this adjustment. Second, a rigidity-adjusted inflation-targeting policy may create the wrong incentives for the adoption by countries of structural changes that would reduce their goods and labour market rigidities. However, this ignores the fact that, once there are rigidities in the price mechanism in all the regions, relative prices also move sluggishly. When asymmetric shocks occur that require adjustment in relative prices, flexibility is beneficial for all the regions in the area.

The policy of stabilising the output gap is immune to this adverse-incentive criticism as it gives a weight to each country similar to its economic size as in the HICP targeting policy. However, it is more difficult to implement since it involves the unobservability of the natural level of output. While, in our context, the natural level indicates the flexible-price equilibrium, there are several other concepts of the natural rate as well as several ways to measure it, as outlined also in McCallum (2001). Thus, a policy of stabilisation of the output gap is neither easy to implement nor easy to communicate to private agents.

These arguments suggest that it may not be desirable to abandon HICP targeting for optimal inflation targeting. However, the broad quantitative target used by the ECB requiring only an overall HICP inflation rate of less than 2% can import some flexibility to monetary policy. This broad target can also permit the ECB to carry out an optimal inflation-targeting policy without disclosing to the public how different countries are weighted.

It follows from this analysis that values of the HICP inflation rate above the threshold do not always require intervention of the ECB, when the sources of a rise in the inflation rate are from sectors or regions characterised by frequent and efficient adjustments in prices. The accountability of the Central Bank should thus be focused on the final goal of price stability as a means of efficiently allocating resources, and not on HICP targeting, which is rather an imperfect measure of deviation from price stability. As our analysis shows, in cases where the inertia in the terms of trade is high and there are important backward-looking components in inflation in some zones of the area, monitoring the output gap too can give the right information on the final goal.

Appendix

In this appendix we derive the utility-based loss function, equation (3.22) in the text. We follow Rotemberg and Woodford (1997) and Woodford (1999b). The average utility flow among all the households belonging to region H is

$$w_t^H = U\left(C_t^H, \xi_{D,t}^H\right) - \frac{\int_0^n V\left(y_t^j, \xi_{S,t}^H\right) dj}{n}, \tag{3.23}$$

while that of region F is

$$w_t^F = U\left(C_t^F, \xi_{D,t}^F\right) - \frac{\int_{1-n}^1 V\left(y_t^j, \xi_{S,t}^F\right) dj}{1-n}. \tag{3.24}$$

The welfare criterion of the Central Bank in the currency area is the discounted value of a weighted average of the average utility flows of the regions,

$$W = E_0 \left\{ \sum_{j=0}^\infty \beta^j \left(n w_{t+j}^H + (1-n) w_{t+j}^F\right) \right\}. \tag{3.25}$$

We take a Taylor expansion of each term of the utility function. Taking a second-order linear expansion of $U(C_t^H, \xi_{D,t}^H)$ around the steady-state value $\bar{C}$, we obtain

$$U\left(C_t^H, \xi_{D,t}^H\right) = U(\bar{C}) + U_C\left(C_t^H - \bar{C}\right) + \frac{1}{2} U_{CC}\left(C_t^H - \bar{C}\right)^2$$
$$+ U_{C\xi_D}\left(C_t^H - \bar{C}\right) \xi_{D,t}^H + o(\|\xi\|^3), \tag{3.26}$$

where in $o(\|\xi\|^3)$ we group all the terms that are of third or higher order in the bound $\|\xi\|$ on the amplitude of the shocks. Furthermore, expanding C_t with a second-order Taylor approximation we obtain

$$C_t^H = \bar{C}\left(1 + \hat{C}_t^H + \frac{1}{2}(\hat{C}_t^H)^2 + o(\|\xi\|^3)\right), \qquad (3.27)$$

where $\hat{C}_t^H = \ln(C_t^H/\bar{C})$. Substituting (3.27) into (3.26) we obtain

$$U\left(C_t^H, \xi_{D,t}^H\right) = U_C \bar{C} \hat{C}_t^H + \frac{1}{2}(U_C \bar{C} + U_{CC} \bar{C}^2)(\hat{C}_t^H)^2$$
$$+ U_{C\xi_D} \bar{C} \hat{C}_t^H \xi_{D,t}^H + \text{t.i.p.} + o(\|\xi\|^3), \qquad (3.28)$$

which can be written as

$$U\left(C_t^H, \xi_{D,t}^H\right)$$
$$= U_C \bar{C} \left[\hat{C}_t^H + \frac{1}{2}(1 - \rho)(\hat{C}_t^H)^2 + \rho \hat{C}_t^H v_t\right] + \text{t.i.p.} + o(\|\xi\|^3),$$

where we have defined $\rho \equiv -U_{cc}\bar{C}/U_c$ and $U_{cc}\bar{C}v_t^H = -U_{C\xi c}\xi_{D,t}^H$ and where in t.i.p. we include all the terms that are independent of monetary policy. Similarly we take a second-order Taylor expansion of $V(y_t(h), \xi_{S,t}^H)$ around a steady state where $y_t(h) = \bar{Y}^H$ for each $j \in [0, n]$, and at each date t, and where $\xi_{S,t}^H = 0$ at each date t. We obtain

$$V\left(y_t(h), \xi_{S,t}^H\right) = V(\bar{Y}^H, 0) + V_y(y_t(h) - \bar{Y}^H) + V_\xi \xi_{S,t}^H$$
$$+ \frac{1}{2}v_{yy}(y_t(h) - \bar{Y}^H)^2 + V_{y\xi}(y_t(h) - \bar{Y}^H)\xi_{S,t}$$
$$+ \frac{1}{2}V_{\xi\xi}(\xi_{S,t}^H)^2 + o(\|\xi\|^3). \qquad (3.29)$$

Here we recall that

$$y(h) = \left(\frac{p(h)}{P_H}\right)^{-\sigma} [(T)^{1-n} C^W]$$

and we take a second order Taylor expansion of $y_t(h)$

$$y_t(h) = \bar{Y}^H \cdot \left(1 + \hat{y}_t(h) + \frac{1}{2} \cdot [\hat{y}_t(h)]^2\right) + o(\|\xi\|^3).$$

We can simplify (3.29) to

$$V\left(y_t(h), \xi_{S,t}^H\right) = V_y \bar{Y}^H \cdot \left[\hat{y}_t(h) + \frac{1}{2} \cdot \hat{y}_t(h)^2 + \frac{\eta}{2} \cdot \hat{y}_t(h)^2\right.$$
$$\left. - \eta \cdot \hat{y}_t(h)\bar{Y}_t^H\right] + \text{t.i.p.} + o(\|\xi\|^3), \qquad (3.30)$$

where $\hat{y}_t(h) = \ln(y_t(h)/\bar{Y}^H)$ and $\bar{Y}_t^H$ has been defined by the relation $V_{y\xi}\xi_{S,t}^H \equiv -V_{yy}\bar{Y}^H\bar{Y}_t^H$. As in the main text we have further defined that $\eta \equiv V_{yy}(\bar{Y}^H, 0)\bar{Y}^H/V_y(\bar{Y}^H, 0)$. Our steady state with zero inflation implies the following conditions, respectively, for region H:

$$(1 - \tau^H)U_C(\bar{C}) = \frac{\sigma}{\sigma - 1}\bar{T}^{1-n}V_y(\bar{T}^{1-n}\bar{C}, 0), \qquad (3.31)$$

and for region F:

$$(1 - \tau^F)U_C(\bar{C}) = \frac{\sigma}{\sigma - 1}\bar{T}^{-n}V_y(\bar{T}^{-n}\bar{C}, 0), \qquad (3.32)$$

where τ^H and τ^F represent proportional taxes on the revenues of the firms of the home and foreign country, respectively. We can rewrite the above conditions as

$$(1 - \Phi^H)U_C(\bar{C}) = \bar{T}^{1-n}V_y(\bar{T}^{1-n}\bar{C}, 0), \qquad (3.33)$$

$$(1 - \Phi^F)U_C(\bar{C}) = \bar{T}^{-n}V_y(\bar{T}^{-n}\bar{C}, 0), \qquad (3.34)$$

after having defined

$$(1 - \Phi^H) \equiv (1 - \tau^H)\frac{\sigma - 1}{\sigma},$$

$$(1 - \Phi^F) \equiv (1 - \tau^F)\frac{\sigma - 1}{\sigma}.$$

In the efficient equilibrium, we have $\Phi^H = \Phi^F = 0$. In this case we get that $\bar{Y}^H = \bar{Y}^F = \bar{C}$. By using (3.33) we can write (3.30) as

$$V\left(y_t(h), \xi_{S,t}^H\right) = U_C\bar{C} \cdot \left[(1 - \Phi) \cdot \hat{y}_t(h) + \frac{1}{2} \cdot \hat{y}_t(h)^2 + \frac{\eta}{2} \cdot \hat{y}_t(h)^2\right.$$
$$\left. - \eta \cdot \hat{y}_t(h)\bar{Y}_t^H\right] + \text{t.i.p.} + o(\|\xi\|^3). \qquad (3.35)$$

Here we integrate (3.35) across the households belonging to region H, obtaining

$$\frac{\int_0^n V\left(y_t(h), \xi_{S,t}^H\right)dh}{n} = U_C\bar{C} \cdot \left\{(1 - \Phi) \cdot E_h\hat{y}_t(h) + \frac{1}{2} \cdot [\text{var}_h\hat{y}_t(h)\right.$$
$$+ [E_h\hat{y}_t(h)]^2] + \frac{\eta}{2} \cdot [\text{var}_h\hat{y}_t(h) + [E_h\hat{y}_t(h)]^2]$$
$$\left. - \eta E_h\hat{y}_t(h)\bar{Y}_t^H\right\} + \text{t.i.p.} + o(\|\xi\|^3). \qquad (3.36)$$

We take a second-order approximation of the aggregators, obtaining

$$\hat{Y}_{H,t} = E_h\hat{y}_t(h) + \frac{1}{2}\left(\frac{\sigma - 1}{\sigma}\right)\text{var}_h\hat{y}_t(h) + o(\|\xi\|^3). \qquad (3.37)$$

Finally substituting (3.37) into (3.36), we obtain

$$\frac{\int_0^n V\left(y_t(h), \xi_{S,t}^H\right)}{n} = U_C \bar{C} \cdot \left[(1 - \Phi^H) \cdot \hat{Y}_{H,t} + \frac{1}{2} \cdot [\hat{Y}_{H,t}]^2 + \frac{\eta}{2} \cdot [\hat{Y}_{H,t}]^2 \right.$$

$$\left. + \frac{1}{2}(\sigma^{-1} + \eta) \cdot \text{var}_h \hat{y}_t(h) - \eta \hat{Y}_{H,t} \bar{Y}_t^H \right]$$

$$+ \text{t.i.p.} + o(\|\xi\|^3). \tag{3.38}$$

Combining (3.38) and (3.28) into (3.23), we obtain

$$w_t^H = U_C \bar{C} \left[\hat{C}_t^H + \frac{1}{2}(1 - \rho)(\hat{C}_t^H)^2 + \rho \hat{C}_t^H v_t^H - (1 - \Phi^H) \cdot \hat{Y}_{H,t} \right.$$

$$\left. - \frac{1}{2} \cdot [\hat{Y}_{H,t}]^2 - \frac{\eta}{2} \cdot [\hat{Y}_{H,t}]^2 - \frac{1}{2}(\sigma^{-1} + \eta) \cdot \text{var}_h \hat{y}_t(h) + \eta \hat{Y}_{H,t} \bar{Y}_t^H \right]$$

$$+ \text{t.i.p.} + o(\|\xi\|^3), \tag{3.39}$$

while for region F we have

$$w_t^F = U_C \bar{C} \left[\hat{C}_t^F + \frac{1}{2}(1 - \rho)(\hat{C}_t^F)^2 + \rho \hat{C}_t^F v_t^F - (1 - \Phi^F) \cdot \hat{Y}_{F,t} - \frac{1}{2} \cdot [\hat{Y}_{F,t}]^2 \right.$$

$$\left. - \frac{\eta}{2} \cdot [\hat{Y}_{F,t}]^2 - \frac{1}{2}(\sigma^{-1} + \eta) \cdot \text{var}_f \hat{y}_t(f) + \eta \hat{Y}_{F,t} \bar{Y}_t^F \right]$$

$$+ \text{t.i.p.} + o(\|\xi\|^3). \tag{3.40}$$

Taking a linear combination of (3.39) and (3.40) with weight n, we obtain

$$w_t = U_C \bar{C} \left\{ \frac{n}{2}(1 - \rho)(\hat{C}_t^H)^2 + \frac{1 - n}{2}(1 - \rho)(\hat{C}_t^F)^2 + n\rho \hat{C}_t^F v_t^F \right.$$

$$+ (1 - n)\rho \hat{C}_t^H v_t^H - \frac{1}{2} \cdot [n(\hat{Y}_{H,t})^2 + (1 - n)(\hat{Y}_{F,t})^2]$$

$$- \frac{1}{2}\eta \cdot [n\hat{Y}_{H,t}^2 + (1 - n)\hat{Y}_{F,t}^2] + \eta \cdot [n\hat{Y}_{H,t} \bar{Y}_t^H + (1 - n)\hat{Y}_{F,t} \bar{Y}_t^F]$$

$$\left. - \frac{1}{2}(\sigma^{-1} + \eta) \cdot [n\text{var}_h \hat{y}_t(h) + (1 - n)\text{var}_f \hat{y}_t(f)] \right\}$$

$$+ \text{t.i.p.} + o(\|\xi\|^3), \tag{3.41}$$

and after substituting the expressions for $\hat{Y}_{H,t}, \hat{Y}_{F,t}$ we get

$$w_t = U_C \bar{C} \left\{ \frac{n}{2}(1 - \rho)(\hat{C}_t^H)^2 + \frac{1 - n}{2}(1 - \rho)(\hat{C}_t^F)^2 + n\rho \hat{C}_t^F v_t^F \right.$$

$$+ (1 - n)\rho \hat{C}_t^H v_t^H + \eta [\hat{C}_t^W \bar{Y}_t^W + n(1 - n)\hat{T}_t \bar{Y}_t^R]$$

$$-\frac{1}{2}\big[(\hat{C}_t^W)^2 + n(1-n)\hat{T}_t^2\big] - \frac{1}{2}\eta \cdot \big[(\hat{C}_t^W)^2 + n(1-n)\hat{T}_t^2$$
$$+ 2\hat{C}_t^W g_t^W - 2n(1-n)\hat{T}_t g_t^R\big]$$
$$-\frac{1}{2}(\sigma^{-1}+\eta) \cdot [n\mathrm{var}_h \hat{y}_t(h) + (1-n)\mathrm{var}_f \hat{y}_t(f)]\bigg\}$$
$$+ \text{t.i.p.} + o(\|\xi\|^3), \tag{3.42}$$

which can be written as

$$w_t = -U_C \bar{C}\bigg\{\frac{1}{2}(\rho+\eta)\big[\hat{C}_t^W - \tilde{C}_t^W\big]^2 + \frac{1}{2}(1+\eta)n(1-n)[\hat{T}_t - \tilde{T}_t]^2$$
$$+\frac{1}{2}(\sigma^{-1}+\eta) \cdot [n\mathrm{var}_h \hat{y}_t(h) + (1-n)\mathrm{var}_f \hat{y}_t(f)]\bigg\}$$
$$+ \text{t.i.p.} + o(\|\xi\|^3). \tag{3.43}$$

The natural rate of world consumption and the terms of trade, which will arise when prices are flexible, are defined as

$$\tilde{C}_t^W \equiv \frac{\rho}{\rho+\eta}v_t^W + \frac{\eta}{\rho+\eta}(\bar{Y}_t^W - g_t^W),$$
$$\tilde{T}_t \equiv \frac{\eta}{1+\eta}(g_t^R - \bar{Y}_t^R),$$
$$\tilde{C}_t^R \equiv v_t^R.$$

After having defined $y_t^W \equiv \hat{C}_t^W - \tilde{C}_t$ we obtain

$$w_t = -U_C \bar{C}\bigg\{\frac{1}{2}(\rho+\eta)\big[y_t^W\big]^2 + \frac{1}{2}(1+\eta)n(1-n)[\hat{T}_t - \tilde{T}_t]^2$$
$$+\frac{1}{2}(\sigma^{-1}+\eta) \cdot [n\mathrm{var}_h \hat{y}_t(h) + (1-n)\mathrm{var}_f \hat{y}_t(f)]\bigg\}$$
$$+ \text{t.i.p.} + o(\|\xi\|^3). \tag{3.44}$$

Here we derive $\mathrm{var}_h \hat{y}_t(h)$ and $\mathrm{var}_f \hat{y}_t(f)$ as in Woodford (1999b) and Steinsson (2000). We have that

$$\mathrm{var}_h\{\log y_t(h)\} = \sigma^2 \mathrm{var}_h\{\log p_t(h)\}.$$

Defining $\bar{p}_t \equiv E_h \log p_t(h)$, we have

$$\mathrm{var}_h\{\log p_t(h)\} = \mathrm{var}_h\{\log p_t(h) - \bar{p}_{t-1}\}$$
$$= E_h\{[\log p_t(h) - \bar{p}_{t-1}]^2\} - (\Delta \bar{p}_t)^2$$
$$= \alpha^H E_h\{[\log p_{t-1}(h) - \bar{p}_{t-1}]^2\}$$
$$+ (1-\alpha^H)(1-\omega^H)\big[\log \tilde{p}_t^f(h) - \bar{p}_{t-1}\big]^2$$
$$+ (1-\alpha^H)\omega^H\big[\log \tilde{p}_t^b(h) - \bar{p}_{t-1}\big]^2 - (\Delta \bar{p}_t)^2.$$

We have also that

$$\bar{p}_t - \bar{p}_{t-1} = (1 - \alpha^H)(1 - \omega^H)\left[\log \tilde{p}_t^f(h) - \bar{p}_{t-1}\right]$$
$$+ (1 - \alpha^H)\omega^H\left[\log \tilde{p}_t^b(h) - \bar{p}_{t-1}\right]$$
$$= (1 - \alpha^H)(\log \tilde{p}_t^*(h) - \bar{p}_{t-1}),$$

and that

$$\log \tilde{p}_t^b(h) - \bar{p}_{t-1} = \log \tilde{p}_t^*(h) + \pi_{t-1}^H - \bar{p}_{t-1},$$
$$= (\log \tilde{p}_{t-1}^*(h) - \bar{p}_{t-2}) + o(\|\xi\|^2),$$

where we have used

$$\bar{p}_t = \log P_{H,t} + o(\|\xi\|^2).$$

We have also that

$$\log \tilde{p}_t^f(h) - \bar{p}_{t-1} = \frac{1}{1 - \omega^H}\log \tilde{p}_t^*(h) - \frac{\omega^H}{1 - \omega^H}\left(\log \tilde{p}_{t-1}^*(h) + \pi_{t-1}^H\right) - \bar{p}_{t-1}$$
$$= \frac{1}{1 - \omega^H}(\log \tilde{p}_t^*(h) - \bar{p}_{t-1}) - \frac{\omega^H}{1 - \omega^H}(\log \tilde{p}_{t-1}^*(h) - \bar{p}_{t-2})$$
$$+ o(\|\xi\|^2).$$

We have then

$$\text{var}_h\{\log p_t(h)\} = \alpha^H \text{var}_h\{\log p_{t-1}(h)\} + \frac{1}{(1 - \alpha^H)(1 - \omega^H)}[\Delta \bar{p}_t - \omega^H \Delta \bar{p}_{t-1}]^2$$
$$+ \frac{\omega^H}{(1 - \alpha^H)}[\Delta \bar{p}_{t-1}]^2 - (\Delta \bar{p}_t)^2 + o(\|\xi\|^3),$$

which can be rewritten as

$$\text{var}_h\{\log p_t(h)\} = \alpha^H \text{var}_h\{\log p_{t-1}(h)\} + \frac{\alpha^H}{(1 - \alpha^H)}\left(\pi_t^H\right)^2$$
$$+ \frac{\omega^H}{(1 - \alpha^H)(1 - \omega^H)}(\Delta \pi_t)^2 + o(\|\xi\|^3).$$

After integration of the above equation we obtain

$$\text{var}_h\{\log p_t(h)\} = (\alpha^H)^{t+1}\text{var}_h\{\log p_{-1}(h)\}$$
$$+ \sum_{s=0}^{t}(\alpha^H)^{t-s}\left(\frac{\alpha^H}{1 - \alpha^H}\left(\pi_s^H\right)^2 + \frac{\omega^H}{(1 - \alpha^H)(1 - \omega^H)}(\Delta \pi_s)^2\right)$$
$$+ o(\|\xi\|^3),$$

where we note that the first term in the right-hand side is independent of the policy chosen after period $t \geq 0$. After taking the discounted value, with the discount factor β, we obtain

$$\sum_{t=0}^{\infty} \beta^t \operatorname{var}_h\{\log p_t(h)\} = \frac{1}{(1-\alpha^H \beta)} \sum_{t=0}^{\infty} \beta^t \frac{\alpha^H}{1-\alpha^H} \left(\pi_t^H\right)^2$$

$$+ \frac{\omega^H}{(1-\alpha^H)(1-\omega^H)} \left(\Delta\pi_t^H\right)^2$$

$$+ \text{t.i.p.} + o(\|\xi\|^3).$$

The same derivations apply also for the foreign country, except that now $\omega^F = 0$. We can then obtain

$$\sum_{t=0}^{\infty} \beta^t \operatorname{var}_f\{\log p_t(f)\}$$

$$= \frac{1}{(1-\alpha^F \beta)} \sum_{t=0}^{\infty} \beta^t \frac{\alpha^F}{1-\alpha^F} \left(\pi_t^F\right)^2 + \text{t.i.p.} + o(\|\xi\|).$$

We define

$$d^H \equiv \frac{\alpha^H}{(1-\alpha^H)(1-\alpha^H \beta)},$$

$$d^F \equiv \frac{\alpha^F}{(1-\alpha^F)(1-\alpha^F \beta)}.$$

We can simplify the currency union's welfare criterion to

$$W_t = -\Omega \sum_{j=0}^{\infty} \beta^j L_{t+j}. \tag{3.45}$$

where

$$L_{t+j} = \Lambda\left[y_{t+j}^W\right]^2 + n(1-n)\Gamma[\hat{T}_{t+j} - \tilde{T}_{t+j}]^2 + \gamma\left(\pi_{t+j}^H\right)^2$$

$$+ \gamma\xi^H\left(\Delta\pi_{t+j}^H\right)^2 + (1-\gamma)\left(\pi_{t+j}^F\right)^2 + \text{t.i.p.} + o(\|\xi\|^3),$$

where we have defined

$$\Omega \equiv \frac{1}{2} U_C \bar{C}(n d^H + (1-n)d^F)\sigma(1+\sigma\eta)$$

$$\Lambda \equiv \frac{1}{\sigma} \frac{\rho + \eta}{1+\sigma\eta} \frac{1}{n d^H + (1-n)d^F},$$

$$\Gamma \equiv \frac{1}{\sigma} \frac{1+\eta}{1+\sigma\eta} \frac{1}{n d^H + (1-n)d^F},$$

$$\gamma \equiv \frac{nd^H}{nd^H + (1-n)d^F},$$

$$\xi^H \equiv \frac{\omega^H}{\alpha^H(1-\omega^H)}.$$

REFERENCES

Alesina, A., O. Blanchard, J. Galí, F. Giavazzi and H. Uhlig, 2001, *Defining a Macroeconomic Framework for the Euro Area (Monitoring the European Central Bank,* vol. 3), London: CEPR.

Amato, J. and T. Laubach, 2002, 'Rule-of-Thumb Behaviour and Monetary Policy', Finance and Economics Discussion Series no. 2002–5, Board of Governors Federal Reserve System.

Backus, D., P. Kehoe and F. Kydland, 1992, 'International Real Business Cycles,' *Journal of Political Economy* 100, 745–75.

Benigno, P., 2001, 'Optimal Monetary Policy in a Currency Area', CEPR Discussion Paper no. 2755.

Benigno, P. and D. López-Salido, 2001, 'Inflation Dynamics and Optimal Monetary Policy in Europe', unpublished manuscript, New York University.

Calvo, G., 1983, 'Staggered Prices in a Utility Maximizing Framework', *Journal of Monetary Economics* 12, 383–98.

Christiano, L. and M. Eichenbaum, 1992, 'Current Real Business Cycle Theories and Aggregate Labor Market Fluctuations', *American Economic Review* 82(3), 430–50.

Erceg, C., D. Henderson and A. Levin, 2000 'Optimal Monetary Policy with Staggered Wage and Price Contracts', *Journal of Monetary Economics* 46(2), 281–313.

Galí, J. and M. Gertler, 1999, 'Inflation Dynamics: A Structural Econometric Analysis', *Journal of Monetary Economics* 44, 195–222.

Goodfriend, M. S. and R. G. King, 1997, 'The New Neoclassical Synthesis and the Role of Monetary Policy', in B. S. Bernanke and J. Rotemberg (eds.), *NBER Macroeconomic Annual 1997*, Cambridge, MA: MIT Press, pp. 231–82.

Hansen, G., 1985, 'Indivisible Labor and the Business Cycle', *Journal of Monetary Economics*, 16, 309–27.

Kehoe, P. and F. Perri, 2000, 'International Business Cycles with Endogenous Incomplete Markets', unpublished manuscript, Federal Reserve Bank of Minneapolis, Staff Report 265.

Killingsworth, M. and J. Heckman, 1986, 'Female Labor Supply: A Survey', in O. Ashenfelter and R. Layard (eds.), *Handbook of Labor Economics*, vol. 1, Amsterdam: Elsevier Science, pp. 103–204.

King, R. and A. L. Wolman, 1998, 'What Should Monetary Authority Do when Prices Are Sticky?', in J. B.Taylor (ed.), *Monetary Policy Rules*, Chicago: University of Chicago Press for NBER.

Kollmann, R., 2001, 'The Exchange Rate in a Dynamic-Optimizing Current Account Model with Nominal Rigidities: A Quantitative Investigation', *Journal of International Economics* 55 (2), 243–62.

Lane, P. R., 2001, 'The New Open Economy Macroeconomics: A Survey', *Journal of International Economics* 54(2), 235–66.

Lucas, R., 1987, *Models of Business Cycles*, Oxford: Blackwell.

McCallum, B., 2001, 'Should Monetary Policy Respond Strongly to Output Gaps?', unpublished manuscript, Carnegie Mellon University.

Rotemberg, J. and M. Woodford, 1997, 'An Optimization-Based Econometric Framework for the Evaluation of Monetary Policy', in B. S. Bernanke and J. Rotemberg (eds.), *NBER Macroeconomic Annual 1997*, Cambridge, MA: MIT Press, pp. 297–346.

Steinsson, J., 2000, 'Optimal Monetary Policy in an Economy with Inflation Persistence', unpublished manuscript, Princeton University.

Svensson, L. E., 2000, 'Open Economy Inflation Targeting', *Journal of International Economics* 50, 155–83.

Woodford, M., 1999a, 'Optimal Monetary Policy Inertia', NBER Working Paper no. 7261.

1999b, 'Inflation Stabilisation and Welfare,' unpublished manuscript, Princeton University.

2000, 'Optimal Models with Nominal Rigidities', unpublished manuscript, Princeton University.

Yun, Tack, 1996, 'Nominal Price Rigidity, Money Supply Endogeneity, and Business Cycles', *Journal of Monetary Economics* 37, 345–70.

4 Inflation modelling in the euro area

*Fabio C. Bagliano, Roberto Golinelli
and Claudio Morana*

1 Introduction

Controlling inflation, at least in the long run, is widely regarded as the primary, and sometimes the only, goal of monetary policy. To this aim, in many countries central banks have explicitly adopted inflation-targeting strategies, setting precise quantitative targets for the monetary authorities' actions. Though not an inflation targeter, the European Central Bank (ECB) adopted a monetary policy strategy aimed at maintaining an annual inflation rate below 2% over a medium-term horizon (ECB 1999). This strategy is based on an announced reference value for M3 money growth and on the outlook of price developments in the euro area. The analysis of the behaviour of monetary aggregates and their components relies on a number of tools recently summarised in ECB (2001). The aim of this chapter is to provide an empirical investigation of the interrelationships among money, prices, interest rates and output in the euro area with a particular focus on the behaviour of the inflation rate over a long-run horizon. In fact, one of the main open issues in inflation analysis stems from the fact that short-run fluctuations of the observed inflation rate may be due to only temporary disturbances to which monetary policy should not respond. How to construct a reliable empirical measure of the underlying, long-run trend of inflation – '*core*' inflation – has therefore become a crucial issue in monetary policy design.

Core inflation series have been constructed following different methodologies (see Wynne 1999 for a thorough overview and assessment of different measures). Some measures are obtained from the cross-sectional distribution of individual price items, either by excluding from the price index some categories of goods (such as energy and food items) which are believed to be high-variance components, or by computing more efficient, 'limited influence'

This paper was originally prepared for the EMU Macroeconomic Institutions Conference, Università di Milano-Bicocca, 20–22 September 2001. We thank our discussant, Gianni Amisano, conference participants, and Steven Durlauf for many useful comments. Financial support from MIUR (F. C. Bagliano and R. Golinelli) and CNR (F. C. Bagliano) is gratefully acknowledged.

estimators of the central tendency of the distribution, such as the (weighted) median popularised by Bryan and Cecchetti (1994) and Cecchetti (1997) for the USA. Other measures are derived from univariate statistical techniques, such as simple moving averages computed over a variable time span (from 3–6 up to 36 months) or more sophisticated methodologies (i.c. unobserved component models, or the one-sided low-pass filter proposed by Cogley 2002). Finally, Quah and Vahey (1995) applied to the UK a bivariate structural vector autoregressive (SVAR) approach to core inflation estimation based on long-run output neutrality of permanent shocks to the inflation rate.

We propose a different, explicitly *forward-looking*, measure of core inflation, based on (appropriately estimated and tested) long-run relations among major macroeconomic variables. This measure may provide useful information in the light of the 'two-pillar' monetary policy strategy of the ECB, which considers: (i) the deviations of M3 growth from a reference value (a money growth indicator), and (ii) a broadly based assessment of the outlook for future price developments in the euro area as a whole (ECB 1999, 2000). This framework is motivated by the (alleged) close long-run relationship between money growth and inflation. Recent results have provided some evidence of stable long-run relationships among money, output, interest rates and inflation over the last two decades for the EMU countries (Brand and Cassola 2000, Gerlach and Svensson 2001, Golinelli and Pastorello 2002). We use such information to construct a forward-looking measure of core inflation consistent with the long-run features of the euro area macroeconomy.

To this aim, we consider a multivariate framework, capturing the dynamic interactions among the inflation rate, real money balances, short- and long-term interest rates and output, extending the analysis in Bagliano, Golinelli and Morana (2002). A stylised macroeconomic model is set up in section 2 to provide a theoretical rationale for the potential long-run relationships among those variables. The existence of valid cointegrating relations is then explored using euro area data for the 1979–2001 period. The problem of structural breaks in the behaviour of the long-term real interest rate is addressed by means of a Markov-switching model for the real rate. In order to decompose observed inflation into a non-stationary (stochastic) trend component, capturing the effect of permanent shocks only, and a stationary transitory element, we adopt a common trends approach. The permanent, 'core' inflation component bears the interpretation of the long-run inflation forecast conditional on an information set including several important macroeconomic variables. The main advantage of this measure of core inflation lies in its forward-looking nature, capturing the long-term element of the inflation process (of particular interest from the monetary policy perspective) consistent with the long-run properties of the macroeconomic system. Section 3 describes the common trends methodology and presents empirical results. Several properties of the estimated core inflation process are then assessed, namely its relative volatility with respect to observed inflation and its ability to forecast future headline inflation rates. Further features of the permanent-transitory decomposition of the inflation rate are analysed in section 4, where the nature of the non-core inflation fluctuations and the convergence of the observed rate to the core inflation rate are discussed. Finally, our main message is summarised in the concluding section 5: the ECB should take into proper account a forward-looking measure of the core inflation rate consistent with its whole monetary policy framework, based on strong and stable long-run relationships between inflation and other major macroeconomic variables.

2   Long-run analysis of a small-scale macro system

To organise thinking about the long-run relationships among inflation, output, money and interest rates we start with a general equation for inflation determination, nesting a traditional backward-looking Phillips curve, whereby inflation is mainly determined by the 'output gap', and a P^* model (see Hallman, Porter and Small 1991), which assumes that inflation dynamics is governed by the 'price gap'. The latter model has recently received strong support for the euro area from Gerlach and Svensson (2001). Ignoring additional dynamic terms and exogenous variables, the equation for the inflation rate is of the form:

$$\pi_t = \pi^e_{t,t-1} + \alpha_y(y_{t-1} - y^*_{t-1}) + \alpha_m(p_{t-1} - p^*_{t-1}) + \varepsilon^\pi_t, \qquad (4.1)$$

where π_t is the annualised inflation rate in quarter t ($\pi_t \equiv 4(p_t - p_{t-1})$) and $\pi^e_{t,t-1}$ is the expected inflation rate as of quarter $t - 1$, $y - y^*$ measures the output gap, with y^* denoting potential output, and $p - p^*$ is the 'price gap', the key determinant of inflation in the P^* model, to be more precisely defined below. Finally, ε^π represents a random shock to inflation. The empirical specification of equation (4.1) requires us to model inflationary expectations. As in other studies which use a backward-looking Phillips curve (e.g. Taylor 1999, Rudebusch and Svensson 1999, Staiger, Stock and Watson 2001), the expected inflation rate $\pi^e_{t,t-1}$ is set equal to π_{t-1}.[1] Therefore we get:

$$\Delta \pi_t = \alpha_y(y_{t-1} - y^*_{t-1}) + \alpha_m(p_{t-1} - p^*_{t-1}) + \varepsilon^\pi_t. \qquad (4.2)$$

Moreover, we assume:

$$y^*_t = \beta^y_0 + y^*_{t-1} + \varepsilon^y_t \qquad (4.3)$$

$$m_t - p_t = \beta^m_0 + \beta^m_1 y_t + \beta^m_2 (l_t - s_t) + \varepsilon^m_t \qquad (4.4)$$

$$p^*_t = m_t - \left[\beta^m_0 + \beta^m_1 y^*_t + \beta^m_2(s^*_t - l^*_t)\right] \qquad (4.5)$$

---

[1] Gerlach and Svensson (2001) adopt a different specification, setting $\pi^e_{t,t-1}$ as a weighted average of π_{t-1} and of the central bank's inflation objective.

$$l_t = \beta_0^f + \pi_{t+1,t}^e + \varepsilon_t^f \qquad (4.6)$$

$$l_t = \beta_0^s + s_t + \varepsilon_t^s. \qquad (4.7)$$

In (4.3) potential output follows a random walk. Real money demand is specified by (4.4), where the long–short interest rate differential $(l - s)$ proxies the opportunity cost of money holdings. Equation (4.5) defines p_t^* as the price level consistent with the current money stock, potential output and long-run equilibrium values for the short and long interest rates (s^* and l^*), according to the P^* model. Finally, (4.6) and (4.7) capture a Fisher parity and a term structure relation respectively. All structural parameters (βs) are positive and the εs are random shocks. In a long-run equilibrium, the following relations hold:

$$y = y^*$$
$$\pi = \pi^e$$
$$l^* = \beta_0^f + \pi$$
$$l^* = \beta_0^s + s^*$$
$$m^* - p^* = \beta_0 + \beta_1^m y^*,$$

where m^* denotes long-run equilibrium nominal money balances and $\beta_0 \equiv \beta_0^m + \beta_2^m \beta_0^s$.

In the above framework, the inflation rate and output are non-stationary, $I(1)$, and the output gap is stationary, $I(0)$. Moreover, the long-term interest rate is $I(1)$ and cointegrated with the inflation rate, so that $l - \pi$ is $I(0)$, and the short-term rate is $I(1)$ and cointegrated with the long rate, so as to make $l - s$ stationary. From (4.4) real money balances are $I(1)$ and cointegrated with output; if the cointegration parameter $\beta_1^m \neq 1$, also money velocity is non-stationary. Then, the first step of our empirical analysis looks at the integration and cointegration properties of the series, to check their consistency with the above macroeconomic framework.

In order to proceed with the empirical analysis, we need euro-area variables over a time span pre-dating the launch of the euro at the beginning of 1999. For the pre-euro period (up to 1998Q4) aggregate variables for the euro area were constructed by aggregating the historical data of the twelve current member countries. This approach is based on the assumption that the artificial euro-area data before monetary union are appropriate for analysing and forecasting the area-wide behaviour under EMU.[2]

---

[2] Despite this caveat, the aggregation route was followed by several other recent studies: Gerlach and Svensson (2001) and Galí, Gertler and López-Salido (2001) recently used area-aggregated data to study the EMU inflation rate, and Golinelli and Pastorello (2002) find some results in favour of the statistical poolability of single-country money demand functions. The latter results are partly supported by Dedola, Gaiotti and Silipo (2001), who find that the area-wide money

In the present analysis, we use quarterly variables at an area-wide level over the 1978Q4–2001Q3 period. We measure (the log of) real money balances $(m - p)$ by the (log of the) index of nominal M3 (published by the ECB) deflated by the (log of the) Harmonised Index of Consumer Prices (HICP) used by the ECB; output (y) is measured by (the log of) real GDP, the nominal short and long-term interest rates $(s$ and $l)$ are the T-bill and the government bond rates, the inflation rate (π) is the annualised quarterly rate of change of the HICP, and the output gap $(ygap \equiv y - y^*)$ is measured by the rate of capacity utilisation in the manufacturing sector measured by the OECD.[3]

The results of unit-root Dickey-Fuller ADF tests reported in table 4.1 are clear-cut: with the only exception of *ygap*, which is stationary, all the variables of interest are first order integrated. Moreover, the lower part of the table reports ADF test statistics for a number of additional variables: if the (null) unit-root hypothesis is rejected, then the corresponding $I(1)$ series are cointegrated with a $(1, -1)$ cointegrating vector. The results show that money velocity is $I(1)$ even when a linear trend is allowed in the specification of the test, the term interest rate differential is stationary (short and long-term rates are cointegrated), whereas the short- and long-term real interest rates are not stationary. As a whole, the evidence is consistent with the features of the above theoretical framework, except for the behaviour of the real interest rate series.

The missing Fisher parity relation deserves more careful scrutiny. To this aim, the lower panel of figure 4.1 plots the long-term real (ex-post) interest rate and the term interest rate differential for the euro area over the whole 1978Q4–2001Q3 period. While the interest rate differential fluctuates quite persistently around a constant mean, the real long-term interest rate shows a much lower mean for the sub-periods 1978–81 and 1997–2001, possibly suggesting that the non-stationarity detected by the ADF test is spurious, and due to a neglected structural change in the constant term of the Fisher parity relation.[4] For example, the introduction of the single monetary policy explicitly aimed at a price stability objective may have reduced inflation uncertainty and therefore the inflation risk premium embodied in the level of the

demand equation is not significantly affected by aggregation bias. Brand and Cassola (2000) and Coenen and Vega (2001) also study money demand only at an area-wide level. On the other side, Marcellino, Stock and Watson (2003), and Espasa, Albacete and Senra (2002) provide evidence against the use of aggregate models and prefer to forecast a number of euro-area variables at country level. Against this view, Bodo, Golinelli and Parigi (2000) show that the area-wide model is better than single country models in forecasting industrial production. Finally, a completely different approach is followed by Rudebusch and Svensson (2002), who use a model estimated on US data to discuss euro-area policy issues.

[3] The data used in the empirical analysis are updated from Golinelli and Pastorello (2002). The data set is available for downloading at http://www.spbo.unibo.it/pais/golinelli/, where further details on the sources are also provided.

[4] Moreover, the Hansen (1992) instability test confirms the presence of instability in the mean real interest rate at the 5% significance level ($L_c = 1.40$).

Table 4.1. *Unit root ADF tests, 1978Q4–2001Q3*

Variable	ADF	k	Model
$m - p$	−3.09	2	c,t
$\Delta(m-p)$	−3.73**	1	c
y	−1.56	0	c,t
Δy	−5.65**	0	c
s	−1.29	1	c
Δs	−5.44**	0	c
l	−1.05	1	c
Δl	−5.15**	0	c
π	−1.36	1	c
$\Delta \pi$	−9.49**	1	c
$ygap$	−3.63**	2	c
$y-(m-p)$	−2.60	1	c,t
$s - \pi$	−1.88	2	c
$l - \pi$	−2.39	1	c
$l - s$	−3.40*	1	c

Notes: * and ** denote rejection of the null hypothesis of unit root at the 5% and 1% level, respectively. MacKinnon critical values are: −2.89 (5%) and −3.50 (1%) for models with constant only (c); −3.46 and −4.06 for models with constant and trend (c, t). k denotes the number of lags in the test, selected following the general-to-specific procedure advocated by Ng and Perron (1995) with $k_{\max} = 5$.

long-term interest rate over the last part of the sample. Then, instead of equation (4.6), a more appropriate specification of the Fisher relation for the euro area could be the following, allowing for changes in the mean real interest rate:

$$l_t = \beta_0^f(r_t) + \pi_t + \varepsilon_t^f, \qquad (4.8)$$

where r_t is a random variable indexing the risk premium regime.

Structural change in the real interest rate has been investigated by means of a Markov-switching model (Hamilton, 1989), allowing us to detect potential break points endogenously, with no a priori assumption concerning their number and timing. Table 4.2 summarises the main features of the estimated Markov-switching model. According to the LR and specification tests, a two-regime model for the intercept in (4.8), with a first-order autoregressive term, can be

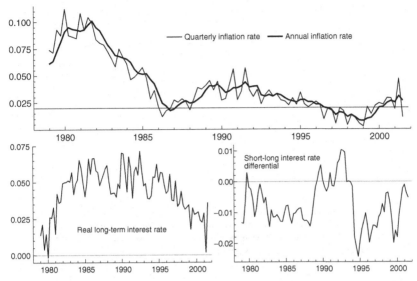

Figure 4.1 Quarterly and annual euro-area inflation rates, real long-term interest rate and short-long interest rate differential 1978Q4−2001Q3
Note: The quarterly inflation rate π is annualised; the annual inflation rate is computed as $\sum_{i=0}^{3} \pi_{t-i}$; the real long-term interest rate is obtained as $l - \pi$, the interest rate differential is computed as $s - l$.

selected, suggesting that the persistence in the real interest rate is not fully explained by the break process only.[5] As shown in the table, the estimated mean ex-post real interest rate is 2.6% in the 'low' regime and 5.2% in the 'high' regime. The estimated mean real interest rate is plotted in the upper panel of figure 4.2, together with the observed rate. In the lower panel of the figure, the estimated smoothed probabilities of the two regimes are shown: the 'low' real interest rate regime ends in 1981Q3 and starts again in 1997Q3, suggesting that the fall in the risk premium pre-dated the introduction of the common monetary policy in 1999,[6] whereas the 'high' real rate regime spans the 1981Q4−1997Q2 period. This finding points to an important contribution of

---

[5] The p-value of the LR test for the null of a single regime model against the two-regime model (computed as in Davies, 1987 to account for the non-standard asymptotic distribution of the test), is 0.002. The p-value of the test for two against three regimes is 1. Similar results are obtained by using the Perron (1997) DF test with endogenous break point: over the period 1981Q4 to 2001Q3 the long-term real interest rate is stationary with a break in 1997Q2 (the test statistic is −6.5 against the 1% critical value of −5.77).

[6] On the other hand, if the reference date is the Maastricht Treaty (February 1992), our findings are consistent with a lagged adjustment of the risk premium. The reduction may have taken place once the macroeoconomic convergence in the euro area and the compatibility with the Maastricht parameters were unambiguous.

Table 4.2. *Regime switching analysis of the long-term real interest rate.*

	Regime 1	Regime 2
Regime 1	0.952	0.016
Regime 2	0.048	0.984
Mean	2.58	5.19
	(0.21)	(0.13)
Duration (quarters)	21	61
Number of observations	29	63

Notes: The first four rows of the table report the transition matrix $(p_{ij} = \Pr\{r(t) = i \mid r(t-1) = j\})$. Mean denotes the estimated ex-post real interest rate in the two regimes. Duration denotes the average duration of each regime in quarters. The number of observations in each regime is reported in the last row.

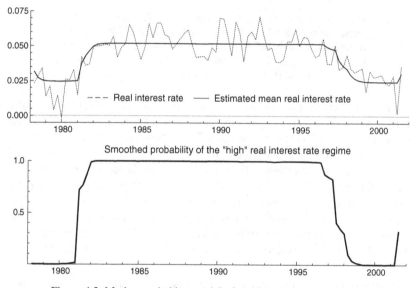

Figure 4.2 Markov-switching model of real interest rate

monetary unification to economic growth, through a reduced cost of investment financing.

The existence of two different regimes in the real interest rate behaviour has relevant consequences for the long-run empirical modelling of our set of six variables of interest ($m - p$, y, s, l, π and $ygap$). In fact, when tests for the cointegration rank and the forecasting ability are performed on a VAR(3) system over the 1981Q4−1997Q2 period only (identified above by the Markov-switching model as the 'high' real interest rate regime), the Johansen (1995) trace statistics support the existence of four cointegrating relationships at the 10% significance level. However, the one-step (ex-post) parameter constancy forecast test over the period 1998–2001 reveals strong evidence of a significant shift and, accordingly, the cointegration test over the full sample detects fewer than four cointegrating relationships. In short, the extension of the sample period leads to forecast failure and missing cointegration owing to parameter instability.

In order to capture the structural change in the long-run Fisher relation detected above, we include in the basic VAR system a step dummy variable (RP) taking the value of 1 during the 'high' real rate regime (1981Q4−1997Q2), and 0 in the 'low' rate regime (1978Q4−1981Q3 and 1997Q3−2001Q3). Prior to presenting the results, the next subsection shows how the standard methodology is extended to include a dummy variable in the cointegrating space.

2.1   Methodology

The standard vector error-correction mechanism (VECM) representation of the model, controlling for a linear trend in the level of the variables, can be written as

$$\Pi^*(L)\,\Delta\mathbf{x}_t = \nu + \Pi(1)\,\mathbf{x}_{t-1} + \varepsilon_t, \tag{4.9}$$

where $\mathbf{x}_t$ is the vector of n $I(1)$ cointegrated variables of interest, ν is the vector of intercept terms, $\varepsilon_t \sim NID\,(0, \Sigma)$; $\Pi(L) = \mathbf{I}_n - \sum_{i=1}^{p} \Pi_i L^i$, $\Pi^*(L) = \mathbf{I}_n - \sum_{i=1}^{p-1} \Pi_i^* L^i$ and $\Pi_i^* = -\sum_{j=i+1}^{p} \Pi_j$ $(i = 1, \dots, p-1)$. If there are $0 < k < n$ cointegration relationships among the variables, $\Pi(1)$ is of reduced rank k and can be expressed as the product of two $(n \times k)$ matrices: $\Pi(1) = \alpha\beta'$, where β contains the cointegrating vectors, such that $\beta'\mathbf{x}_t$ are stationary linear combinations of the $I(1)$ variables, and α is the matrix of factor loadings. When one of the cointegrating vectors (i.e. the kth vector) contains a switching intercept modelled by dummy variables, it is possible to rewrite the β matrix as

$$\underset{(n+q)\times k}{\bar{\beta}} = \begin{pmatrix} \underset{n\times k}{\beta} \\ \underset{q\times(k-1)}{\mathbf{0}} \quad \underset{q\times 1}{\beta^*} \end{pmatrix},$$

where β^* is the $q \times 1$ subvector containing the parameters of the q deterministic variables in the kth cointegrating vector. If there are q regimes, $q-1$ regimes may be normalised relative to the qth regime; this amounts to measuring the switches relative to a constant intercept term, therefore requiring a constant term and $q-1$ intervention dummies. The VECM representation can then be

Table 4.3. *Cointegration parameter estimates*

	Loading coeff. (α)				Restricted cointegrating vectors (β')					
					$m-p$	y	s	l	π	$ygap$
$m-p$	−0.091 (0.023)	0	0	0						
y	0	−0.176 (0.094)	0	0	1	−1.583 (0.026)	0	0	0	0
s	0	0	0	0.055 (0.024)	0	0	1	−1	0	0
l	0	0.129 (0.056)	−0.144 (0.046)	0	0	0	0	1	−1	0
π	0.213 (0.061)	0	0.378 (0.138)	0.151 (0.062)	0	0	0	0	0	1
$ygap$	0	0	0	−0.136 (0.034)						

Overidentifying restrictions test: $\chi^2(22) = 21.6$ (p-value 0.48)

rewritten as

$$\Pi^*(L)\,\Delta\mathbf{x}_t = \nu + \alpha\,\bar{\boldsymbol{\beta}}'\,\bar{\mathbf{x}}_{t-1} + \varepsilon_t, \qquad (4.10)$$

where $\bar{\mathbf{x}}'_t = (\mathbf{x}'_t \, 1 \, \mathbf{d}'_t)$ and $\mathbf{d}_t$ is a $(q - 1) \times 1$ subvector including the $q - 1$ intervention dummies. Denoting the last column of α by α_k, equation (4.10) can be expressed in an estimable form as:

$$\Pi^*(L)\Delta\mathbf{x}_t = \nu^* + \alpha_k\,\beta_2^{*\prime}\,\mathbf{d}_{t-1} + \alpha\beta'\mathbf{x}_{t-1} + \varepsilon_t, \qquad (4.11)$$

where $\nu^* = \nu + \alpha_k\beta_1^*$, β_1^* and β_2^* denote respectively the first and the last $q -$ 1 elements of β^*, and $\mathbf{d}_t$ contains the $q - 1$ intervention dummies. In practice the model can be estimated leaving the deterministic components unrestricted.

2.2   Long-run results

The previously estimated VAR(3) system is then extended to include the (un-restricted) dummy variable *RP* to capture regime shifts in the long-term real interest rate behaviour. The estimation period now spans the full sample, from 1978Q4 to 2001Q3. Diagnostic tests on the whole system do not detect any sign of autocorrelation (supporting the choice of a three-lag specification) and heteroscedasticity. Only some residual non-normality is detected in the *ygap* equation.

Since formal Johansen's (1995) tests for the cointegration rank cannot be used owing to the presence of the *RP* dummy variable, we rely on visual inspection

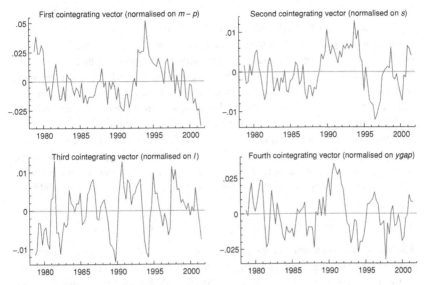

Figure 4.3 Restricted cointegrating vectors

and proceed under the assumption that there exist four valid cointegrating relationships among the variables in **x**. In accord with the theoretical framework illustrated above, we interpret such relationships as a long-run money demand function involving $m - p$ and y, a term structure equation between s and l, a Fisher parity relation linking l and π, and a long-run constant rate of capacity utilisation (stationarity of $ygap$). The LR test of the resulting set of seven overidentifying restrictions on the coefficients of β yields a $\chi^2(7)$ statistic of 9.1, with a corresponding p-value of 0.25, strongly supporting the chosen identification scheme. If additional zero restrictions are imposed on the loading parameter in α we obtain a $\chi^2(22)$ test statistic of 21.6 with a p-value of 0.48. The restricted loading factors and cointegration parameter estimates are reported in table 4.3, and the four (restricted) cointegrating vectors are shown in figure 4.3. The money demand long-run elasticity to income is very precisely estimated and considerably larger than unity (in line with the results in Gerlach and Svensson 2001), explaining the $I(1)$ feature of money velocity mentioned above.[7] Recursive estimation over the 1995–2001 subperiod shows that this elasticity

---

[7] When the term structure and the Fisher long-run relations are estimated without imposing $(1, -1)$ cointegrating vectors, the following results are obtained:

$$l = 0.951s; \quad l = 1.048\pi$$
$$(0.069) \quad\quad (0.074)$$

supporting the imposed restrictions.

is remarkably stable over time. The estimated loading parameters show that positive deviations from the equilibrium relation between $m - p$ and y cause a strong upward pressure on inflation and output and an error-correcting reaction of real money balances. An increase of the short-term interest rate relative to the long rate determines a negative reaction of output and an equilibrating response of the long-term rate. The long-term interest rate exhibits error-correcting behaviour also in response to positive deviations from the Fisher parity relation with the inflation rate. Finally, increases in the capacity utilisation rate have a positive impact on inflation (a 'Phillips curve') and on the short-term interest rate (a 'Taylor rule' effect). The whole set of overidentifying restrictions on the loading factors and the cointegrating vector parameters is never rejected at the 5% significance level when the system is estimated recursively from 1995.

3   Permanent and transitory components of inflation

The long-run (cointegration) properties of the data analysed in the previous section may then be used to disentangle the short- and long-run ('*core*') components of the variables analysed, as shown by Stock and Watson (1988) and Gonzalo and Granger (1995). To this aim, we apply the common trends methodology of King et al. (1991) and Mellander, Vredin and Warne (1992) to our small-scale macroeconomic system and focus in particular on the inflation rate. In this context, core inflation is interpreted as the long-run forecast of the inflation rate conditional on the information contained in the variables of the system and consistent with the long-run cointegration properties of the data. A similar definition of core inflation is adopted by Cogley and Sargent (2001) in their analysis of the dynamic behaviour of post-war US inflation. Moreover, in a multivariate system, structural shocks are likely to be identified more precisely than, for example, in the bivariate approach of Quah and Vahey (1995), and the forecast error variance decomposition can yield meaningful information about the dynamic effects of different disturbances on the inflation process. The rest of this section outlines and applies this econometric methodology to euro-area data.

3.1   Econometric methodology

As in Mellander, Vredin and Warne (1992) and Warne (1993), the cointegrated VAR in (4.11) can be inverted to yield the following stationary Wold representation for $\Delta \mathbf{x}_t$ (henceforth, deterministic terms, including the constant vector ν^* and the dummy variable vector $\mathbf{d}$ capturing different real interest rate regimes are omitted for ease of exposition):

$$\Delta \mathbf{x}_t = \mathbf{C}(L)\,\varepsilon_t, \qquad\qquad\qquad (4.12)$$

where $C(L) = I + C_1 L + C_2 L^2 + \ldots$ with $\sum_{j=0}^{\infty} j \mid C_j \mid < \infty$. From the representation in (4.12) the following expression for the levels of the variables can be derived by recursive substitution:

$$\mathbf{x}_t = \mathbf{x}_0 + \mathbf{C}(1) \sum_{j=0}^{t-1} \varepsilon_{t-j} + \mathbf{C}^*(L)\varepsilon_t, \qquad (4.13)$$

where $\mathbf{C}^*(L) = \sum_{j=0}^{\infty} \mathbf{C}_j^* L^j$ with $\mathbf{C}_j^* = -\sum_{i=j+1}^{\infty} \mathbf{C}_i$. $\mathbf{C}(1)$ captures the long-run effect of the reduced form disturbances in ε on the variables in $\mathbf{x}$ and $\mathbf{x}_0$ is the initial observation in the sample.

In order to obtain an economically meaningful interpretation of the dynamics of the variables of interest from the reduced form representations in (4.12) and (4.13), the vector of reduced form disturbances ε must be transformed into a vector of underlying, 'structural' shocks, some with *permanent* effects on the level of $\mathbf{x}$ and some with only *transitory* effects. Let us denote this vector of i.i.d. structural disturbances as $\varphi_t \equiv \left(\begin{smallmatrix} \psi_t \\ \nu_t \end{smallmatrix} \right)$, where ψ and ν are subvectors of $n - k$ and k elements, respectively. The structural form for the first difference of $\mathbf{x}_t$ is:

$$\Delta \mathbf{x}_t = \mathbf{\Gamma}(L)\varphi_t \qquad (4.14)$$

where $\mathbf{\Gamma}(L) = \mathbf{\Gamma}_0 + \mathbf{\Gamma}_1 L + \ldots$. Since the first element of $\mathbf{C}(L)$ in (4.12) is $\mathbf{I}$, equating the first term of the right-hand sides of (4.12) and (4.14) yields the following relationship between the reduced form and the structural shocks:

$$\varepsilon_t = \mathbf{\Gamma}_0 \varphi_t, \qquad (4.15)$$

where $\mathbf{\Gamma}_0$ is an invertible matrix. Hence, comparison of (4.14) and (4.12) shows that

$$\mathbf{C}(L)\mathbf{\Gamma}_0 = \mathbf{\Gamma}(L),$$

implying that $\mathbf{C}_i \mathbf{\Gamma}_0 = \mathbf{\Gamma}_i \, (\forall i > 0)$ and $\mathbf{C}(1)\mathbf{\Gamma}_0 = \mathbf{\Gamma}(1)$. In order to identify the elements of ψ_t as the permanent shocks and the elements of ν_t as the transitory disturbances, the following restriction on the long-run matrix $\mathbf{\Gamma}(1)$ must be imposed:

$$\mathbf{\Gamma}(1) = (\mathbf{\Gamma}_g \, \mathbf{0}), \qquad (4.16)$$

with $\mathbf{\Gamma}_g$ an $n \times (n - k)$ submatrix. The disturbances in ψ_t are then allowed to have long-run effects on (at least some of) the variables in $\mathbf{x}_t$, whereas the shocks in ν_t are restricted to have only transitory effects.

From (4.14) the structural form representation for the endogenous variables in levels is derived as

$$\mathbf{x}_t = \mathbf{x}_0 + \mathbf{\Gamma}(1) \sum_{j=0}^{t-1} \varphi_{t-j} + \mathbf{\Gamma}^*(L)\varphi_t = \mathbf{x}_0 + \mathbf{\Gamma}_g \sum_{j=0}^{t-1} \psi_{t-j} + \mathbf{\Gamma}^*(L)\varphi_t, \quad (4.17)$$

where the partition of ϕ and the restriction in (4.16) have been used and $\Gamma^*(L)$ is defined analogously to $\mathbf{C}^*(L)$ in (4.13). The permanent part in (4.17), $\sum_{j=0}^{t-1} \psi_{t-j}$, may be expressed as an $(n - k)$-vector random walk τ with innovations ψ:

$$\tau_t = \tau_{t-1} + \psi_t = \tau_0 + \sum_{j=0}^{t-1} \psi_{t-j}. \tag{4.18}$$

Using (4.18) in (4.17), we finally obtain the common trend representation of Stock and Watson (1988) for $\mathbf{x}_t$:

$$\mathbf{x}_t = \underbrace{\mathbf{x}_0 + \Gamma_g \tau_t}_{} + \underbrace{\Gamma^*(L)\varphi_t}_{} \tag{4.19}$$

$$\Rightarrow \mathbf{x}_t = \qquad \mathbf{x}_t^c \qquad + \qquad \mathbf{x}_t^{nc},$$

where $\mathbf{x}_t^c$ and $\mathbf{x}_t^{nc}$ correspond to the 'trend' and 'cycle' components in the Beveridge–Nelson–Stock–Watson decomposition of $\mathbf{x}_t$. According to (4.19) the trend behaviour of the variables is determined by the permanent disturbances only, whereas the cyclical component is determined by all innovations in the system, both permanent and transitory. This implies that permanent innovations also induce transitory dynamics.

As shown in detail by Stock and Watson (1988), King et al. (1991) and Warne (1993), the identification of separate permanent shocks requires a sufficient number of restrictions on the long-run impact matrix Γ_g in (4.19). Part of these restrictions are provided by the cointegrating relations and the consistent estimation of $\mathbf{C}(1)$; additional ones are suggested by economic theory (e.g. long-run neutrality assumptions). Finally, having estimated Γ_g, the behaviour of the variables in $\mathbf{x}_t$ due to the permanent disturbances only, interpreted as the long-run forecast of $\mathbf{x}_t$, may be computed as $\mathbf{x}_0 + \Gamma_g \tau_t$. Formally, such a long-run forecast can be expressed as

$$\lim_{h \to \infty} E_t \mathbf{x}_{t+h} = \mathbf{x}_0 + \Gamma_g \tau_t, \tag{4.20}$$

capturing the values to which the series are expected to converge once the effect of the transitory shocks have died out (Cogley and Sargent 2001). Moreover, from the moving average representation in (4.14), impulse responses and forecast error variance decompositions may be calculated to gauge the relative importance of permanent and transitory innovations in determining fluctuations of the endogenous variables.

3.2   Results

In our common trends framework, the existence of four cointegrating vectors in the six-variable system implies the presence of two sources of shocks having permanent effects on at least some of the variables in $\mathbf{x}'$ ($m - p$, y, s, l, π and $ygap$). As previously mentioned, the four (restricted) cointegrating vectors provide a set of restrictions that can be used to identify the elements of Γ_g in (4.19). However, one additional restriction is needed to achieve identification. To this aim, we make the following assumption on the nature of the two permanent shocks in the system: we consider a *real* shock (ψ_r) and a *nominal* disturbance (ψ_n). The permanent part (4.18) of the common trends representation is then given by the following bivariate random walk:

$$\begin{pmatrix} \tau_r \\ \tau_n \end{pmatrix}_t = \begin{pmatrix} \mu_r \\ \mu_n \end{pmatrix} + \begin{pmatrix} \tau_r \\ \tau_n \end{pmatrix}_{t-1} + \begin{pmatrix} \psi_r \\ \psi_n \end{pmatrix}_t, \tag{4.21}$$

where μ is a vector of constant drift terms. Consistent with the theoretical framework sketched in section 2, as an additional restriction we assume that output is not affected in the long run by the nominal shock (a long-run neutrality assumption). Letting γ_{ij} denote the generic element of Γ_g, this neutrality assumption implies $\gamma_{22} = 0$. Given the long-run relationship linking output and real money balances only, an implication of the long-run neutrality restriction is that the nominal trend does not have a long-run impact on real money balances as well ($\gamma_{12} = 0$). In addition, the same long-run money demand relation implies that the response of $m - p$ to the real permanent shock (γ_{11}) is given by $\beta_1^m \gamma_{21}$, with the estimated value of β_1^m being 1.583 (see results in table 4.3). Moreover, the cointegration properties of the interest rates and inflation also imply that $\gamma_{31} = \gamma_{41} = \gamma_{51}$ and $\gamma_{32} = \gamma_{42} = \gamma_{52}$: in the long-run a permanent disturbance (either real or nominal) has the same effect on s, l and π. Finally, since the output gap is a stationary variable and therefore not affected by permanent shocks in the long run, we have $\gamma_{61} = \gamma_{62} = 0$. The common trends representation of the variables in levels (4.19) becomes therefore the following:

$$\begin{pmatrix} m - p \\ y \\ s \\ l \\ \pi \\ ygap \end{pmatrix}_t = \begin{pmatrix} m - p \\ y \\ s \\ l \\ \pi \\ ygap \end{pmatrix}_0 + \begin{pmatrix} \beta_1^m \gamma_{21} & 0 \\ \gamma_{21} & 0 \\ \gamma_{31} & \gamma_{32} \\ \gamma_{31} & \gamma_{32} \\ \gamma_{31} & \gamma_{32} \\ 0 & 0 \end{pmatrix} \begin{pmatrix} \tau_r \\ \tau_n \end{pmatrix}_t + \Gamma^*(L) \begin{pmatrix} \psi_r \\ \psi_n \\ \nu_1 \\ \nu_2 \\ \nu_3 \\ \nu_4 \end{pmatrix}_t, \tag{4.22}$$

where the ν_is ($i = 1,2,3,4$) are purely transitory disturbances (uncorrelated with the permanent shocks) to which, given the main focus of our analysis, we do not attribute any structural economic interpretation.

The estimated core inflation series from the common trends model is then computed as $\hat{\pi}_t^c = \pi_0 + \hat{\gamma}_{31} \hat{\tau}_{r,t} + \hat{\gamma}_{32} \hat{\tau}_{n,t}$. Such a measure captures the

Table 4.4. *Common trends model*

Variable	Long-run effects (Γ_g)		Long-run(∞) forecast error variance explained by:	
	ψ_r	ψ_n	ψ_r	ψ_n
$m - p$	0.980*	0	1	1
	(0.395)			
y	0.619*	0	1	0
	(0.249)			
s	1.104	0.384**	0.069	0.931**
	(0.177)	(0.085)	(0.225)	(0.225)
l	0.104	0.384**	0.069	0.931**
	(0.177)	(0.085)	(0.225)	(0.225)
π	0.104	0.384**	0.069	0.931**
	(0.177)	(0.085)	(0.225)	(0.225)
$ygap$	0	0	0	0

Notes: ψ_r and ψ_n denote the real and nominal permanent shocks respectively; asymptotic standard errors in parentheses; * and ** denote statistical significance at the 5% and 1% level, respectively.

long-run effects on inflation of the two identified permanent disturbances and bears the interpretation of the (conditional) forecast of the inflation rate over a long-term (infinite) horizon, when all transitory fluctuations in the inflation rate have vanished.

The main results from the estimation of the common trends model are shown in table 4.4, where the estimated elements of the long-run impact matrix Γ_g (with asymptotic standard errors in parentheses) and the long-run forecast error variance decomposition of all variables are reported. The estimated long-run effects of permanent shocks show that the real shock (ψ_r), which is the only determinant of the long-run behaviour of real money balances and output, plays only a marginal role in explaining the long-run features of the two interest rates and the inflation rate, which are dominated by nominal disturbances (ψ_n). This finding supports the separation of the long-run properties of real money balances and output on the one hand and nominal interest rates and inflation on the other (as noted also by Cassola and Morana 2002 in a larger system of euro-area variables). Therefore, the measure of core inflation derived from the common trends model is almost entirely explained by the nominal trend. This conclusion is supported also by the result of the forecast error variance decomposition reported in table 4.4, showing that in the long run more than 90% of the inflation rate variability is attributable to the nominal permanent disturbance.

The upper panel of figure 4.4 plots the estimated core inflation series, π^c, the measured HICP inflation, and the 'non-core' inflation rate ($\pi^{nc} \equiv \pi - \pi^c$),

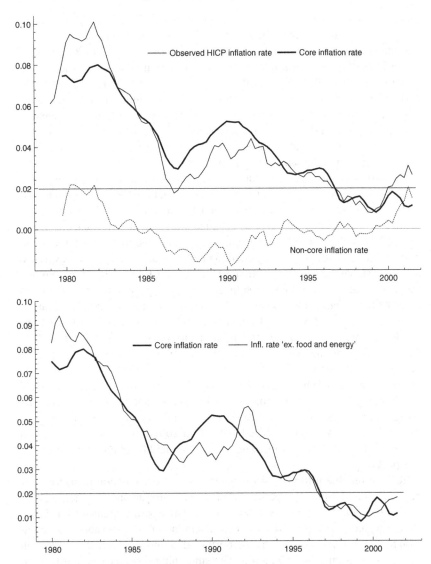

Figure 4.4 Observed annual inflation rates and common trend core and non-core inflation measure

all expressed as annual rates (four-quarter lagged moving averages) over the whole 1979–2001 period. In the lower panel, the common trend measure of core inflation is compared with a widely used measure of the underlying trend in the inflation rate, namely the rate of change of the CPI price level excluding 'food and energy' goods. As shown in the figure, in the 1980s the core inflation rate shows more limited fluctuations, ranging from 3% to 8%, with respect to both observed inflation measures, which vary widely between 2% and 10%. In particular, core inflation displays a lower peak during the oil-shock episode of the early 1980s (around 8% against 9–10% observed inflation rate), whereas this pattern is reversed during the counter-shock in the mid-1980s. Starting in the early 1990s, the various inflation rates show more similar behaviour, though with some notable exceptions, namely in 1991, when the core rate began to decrease rapidly in the face of broadly stable (HICP) or increasing ('ex food and energy') actual inflation. Then, all inflation measures declined below the 2% level at around the same time in the second half of 1996.

Of particular interest is the relative behaviour of the actual and core inflation series since the introduction of the euro in January 1999. Initially, the core and the HICP rates increased from around 1% in early 1999 up to around 2% in mid-2000 (in 2000Q2 the core inflation rate was at 1.8% and the HICP rate at 2.1%). Such an increase is commonly attributed to the sharp rise in oil prices, since the consumer price inflation rate 'excluding food and energy items' remained stable within a 1–1.2% range. However, the forward-looking, common trends measure of core inflation signals that the long-run inflation forecast as of 2000Q2 was very close to the HICP observed inflation, even though the 'ex food and energy' index showed a lower and stable inflation rate. This evidence can lend some support to the prudent monetary policy attitude of the ECB in 1999 and 2000 in the management of policy interest rates. From 2000Q3, the behaviour of the estimated core inflation rate started to diverge from that of the two observed rates. While the HICP continued to increase up to 3.1% in 2001Q2 before going back to 2.6% in the following quarter, and the CPI 'ex food and energy' rate reached 1.8% in 2001Q3, the core inflation rate declined duing the second half of 2000 and stabilised at 1.1% in 2001. The increase in inflation observed in 2001 does not, then, necessarily signal higher long-term inflation prospects.

To give reliable information for policy use, a core inflation measure must possess some desirable properties, as stressed by Bryan and Cecchetti (1994) and Wynne (1999). First, the estimated core inflation series should display lower variability and higher persistence than actual inflation. As noted above, the common trends measure of core inflation portrayed in figure 4.4 is less volatile than measured consumer price inflation. The smoothing property of the estimated core inflation is further illustrated in panel A of table 4.5, which reports correlation coefficients among changes in the quarterly and annual (four-quarter moving average) inflation rates, including observed inflation and the common trends core and non-core measures, denoted by $\Delta\pi^c$ and $\Delta\pi^{nc}$ respectively, with $\Delta\pi \equiv \Delta\pi^c + \Delta\pi^{nc}$. Standard deviations in percentage points are shown on the diagonal. These latter statistics show that there is a remarkable difference in variability between the core and the non-core component: standard

Table 4.5. *Assessment of the common trend core inflation measure*

	A. Correlations				
	$\Delta\pi$	$\Delta\pi^c$	$\Delta\pi^{nc}$	$\Delta\pi^c_{NFE}$	$\Delta\pi^{nc}_{NFE}$
	Quarterly inflation rates: 1979Q2–2001Q3				
$\Delta\pi$	0.290				
$\Delta\pi^c$	0.384	0.100			
$\Delta\pi^{nc}$	0.938	0.042	0.268		
$\Delta\pi^c_{NFE}$	0.044	−0.033	0.060	0.259	
$\Delta\pi^{nc}_{NFE}$	0.723	0.315	0.675	−0.647	0.380
	Annual inflation rates: 1980Q1–2001Q3				
$\Delta\pi$	0.358				
$\Delta\pi^c$	0.509	0.210			
$\Delta\pi^{nc}$	0.806	−0.099	0.306		
$\Delta\pi^c_{NFE}$	0.478	0.120	0.470	0.293	
$\Delta\pi^{nc}_{NFE}$	0.639	0.434	0.440	−0.371	0.335

B. *Results from bivariate VAR systems*: 1979Q4–2001Q3

	F test (p-value) on 2 lags of:			Coefficient estimate on:	
Equation for:	$\Delta\pi$	$\Delta\pi^c$	$\Delta\pi^c_{NFE}$	$(\pi - \pi^c)_{t-1}$	$(\pi - \pi^c_{NFE})_{t-1}$
$\Delta\pi$	0.009**	0.643		−0.215*	
				(0.107)	
$\Delta\pi^c$	0.941	0.816		0.013	
				(0.045)	
$\Delta\pi$	0.037*		0.761		−0.165
					(0.126)
$\Delta\pi^c_{NFE}$	0.579		0.192		0.332**
					(0.109)

Notes: $\Delta\pi$ denotes the first difference of the measured HICP inflation rate; $\Delta\pi^c$ and $\Delta\pi^c_{NFE}$ denote the first differences of the common trend measure of core inflation and of the CPI 'excluding food and energy' inflation rates respectively; $\Delta\pi^{nc}$ and $\Delta\pi^{nc}_{NFE}$ are the associated non-core inflation changes, defined as $\Delta\pi^{nc} = \Delta\pi - \Delta\pi^c$ and $\Delta\pi^{nc}_{NFE} = \Delta\pi - \Delta\pi^c_{NFE}$. The figures on the main diagonals in panel A are standard deviations in percentage points (quarterly inflation rates are not annualised). * and ** denote statistical significance at the 5% and 1% levels, respectively.

deviations are 0.10 and 0.27 for $\Delta\pi^c$ and $\Delta\pi^{nc}$ respectively in quarterly data (0.21 and 0.31 in annual data), with a standard deviation of changes in the observed inflation rate of 0.29 (0.36). We also note that quarterly changes in observed inflation are much more closely correlated with changes in the non-core component (the correlation coefficient is 0.94) than with changes in the estimated core rate (0.38), and that there is a very low correlation between core and non-core inflation changes (0.04 in quarterly and -0.10 in annual data).

Panel A of Table 4.5 also reports standard deviations and correlations of the change in the CPI inflation rate 'excluding food and energy' goods, $\Delta \pi_{NFE}^{c}$ (the associated transitory inflation component is denoted by $\Delta \pi_{NFE}^{nc} \equiv \Delta \pi - \Delta \pi_{NFE}^{c}$). The standard deviations of changes in both inflation components obtained from the ex-food and energy price level are large (0.26 for $\Delta \pi_{NFE}^{c}$ and 0.38 for $\Delta \pi_{NFE}^{nc}$ in quarterly data), suggesting that this inflation indicator does not possess the smoothing property displayed by the common trends core inflation measure.

A second desirable property of a core inflation measure is the ability to forecast future headline inflation rates. The long-run forecasting power of our common trends measure is warranted, since it is estimated as the long-run conditional forecast of inflation. This property can be formally assessed by means of a bivariate VAR system including the observed inflation rate and core inflation π^{c}. As argued by Freeman (1998), the integration and cointegration properties of the inflation series require an error-correction representation to perform appropriate Granger-causality tests. In fact, both π and π^{c} are nonstationary, $I(1)$ series, whereas the associated non-core component π^{nc} displays stationarity, which may be interpreted as evidence of cointegration between the core inflation measure and the actual inflation rate, since $\pi^{nc} \equiv \pi - \pi^{c}$. The specification of the bivariate system is then the following:

$$\Delta \pi_t = \delta_{10} + \sum_{i=1}^{2} \delta_{11}(i) \Delta \pi_{t-i} + \sum_{i=1}^{2} \delta_{12}(i) \Delta \pi_{t-i}^{c} + \rho_{\pi}(\pi - \pi^{c})_{t-1} + u_{1t}$$

$$\Delta \pi_t^{c} = \delta_{20} + \sum_{i=1}^{2} \delta_{21}(i) \Delta \pi_{t-i} + \sum_{i=1}^{2} \delta_{22}(i) \Delta \pi_{t-i}^{c} + \rho_{c}(\pi - \pi^{c})_{t-1} + u_{2t},$$

$$(4.23)$$

where two lags are sufficient to eliminate residual serial correlation. Panel B of table 4.5 reports the results of the F-tests on each block of lagged regressors and the coefficient estimates of the error-correction coefficients ρ_{π} and ρ_{c}. Although lags of $\Delta \pi^{c}$ do not have additional predictive power for the actual inflation rate, a sizeable and significant error-correction coefficient ρ_{π} (-0.22) is estimated, showing a tendency of actual inflation to adjust to the core component, whereas no adjustment is detected in the behaviour of π^{c}. We also estimated the bivariate system in (4.23) with π_{NFE}^{c} in the place of π^{c}. The ex-food and energy inflation measure does not show any strong additional predictive power for the observed inflation rate. Moreover, the positive and strongly significant estimated error-correction coefficient on $(\pi - \pi^c_{NFE})_{t-1}$ suggests that past values of the inflation rate above the 'underlying' component measured by π^c_{NFE} cause an increase in π^c_{NFE} itself, reflecting the transmission of transitory shocks to the permanent component of inflation and casting some doubts on the usefulness of this measure as an indicator of the long-run inflation trend.

4   A closer look at the properties of inflation components

The common trends model applied in the preceding section decomposes observed inflation into a long-run, core component and a transitory, non-core element. In this section we analyse several features of this decomposition, starting from the sources of temporary fluctuations in the inflation rate captured by the non-core component. Then, we investigate how long it takes for the inflation rate to converge to the core inflation rate, interpreted as a long-run inflation forecast. Finally, we compare the estimated core inflation rate with the inflation forecast at various horizons obtained from a structural dynamic model encompassing the VAR.

4.1   The nature of the cyclical inflation component

By construction, the common trends core inflation measure embeds only the information contained in the permanent shocks hitting the system, abstracting from the more volatile dynamics generated by transitory shocks. However, the latter disturbances may not be the only sources of inflation fluctuations around the core component. In fact, an important property of the Beveridge–Nelson–Stock–Watson decomposition is that the 'cyclical' (here interpreted as the 'non-core') component π^{nc} is explained not only by transitory shocks, but also by permanent shocks. Proietti (1997) has proposed a methodology to disentangle in cyclical fluctuations the contribution of permanent shocks from the effect of transitory disturbances. Following Cassola and Morana (2002), a similar decomposition of the cycles can be obtained by rewriting the vector of cyclical components $\mathbf{x}^{nc}$ as

$$\mathbf{x}^{nc}_t = \mathbf{\Gamma}^*(L)\,\boldsymbol{\varphi}_t = \mathbf{\Gamma}^*_1(L)\,\boldsymbol{\psi}_t + \mathbf{\Gamma}^*_2(L)\,\boldsymbol{v}_t. \tag{4.24}$$

The vector $\mathbf{\Gamma}^*_1(L)\boldsymbol{\psi}_t$ gives the contribution of permanent innovations to the overall cycle (henceforth referred to as the 'dynamics *along* the attractor', DAA), while the vector $\mathbf{\Gamma}^*_2(L)\boldsymbol{v}_t$ measures the contribution of the transitory innovations to the overall cycle ('dynamics *towards* the attractor', DTA).

The latter kind of short-run dynamics have the error-correction process as generator and, therefore, are disequilibrium fluctuations, while the dynamics along the attractor may be related to the overshooting of the variables

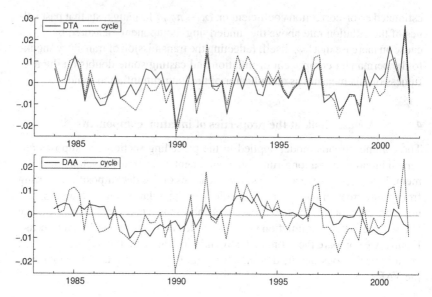

Figure 4.5 Non-core quarterly inflation rate 1984Q1−2001Q3
Note: The quarterly non-core inflation rate is decomposed into 'dynamics towards the attractor' (DTA) and the 'dynamics along the attarctor' (DAA) components.

to permanent innovations, i.e. they are the transitional dynamics which take place following a shock to the common trend. Since along the attractor the cointegration relationships are satisfied, the DAA adjustment captures equilibrium fluctuations. This distinction is of particular interest here since it allows us to attribute deviations of observed inflation from its core rate to the effects of transitory shocks and to the overshooting of the system to permanent shocks.

The decomposition of the non-core quarterly inflation rate into the DTA and DAA components is plotted in figure 4.5. After some experimentation we concluded that twenty lags are sufficient to reconstruct the cyclical components, so that our analysis focuses on the period starting in 1984Q1. As shown in the figure, both cyclical components are important determinants of the short-run inflation dynamics, with the DTA capturing most of the fluctuations. Over the reconstruction period the DTA explain about 50% of the unconditional variance of non-core inflation, while the contribution of the DAA is 38%.[8] Of the latter proportion, 49% is explained by the real permanent shock ψ_r and 32% by the nominal permanent disturbance ψ_n.

[8] The fractions of variance need not sum to one, since the orthogonality of structural shocks holds only on the entire estimation period, 1978Q1−2001Q3.

4.2   Convergence to the core inflation rate

Our proposed measure of core inflation bears the interpretation of long-run inflation forecast, i.e. $\pi_t^c = \lim_{h \to \infty} E_t \pi_{t+h}$. Although a long-run perspective is consistent with the monetary policymakers' ability to influence the price level, an infinite horizon is not literally appropriate for the purposes of policy analysis; for example, the ECB price stability objective is explicitly referred to as a 'medium-term' horizon. Then, for the common trend measure of core inflation to provide useful information to policymakers on the consistency of current inflation developments with their longer-term price stability goal, it is important to assess how long it takes for transitory and permanent shocks to exhaust their effects on the non-core inflation component π^{nc}, i.e. how long it takes for the observed inflation rate π to converge to the long-run forecast π^c.

In order to provide some empirical evidence on this issue, we estimated the impulse response functions of the non-core inflation rate to the various structural disturbances. Figure 4.6 shows the impulse responses of the non-core inflation rate to the real and nominal permanent shocks, to a composite permanent shock, i.e. the sum of the two permanent shocks, capturing the 'dynamics along the attractor', and to a composite transitory shock, i.e. the sum of the four transitory shocks, capturing the 'dynamics towards the attractor'.

As shown in the figure, both composite disturbances have short-lived effects on non-core inflation; in particular, transitory shocks tend to be inflationary whereas permanent disturbances tend to be deflationary, and complete convergence to the reference value is achieved within six and twenty quarters for the DTA shock and the DAA shock, respectively (consistent with the result of the decomposition of the overall short-run inflation fluctuations in the previous subsection). As far as the DAA composite disturbance is concerned, the response of non-core inflation is dominated by the reaction to the real permanent shock, with inflation falling as productivity increases. According to the estimated significance bands (one standard error), the responses of π^{nc} are not statistically different from zero after only a few quarters (one and six quarters for DTA and DAA shocks, respectively), suggesting that the overall inflation rate quickly reverts to its long-run, core component. The empirical evidence therefore supports the proposed core inflation measure as a potentially useful indicator of long-run inflation prospects over a horizon appropriate for monetary policy evaluation.

4.3   Forecasting inflation from a structural dynamic model

Finally, we compare the estimated core inflation from the common trends model with the forecast of a structural econometric model (SEM) derived from the cointegrated VAR system previously estimated. Starting from the cointegrated

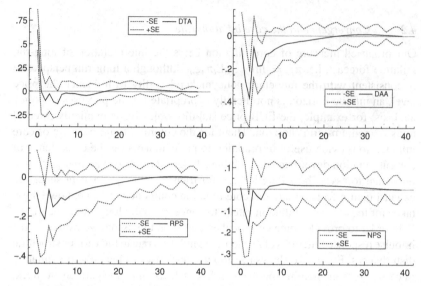

Figure 4.6 Responses of the non-core quarterly inflation rate to shocks.
Note: The upper panels show the impulse response functions of the non-core quarterly inflation rate π^{nc} to composite transitory shocks (DTA), and to composite permanent shocks (DAA). The lower panels show the impulse response functions of π^{nc} to the real permanent shock ψ_r (RPS), and to the nominal permanent disturbance ψ_n (NPS). One-standard error confidence bands have been computed by Monte Carlo simulations, with 1000 replications.

VAR set up in section 2.2, we followed a 'general-to-specific' modelling strategy (Hendry and Mizon, 1993). Zero restrictions were imposed in successive steps on several lags of the endogenous variables in the six equations of the system; after each step a test of the overidentifying restrictions was performed, supporting the restrictions imposed. The FIML estimates of the final specification of the SEM are shown in table 4.6, where deterministic terms are not reported for brevity.

The system diagnostic tests show the data congruence of the SEM and recursive one-step and break-point Chow tests support parameter stability. The tracking of the model is good (the residual standard errors are relatively small) and the test of the whole set of overidentifying restrictions has a p-value of 0.96 (beside the zero restrictions, one additional parameter restriction is imposed in the Δy equation, with a p-value of 0.53). Moreover, the residual correlation matrix shows low coefficients (usually lower than 0.3), suggesting the success of the modelling strategy. Finally, the static long-run real interest rate estimates reported in the bottom part of table 4.6. are consistent with both the Markov-switching results in section 2.2 and with those in Gerlach and Schnabel (2000).

Table 4.6. *The structural dynamic model (FIML estimates)*

	Equation for:					
	$\Delta(m-p)$	Δy	Δs	Δl	$\Delta\pi$	$\Delta ygap$
$\Delta(m-p)_{t-1}$	0.416 (0.089)	–	–	–	–	–
$\Delta(m-p)_{t-2}$	0.219 (0.088)	0.351 (0.090)	–	0.160 (0.059)	–	–
Δy_{t-1}	–	–	0.116 (0.064)	–	–	0.362 (0.093)
Δy_{t-2}	0.118 (0.062)	–	–	–	–	0.239 (0.097)
Δs_{t-1}	–	–	0.191 (0.099)	–	–	–
Δs_{t-2}	−0.150 (0.080)	−0.197 (–)	−0.244 (0.094)	−0.174 (0.076)	–	−0.318 (0.140)
Δl_{t-1}	−0.340 (0.090)	–	0.380 (0.121)	0.623 (0.090)	–	–
Δl_{t-2}	–	–	–	–	–	0.419 (0.156)
$\Delta\pi_{t-1}$	0.093 (0.041)	–	0.072 (0.037)	−0.117 (0.046)	−0.337 (0.122)	
$\Delta\pi_{t-2}$	–	0.197 (0.043)	–	−0.082 (0.032)	−0.191 (0.091)	–
$\Delta ygap_{t-1}$	–	0.196 (0.079)	–	–	–	0.223 (0.093)
$\Delta ygap_{t-2}$	–	–	–	0.095 (0.047)	–	0.261 (0.088)
$[(m-p)-1.58y]_{t-1}$	−0.079 (0.020)	–	–	–	0.185 (0.050)	–
$(s-l)_{t-1}$	–	−0.106 (0.072)	–	0.127 (0.045)	–	–
$(l-\pi)_{t-1}$	–	–	–	−0.153 (0.041)	0.370 (0.110)	–
$ygap_{t-1}$	–	–	0.068 (0.020)	–	0.176 (0.050)	−0.110 (0.027)
St. error regression	0.0036	0.0047	0.0039	0.0032	0.0094	0.0048

Misspecification tests:

AR(5) F: 1.08 [0.28]   Heter. F: 0.97 [0.65]   Norm. $\chi^2(2)$: 23.4 [0.03]

Tests of overidentifying restrictions:

Zero restrictions $\chi^2(63)$: 44.7 [0.96]   Other restrictions $\chi^2(1)$: 0.4 [0.53]

Static long-run:

Δy^* (annualised): 0.0249 $\beta_0^f = l^* - \pi^*$, low-rate regime: 0.0331
(0.003),   (0.0025)

difference high–low rate regimes: 0.0191
(0.0028)

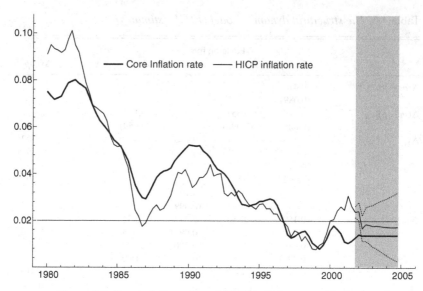

Figure 4.7 Core inflation rate and HICP inflation rate with forecast from a
multiple-equation structural dynamic model
Note: One-standard forecast error bands are shown. The shaded area indicates
the forecast period: 2001Q4–2004Q4.

Turning to the inflation forecasting issue, figure 4.7 displays the annual HICP
inflation rate with point forecast values for the period 2001Q4–2004Q4 from
the estimated SEM. The inflation rate is forecast to decline rapidly from the
2.6% level reached in 2001Q3 and stabilise in the 1.7–1.8% range from 2002Q2.
Over a two- to three- year horizon these values are broadly consistent with the
long-run inflation forecast measured by the common trends core inflation series,
which predicts an annual inflation rate around 1.4%.[9]

5   Conclusions

A common trends model has been used to estimate the underlying, 'core' inflation behaviour for the euro area from 1978 to 2001. In this framework core
inflation is interpreted as the long-run forecast of inflation conditional on the
information contained in money growth, output fluctuations and movements of
the term structure of interest rates.

---

[9] The relatively wide one-standard forecast error bands, computed taking into account the error
variance only, show that, despite the overall good statistical performance of the econometric
model, forecasting accuracy is still insufficient to make point inflation forecast from the SEM a
reliable guide for policymakers.

A price stability-oriented monetary policy has to be forward looking and respond only to shocks having long-lasting effects on the inflation rate. The common trends core inflation measure may be useful for monetary policy purposes since it embodies long-run economic restrictions strongly supported by the data and bears the interpretation of a long-run forecast, affected only by permanent disturbances to the inflation rate.

Our empirical exercise on euro-area data shows that purely transitory shocks have short-lived effects on the inflation rate and the estimated core measure captures the permanent component of inflation fluctuations over a medium-term horizon consistent with the monetary policy strategy of the European Central Bank. An important implication of our results is that deviations of core inflation, rather than actual inflation, from the price stability objective convey the appropriate signals for policy action. This conclusion partly contrasts with a large body of the monetary policy literature, where policy behaviour is modelled by means of a standard Taylor rule.[10]

As a final word of caution, we observe that a core inflation rate estimated from a common trend model depends on the specification of the system in terms of variables included, sample period, dynamic specification, and other modelling choices. However, the core inflation series obtained from the small-scale macroeconomic model used in this chapter, featuring long-run relationships between real money balances, output, inflation and interest rates, seems a useful benchmark to evaluate the properties of other measures of core inflation currently used in the monetary policy debate. As a first step in this direction we compared the smoothing and forecasting properties of the common trends core inflation with those of the 'ex food and energy' CPI inflation rate. The comparison lends support to our core inflation measure as a more reliable indicator of the long-run inflation trend.

REFERENCES

Bagliano, F. C., R. Golinelli and C. Morana, 2002, 'Core Inflation in the Euro Area', *Applied Economic Letters* 9, 353–7.

Bodo, G., R. Golinelli and G. Parigi, 2000, 'Forecasting Industrial Production in the Euro Area', *Empirical Economics* 25(4), 541–61.

Brand, C. and N. Cassola, 2000, 'A Money Demand System for Euro Area M3', European Central Bank Working Paper no. 39.

Bryan, M. F. and S. G. Cecchetti, 1994, 'Measuring Core Inflation', in N. G. Mankiw (ed.), *Monetary Policy*, Chicago: University of Chicago Press for NBER, pp. 195–215.

---

[10] A first application of a modified monetary policy rule which determines short-term interest rates according to the deviations of core inflation from the price stability objective is provided by Cassola and Morana (2002).

Cassola, N. and C. Morana, 2002, 'Monetary Policy and the Stock Market in the Euro Area', European Central Bank Working Paper no. 119.

Cecchetti, S. G., 1997, 'Measuring Short-Run Inflation for Central Bankers', *Federal Reserve Bank of St. Louis Review* 79(3), 143–56.

Coenen, G. and J. L. Vega, 2001, 'The Demand for M3 in the Euro Area', *Journal of Applied Econometrics* 16(6), 727–48.

Cogley, T., 2002, 'A Simple Adaptive Measure of Core Inflation', *Journal of Money, Credit and Banking* 34(1), 94–113.

Cogley, T. and T. J. Sargent, 2001, 'Evolving Post-World War II U.S. Inflation Dynamics', in B. S. Bernanke and K. Rogoff (eds.), *NBER Macroeconomics Annual 2001*, Cambridge, MA: MIT Press, pp. 331–72.

Davies, R. B., 1987, 'Hypothesis Testing when a Nuisance Parameter is Present Only Under the Alternative', *Biometrika* 74, 33–43.

Dedola L., E. Gaiotti and L. Silipo, 2001, 'Money Demand in the Euro Area: Do National Differences Matter?', Bank of Italy Discussion Paper no. 405.

Espasa, A., R. Albacete and E. Senra, 2002, 'Forecasting EMU Inflation: A Disaggregated Approach by Countries and Components', *European Journal of Finance* 8(4), 402–21.

European Central Bank, 1999, 'The Stability-Oriented Monetary Policy Strategy of the Eurosystem', *Monthly Bulletin*, January, 39–49.

    2000, 'The Two Pillars of the ECB's Monetary Policy Strategy', *Monthly Bulletin*, November, 37–48.

    2001, 'Framework and Tools of Monetary Analysis', *Monthly Bulletin*, May, 41–58.

Freeman, D. G., 1998, 'Do Core Inflation Measures Help Forecast Inflation?', *Economics Letters* 58, 143–7.

Galí, J., M. Gertler and J. D. López-Salido, 2001, 'European Inflation Dynamics', *European Economic Review* 45(7), 1237–70.

Gerlach, S. and G. Schnabel, 2000, 'The Taylor Rule and Interest Rates in the EMU Area', *Economics Letters* 67, 165–71.

Gerlach, S. and L. E. O. Svensson, 2001, 'Money and Inflation in the Euro Area: A Case of Monetary Indicators?', Bank for International Settlements Working Paper no. 98, January.

Golinelli, R. and S. Pastorello, 2002, 'Modelling the Demand for M3 in the Euro Area', *European Journal of Finance* 8(4), 371–401.

Gonzalo, J. and C. W. J. Granger, 1995, 'Estimation of Common Long-Memory Components in Cointegrated Systems', *Journal of Business and Economic Statistics* 13, 27–35.

Hallman, J. J., R. D. Porter and D. H. Small, 1991, 'Is the Price Level Tied to the M2 Monetary Aggregate in the Long Run?', *American Economic Review* 81(4), 841–58.

Hamilton, J. D., 1989, 'A New Approach to the Economic Analysis of Nonstationary Time Series and the Business Cycle', *Econometrica* 57, 357–84.

Hansen, B. E., 1992, 'Tests for Parameter Instability in Regressions with I(1) Processes', *Journal of Business and Economics Statistics* 10, 321–35.

Hendry, D. F. and G. E. Mizon, 1993, 'Evaluating Dynamic Econometric Models by Encompassing the VAR', in P. C. B. Phillips (ed.), *Models, Methods and Applications of Econometrics*, Oxford: Basil Blackwell, pp. 272–300.

Johansen, S., 1995, *Likelihood-Based Inference in Cointegrated Vector Autoregressive Models*, Oxford: Oxford University Press.

King, R. J., C. Plosser, J. H. Stock and M. W. Watson, 1991, 'Stochastic Trends and Economic Fluctuations', *American Economic Review* 81, 819–40.

Marcellino, M., J. H. Stock and M. W. Watson, 2003, 'Macroeconomic Forecasting in the Euro Area: Country Specific Versus Area-wide Information', *European Economic Review* 47(1), 1–18.

Mellander, E., A. Vredin and A. Warne, 1992, 'Stochastic Trends and Economic Fluctuations in a Small Open Economy', *Journal of Applied Econometrics* 7, 369–94.

Ng, S. and P. Perron, 1995, 'Unit Root Tests in ARIMA Models with Data-Dependent Methods for the Selection of the Truncation Lag', *Journal of the American Statistical Association* 90(429), 268–81.

Perron, P., 1997, 'Further Evidence on Breaking and Trend Functions in Macroeconomic Variables', *Journal of Econometrics* 55, 355–85.

Proietti, T., 1997, 'Short-Run Dynamics in Cointegrating Systems', *Oxford Bulletin of Economics and Statistics* 59(3), 403–22.

Quah, D. and S. P. Vahey, 1995, 'Measuring Core Inflation', *Economic Journal* 105, 1130–44.

Rudebusch, G. D. and L. E. O. Svensson, 1999, 'Policy Rules for Inflation Targeting', in J. B. Taylor (ed.), *Monetary Policy Rules*, Chicago: University of Chicago Press for NBER, pp. 203–46.

2002, 'Eurosystem Monetary Targeting: Lessons from US Data', *European Economic Review* 46(3), 417–42.

Staiger, D., J. H. Stock and M. W. Watson, 2001, 'Prices, wages and the US NAIRU in the 1990s', NBER Working Paper no. 8320.

Stock, J. H. and M. W. Watson, 1988, 'Testing for Common Trends', *Journal of the American Statistical Association* 83, 1097–107.

Taylor, J. B., 1999, 'The Robustness and Efficiency of Monetary Policy Rules as Guidelines for Interest Rate Setting by the European Central Bank', *Journal of Monetary Economics* 43, 655–79.

Warne, A., 1993, 'A Common Trends Model: Identification, Estimation and Inference', IIES, Stockholm University, Seminar Paper no. 555.

Wynne, M. A., 1999, 'Core Inflation: A Review of Some Conceptual Issues', European Central Bank Working Paper no. 5.

Part II

Fiscal policies

5 The interaction between monetary and fiscal policies in a monetary union: a review of recent literature

Roel Beetsma and Xavier Debrun

1 Introduction

The creation of the European Monetary Union (EMU) has given a new impulse to research on the interactions between monetary and fiscal policies. The key considerations in this research concern (1) the question of how fiscal policy impacts on the credibility of the common monetary policy and (2) to what extent fiscal policy can or should take over the role of monetary policy in stabilising country-specific shocks.

Central bankers often regard fiscal discipline as a prerequisite for a credible monetary policy. Accordingly, the Delors Report (1989),[1] which provides the blueprint for the foundation of a monetary union in Europe, emphasised fiscal discipline as a prerequisite for a successful monetary union. This view has found its way into the Treaty on the European Union (the 'Maastricht Treaty'), which sets out the institutional framework for EMU. The Treaty includes restrictions on deficit and debt, both as an entry criterion for EMU and as a permanent provision for countries to stick to, once membership is granted. Violation of these restrictions might activate the so-called 'Excessive Deficit Procedure'.

The provisions for fiscal policy in the Treaty have failed to mitigate concerns about fiscal discipline in EMU. The reason is that, once countries have entered EMU, the Treaty provides only little scope for forcing fiscal discipline on the union participants. As a result, Germany, frightened by the possibility that undisciplined fiscal policies might undermine the common monetary policy, floated the idea of a 'stability pact'. The pact was concluded in 1997 under the name of 'Stability and Growth Pact' (SGP). It clarifies and strengthens the Excessive Deficit Procedure, by specifying both the sanctions in the case of defiance of the fiscal restrictions and the formal procedure leading up to

The views expressed in this chapter are those of the authors and not necessarily those of the institutions they are affiliated with.

[1] The Delors Report (1989) was the result of the work by the Committee for the Study of Economic and Monetary Union, also sometimes called the 'Delors Committee' after its chairman, at that time President of the European Commission. Among the other participants were the presidents of the national central banks in the European Community.

their adoption.[2] In addition, the SGP requires the EMU participants to submit stability programmes, which will be reviewed by the European Commission and peer reviewed by the other members of the system. The stability programmes set out the countries' medium-term budgetary targets as well as the adjustment path leading to these targets. The countries are supposed to strive for budgets that are close to balance or in surplus in the medium run so that full use can be made of the automatic stabilisers, without violating the formal deficit criterion of 3% of GDP (see Buti, Franco and Ongena 1998).

The fiscal criteria imposed by the Treaty and the SGP have been severely criticised by the economics profession. The most important criticism probably concerns the allegation that the criteria reduce flexibility in using fiscal policy to stabilise country-specific shocks. This role is supposed to acquire particular importance when monetary policy is shifted to the supranational level and can no longer respond to country-specific shocks. Another criticism sometimes voiced is that the sanctions envisaged by the SGP worsen the situation of countries already in a precarious financial situation. Furthermore, even if it is not outright harmful, many economists simply view the SGP as unnecessary, because they believe that financial markets are able to discipline governments by raising the interest rate if deficits or debt get out of hand. Finally, some of the commentators acknowledge the need for fiscal restrictions, but they believe that the current ones are ill designed (e.g., Canzoneri and Diba 2001).

Although sceptical views of the fiscal rules have been widely expressed, some economists have pointed out that the current rules, imperfect as they may be, perform a useful role. Willett (1999) points to the fact that their simplicity also provides clarity. The criteria form an easy benchmark for the public and other authorities to hold individual governments accountable for their fiscal behaviour. Moreover, it is argued that, as long as countries stick to their stability programmes, they retain enough room to deal with country-specific shocks (Buti, Franco and Ongena 1998). In those cases, where fiscal flexibility is insufficient, countries could probably make legitimate appeals to the formal exceptions that the SGP provides. Finally, the argument that financial markets provide sufficient discipline is undermined by the observation that financial markets often react in a rather discontinuous way. Over long intervals, an increase in the public debt may have only a marginal effect on the interest rate, and then, suddenly, after some threshold level has been crossed, all the credit may be cut off. In addition, it should be noted that in the past in many instances financial markets have failed to discipline profligate governments.

In this chapter, we try to provide an overview of the recent literature on the interactions between monetary and fiscal policies in the context of EMU.

---

[2] The details of the Pact can be found in, for example, Artis and Winkler (1998) and the contributions in Brunila et al. (2001).

Given that the literature on this subject is expanding fast, it is impossible to be exhaustive in any discussion. In addition, some aspects of the interactions may receive less attention than some readers would like to see. This chapter is organised according to the key issues identified above. Section 2 deals with the issue of how fiscal policy affects the credibility of the common monetary policy. It starts with a simple model of the interactions between monetary and fiscal policy operating under an explicit government budget constraint and then shows how fiscal policies affect the average stance of the monetary policy in various settings. We also discuss the recent work by Dixit and Lambertini (2001, 2003a, b), who demonstrate that fiscal discretion may undo the effects of monetary policy commitment and who also point to the importance of consensus among fiscal and monetary policymakers about macroeconomic objectives. The section concludes with a brief discussion of the fiscal theory of the price level (FTPL), which argues that under 'fiscal dominance' the central bank loses the control over the price level, which is now determined by the government budget constraint. Hence, some of the proponents of FTPL argue that the role of the fiscal criteria in the Treaty and the SGP is to put the ECB in a leadership position against the fiscal authority. Section 3 investigates the implications of monetary union for the stabilisation of shocks and how the role of fiscal policy is affected in this respect. The section discusses these issues for the case of decentralised (national) fiscal policies, as is largely the reality now in Europe, but also for the case of centralised fiscal policy at the European level, which provides more scope for the stabilisation of country-specific shocks. Although the latter is still a hypothetical situation, one could well imagine a move towards European-level fiscal policies in the longer run. In section 4 we discuss the institutional adjustments proposed to deal with the potentially negative impact of undisciplined fiscal policies on the credibility of the monetary policy and the potentially enhanced burden on fiscal policy in the stabilisation of shocks. A key trade-off in designing appropriate institutions is that between the credibility of the fiscal policies and their flexibility. The section does not limit itself to the discussion of the actual institutional arrangements, but also assesses the alternative proposals that have been offered in the literature. Finally, section 5 concludes.

2   Credibility issues

The Maastricht Treaty assigns to the European Central Bank (ECB) the objective of maintaining price stability. As part of its monetary policy strategy, the ECB has defined price stability as a percentage change in the Harmonised Index of Consumer Prices between 0% and 2% on a yearly basis. The implications of fiscal policies for the conduct of monetary policy and, thus, inflation have received renewed interest since the signing of the Treaty. The Treaty considers disciplined fiscal policies a prerequisite for achieving this goal of low and stable inflation. Therefore, it imposes fiscal criteria for admission into and participation in EMU. In particular, the Treaty requires countries to keep their deficits below 3% of GDP and public debt below 60% of GDP. Violation of these criteria may trigger the Excessive Deficit Procedure, which has been clarified and strengthened with the adoption of the Stability and Growth Pact. Fiscal and monetary policies may interact in various ways. In this section we investigate the implications of fiscal policy for the credibility of the low and stable inflation policy pursued by the ECB.

2.1   The credibility problem in monetary policy

Credibility problems have a long history in research on monetary policy. They are often identified with the existence of an 'inflation bias'. That is, the inflation rate is suboptimally high, because the ex-ante, optimal low-inflation policy is time inconsistent. The high-inflation problem has received an immense amount of attention in the economic literature, partly as a result of the high inflation that plagued the industrialised world in the aftermath of the oil crises, at the end of the 1970s and the beginning of the 1980s. Early studies of time-consistency problems in policymaking are Kydland and Prescott (1977) and, more specifically, in connection with monetary policy, Calvo (1978), Barro (1983) and Barro and Gordon (1983a, b).

The classic work by Barro and Gordon analyses the inflation bias in a model with a suboptimally high natural unemployment rate. In this setting, the monetary authority tries to exploit existing nominal wage contracts, by relaxing monetary policy. The resulting reduction in the real wage rate raises the demand for labour. In equilibrium, however, the incentive to stimulate the economy in this way is anticipated and the inflation expectations incorporated in the nominal wage contracts adjust accordingly. Therefore, the natural unemployment rate is unaffected.

2.2   The link between fiscal policy and the inflation problem

One of the earliest analyses of the interaction between monetary and fiscal policy is the article by Sargent and Wallace (1981). They depict a game of chicken between a monetary authority and a fiscal authority. Together, fiscal and monetary policies are constrained by the requirement that the combined sum of the primary surpluses and seigniorage revenues generated by the respective authorities should ensure the solvency of the government. The authors distinguish two strategic regimes: when the monetary authority is dominant, it is able to commit to a certain monetary policy, so that, at some point, the fiscal authority will adjust its path of surpluses to ensure that the present-value government budget constraint is indeed fulfilled. When the fiscal authority is dominant, it is able to commit to a path of fiscal surpluses, and sooner or later, the monetary authority has to give in and generate the seigniorage revenues needed to guarantee government solvency. In particular, under this latter regime, lower inflation in the short run leads to higher inflation in the long run.

In the remainder of this section, we discuss a variety of frameworks that have been used recently to explore the interactions between monetary and fiscal policy, in particular in connection with EMU.

2.2.1 Models with an explicit government budget constraint Alesina and Tabellini (1987) argue forcefully that the ultimate source of the inflation problem is a lack of non-distortionary tax revenues and not the policymaker's over-ambitious employment target. We can illustrate this in the context of the following model, which has been extended into various directions by other authors. In its simplest form, the model features a single authority who shares society's preferences (and, thus, is benevolent) and controls both the monetary and fiscal policy instruments. Its loss function is given by:

$$L_F = \frac{1}{2}[\alpha_\pi(\pi - \pi^*)^2 + (x - x^*)^2 + \alpha_g(g - g^*)^2], \qquad (5.1)$$

where π is inflation, x is output (or employment) and g is public spending (as a share of output in the absence of inflation surprises and distortionary taxes – see below – which we term the *non-distortionary output level*). Further, π^*, x^* and g^* are the bliss points for inflation, output and public spending, respectively. Because of distortions in labour markets and product markets (which are not explicitly modelled), we assume that $x^* > 0$, so that the non-distortionary output level is lower than the bliss point for output. Finally, the constants α_π and α_g are the weights that the government attaches to inflation and public spending relative to output.

Output is given by the following short-run aggregate supply curve:

$$x = \nu(\pi - \pi^e - \tau), \qquad (5.2)$$

where π^e is (rationally) expected inflation and τ is the rate of a tax on the revenues generated by firms.[3] This tax is distortionary: $x < 0$ when inflation surprises are absent and $\tau > 0$. Finally, the government operates under a budget constraint, which, expressed in shares of non-distortionary output, can be approximated by:

$$g + [1 + \rho + \lambda(\pi^e - \pi)]d = \tau + \kappa\pi + \theta, \qquad (5.3)$$

---

[3] The derivation of this equation can be found in Beetsma and Bovenberg (1998).

where d is debt inherited from the past, ρ is the real interest rate, λ is the share of the public debt that is not indexed for unexpected inflation, τ is revenues from the distortionary tax, $\kappa\pi$ is seigniorage revenues (based on the assumption that real money holdings is a constant share κ of non-distortionary output) and θ is the (maximum) amount of lump-sum (non-distortionary) tax revenues that can be raised. We can rewrite equation (5.3) as follows:

$$g^* + (1+\rho)d + x^*/v - \kappa\pi^* - \theta = (g^* - g) + (\tau + x^*/v)$$
$$+ \kappa(\pi - \pi^*) + \lambda d(\pi - \pi^e). \qquad (5.4)$$

Next, rewrite the supply curve (5.2) as:

$$\tau + x^*/v = (x^* - x)/v + (\pi - \pi^e), \qquad (5.5)$$

and combine this with (5.4) to give:

$$K = (g^* - g) + (x^* - x)/v + (1 + \lambda d)(\pi - \pi^e) + \kappa(\pi - \pi^*), \qquad (5.6)$$

where

$$K \equiv g^* + (1+\rho)d_0 + x^*/v - \kappa\pi^* - \theta \qquad (5.7)$$

is the so-called *overall financing requirement*. This concept is useful because it is an exogenous measure of everything that causes losses to society. Further, all the outcomes can be expressed in terms of this measure. The *financing sources* of the overall financing requirement – the right-hand side of (5.6) – are a shortfall of spending from its bliss point (the *spending shortfall*), $g^* - g$, a (scaled) shortfall of output from its bliss point (the *output shortfall*), $(x^* - x)/v$, the inflation surprise, $\pi - \pi^e$, and the difference between actual seigniorage revenues and seigniorage revenues when the bliss point for inflation is reached.

Suppose that the authority is not able to commit and minimises its loss function over the inflation rate (which it controls directly) and the distortionary tax rate, subject to the government budget constraint. Then, the outcomes of the variables that enter the loss function (5.1) are given by:

$$\pi - \pi^* = [((\kappa + 1)/\alpha_\pi)/N]K, \qquad (5.8)$$

$$(x^* - x)/v = [(1/v^2)/N]K, \qquad (5.9)$$

$$g^* - g = [(1/\alpha_g)/N]K, \qquad (5.10)$$

where

$$N \equiv 1/v^2 + 1/\alpha_g + \kappa((\kappa + 1) + \lambda d)/\alpha_\pi. \qquad (5.11)$$

Clearly, as components of K, the spending target, initial public debt and the 'over-ambitious' output target all play a 'symmetric' role in generating an inflation bias, $\pi - \pi^*$. Moreover, it is clear that, when sufficient lump-sum taxes are available, the overall financing requirement can be set to zero, so that all variables – inflation, output and public spending – reach their targets. Using the rewritten government budget constraint (5.4), this implies that $\tau = -x^*/v$. In other words, sufficient lump-sum tax revenues allow the government to subsidise firms' revenues to an extent that is necessary to eliminate the pre-existing product- and labour-market distortions. We also observe that the financing sources are applied in fixed proportions, irrespective of the size of the overall financing requirement. Not surprisingly, the relative intensity of the use of the various financing sources depends on parameters of the model. A higher inflation weight, α_π, reduces reliance on inflation, while a higher spending weight, α_g, reduces reliance on public spending. Further, larger real money holdings raise the benefit from an increase in inflation, so that this source of financing becomes more important. Finally, an increase in v boosts the incentive for an inflation surprise and, thus, inflation itself. In addition, a given tax rate becomes more distortionary so that, in equilibrium, the output shortfall is higher.

The simple setup presented above has been extended in various directions. First, there has been a tendency towards more central bank independence in the past ten to twenty years, in particular in industrialised countries. Many papers model fiscal and monetary policy as being conducted by separate authorities. The equilibrium outcomes for the policy instruments and other variables are the result of some game between these authorities. While fiscal policy is still conducted by the benevolent authority with the loss function given by (5.1), monetary policy may be conducted by a central bank with loss function

$$L_M = \frac{1}{2}[\alpha_{\pi M}(\pi - \pi^T)^2 + (x - x^*)^2 + \alpha_{gM}(g - g^*)^2]. \qquad (5.12)$$

The relative weights that the central bank attaches to inflation and public spending may differ from the corresponding weights of society or the fiscal authority. In particular, when $\alpha_{\pi M} > \alpha_\pi$, the central bank is said to be 'conservative' (in the sense of Rogoff 1985a). The Maastricht Treaty assigns price stability as the primary objective for the ECB. Stabilisation of the euro-area economy is allowed only if it is without prejudice to price stability. This almost lexicographic ordering of preferences would correspond to a very high value of $\alpha_{\pi M}$. Further, π^T is an inflation target assigned to the central bank. This target may be different from society's bliss point for inflation, π^*. This way of modelling the inflation target follows Svensson (1997). Although the ECB has not adopted a formal inflation target as many central banks nowadays have, it has publicly declared that it will strive for a medium-term rate of inflation of between 0% and 2%, which it considers to be consistent with price stability. Whether the ECB formally follows a policy of inflation targeting seems more a matter of semantics than anything else. Although it has announced it will follow a two-pillar strategy with a reference value for money growth and an indicator for expected inflation, it is expected to follow a pragmatic course (as the Bundesbank is often said to have done in the past) by giving priority to the inflation objective, rather than the reference money growth, whenever there is a conflict between the two. Finally, α_{gM} may differ from α_g. In particular, its statute forbids the ECB to help governments in financial trouble (the 'no-bail-out clause'). Such a statute might be represented by a low or even zero value of α_{gM}.

Apart from the specification of the objective of the monetary authority, another important consideration is the type of game between the authorities. More specifically, the question is in what order the players move. While monetary policy is sometimes considered to be the 'swing policy' (Debelle 1993), as it can be adjusted almost instantaneously, fiscal policy adjustments take time to materialise. For example, they have to be prepared, voted on in parliament and then implemented. The difficulty in adjusting fiscal policy may provide the fiscal authority with a pre-commitment capacity *vis-à-vis* the monetary authority and, for this reason, the fiscal authority is often modelled as having a first-mover advantage against the monetary authority (Debelle and Fischer 1997). Beetsma and Bovenberg (1997a) analyse in detail the outcomes of the current model (though with $\pi^T = \pi^* = 0$) under the three possible leadership assumptions: the fiscal authority acting as a Stackelberg leader against the central bank, the central bank acting as a Stackelberg leader and the two authorities playing Nash. Assuming that $K > 0$, the model produces the somewhat counterintuitive result that the inflation bias is highest under monetary leadership. The result arises from the assumption that the central bank, when choosing the inflation rate, does not take into account the direct effect of higher inflation on the government budget constraint (because the central bank is independent). However, monetary leadership forces the central bank to internalise the effect in an indirect way via the fiscal reaction function: an increase in inflation, through an increase seigniorage, leads to a reduction in the tax rate.

Beetsma and Bovenberg (1998) extend the setup to a model of a monetary union with $n > 1$ countries and, thus, n fiscal authorities.[4] The fiscal authorities act as Stackelberg leaders against the common central bank (CCB), whose loss function is now given by:

$$L_{CCB} = \frac{1}{2}\left[\alpha_{\pi M}(\pi - \pi^T)^2 + \frac{1}{n}\sum_{i=1}^{n}(x_i - x^*)^2\right], \tag{5.13}$$

where i indexes the country. The CCB attaches an equal weight to each country's deviation of output from its bliss point. For illustrative purposes, let us assume

---

[4] Van Aarle and Huart (1999) explore a two-country model of monetary union. Their analysis assigns quite a lot of importance to (the distribution of) seigniorage. The analysis also explores fiscal federalism in EMU.

that $\alpha_{\pi M} = \alpha_\pi$. Then, the CCB's reaction function is given by:

$$\pi = \frac{\alpha_\pi}{1 + \alpha_\pi} \pi^T + \frac{1}{1 + \alpha_\pi} \left[\pi^e + \frac{1}{n} \sum_{i=1}^{n} (\tau_i + x^*) \right].$$ (5.14)

Their leadership position induces the fiscal authorities to raise the tax rate strategically. This forces the CCB to raise inflation, in order to protect employment, as is evident from (5.14). The implied increase in seigniorage and the erosion of the real value of outstanding public debt are used to finance extra public spending. Fiscal leadership thus results in a spending bias and higher inflation. However, as the number of countries increases, the 'strategic position' of each fiscal authority against the CCB weakens, and the public spending bias and the inflation rate shrink.

The analyses discussed so far are one-shot analyses. A number of papers have extended the model to a dynamic one, in which public debt plays an explicit role. For example, Van Aarle, Bovenberg and Raith (1997) extend the analysis of Tabellini (1986) and explore the dynamics of public debt in a two-country infinite-horizon model with a common central bank. Levine and Pearlman (1992) analyse a dynamic model of a two-country monetary union under different assumptions about the ECB's monetary policy. Levine and Brociner (1994) study fiscal policy coordination within EMU in a dynamic game framework. Beetsma and Bovenberg (1997b) extend the basic, single-country model discussed above to a two-period setting, so that the fiscal authority is allowed to accumulate public debt. All public debt is indexed (real). Each period, the central bank and the fiscal authority are involved in a Nash game. However, because the fiscal authority's problem has now become dynamic, in the first period, when it selects public debt, it tries to exploit the reaction functions of the players in the second period (who take public debt as given). In the presence of a conflict between the fiscal and monetary authority about the inflation objective, the former will use public debt strategically in order to affect future monetary policy. In particular, if $\alpha_{\pi M}$ is sufficiently high relative to α_π, the fiscal authority issues more public debt in the first period. This raises the need for second-period tax revenues and, hence, the need for the central bank to relax monetary policy. Equilibrium inflation in the second period will thus be higher. The opposite is the case if $\alpha_\pi / \alpha_{\pi M}$ is above a certain level. While, on the one hand, an increase in $\alpha_{\pi M}$ leads to a shift from seigniorage to other financing sources in each period (an *intra*temporal effect), it may also lead to a (strategic) increase of the public debt (an *inter*temporal effect). This latter effect may actually dominate the intratemporal effect on second-period inflation and thus lead to higher second-period inflation. This result thus reproduces results that are analogous to those of Sargent and Wallace (1981), but in a setting with an explicitly modelled Nash game between the monetary and the fiscal authority in each period. If $\alpha_{\pi M}$ is sufficiently high, though, the intratemporal effect dominates the intertemporal effect.

Beetsma and Bovenberg (1999) extend Beetsma and Bovenberg (1997b) by increasing the number of countries to $n > 1$. The countries form a monetary union, so that the common central bank (CCB), which sets the inflation rate for the entire union, is involved in a game against the n fiscal authorities. Debt policy conducted by the fiscal authorities is driven by two considerations. On the one hand, the discount factor of the fiscal authorities may, for political reasons, be lower than the social discount factor. This would lead to suboptimally high (from society's perspective) public debt. On the other hand, by restraining public debt accumulation, a fiscal authority reduces the need for future tax revenues. Hence, output losses arising from tax distortions will be smaller and the central bank's incentive to raise inflation is weakened. While inflation expectations for the current period are predetermined, future inflation expectations, and therefore also the future inflation bias, can be affected by the current-period debt policy. For this reason, the fiscal authorities have an incentive to restrain public debt accumulation. Because each individual country's debt policy has only a '1 over n' effect on the common inflation rate, the debt restraining effect diminishes as the monetary union grows larger.[5] The resulting increase in the equilibrium debt level actually enhances welfare if the fiscal authorities share the social discount factor, but it may reduce welfare when the government's discount factor is lower than the social discount factor.

2.2.2   *Short-run analyses*

Another strand of literature neglects the intertemporal issues brought about by the budget constraint to strictly focus on the short-term strategic interaction between fully separate monetary and fiscal authorities. Dixit (2001) and Dixit and Lambertini (2001, 2003a, b) adopt this approach to explore in detail the role of monetary commitment, leadership position and alignment of the authorities' objectives for the macroeconomic outcomes.[6] They also discuss the potential desirability of formal fiscal restraints independently of the government's solvency constraint.

To illustrate that approach, we consider a version of the Dixit and Lambertini models with a monetary union which consists of n countries. Output x_i in country i is given by:

$$x_i = \bar{x}_i + \sum_{j=1}^{n} \gamma_{ij} \tau_j + v_i(\pi - \pi^e), \quad i = 1, \dots, n, \tag{5.15}$$

---

[5] A analogous incentive effect can be found in analyses of the effect of monetary unification on the behaviour of non-atomistic trade unions (see Cukierman and Lippi 2001). With the move from a national monetary policy to a monetary union, the influence of an individual trade union's wage demands on inflation is reduced. Thus, each union perceives the cost of demanding a higher wage to be smaller and, in equilibrium, unemployment and inflation will be higher.

[6] Related contributions include the short-term version of Agell, Calmfors and Jonsson (1996) and Debrun (1999, 2000).

where $\bar{x}_i$ is the natural output level and τ_j a more general representation of fiscal policy than before. It may capture public spending on goods and services, public investment, subsidies and changes in distortionary taxation. Fiscal policy is discretionary in the sense that, after shocks have occurred (see below), it can be freely chosen by the fiscal authorities. An increase in τ_j indicates a fiscal expansion. The effect of an increase in τ_i on x_i can be positive or negative, depending on the type of fiscal policy enacted. Observe that fiscal policies may also have cross-country spillover effects that can be positive (e.g. demand effects) or negative (e.g. crowding out effects).

The common inflation rate is:

$$\pi = \pi_0 + \sum_i c_i \tau_i. \tag{5.16}$$

Hence, in general the common inflation rate is affected by the fiscal policies conducted in the various countries. The effects of fiscal policy on inflation may capture the effects that taxes have on firms' costs or the need for the central bank to accommodate fiscal expansions at least to some extent. A fiscal expansion may have either a positive or negative effect on inflation. Observe that fiscal policy not only exerts international spillovers via output, but also via inflation. All of the $\bar{x}_i$, γ_{ij}, ν_i and c_i are allowed to be stochastic.

We conclude the description of the model with the specification of the authorities' loss functions. In contrast to the work discussed above, public spending no longer explicitly enters the loss functions. The loss function of the fiscal authority of country i is

$$L_{Fi} = \frac{1}{2}\left[\left(\pi - \pi_i^F\right)^2 + \xi_i^F\left(x_i - x_i^F\right)^2\right]. \tag{5.17}$$

Hence, the bliss points for inflation, π_i^F, and output, x_i^F, may differ across countries. Also, the trade-off, ξ_i^F, between output variability and inflation variability around their bliss points may differ across the union members. The union has a common central bank (CCB) with the loss function:

$$L_{CCB} = \frac{1}{2}\left[(\pi - \pi^M)^2 + \sum_{i=1}^{n} \xi_i^M\left(x_i - x_i^M\right)^2\right], \tag{5.18}$$

where π^M and x_i^M are the CCB's targets for inflation and output in the member countries. Observe that the CCB may attach different weights to the output levels of different countries. The CCB is conservative in Dixit and Lambertini's terminology when

$$\pi^M < \pi_i^F, x_i^M < x_i^F, \xi_i^M \le \xi_i^F/n, \text{ for all } i, \tag{5.19}$$

that is, when the CCB's targets for inflation and output in a country are lower than the corresponding targets of its government and when the CCB's relative weight on output is less than the government's relative weight, corrected for the fact that the country is only one out of n countries. This definition of conservatism is more restrictive than Rogoff's (1985a), but it defines a situation that leads to some unambiguous results.

The general description of the timing is as follows. In stage (1) the central bank chooses a rule for $\pi_0 = \pi_0 (z)$ when there is commitment. Here, z is a future state. Under discretion nothing happens at this moment. In stage (2), the private sector forms inflation expectations π^e. Then, in stage (3) a state z materializes. That is, a realisation of the stochastic shocks $\bar{x}_i$, γ_{ij}, ν_i and c_i occurs. Finally, in stage (4), under monetary commitment, the CCB simply executes its rule. Under monetary discretion, the various authorities choose their ex-post optimal policies. The authorities may be involved in a Nash game, or, alternatively, there may be monetary leadership or fiscal leadership.

Several important results emerge from the analysis. First, when the authorities are involved in a Nash game, then with a conservative CCB and assuming that all the γ_{ii} and c_i are positive, the outcomes for inflation and output are more extreme than the targets of the CCB and the fiscal authorities:

$$\pi < \pi^M \leq \pi_i^F, x_i > x_i^F > x_i^M, \text{for all } i. \tag{5.20}$$

Hence, the non-cooperative race between the CCB, which tries to push inflation below the fiscal authorities' bliss points, and the fiscal authorities, who try to push output beyond the CCB's ideal levels, leads to a bad policy mix, in which inflation is too low and output is too high for the taste of any of the policymakers.[7] The results of this model validate the concerns of many observers that a highly conservative ECB may lead to an undesirable combination of monetary and fiscal policies (see, for instance, Wyplosz 1999a). When the bliss points of all the authorities coincide, that is, when

$$\pi^M = \pi_i^F = \pi^*, x_i^M = x_i^F = x_i^*, \text{for all } i,$$

then, for all shock realisations z,

$$\pi(z) = \pi^*, x_i(z) = x_i^*, \text{for all } i.$$

Hence, in this special case, all the targets are attained. This finding leads Dixit and Lambertini to conclude that it is probably more important to achieve consensus on the macroeconomic objectives than to have a conservative ECB.

The second major result is that fiscal freedom (discretion) destroys monetary commitment. In particular, monetary commitment and discretionary monetary

---

[7] In reality, both too low inflation and too high output are bad for a variety of reasons. Some inflation may be needed to 'grease the wheels of the economy', for example because nominal wages tend to be downwardly rigid. Too high output can be bad because individuals have too little leisure and, if it is the result of a too expansive fiscal policy, the consequence may be too much debt accumulation and higher future interest rates.

leadership yield the same equilibria. The reason is that the fiscal reaction functions impose constraints on the monetary authority's problem that make the rational expectations constraint redundant. Therefore, Dixit and Lambertini argue in favour of restrictions of the type imposed under the SGP, which modify the fiscal reaction functions, thereby restoring the role of the rational expectations constraint and, thus, of the commitment power given to the ECB.

2.2.3   The fiscal theory of the price level (FTPL)   A new line of research in the analysis of the interaction between monetary and fiscal policies concerns the 'fiscal theory of the price level' (FTPL), pioneered by Leeper (1991), Sims (1994) and Woodford (1995, 1998). The origins of this literature date back to the chicken game between the monetary and fiscal authorities in Sargent and Wallace (1981). However, in contrast to Sargent and Wallace, the real value of the outstanding stock of public debt is no longer fixed. The FTPL assigns a crucial role to the presence of nominal debt. Even if both the monetary and fiscal authorities stick to their pre-announced paths for the money supply and the fiscal surplus, the intertemporal government budget constraint will be fulfilled. The reason is that the price level changes to make the real value of the outstanding public debt consistent with the fulfilment of the government budget constraint. Hence, in the 'fiscal dominance' regime, where the fiscal authority precommits to a path of surpluses, the monetary authority loses the control over the price level. This finding provides a new rationale for fiscal rules such as the SGP: such rules help to avoid a situation of fiscal dominance.

We illustrate the idea briefly by using the simple framework of Canzoneri and Diba 2001, and Canzoneri, Cumby and Diba 2001b). In nominal terms, the period-t government budget constraint is written as:

$$B_t = T_t - G_t + M_{t+1} - M_t + B_{t+1}/(1+i_t), \tag{5.21}$$

where B_t is the outstanding public debt at the start of period t, T_t is tax revenues, G_t is public spending and M_t is the amount of base money at the start of period t. All these variables are in nominal terms. Finally, i_t is the nominal interest rate. By iterating forward, we can rewrite the government budget constraint as:

$$\frac{M_t + B_t}{P_t y_t} = E_t \sum_{j=t}^{\infty} \delta_j \left[\frac{T_j - G_j}{P_j y_j} \right] + E_t \sum_{j=t}^{\infty} \delta_j \left[\frac{M_{j+1}}{P_j y_j} \right] i_j, \tag{5.22}$$

where y_t is real GDP, P_t is the price level and δ_j is a discount factor involving ratios of output growth to real interest rates. The first term on the right-hand side is the discounted sum of surpluses as shares of output, while the second term on the right-hand side is the discounted sum of seigniorage revenues as shares of output. The question is how (5.22) gets fulfilled. If the fiscal authorities actively pursue fiscal solvency, the economy is in the monetary dominant regime and monetary policy has control over the price level. The fiscal authorities then adjust their primary surpluses, taking the price level as given. However, when the ratios of primary surpluses and seigniorage evolve exogenously over time, then the nominal income $P_t y_t$ adjusts endogenously to assure that (5.22) is satisfied. This is the fiscal dominant regime. Although the central bank may be formally independent, it loses control of the nominal GDP and, thus, of the price level. In the words of Canzoneri and Diba (2001), the central bank is not *functionally* independent of the fiscal authorities.

Bergin (2000) explores the FTPL in the context of a monetary union. Under fiscal dominance, international spillovers from fiscal policy can arise in the model, because the price level is determined jointly by the budget constraints of union participants. In particular, if a country decides to increase its public debt without backing the increase by a rise in future taxes, then the price level rises throughout the entire union. It should be observed that maintaining price stability does no longer require all the governments to be solvent, because one government's surplus can offset another government's debt. Leith and Wren-Lewis (2002) develop a two-country open-economy model with overlapping generations of non-Ricardian consumers and imperfectly competitive firms that adjust their prices only infrequently. Because of the assumed demographic structure, respectively the sluggish price adjustment, both debt policy and monetary policy have real effects in the two countries. The authors consider a monetary union combined with independent, national fiscal policies. They simulate the adjustment of the economies in response to demand and supply shocks, which may be symmetric or asymmetric. Fiscal (debt) stabilisation can take place via feedback rules for taxes or for spending and these feedback rules are allowed to differ between the two countries. The optimal adjustment speed of the public debt depends on the type of instrument (spending or taxes) used and on the type of shock hitting the economies. The authors point out that, while asymmetric fiscal policy responses have only a limited effect on inflation, differences in nominal inertia have much more serious consequences.

3   Stabilisation issues

The formation of a currency union drastically affects the use of monetary and fiscal policies as instruments for macroeconomic stabilisation. First of all, centralisation of monetary decisions leads to an automatic coordination of monetary responses to *symmetric* shocks (Canzoneri and Gray 1985). This represents an undeniable benefit of monetary unification as the externalities associated with potentially divergent national monetary policies are credibly internalised. Although the literature often concludes that the gains from international coordination are likely to be small,[8] centralised monetary decisions may have specific merits for a group of countries with a clear revealed preference for fixed exchange rates. This was the case for the member states of the European Monetary System (EMS).[9] The reason is that centralisation eliminates the costs of currency crises and ample reserve fluctuations that would otherwise occur in response to actual or expected differences in national monetary policies (Debrun 2001). The second key consequence of monetary unification for the design of macroeconomic stabilisation policies is that country-specific, or *asymmetric*, disturbances are much harder to deal with because monetary policy can only serve union-wide objectives.[10] An additional difficulty comes from the fact that the effects of the common monetary policy may differ across countries owing to different transmission mechanisms (Favero and Giavazzi 1999).

The lack of country-specific monetary strategies to deal with asymmetric shocks leads to the question about the existence of alternative channels to absorb these shocks. When factor markets are perfectly flexible, there is no need to develop policies for the stabilisation of asymmetric shocks as production factors move instantaneously to that part of the union where undercapacity prevails. As Mundell (1961) argues, labour mobility is an important criterion in judging whether a group of countries constitutes an optimum currency area. In reality, however, labour mobility is notoriously low, both within and across countries. Hence, this channel of adjustment plays only a minor role. In addition, despite the huge international capital flows we observe nowadays, cross-border asset holdings still seem to be much smaller than predicted by standard theoretical models (see Gordon and Bovenberg 1996). Rather than spreading investments over countries, in order to limit the impact of country-specific shocks on disposable income, agents invest most of their savings locally (Obstfeld and Rogoff 2000). The findings by Yosha and Sorensen (1998) confirm the negligible role of capital income flows in absorbing the effects of country-specific shocks in Europe. This contrasts with the United States, where capital markets are found to play a considerable role in diversifying away local shocks (Asdrubali, Sorensen and Yosha 1996).

The failure of market mechanisms in dealing with country-specific shocks poses considerable challenges for the design of fiscal policies, as they remain

---

[8] The seminal paper is by Oudiz and Sachs (1984). Mooslechner and Schuerz (1999) provide a recent and comprehensive survey of the vast literature on international policy coordination.

[9] Reviewing the monetary history of the European Community, von Hagen (1993, p. 512) notes: 'the common desire for monetary co-ordination and exchange rate stability has led the EC to approach policy co-ordination strategically through exchange rate management'.

[10] Wyplosz (1999a) proposes the adoption of 'monetary federalism' by the ECB. According to that argument, the central bank should pay particular attention to countries affected by severe disturbances instead of strictly focusing on area-wide aggregates.

the only tool available to influence national aggregate conditions.[11] The nature of those challenges depends upon the degree of centralisation of the fiscal decisionmaking process within the currency area. In a *decentralised fiscal system* like the euro area, the pivotal issues concern (i) the flexibility with which national budgets play a countercyclical role, (ii) the extent to which more activist national policies may exacerbate fiscal coordination problems within the area and (iii) the greater difficulty of achieving a well-balanced policy mix in individual countries. In more *centralised fiscal regimes* like the United States, Canada or pre-EMU Germany, the key economic issue is the efficiency of the insurance or risk-sharing service provided by fiscal transfers from booming regions to contracting ones. Such transfers operate either directly through a redistributive scheme among decentralised entities or indirectly through national/federal social security systems (automatic stabilisers).

The rest of this section offers an overview of the recent literature's main findings on those issues and distinguishes between the 'polar' cases of complete decentralisation of fiscal policies (subsection 3.1) and complete centralisation (subsection 3.2).

3.1   Decentralised fiscal policies

The main lesson from the optimum currency area literature is that in the absence of adjustment mechanisms (e.g. international labour mobility) or cross-country (centralised) risk-sharing schemes (e.g. cross-border asset holdings), the stabilisation of country-specific disturbances rests entirely on national fiscal policies. We first review the case for increased fiscal activism in a currency union and assess its empirical relevance. Then, we address the consequences of active fiscal stabilisation policies on the strategic interplay between monetary and fiscal authorities.

3.1.1   Greater fiscal activism?   The greater need for countercyclical fiscal actions may manifest itself in two ways. First, the desirable economic size of governments participating in currency unions may be larger than the one of governments still in control of their monetary policy. Greater government size would reflect increased reliance on *automatic stabilisers*. The latter could take the form of generous social security systems providing effective insurance against aggregate shocks hitting the economy. In principle, automatic stabilisers allow for flexible and timely countercyclical responses of fiscal policy and appear as an attractive option for countries deprived of stabilisation tools other

---

[11] In the absence of fiscal stabilisation policies also, adjustment to asymmetric shocks necessarily takes place through changes in relative prices that impose lower inflation or deflation on the region(s) affected by a negative shock and higher inflation elsewhere in the union. Those adjustment costs naturally increase with the degree of price rigidity.

than the government's budget (Fatás and Rose 2001). A potential downside of large automatic stabilisers in a currency union is that they do not allow one to distinguish between area-wide fluctuations, which could be addressed by the common monetary policy and country-specific disturbances, which require fiscal measures. In the context of the strategic interaction between fiscal and monetary authorities, this means that national fiscal policies may end up bearing a suboptimally large share of the stabilisation burden. Beetsma, Debrun and Klaassen (2001) provide a formal illustration of that argument and show how large automatic stabilisers create more propitious conditions for free-riding behaviour by the central bank in the form of a bias towards an excessively passive monetary policy. For intuitive reasons, that problem is particularly severe in the case of *symmetric* disturbances.

Besides automatic stabilisers, greater fiscal activism may also take the form of *stronger discretionary interventions*. These may be calibrated to address the country-specific component of the shocks and may mitigate the temptation of the central bank to free ride on stabilisation efforts. However, the overall efficiency of discretionary measures depends on the budgetary procedures prevailing in the member states. In particular, long decision lags and rigid amendment procedures of budget laws may limit their effectiveness or even make them procyclical. Also, the combination of discretionary activism with weak budgetary institutions may threaten fiscal sustainability, as a stimulus could prove hard to reverse and adjustments difficult to implement (e.g., De Grauwe 1994).[12]

Looking at a large sample of countries having adopted 'extreme monetary arrangements' (i.e., currency boards, currency unions or hard pegs), Fatás and Rose (2001) find some empirical support for the greater role of governments in currency unions. Their result most clearly emerges in the case of unilateral currency unions – i.e. countries unilaterally adopting a third currency – which is hardly surprising since those countries have no influence on the common monetary policy. These findings echo other studies suggesting that, in general, an increase in macroeconomic risks leads to bigger governments. For instance, Rodrik (1998) concludes that more open economies tend to have bigger governments because of the need to cope with the macroeconomic impact of larger terms-of-trade volatility.

The concrete relevance of these issues for the policy debate rests on two presumptions: (i) the euro area is characterised by significant asymmetric shocks and (ii) fiscal policies can be used as effective stabilisation tools, meaning that they could effectively deal with idiosyncrasies within the euro area. Existing empirical evidence lends support to both hypotheses. Regarding the symmetry of aggregate disturbances, a large number of papers have consistently reported

---

[12] Von Hagen (1999a) proposes a case study of the role of budgetary institutions in post-reunification Germany.

that shocks among EMU member states are less correlated than among the regions of existing federal monetary unions like the United States or Canada (see, for instance, Bayoumi and Eichengreen 1997). The relevance of such analyses has been criticised on two counts. First, it is notoriously difficult to disentangle 'pure' shocks from policy reactions. In other words, empirical estimates of shock asymmetry may also capture country-specific responses and induced exchange rate adjustments. Second, the degree of synchronisation in business cycles (or the degree of adequacy to optimum currency area criteria) is endogenous to the existence of a currency union (Frankel and Rose 1998), one prominent reason being that currency unions seem to have a dramatic impact on intra-union trade flows (see, for example, Rose and Van Wincoop 2001). Whatever the debate on the exact degree of asymmetry of the shocks, it is conceivable that significant differences in economic situations across the twelve member states of the euro area may occur, triggering the need for country-specific fiscal actions.

As far as the countercyclical effectiveness of fiscal policies is concerned, recent studies carried out with data for industrial countries confirm that the latter have a significant impact on the business cycle. These studies include Galí (1994), Blanchard and Perotti (2002), Giavazzi, Jappelli and Pagano (2000), Fatàs and Mihov (2001) and De Arcangelis and Lamartina (2003). Blanchard and Perotti (2002) strictly focus on time-series evidence for the US, while Galí (1994) and Fatás and Mihov (2001) look at a panel of OECD countries and specifically address the issue of *automatic stabilisers* as an effective tool to reduce the variability of output. Fatàs and Mihov (2001) conclude that a one-percentage-point increase in the government spending to GDP ratio leads to a reduction in output volatility by eight basis points, this even if one takes into account the possible reverse causality discussed above (i.e. less stable economies choose bigger governments). Running identical tests for US states, they show that effect to be significantly greater than in the OECD panel (13 to 40 basis points reduction in output volatility). Fatás and Mihov (2003) extend the analysis of the stabilising properties of fiscal policies to *discretionary measures* and find the latter to be *pro-cyclical* or destabilising. Giavazzi and Pagano (1990) and Giavazzi, Jappelli and Pagano (2000) investigate the non-linear response of economies to fiscal policy impulses due to the conflict between Keynesian and Ricardian (or wealth) effects. The economic consequences of fiscal policies have also been extensively analysed in the specific context of large fiscal adjustments. That strand of literature seeks to identify the determinants of successful (i.e. lasting) adjustments.[13] The contributions in this literature all

---

[13] Giavazzi and Pagano (1990) present case studies of the Irish and Danish adjustments in the 1980s, while Alesina and Perotti (1995) and Alesina and Ardagna (1998) consider a panel of OECD countries. Giavazzi, Jappelli and Pagano (2000) extend their investigation to developing countries as well.

stress the importance of the 'qualitative' aspects of the fiscal package, like its composition in terms of tax increases and spending cuts.

Only a few empirical papers explicitly investigated the potentially important role played by the interaction between monetary and fiscal policies. Lambertini and Tavares (2000) attempt to identify the effect of exchange rate and monetary policies on the success of fiscal adjustments in a panel of OECD countries. They conclude that a depreciation of the exchange rate at an early stage of the adjustment significantly contributes to its success, but they fail to find any significant impact of monetary policy indicators. Their results suggest that fiscal adjustments in the EMU might be harder to achieve than in a regime with independent monetary policies and floating, or at least adjustable, exchange rates. Broader empirical analyses of the interaction between monetary and fiscal policies include Mélitz (1997), Wyplosz (1999b) and von Hagen, Hughes-Hallett and Strauch (2001), who use a variety of panels with annual data for OECD and EU countries. Those authors do not reject the hypothesis that, on average, monetary and fiscal stances counteract one another, lending support to the view that both instruments are *strategic substitutes*. Using time-series analysis based on quarterly data for G7 countries, Muscatelli, Tirelli and Trecroci (2003) identify a recent shift towards less intense conflicts and a greater complementarity between both instruments. They interpret this shift as a consequence of the less activist fiscal policies pursued in the 1990s as a result of the greater attention given to debt stabilisation and formal fiscal discipline. This suggests that if fiscal discipline gains momentum under the SGP and if EMU membership triggers more activist fiscal stabilisation policies, stronger conflicts may again emerge between monetary and fiscal authorities.

The empirical evidence discussed above provides two important lessons for strategic analyses of the policy mix under a monetary union with decentralised fiscal policies. The first lesson is that fiscal policy is a much more complex instrument of macroeconomic management than monetary policy. Fiscal actions are subject to specific constraints (e.g. the government's solvency, long decision and implementation lags), operate through multiple, and sometimes contradictory, transmission channels and respond to objectives other than output stabilisation. As a result, the composition (or the 'quality') of changes in budget balance should matter a great deal when it comes to modelling its effect on real activity and prices. This reality is often overlooked in theoretical analyses of the strategic interaction between monetary and fiscal policymakers. For obvious tractability reasons, these studies tend to rely on two different extensions of the highly stylised Barro–Gordon framework. In the first one, proposed by Alesina and Tabellini (1987) and extended by Debelle and Fischer (1997) and Beetsma and Bovenberg (1997a, b), the government aims at a positive level of expenditure and uses a distortionary tax on firms' revenue as its strategic choice variable. A binding budget constraint implies that expenditure choices are residual. The alternative to Alesina and Tabellini's assumptions is best described in Agell, Calmfors and Jonsson (1996).[14] They propose a dynamic model of the optimal policy mix, assuming that both instruments affect real output exclusively through aggregate demand so that only unexpected policy changes have a (temporary) real impact. These one-dimensional views of fiscal policy imply that monetary and fiscal instruments are either strategic substitutes (demand-side fiscal policy) or strategic complements (supply-side fiscal policy) so that the outcome of those strategic analyses depends in a fundamental way on the assumption about the transmission channel for fiscal policies. Great caution is therefore required when drawing policy implications from such stylised models of the policy mix. Bryson, Jensen and Van Hoose (1993), Castellani and Debrun (2001), Catenaro and Tirelli (2000), Debrun (2000), Levine and Pearlman (2001) and Pina (1999) allow for multiple transmission channels for fiscal policy. In particular, Debrun (2000) identifies three different fiscal 'regimes' under which a national government may choose fiscal policy and shows how these regimes affect the nature of the coordination problem with the common central bank and the features of the optimal fiscal institutions (see section 4).

The second lesson stemming from empirical studies is that the likely enhancement of fiscal stabilisation efforts by individual member states will sharpen two types of conflict among policymakers: the coordination of fiscal policies and the monetary and fiscal policy mix. Despite their shortcomings, the stylised models evoked above provide a flexible framework in which to analyse these issues. The next two subsections present an overview of these studies.

3.1.2   *Fiscal policy coordination among member states*   More active fiscal policies naturally pose the question of the cross-border spillovers or externalities associated with decentralised actions on national fiscal instruments. In principle, the existence of significant spillover effects would justify a certain degree of coordination or centralisation at the supranational level in order to internalise the externalities and deliver collectively more efficient measures (Hamada 1985). The Treaty establishing the European Union (the Amsterdam Treaty) already provides a framework for fiscal coordination through a variety of mechanisms: the Excessive Deficit Procedure (Article 104), the Stability and Growth Pact (Council Regulation 1467/97), the Mutual Surveillance Procedure (Article 99–3) and the Broad Economic Policy Guidelines (Article 99). However, European policymakers as well as some researchers have argued that closer coordination is needed, possibly in the context of the so-called Euro-group, an informal gathering of the finance ministers of the euro area member states.[15]

---

[14] See also Andersen and Schneider (1986) or Nordhaus (1994) among others.

[15] Von Hagen and Mundshenck (2001) provide a detailed description of the policy coordination procedures within the European Union. See also Cangiano and Mottu (1998).

A central element in assessing the need for closer coordination (or even a partial centralisation of fiscal decisionmaking) and the forms such coordination should take is to understand the nature of the international fiscal policy spillovers within the monetary union. Unfortunately, the literature does not provide any clear-cut indication about the sign of these spillovers. In classic analyses of policy coordination (e.g., Mundell 1968; Hamada 1985), ad-hoc fixed-price models generally assume direct, positive demand spillovers. By contrast, many recent models of currency unions conclude to negative spillovers. Cohen and Wyplosz (1989) focus on the negative externality associated with the Union's aggregate balance of payments and insist on the influence of national fiscal policies on the joint real exchange rate. In a similar vein, Andersen and Sorensen (1995) and Jensen (1996) emphasise the contractionary terms-of-trade effect of a *balanced-budget* foreign fiscal expansion on the domestic economy.[16] In a monetary union, public debt accumulation adds other sources of negative spillovers through the common real interest rate and the credibility of monetary policy (see section 2). Levine and Brociner (1994) combine terms-of-trade (negative), real-interest-rate (negative) and external-demand (positive) spillovers in a single model and argue that negative spillovers probably dominate. Eichengreen (1997) conjectures that the *positive* demand spillovers operating through trade flows will be roughly offset by the union-wide crowding-out effects so that the case for fiscal policy coordination is weak. By contrast, Dixon and Santoni (1997) demonstrate the possibility of *positive* demand spillovers in a micro-founded model of EMU with monopolistic competition and unionised labour markets leading to excessive unemployment. Important for their result is the assumption that a 'specie-flow' mechanism is at work to balance intra-EMU trade. Hence, a domestic fiscal expansion entails a trade deficit financed by a decrease in the net foreign assets of the economy. For a given union-wide money supply, the domestic fiscal expansion thus triggers a redistribution of the money stock in favour of the foreign economy, leaving both member states better off. Beetsma, Debrun and Klaassen (2001) also argue that positive spillovers probably dominate ex ante. They point out that the magnitude of the union-wide crowding-out effects (through joint interest and exchange rates) crucially depends on the decision of the central bank to accommodate the fiscal impulse or to counteract it. They argue that since crowding-out effects are endogenous to the outcome of the game, one should restrict the attention to positive ex-ante spillovers.

Although significant spillovers are necessary to make a case for closer fiscal coordination, they are not sufficient to establish that such coordination would be welfare improving. The literature provides various examples of

---

[16] This spillover effect was originally studied by Turnovsky (1988). Catenaro and Tirelli (2000) and Pina (1999) also rely on this channel in their models.

counterproductive international policy coordination (Rogoff 1985b; Kehoe 1989; Carraro and Giavazzi 1991; Canzoneri and Henderson 1991), illustrating a general result of game theory when coordination is limited to a subset of players. In a monetary union, the common central bank emerges as the 'natural' outsider whose adverse reaction to fiscal coordination could make the latter counterproductive. In effect, the Amsterdam Treaty imposes a strict separation of monetary and fiscal powers, making it unlikely for the ECB to participate in any kind of joint decision process with national governments. As a consequence, the 'horizontal' coordination problem (across governments) interacts with a 'vertical' coordination problem (between monetary and fiscal authorities) discussed in subsection 3.2.3 below. The tension between these two problems intensifies as the gap between the objectives of the common central bank and those of the governments gets wider.[17] The resulting risk of counterproductive fiscal coordination manifests itself in two ways. The first is a potential threat to macroeconomic discipline and the second, a conflict on the appropriate policy mix in response to a given set of disturbances.

Various papers illustrate how fiscal coordination may threaten macroeconomic discipline. In a small open economy model, Agell, Calmfors and Jonsson (1996) show that if the authorities can credibly assign their monetary instrument to the exclusive pursuit of price stability (which, according to these authors, they could do by entering EMU), discretionary demand-side fiscal policies may turn more activist and result in an expansive deficit bias analogous to the Barro–Gordon inflation bias. Debrun (2000) considers a similar argument in a model of a monetary union with n heterogeneous members and an independent central bank focusing exclusively on price stability. He shows that 'horizontal' fiscal coordination may aggravate the conflict with the common central bank, providing an incentive for the national governments to appoint excessively 'liberal' central bankers at the ECB Board to smoothen the conflict. However, certain forms of heterogeneity among member states may reverse that result.[18] Jensen (1996), Beetsma and Bovenberg (1998) and Catenaro and Tirelli (2000) argue that fiscal coordination may aggravate the time-inconsistency problem of monetary policy because a joint decision on fiscal policies reinforces the strategic position of governments with respect to the common central bank. In terms of equation (5.14) above, fiscal coordination would eliminate the perception by individual governments that their ability to influence the common monetary policy is diluted to a factor $1/n$. In two closely related papers, Pina (1999) and Catenaro (2000) independently challenge the generality of these results.

---

[17] Most of the time the ECB is assumed to put a greater emphasis on price stability relative to other objectives.

[18] See also Hughes-Hallett and Weymark (2001) for a related argument.

Pointing out that optimal delegation decisions (i.e. the appointment of central bankers) should internalise the horizontal coordination problem, they show that the failure to coordinate fiscal policies distorts those choices and leads to suboptimal appointments of central bankers.

As first established by Canzoneri and Henderson (1991), counterproductive coordination may also emerge independently of time-inconsistency problems when, confronted with a given disturbance, coordination among a subset of governments entails such an adverse reaction by outsiders that all the players would be better off without coordination. In an extension of Buti, In't Veld and Roeger (2001), Beetsma, Debrun and Klaassen (2001) propose a systematic analysis of the counterproductivity issue in a simple two-country model of a monetary union with positive demand externalities. The latter assumption implies that all macroeconomic stabilisation instruments (national fiscal policies and the common monetary policy) are strategic substitutes. With a cautious central bank and governments aware of the limitations of fiscal activism,[19] non-coordination is characterised by horizontal as well as vertical free riding. Since counterproductivity stems from the adverse reaction of the ECB to coordinated fiscal actions,[20] fiscal coordination is more likely to be beneficial the less intense the central bank's reaction is to the disturbances. Such passivity on the side of the ECB is observed in the presence of *asymmetric* shocks because the latter have a limited impact on the EMU aggregates targeted by the ECB. This result is valid for demand as well as supply shocks and it challenges the conventional wisdom according to which joint fiscal actions should be limited to the case of large *symmetric* shocks (Buti and Sapir 1998). In a framework very close to Beetsma, Debrun and Klaassen (2001), Lambertini and Rovelli (2003) independently provide several refinements on the conditions under which fiscal authorities have an incentive to coordinate.

3.1.3   Coordinating the policy mix   The previous subsection has developed arguments where horizontal *fiscal* coordination may be counterproductive because it worsens the vertical coordination problem between the union's common central bank and the national fiscal authorities. The same type of argument has been elaborated to warn of the possible dangers of monetary unification. Hughes-Hallett and Ma (1996) argue that horizontal monetary coordination achieved by means of a monetary union would come at the cost of vertical coordination failures. More specifically, they present entry into a currency union

[19] In fact, they assume that changes in the value of policy instruments are perceived as costly by the policymakers.

[20] For example, in the case of a common adverse demand shock, fiscal coordination leads to more expansive fiscal policies. The additional monetary tightening that this induces may leave both fiscal players worse off.

as a decision to 'change partners' in policy coordination. When adhering to EMU, countries choose a full, horizontal coordination of monetary policies, at the potential cost of a failure to achieve a proper vertical coordination of their monetary–fiscal policy mix. As a result of the architecture established by the Treaty on the European Union, a strict policy assignment emerges where monetary policy stabilises prices at the supranational level and fiscal policy promotes stable and sustained growth in each member state. Using a small international model similar to Oudiz and Sachs (1985), their simulations identify significant costs to such a radical policy assignment. In many cases, the costs of non-coordinated policy mixes exceed the gains from international monetary coordination. They conclude that a full but discretionary coordination between the monetary and fiscal authorities is desirable.[21] However, the costs of 'individually' unbalanced policy mixes may be smaller in a monetary union than with autonomous monetary policies. Indeed, unbalanced policy mixes are often blamed for lasting and probably costly misalignments in the nominal exchange rates of industrial countries. A classic example is the so-called 'Reaganomics' of the early 1980s where a combination of tight money and loose fiscal stance led to a substantial appreciation of the US dollar and a dramatic loss of competitiveness of the American economy. In the EMU, such a phenomenon would require *all* member states to adopt a similar fiscal stance at the same time. In fact, Cohen and Loisel (2001) find evidence that the synchronised fiscal retrenchments of the late 1990s combined with a loosening of monetary policy contributed to a sort of reverse-Reaganomics that might explain the weakness of the euro.

Vertical coordination failures may also imply unsustainable fiscal stances, especially when big governments increase fiscal activism (De Grauwe 1994). Following the Sargent and Wallace (1981) argument developed above in section 2, this might ultimately backlash on central bank independence and price stability. In the light of what happened in the 1980s, such a scenario is not unrealistic. The operation of the European Monetary System between 1979 and 1992 provides an interesting real-world experiment of increased horizontal coordination of monetary policies at the expense of domestic policy mixes. For non-German member states, participation in the EMS also served as credibility-enhancing mechanism of their decisions to assign monetary policy to price stability. Indeed, the increasing rigidity of the EMS until the crises of 1992–3 led to a de facto convergence of national monetary policies towards the German standards while fiscal policies remained discretionary. It is remarkable to observe that over the same period, fiscal performance in all other countries was significantly worse than in Germany. In particular, all countries saw a debt build-up

---

[21] See also Buti, In't Veld and Roeger (2001) for a similar conclusion.

considerably greater than in Germany. Debrun (1999) reports a significant and positive relationship between the increase in debt-to-GDP ratios relative to Germany and the 'institutional shift'[22] implied by shadowing the Bundesbank's policy. This relationship is consistent with the idea that a change in the monetary regime not accompanied by adjustments in the fiscal regime may affect fiscal sustainability.

3.2   Fiscal federalism and macroeconomic stabilisation

As most currency areas are confined within the borders of nation-states, many studies have attempted to capture the extent to which centralised fiscal systems contribute to offsetting regional shocks. In particular, existing federations like the United States, Canada, Germany or Switzerland provide interesting cases where subnational entities (states, provinces, *Länder* or cantons) control a significant part of the general government budget and potentially share with the central authority the task of stabilising economic disturbances. The central normative issue in the fiscal federalism literature is the optimal allocation of the tasks generally attributed to fiscal policy (allocative efficiency, redistribution and macroeconomic stabilisation) among the various levels of government (from central to local). In a macroeconomic perspective, fiscal federalism involves an analysis of the desirable sharing of spending and revenue-raising responsibilities among subnational, national and, in the case of the European Union, supranational policymakers. An important and highly sensitive element of that analysis is the size and direction of the intergovernmental transfers that will inevitably take place as a result of different regional conditions and/or specific devolution arrangements.[23] In a currency union, the formation of a fiscal federation and the intergovernmental transfers it implies naturally emerge as a potential contributor to the stabilisation of regional disturbances. The next two subsections briefly address the two key questions relevant for EMU: (i) Is there a need to centralise the fiscal stabilisation function? (ii) How could this be achieved?

3.2.1   Centralising stabilisation?   The traditional recommendation of the fiscal federalism theory is indeed that the macro stabilisation role of fiscal policy be carried out by the central government (Cangiano and Mottu 1998). This has been justified by various arguments. One of them, implicitly evoked above, is related to the public good nature of stabilisation policy. As highly

---

[22] The shift is measured by the gap between the degree of legal independence of the other central banks and that of the Bundesbank.

[23] Ter-Minassian (1997) provides a detailed overview of fiscal federalism in a macroeconomic perspective.

integrated, neighbouring regions are likely to benefit from stabilisation measures carried out by one of them, a free-riding problem emerges and makes decentralised policies excessively passive. Centralisation then offers a credible solution to that coordination failure. Another justification is that central governments benefit from 'scale' economies in performing the macroeconomic stabilisation function. The determinants of these scale economies include better borrowing conditions, greater revenue-raising capacities and smaller Ricardian effects. The downsizing of Ricardian effects comes from the fact that liabilities resulting from a countercyclical fiscal stimulus (and the expected future repayments through higher taxes) would be shared by the entire federation. This effect drives the results obtained by Bayoumi and Masson (1998), who estimated with Canadian data that a non-liability-creating stabilisation would be two to three times more effective than decentralised stabilisation financed by an increase in the local public debt. Last, but not least, fiscal federations offer interregional risk-sharing opportunities through a variety of transfer mechanisms from booming regions to depressed regions. Such transfers provide a welcome complement to (or a much needed substitute for) market-driven factor mobility (or the absence of it) as a stabilising response to asymmetric shocks. Not surprisingly, many observers and researchers have argued that the EMU would benefit from such a fiscal federation.[24]

In his discussion of the role of fiscal policy in a currency area, Fatás (1998) blends those arguments and proposes a convenient distinction between intertemporal transfers and interregional transfers. The former have already been extensively discussed above and mainly involve the normal operation of automatic stabilisers (through progressive taxation and social transfers), creating a deficit in bad times and a surplus in good times. Those transfers make disposable income less sensitive to the business cycle than pre-tax income. Given consumers' desire to smooth consumption over time, intertemporal transfers make credit-constrained, non-Ricardian consumers better off but leave fully Ricardian ones indifferent. Interregional transfers may either be deliberately organised by the central government, 'forcing' booming regions to assist contracting ones, or emerge automatically through the normal operation of the tax and social security systems. For instance, regions in recession would pay less in taxes and receive more in social security benefits at the expense of a central government's deficit. Interregional transfers (automatic or deliberate) thus work as an insurance mechanism and, in that sense, protect permanent income from region-specific shocks. From a welfare point of view, even perfectly Ricardian consumers would be better off as a result of interregional transfers because they

---

[24] Cooper and Kempf (2000) explore the benefits from monetary union in a two-country model with asymmetric supply shocks. They consider different settings as regards to the degree of centralisation of risk sharing.

could ensure that the fiscal expansion benefiting the contracting region would not be fully financed by future taxes. To conclude, since it is likely that, under EMU, fiscal policy has to offer an extra contribution to macroeconomic stabilisation efforts, fiscal federalism theory suggests that the most efficient way to reinforce fiscal stabilisation instruments would be through the interregional transfers that a fiscal federation can bring about.

A large number of studies have recently tried to estimate the implicit insurance provided by the centralised tax-transfer systems of existing fiscal federations. Von Hagen (1999b) provides a recent survey of this empirical literature. For obvious reasons of data availability, most studies consider the degree of interstate insurance in the United States. Estimates range from 7% to 40% of state-specific shocks being insured automatically through the tax-transfer system, with the majority of estimates falling in an interval of 10–15%. Such a wide range can be explained by the methodological difficulty of disentangling intertemporal (pure stabilisation) from interregional transfers (pure insurance). In that respect, Fatás (1998) argues that the insurance service provided by federal budgets in the United States and other federations have often been overestimated. For instance, earlier estimates by Sala-i-Martin and Sachs (1992) captured the *overall* stabilising effect of the tax system on the state disposable income.[25] The latter could only be identified with interregional transfers (or insurance) under the implausible assumption of no aggregate risk in the federation. Trying to better insulate interregional transfers from intertemporal ones,[26] Fatás (1998) finds that those 'previous estimates of the amount of interstate insurance provided by the US federal budget overestimate the true amount of insurance by a factor 3'. Hence, he concludes that, 'even if a European-wide fiscal system managed to reduce volatility in disposable income by 30 percent, it would be providing less than 10 percent insurance'.

3.2.2   Towards a European fiscal federation?   Considering the heterogeneous membership of the EMU, it is not clear that all potential members of a fiscal federation would gain from it. Economic heterogeneity induces two types of problems. First, regions characterised by more stable output might gain very little from, or could even be destabilised by, the need to 'contribute' to the federal system (Fatás 1998). Second, it appears difficult to design a system that would aim only at minimising the *variability* of income. It seems inevitable that a European fiscal federation would, at least to some extent, lead to a systematic redistribution from rich (or fast-growing) to poor (or slow-growing) countries as the former pay higher taxes and receive lower transfers *on average*. Other

---

[25] Following these authors: 'a one dollar reduction in state personal income reduces disposable income by only 56 to 65 cents' (in Fatás 1998, p. 171).

[26] Recall that intertemporal transfers are already provided by the automatic stabilisers of national budgets in each member state.

problems may arise. They include moral hazard, as in any insurance scheme, or exploitation of the redistribution scheme by politically powerful regions (Bordignon, Manasse and Tabellini 2001). This type of problem is politically sensitive and limits the scope for centralising the tax-transfer systems at the European level.

This brief review of the fiscal federalism literature indicates that the economics of fiscal federations is a political minefield. Hence, it is safe to predict that the establishment of a European fiscal federation is very unlikely in the foreseeable future. It is more reasonable to foresee the development of a more cooperative approach to fiscal policymaking. Furthermore, the prospective enlargement of the E(M)U will certainly not help to tilt the balance towards a significant redistribution mechanism. Concrete proposals for the creation of a European fiscal transfer scheme exist. They are reviewed by Pacheco (2000).[27] Perhaps the only feasible scheme at present would be an intermediate, ad-hoc system based on an extended role of the existing structural funds.

4   Institutional issues

As discussed in sections 2 and 3 above, the interaction between monetary and fiscal policies in a currency union gives rise to two sorts of problems. On the one hand, the nature of the strategic interaction between monetary and fiscal authorities directly affects the anti-inflationary credibility of the common central bank. On the other hand, monetary unification imposes specific constraints on the ability of policymakers to insure their citizens against real aggregate fluctuations in a socially optimal way. In both cases, a large part of the academic literature as well as most observers and policymakers have emphasised the essential contribution of appropriately designed institutions to address these problems. Although most of the theoretical analyses of macroeconomic institutions deal with the time-inconsistency problem of the optimal monetary policy, institutional solutions have also been advocated and formally characterised in the context of international policy coordination (Persson and Tabellini 1996; Jensen 2000) and the coordination of the monetary–fiscal policy mix (Agell, Calmfors and Jonsson 1996; Beetsma and Bovenberg 1997b; Dixit and Lambertini 2003a; Catenaro and Tirelli 2000; Debrun 2000; Castellani and Debrun 2001). However, in theory as well as in practice, the design of a coherent set of institutions supposed to effectively tackle problems as diverse and as interdependent as the credible achievement of price stability, the efficient use of macroeconomic policies as stabilisation instruments, the safeguarding of fiscal discipline and the implementation of a broadly coordinated policy mix represents a tremendous challenge, especially with thirteen decisionmakers (twelve

---

[27] Von Hagen and Hammond (1998) discuss a number of obstacles to setting up such a system.

fiscal authorities plus the ECB) motivated by different aims and facing different economic and political contexts.

The institutional dimension of the current policy debate concerns the strict limitations on public debts and deficits and the establishment of a more formal mechanism for fiscal policy coordination among EMU member states. In this section, we first discuss the rationale for the Excessive Deficit Procedure and the Stability and Growth Pact. We then review the attempts made in the literature to characterise optimal fiscal institutions and compare the latter with existing arrangements. Finally, we provide an overview of the lively debate on the need for additional institutions of fiscal coordination.

4.1   Rationales for existing institutional constraints on fiscal discretion

The academic literature generally provides little support to the fiscal discipline mechanisms embedded in EMU institutional architecture. At best, fiscal restraints are presented as useless, at worst, as counterproductive and, on average, as a 'minor nuisance', to borrow from Eichengreen and Wyplosz (1998). Most of the negative feelings rest on the potential costs induced by the lack of fiscal flexibility in response to country-specific shocks. That point of view was most forcefully expressed in the early literature on the Maastricht fiscal criteria (see, for example, Bean 1992; Buiter, Corsetti and Roubini 1993). More recent studies based on the precise contents of the Stability and Growth Pact are less nit-picking. Buti, Franco and Ongena (1997) and Eichengreen and Wyplosz (1998) provide counterfactual evidence based on the last thirty years showing that a retrospective implementation of the Stability and Growth Pact's provisions would not have entailed dramatic costs in terms of output variability or cumulative output losses. Still, the conventional wisdom about fiscal restraints remains tainted with scepticism. For instance, Dornbusch (1997) argues that '. . . the concern with fiscal criteria lacks a basis once an independent central bank with a precise stability mandate and a no-bail-out provision are in place'. Only very recently have systematic attempts been made in the academic literature to identify a plausible rationale for fiscal restraints and discuss possible ways to amend existing rules.

Part of the difficulty in finding a rationale for Europe's fiscal arrangement stems from the fact that the EMU constitution is a clear effort to institute an 'ideal world' for central bankers. Attempts to justify the introduction of specific assurances regarding fiscal discipline therefore assume that some aspects of the monetary arrangement established by the Treaty are flawed. The main arguments include:

(a) Perfect central bank independence in periods of severe fiscal stress is unrealistic because political pressure would ultimately become too large to be credibly resisted.

(b) Imposing price stability as the overriding objective is not credible because other objectives such as the stability of the financial system may temporarily interfere with it. In particular, bailing out a large public debtor may appear more desirable than a full-scale systemic crisis.
(c) Participation in a monetary union distorts incentives of national governments towards fiscal profligacy, leading to an unsustainable fiscal stance that may ultimately threaten the commitment to price stability.
(d) Following the fiscal theory of the price level, monetary arrangements alone are insufficient to guarantee price stability at all times. In a monetary union with decentralised fiscal policies, the problem is complicated by the fact the single monetary policy is confronted with multiple solvency constraints.

Beetsma and Uhlig (1999) provide a formal analysis of the Stability and Growth Pact that combines a *political* deficit bias (Alesina and Tabellini 1990) with argument (a) above. Hence, without a formal mechanism to discipline governments, the ECB might be forced into implicit debt repudiation through inflation. Eichengreen and Wyplosz (1998) prefer argument (b). They argue that, despite the Treaty's explicit prohibition, bail-out operations similar to the international rescue packages set up in the aftermath of the Mexican and Asian crises in the late 1990s are not unlikely in the EMU. In the same vein, Jahjah (2000) studies a monetary union in which the central bank aims at low inflation and financial stability. As sovereign default by a large debtor might threaten financial stability, he shows that, beyond a certain level of public debt, increasing default risk incites the central bank to choose higher inflation in the hope of alleviating fiscal pressures and ultimately preserving financial stability. Argument (c) has been investigated in various models. Beetsma and Bovenberg (1999) demonstrate that monetary unification leads to excessive debt accumulation when the fiscal authorities are subject to a political distortion. Key to their result is that public debt accumulation leads to future inflation and consequently acts as a disciplinary device on governments' current fiscal decisions (see section 2). In a monetary union, the effectiveness of that disciplinary mechanism is diluted proportionally to the country's relative size in the union and may justify binding institutional restraints on fiscal discretion. Recent developments in the fiscal theory of the price level also offer interesting insights on the role of discipline-enhancing fiscal institutions in a monetary union with decentralised fiscal policies (argument (d)). Authors such as Bergin (2000), Sims (1999) or Woodford (1998) show that the risk of fiscal dominance (or a non-Ricardian regime) is magnified by the number of individual fiscal solvency constraints facing the common monetary policy. Canzoneri, Cumby and Diba (2001a) further show that if more than one member state is characterised by fiscal dominance, the monetary union is unsustainable. Their analysis suggests that the fiscal arrangements of the EMU are sufficient to ensure monetary dominance (or a Ricardian regime), that is the capacity of the central bank to maintain price stability.

All the above arguments rely on the presumption that the common central bank may come to the rescue of individual member states with unsustainable deficits, thereby creating unacceptable externalities. The latter would naturally justify institutional guarantees on the fiscal probity of all participants. One of the main criticisms to that approach is its presumption that some clauses of the Treaty, like the prohibition of monetisation (Article 101) or the prohibition of peer political pressure on the ECB (Article 108) are not credible.[28] In other words, the Excessive Deficit Procedure would be an explicit recognition in the Treaty itself that the provisions concerning monetisation, inflationary bail-out and complete independence are not fully binding. Furthermore, most of the problems underscored above could be alleviated with appropriate debt ceilings. These would allow for more flexibility in the short term than the existing deficit cap to be met every single year. To overcome those criticisms, some authors argue that fiscal restraints are justifiable on the sole basis of the coordination problem that arises from the separation of monetary and fiscal powers. In particular, if monetary and fiscal instruments are to some extent strategic substitutes, a possibility that is not rejected by existing empirical evidence (see section 3), delegating monetary policy to an independent central bank with a specific mandate to achieve price stability creates an unbalanced policy mix characterised by overly restrictive monetary policy (high real interest rates) and an excessively lax fiscal policy (excessive deficits). This point has been extensively developed by Nordhaus (1994). Agell, Calmfors and Jonsson (1996), Debrun (2000) and Castellani and Debrun (2001) exploited similar arguments to justify fiscal restraints in the EMU. When monetary and fiscal policies are strategic complements, Beetsma and Bovenberg (1997b, 1998) show that the fiscal authority, when acting as a Stackelberg leader, can exploit the central bank's preference for full employment by strategically increasing taxes to obtain looser monetary policies. As a result, discipline-enhancing fiscal institutions may be called for.

4.2   Alternative proposals for guaranteeing fiscal discipline

Extending the vast literature on monetary institutions, models of the interaction between monetary and fiscal policies can generate a variety of fiscal arrangements dealing with the coordination failures discussed in subsection 4.1. Models emphasising the possible pressure of governments' intertemporal budget constraints generally conclude that the imposition of debt ceilings is sufficient to ease fiscal threats on monetary stability. Interesting aspects of debt criteria are their simplicity and flexibility. When binding, they are more easily subject to 'dynamic' interpretations (i.e. the country must be converging at a satisfactory pace towards the objective) and do not force the country to a restrictive

---

[28] By extension, implicit bail-out through higher inflation is prohibited as well.

overkill that would ultimately threaten the credibility of the entire procedure. When non-binding, a debt cap allows for a potentially infinite variety of primary balance paths consistent with it. In particular, countries with a large government sector are induced to build up a 'buffer' between the debt ceiling and their cyclically adjusted actual debt level, which leaves them sufficient freedom to absorb severe shocks. Another argument in favour of debt ceilings is that the outstanding stock of public debt is probably the best measure for the severity of the credibility problems and, hence, for the potential pressure on the ECB to relax monetary policy. Although countries have entered EMU with very different debt/GDP ratios, one could well imagine an arrangement that would have set out country-specific time paths for the ceiling on the public debt, until an eventual, constant ceiling was reached. Papers explicitly endorsing the desirability of appropriate debt ceilings include Beetsma and Bovenberg (1999), Chari and Kehoe (1998), Jahjah (2000) and Woodford (1998). However, as pointed out by Canzoneri, Cumby and Diba (2001a), the Amsterdam Treaty and the Stability and Growth Pact put a clear emphasis on deficits. They show the 3% cap on the overall fiscal deficit to be sufficient to guarantee fiscal solvency.

Other papers derive fiscal institutions by analogy with the vast literature on monetary institutions. Beetsma and Bovenberg (1998) show that if the fiscal authority enjoys a Stackelberg leadership position against the central bank, a Rogoff-conservative government (i.e. a government that puts a greater emphasis on price stability than the representative agent) is desirable. The rest of the literature relies on contract metaphors (Walsh 1995). Beetsma and Uhlig (1999) model the role of pecuniary sanctions directly affecting the government budget constraint to eliminate a political deficit bias. Debrun (2000) characterises deficit sanctions in utility terms (analogous to the Walsh contracts for central bankers) and shows the latter to be non-linear, country-specific, and contingent on shocks as well as on the coordination regime among national governments. Castellani and Debrun (2001) demonstrate that, in general, deficit caps represent a sub-optimal solution to monetary-fiscal coordination problems and argue in favour of instrument-specific 'contracts'. They show that the choice of the instrument to be targeted depends on the nature of the strategic interplay between fiscal monetary authorities. In the same vein, Catenaro and Tirelli (2000) show that linear expenditure caps may be efficient. An arrangement that is sometimes advocated to deal with the incentive of shortsighted governments to squeeze out public investment is the use of a capital budgeting rule. It requires that each additional euro of deficit be spent on additional public investment. Peletier, Dur and Swank (1999) compare the performance of a deficit rule and a capital-budgeting rule in a model that yields a deficit bias in the absence of fiscal restrictions. The reason is that the current government wants to increase current public consumption at the expense of future spending. A deficit rule induces the government to reduce public investment in order to increase current consumption. A capital budgeting rule would prevent such a perverse change in behaviour. However, it has its own disadvantages, such as the problem that it precludes the possibility of shifting part of the expected proceeds on the public investment to the present and the incentive it may provide to disguise public consumption as public investment.

From a theoretical perspective, the contract metaphor is convenient to characterise the institutional environment fiscal policymakers face, and address the optimal design of these institutions in a general and explicit way. That literature suggests that legislation introducing specific fiscal criteria as well as compliance incentives for the government is an efficient means to deal with the lack of coordination of the policy mix. In a rather intuitive way, all the optimal institutional frameworks mentioned above prescribe that when the choice of an instrument (deficit, expenditure, effective tax rate, . . .) diverges from its most desirable value, the government should face punishment calibrated to incite compliance.

The appealing features of the contractual approach should remind us of some obvious caveats. One of the main shortcomings of that approach is that it remains silent on the effectiveness of these institutions. In fact, making desirable policies more credible through institutional reforms might simply transform the problem of non-credible policies into a problem of non-credible institutions (McCallum 1995; Jensen 1997). There is no doubt that a practically irreversible arrangement such as an international treaty lends more credibility to a fiscal stability rule than less visible or less transparent legal provisions.[29] Another sensitive point is that, even in the context of simple models, contracts are often extremely demanding in terms of information. For instance they require certainty, or at least consensus, about some key economic relations. They also postulate that the optimal policies under a hypothetical regime can effectively be translated into a set of desirable targets. Finally, by contrast with monetary institutions, enforcement of fiscal arrangements may be a problem when the agent (the national government) has a direct impact on the decisions of the principal (Council of Ministers). It would be naive not to suspect collusion among member states when it comes to formally sanctioning decisions of one of them, especially when the latter is influential.[30] To the best of our knowledge, only Casella (1999) addresses the issue of implementation in a systematic way. She proposes a market-based solution (tradable deficit permits) that could be considered if the Stability and Growth Pact is ever to be seriously renegotiated. Eichengreen and Wyplosz (1998) and Buti, Franco and Ongena (1997) indirectly address the implementation of the Stability and Growth Pact on the basis

---

[29] The lack of transparency in budget figures is a tremendously important issue neglected in the theoretical literature.

[30] The initial events surrounding Germany's increasing deficit serve as a good illustration. While the European Commission originally recommended the issuance of a formal warning at the ECOFIN Council meeting (on 12 February 2002), Germany's lobby proved effective at preventing this warning. The result was a compromise that allowed all the players to save face and that extracted a German promise to make the necessary adjustments for the fulfilment of the SGP.

of counterfactual evidence. Their results suggest that the Pact's constraints are not excessively restrictive and should not dramatically impair the use of fiscal policies as stabilisation instruments.

4.3   Institutions for fiscal policy coordination

The current framework of fiscal and fiscal–monetary coordination is based on formal mechanisms instituted by the Treaty and a series of informal procedures.[31] Formal mechanisms include the Excessive Deficit Procedure (EDP), the Mutual Surveillance Procedure (MSP) and the Broad Economic Policy Guidelines (BEPG). Both the MSP and the BEPG ensure broad consistency among all economic policies within the European Union and involve the ECOFIN, the European Commission and national governments. The EDP distinguishes itself by its rule-based approach and the possibility of sanctions. Informal coordination mechanisms mainly involve the euro group, which gathers euro area finance ministers, and the Cologne process, which consists of bi-annual informal meetings of delegates from trade unions, the European Commission, the European Central Bank, ECOFIN and non-euro-area central banks. The aim of the Cologne process is to establish some degree of coordination between macroeconomic policies and wage negotiations. Overall, those various procedures serve the same goal: to ensure coordination of the entire policy mix around the objective of macroeconomic discipline. In particular, vertical coordination (between monetary and fiscal policies) is specifically limited to the preservation of fiscal probity in all member states. It seems at present that further vertical coordination (on stabilisation policies, for instance) will necessarily take place in a non-binding context because of the potential contradictions between a rule-based approach and the statutory independence of the ECB.

As far as horizontal coordination is concerned, it is sometimes argued that the existing mechanisms do not provide a sufficient degree of commitment to deal effectively with the internalisation of potentially significant externalities. More efficient stabilisation policies would therefore require a more formal approach to horizontal fiscal coordination.

In general, the theoretical literature distinguishes two types of coordination (e.g. Beetsma and Bovenberg 2001): ex-ante coordination and ex-post coordination, depending on the means by which coordination is implemented. Ex-ante coordination operates through formal agreements recognised by the parties as international obligations (pacts, treaties, regulations issued by supranational institutions). Ex-post coordination is ad hoc and takes place on the basis of the current state of affairs. The Eurogroup can be viewed as a forum for ex-post fiscal coordination. By contrast, ECOFIN has well-defined policy prerogatives

---

[31] See von Hagen and Mundschenk (2001) for a recent and comprehensive overview of policy coordination institutions within the euro area.

and its decisions in those matters are legally binding. In practice, however, the distinction between ex-post and ex-ante coordination is not always so clear-cut. For instance the functioning of the Stability and Growth Pact seems to leave room for discretion, ad-hoc adjustments and perhaps political bargaining. Ultimately, the important difference between ex-ante and ex-post coordination is that the former implies a much stronger commitment of the parties involved because any violation of the agreement would be public and possibly subject to explicit punishment.

Beetsma, Debrun and Klaassen (2001) formally study the benefits of purely horizontal coordination of fiscal stabilisation policies in a monetary union without a time-inconsistency problem. They argue that fiscal coordination not based on a strong pre-commitment capacity of the fiscal authorities is likely to be counterproductive. The reason is that national governments jointly play Nash against the central bank, inciting the latter to free-ride on stabilisation efforts. This counterproductivity result is reversed when the governments enjoy a pre-commitment capacity, for instance through institutionalised coordination. The point is that a formal joint decision process allows the fiscal authorities to enjoy a first-mover advantage (Stackelberg leadership) and perfectly anticipate the adverse reaction of the ECB, forcing it to bear a greater share of the stabilisation burden.[32] Onorante (2003) argues that horizontal coordination may lead the fiscal authorities to abuse their power relative to the ECB. He favours rule-based coordination (such as the SGP) above horizontal fiscal coordination of the type considered here. Godbillon and Sidiropoulos (2001) study the joint design of centralised monetary and fiscal authorities by a group of countries. They show that the optimal institutional setting is an independent central bank that exclusively targets union-wide aggregates and a common fiscal authority made up of country representatives defending national interests. Such a combination deals with the inflation bias problem and delivers a more efficient stabilisation of idiosyncratic real disturbances than alternative regimes. In an operational perspective, a large number of concrete proposals have been made to amend the existing framework of policy coordination in the EMU. They include Wyplosz (1999a,b), von Hagen and Mundshenck (2001) and Lossani, Natale and Tirelli (2001).

5   Concluding remarks

This chapter was an attempt to review the recent literature on the interactions between monetary and fiscal policies in a monetary union. We analysed how fiscal policy affects the credibility of monetary policy and we discussed the

---

[32] Clearly, this capacity to strategically exploit the first-mover advantage hinges crucially on the assumption of complete information. Should the governments be uncertain about the ECB's reaction, it is not clear this result would still hold (see also Alesina et al. 2001).

implications of monetary union for the role of fiscal policy in stabilising country-specific shocks. Regarding the latter, we distinguished between decentralised fiscal institutions and fiscal federalism. We also paid attention to existing institutional arrangements to curb fiscal profligacy and the alternatives suggested by the literature. Finally, we discussed the need and the feasibility of intensified fiscal coordination.

Many open issues remain to be investigated. One concerns the more detailed modelling of the SGP and its effects on the economies. Most models of the SGP are highly stylised and miss many of the Pact's complexities, including the wide discretion margins left by the procedure ultimately leading to formal sanctions. In particular, more needs to be done to understand the strategic interactions between the players when it comes to voting in ECOFIN Council. Further, and related to the latter issue, formal analyses generally assume the Pact to be credible, while informal assessments by commentators often cast serious doubts on a strict execution of the Pact's provisions. Hence, it may be worthwhile to formally address the consequences of imperfectly credible fiscal institutions. Finally, we believe the relevance of the stability programmes, which provide for a regular assessment on the countries' fiscal policies, has not been properly reflected in the formal analyses of the SGP. Although the failure to adhere to the stability programmes in itself cannot lead to formal sanctions (non-interest-bearing deposits and fines), the programmes play an important role in information sharing and offer opportunities for peer pressure in case of deviations from proper fiscal policies. These aspects form a largely unexplored area at the moment. Another set of issues that deserves further attention is the design of alternative channels for the stabilisation of asymmetric shocks, given that monetary policy can no longer be directed towards that purpose. In particular, further analysis of the design of fiscal insurance systems (horizontal transfers between countries hit by different shocks) and of systems for fiscal federalism in the context of the EMU would be welcome. Although their political feasibility is still remote, one might expect that, with the ongoing European integration, they should receive serious consideration. In that respect, it may be useful to recall that a few decades ago most people would have found the idea of a common currency in Europe inconceivable. Finally, the issue that is probably perceived as most pressing at the moment is macroeconomic policy coordination. More clarity needs to be gained about the desirability of enhanced fiscal coordination and how such coordination can be implemented in practice, taking into account the individual incentives to deviate from coordination agreements.

REFERENCES

Agell, Jonas, L. Calmfors and G. Jonsson, 1996, 'Fiscal Policy when Monetary Policy Is Tied to the Mast', *European Economic Review* 40, 1413–40.

Alesina, A. and S. Ardagna, 1998, 'Tales of Fiscal Adjustment', *Economic Policy* 27, 487–546.

Alesina, A., O. J. Blanchard, J. Galí, F. Giavazzi and H. Uhlig, 2001, *Defining a Macroeconomic Framework for the Euro Area (Monitoring the European Central Bank*, vol. 3), London: CEPR.

Alesina, Alberto and R. Perotti, 1995, 'Fiscal Expansions and Fiscal Adjustments in OECD Countries', *Economic Policy* 21, 207–48.

Alesina, A. and G. Tabellini, 1987, 'Rules and Discretion with Noncoordinated Monetary and Fiscal Policies', *Economic Inquiry* 25, 619–30.

1990, 'A Positive Theory of Fiscal Deficits and Government Debt', *Review of Economic Studies* 57, 403–14.

Andersen, T. and F. Schneider, 1986, 'Coordination of Fiscal and Monetary Policy under Different Institutional Arrangements', *European Journal of Political Economy* 2, 169–91.

Andersen, T. and J. R. Sorensen, 1995, 'Unemployment and Fiscal Policy in an Economic and Monetary Union', *European Journal of Political Economy* 11, 27–43.

Artis, M. and B. Winkler, 1998, 'The Stability Pact: Safeguarding the Credibility of the European Central Bank', *National Institute Economic Review* 163, 87–98.

Asdrubali, P., B. E. Sorensen and O. Yosha, 1996, 'Channels of Interstate Risk Sharing: United States 1963–1990', *Quarterly Journal of Economics* 111, 1081–110.

Barro, R. J., 1983, 'Inflationary Finance under Discretion and Rules', *Canadian Journal of Economics* 16, 1–16.

Barro, R. J. and D. B. Gordon, 1983a, 'Rules, Discretion and Reputation in a Model of Monetary Policy', *Journal of Monetary Economics* 12, 101–21.

1983b, 'A Positive Theory of Monetary Policy in a Natural Rate Model', *Journal of Political Economy* 91, 589–610.

Bayoumi, T. and B. Eichengreen, 1997, 'Shocking Aspects of European Monetary Unification', in B. Eichengreen (ed.), *European Monetary Unification: Theory, Practice and Analysis*, Cambridge: Cambridge University Press, pp. 73–109.

Bayoumi, T. and P. Masson, 1998, 'Liability-Creating Versus Non-Liability-Creating Fiscal Stabilisation Policies: Ricardian Equivalence, Fiscal Stabilisation, and EMU', *Economic Journal* 108, 1026–45.

Bean, C., 1992, 'Economic and Monetary Union in Europe', *Journal of Economic Perspectives* 6, 31–52.

Beetsma, R. M. W. J. and A. L. Bovenberg, 1997a, 'Designing Fiscal and Monetary Institutions in a Second-Best World', *European Journal of Political Economy* 13, 53–79.

1997b, 'Central Bank Independence and Public Debt Policy', *Journal of Economic Dynamics and Control* 21, 873–894.

1998, 'Monetary Union without Fiscal Coordination May Discipline Policymakers', *Journal of International Economics* 45, 239–58.

1999, 'Does Monetary Unification Lead to Excessive Debt Accumulation?', *Journal of Public Economics* 74, 299–325.

2001, 'Structural Distortions and Decentralised Fiscal Policies in EMU', Discussion Paper no. 2851, CEPR, London.

Beetsma, R. M. W. J., X. Debrun and F. Klaassen, 2001, 'Is Fiscal Policy Coordination in EMU Desirable?', *Swedish Economic Policy Review* 8, 57–98.

Beetsma, R. M. W. J. and H. Uhlig, 1999, 'An Analysis of the Stability and Growth Pact', *Economic Journal* 109, 546–571.

Bergin, P. R., 2000, 'Fiscal Solvency and Price Level Determination in a Monetary Union', *Journal of Monetary Economics* 45, 37–53.

Blanchard, O. J. and R. Perotti, 2002, 'An Empirical Characterization of the Dynamic Effects of Changes in Government Spending and Taxes on Output', *Quarterly Journal of Economics* 117, 1329–68.

Bordignon, M., P. Manasse and G.Tabellini, 2001, 'Optimal Regional Redistribution under Asymmetric Information', *American Economic Review* 91, 709–23.

Brunila, A., M. Buti and D. Franco (eds.), 2001, *The Stability and Growth Pact*, New York: Palgrave.

Bryson, J., H. Jensen and D.Van Hoose, 1993, 'Rules, Discretion and International Monetary and Fiscal Policy Coordination', *Open Economies Review* 4, 117–32.

Buiter, W. H., G. Corsetti and N. Roubini, 1993, 'Excessive Deficits: Sense and Nonsense in the Treaty of Maastricht', *Economic Policy* 8, 57–100.

Buti, M., D. Franco and H. Ongena, 1997, 'Budgetary Policies During Recessions – Retrospective Application of the Stability and Growth Pact to the Post-War Period', Economic Paper no. 121, Brussels: European Commission.

1998, 'Fiscal Discipline and Flexibility in EMU: The Implementation of the Stability and Growth Pact', *Oxford Review of Economic Policy* 14, 81–97.

Buti, M., J. In't Veld and W. Roeger, 2001, 'Stabilising Output and Inflation in EMU: Policy Conflicts and Co-operation under the Stability Pact', *Journal of Common Market Studies* 39, 801–28.

Buti, M. and A. Sapir (eds.), 1998, *Economic Policy in EMU – A Study by the European Commission Services*, Oxford: Clarendon Press.

Calvo, G. A., 1978, 'On the Time Inconsistency of Optimal Policy in a Monetary Economy', *Econometrica* 46, 1411–28.

Cangiano, M. and E. Mottu, 1998, 'Will Fiscal Policy be Effective Under EMU?', Working Paper no. 98/176, IMF, Washington, DC.

Canzoneri, M. B., R. E. Cumby and B. T. Diba, 2001a, 'Fiscal Discipline and Exchange Rate Systems', *Economic Journal* 111, 667–90.

2001b, 'Is the Price Level Determined by the Needs for Fiscal Solvency?', *American Economic Review* 91, 1221–38.

Canzoneri, M. B. and B. T. Diba, 2001, 'The SGP: Delicate Balance or Albatross?', in Brunila et al., pp. 53–74.

Canzoneri, M. B. and J. A. Gray, 1985, 'Monetary Policy Games and the Consequences of Noncooperative Behaviors', *International Economic Review* 26, 547–64.

Canzoneri, M. B. and D. W. Henderson, 1991, *Monetary Policy in Interdependent Economies: A Game-Theoretic Approach*, Cambridge, MA: MIT Press.

Carraro, C. and F. Giavazzi, 1991, 'Can International Policy Co-ordination Really Be Counterproductive?' in C. Carraro et al. (eds.), *International Economic Policy Co-ordination*, Oxford: Blackwell, pp. 184–98.

Casella, A., 1999, 'Tradable Deficit Permits: Efficient Implementation of the Stability Pact in the European Monetary Union', *Economic Policy* 29, 321–47.

Castellani, F. and X. Debrun, 2001, 'Central Bank Independence and the Design of Fiscal Institutions', Working Paper no. 01/205, IMF, Washington, DC.

Catenaro, M., 2000, 'Macroeconomic Policy Interactions in the EMU: A Case for Fiscal Policy Co-ordination', Working Paper no. 0003, University of Surrey.

Catenaro, M. and P. Tirelli, 2000, 'Reconsidering the Pros and Cons of Fiscal Policy Coordination in a Monetary Union: Should We Set Public Expenditure Targets?', mimeo, University of Milan-Bicocca.

Chari, V.V. and P. Kehoe, 1998, 'On the Need for Fiscal Constraints in a Monetary Union', Working Paper no. 589, Federal Reserve Bank of Minneapolis.

Cohen, D. and O. Loisel, 2001, 'Why Was the Euro Weak? Markets and Policies', *European Economic Review* 45, 988–94.

Cohen, D. and C. Wyplosz, 1989, 'The European Monetary Union: An Agnostic Evaluation', in R. C. Bryant et al. (eds.), *Macroeconomic Policies in an Interdependent World*, Washington, DC: Brookings Institution; London: CEPR, pp. 311–37.

Cooper, R. and H. Kempf, 2000, 'Designing Stabilisation Policy in a Monetary Union', mimeo, Boston University/Université Paris-1 Panthéon-Sorbonne.

Cukierman, A. and F. Lippi, 2001, 'Labour Markets and Monetary Union: A Strategic Analysis', *Economic Journal* 111, 541–65.

De Arcangelis, G. and S. Lamartina, 2001, 'Fiscal Shocks and Policy Regimes in Some OECD countries', chapter 9 in this volume.

Debelle, G., 1993, 'Central Bank Independence: A Free Lunch?', mimeo, MIT.

Debelle, G. and S. Fischer, 1997, 'How Independent Should a Central Bank Be?', in S. C. W. Eijffinger et al. (eds.), *Independent Central Banks and Economic Performance*, Cheltenham: Elgar, pp. 462–88.

Debrun, X., 1999, 'Macroeconomic Policies in the European Monetary Union: Credibility, Coordination and Institutions', Ph.D. Dissertation no. 597, University of Geneva.

2000, 'Fiscal Rules in a Monetary Union: A Short Run Analysis', *Open Economies Review* 11, 323–58.

2001, 'Bargaining over EMU vs. EMS: Why Might the ECB Be the Twin Sister of the Bundesbank?', *Economic Journal* 111, 566–90.

De Grauwe, P., 1994, *The Economics of Monetary Integration*, 2nd edn, Oxford: Oxford University Press.

Delors Report 1989, *Report on Economic and Monetary Union*, Luxemburg: EC Publication Office.

Dixit, A., 2001, 'Games of Monetary and Fiscal Interactions in the EMU', *European Economic Review* 45, 589–613.

Dixit, A. and Luisa Lambertini, 2001, 'Monetary-Fiscal Policy Interactions and Commitment Versus Discretion in a Monetary Union', *European Economic Review* 45, 977–87.

2003a, 'Symbiosis of monetary and fiscal policies in a monetary union', *Journal of International Economics* 60, 235–47.

2003b, 'Interactions of Commitment and Discretion in Monetary and Fiscal Policies', forthcoming, *American Economic Review*.

Dixon, H. D. and M. Santoni, 1997, 'Fiscal Policy Coordination with Demand Spillovers and Unionised Labour Markets', *Economic Journal* 107, 403–17.

Dornbusch, R., 1997, 'Fiscal Aspects of Monetary Integration', *American Economic Review* 87, 221–3.

Eichengreen, B., 1997, 'Saving Europe's Automatic Stabilisers', *National Institute Economic Review* 159, 92–9.

Eichengreen, B. and C. Wyplosz, 1998, 'The Stability Pact: More than a Minor Nuisance?', *Economic Policy* 26, 65–104.

Fatás, A., 1998, 'Does EMU Need a Fiscal Federation?', *Economic Policy* 26, 165–92.

Fatás, A. and I. Mihov, 2001, 'Government Size and Automatic Stabilisers: International and Intranational Evidence', *Journal of International Economics* 55, 3–28.

2003, 'The Case for Restricting Fiscal Policy Discretion', forthcoming, *Quarterly Journal of Economics*.

Fatás, A. and A. K. Rose, 2001, 'Do Monetary Handcuffs Restrain Leviathan? Fiscal Policy in Extreme Exchange Rate Regimes', *IMF Staff Papers*, 47, Special Issue, 40–61.

Favero, C. and F. Giavazzi, 1999, 'The Transmission Mechanism of Monetary Policy in Europe: Evidence from Banks' Balance Sheets', NBER Working Paper no. 7231, Cambridge, MA.

Frankel, J. and A. Rose, 1998, 'The Endogeneity of the Optimum Currency Area Criteria', *Economic Journal* 108, 1009–25.

Galí, J. 1994, 'Government Size and Macroeconomic Stability', *European Economic Review* 38, 117–32.

Giavazzi, F., T. Jappelli and M. Pagano, 2000, 'Searching for Non-linear Effects of Fiscal Policy: Evidence from Industrial and Developing Countries', *European Economic Review* 44, 1259–89.

Giavazzi, F. and M. Pagano, 1990, 'Can Severe Fiscal Contractions Be Expansionary? Tales of Two Small European Countries', in O. J. Blanchard and S. Fischer (eds.), *NBER Macroeconomics Annual 1990*, Cambridge, MA: MIT Press, pp. 75–111.

Godbillon, B. and M. Sidiropoulos, 2001, 'Designing Fiscal Institutions in a Monetary Union', *Open Economies Review* 12, 163–79.

Gordon, R. H. and A. L. Bovenberg, 1996, 'Why Is Capital so Immobile Internationally? Possible Explanations and Implications for Capital Income Taxation', *American Economic Review* 86, 1057–75.

Hamada, K., 1985, *The Political Economy of International Monetary Interdependence*, Cambridge, MA: MIT Press.

Hughes-Hallett, A. and Y. Ma, 1996, Changing Partners: The Importance of Coordinating Fiscal and Monetary Policies within a Monetary Union, *Manchester School* 64, 115–34.

Hughes-Hallett, A. and D. N. Weymark, 2001, 'The Cost of Heterogeneity in a Monetary Union', Working Paper no. 01-W28, Vanderbilt University, Nashville.

Jahjah, S., 2000, 'Inflation, Debt and Default in a Monetary Union', Working Paper no. 00/179, IMF, Washington, DC.

Jensen, H., 1996, 'The Advantage of International Fiscal Cooperation under Alternative Monetary Regimes', *European Journal of Political Economy* 12, 485–504.

1997, 'Credibility of Optimal Monetary Delegation', *American Economic Review* 87, 911–20.

2000, 'Optimal Monetary Policy Cooperation through State-Independent Contracts with Targets', *European Economic Review* 44, 517–39.

Kehoe, P. J., 1989, 'Policy Coordination among Benevolent Governments may Be Undesirable', *Review of Economic Studies* 56, 289–96.

Kydland, F. E. and E. C. Prescott, 1977, 'Rules Rather than Discretion: The Inconsistency of Optimal Plans', *Journal of Political Economy* 85, 473–92.

Lambertini, Luca and R. Rovelli, 2003, 'Independent or Coordinated? Monetary and Fiscal Policy in EMU', chapter 6 in this volume.

Lambertini, Luisa and J. Tavares, 2000, 'Exchange Rates and Fiscal Adjustments: Evidence from OECD and Implications for EMU', mimeo, University of California at Los Angeles.

Leeper, E., 1991, 'Equilibria under "Active" and "Passive" Monetary and Fiscal Policies', *Journal of Monetary Economics* 27, 129–47.

Leith, C. and S. Wren-Lewis, 2002, 'Interactions between Monetary and Fiscal Policy under EMU', chapter 8 in this volume.

Levine, P. and A. Brociner, 1994, 'Fiscal Policy Coordination and EMU', *Journal of Economic Dynamics and Control* 18, 699–729.

Levine, P. and J. Pearlman, 1992, 'Fiscal and Monetary Policy under EMU: Credible Inflation Targets or Unpleasant Monetary Arithmetic?', Discussion Paper No. 701, CEPR, London.

2001, 'Monetary Union: The Ins and Outs of Strategic Delegation', *Manchester School* 69, 285–309.

Lossani, M., P. Natale and P. Tirelli, 2001, 'Macroeconomic Policies and Institutions in Europe: Some Considerations and a Proposal', mimeo, University of Milan-Bicocca.

McCallum, B. T., 1995, 'Two Fallacies Concerning Central-Bank Independence', *American Economic Review* 85, 207–11.

Mélitz, J., 1997, 'Some Cross-Country Evidence about Debt, Deficits and the Behaviour of Monetary and Fiscal Authorities', Discussion Paper no. 1653, CEPR, London.

Mooslechner, P. and M. Schuerz, 1999, 'International Macroeconomic Policy Coordination: Any Lesson for EMU? A Selective Survey of the Literature', *Empirica* 26, 171–99.

Mundell, R. A., 1961, 'A Theory of Optimum Currency Areas', *American Economic Review* 51, 657–65.

1968, *International Economics*, London: Macmillan.

Muscatelli, A., P. Tirelli and C. Trecroci, 2003, 'Monetary and Fiscal Policy Interactions over the Cycle: Some Empirical Evidence', chapter 10 in this volume.

Nordhaus, W., 1994, 'Policy Games: Coordination and Independence in Monetary and Fiscal Policies', *Brookings Papers on Economic Activity* 2, 139–216.

Obstfeld, M. and K. Rogoff, 2000, 'The Six Major Puzzles in International Macroeconomics: Is there a Common Cause?', Working Paper no. 7777, NBER, Cambridge, MA.

Onorante L., 2003, 'Interaction of Fiscal Policies on the Euro Area: The ECB View', chapter 7 in this volume.

Oudiz, G. and J. Sachs, 1984, 'Macroeconomic Policy Coordination Among Industrial Economies', *Brookings Papers on Economic Activity* 1, 1–75.

1985, 'International Policy Coordination in Dynamic Macroeconomic Models', in W. H. Buiter and R.C. Marston (eds.), *International Economic Policy Coordination*, Cambridge: Cambridge University Press, pp. 274–319.

Pacheco, L. M., 2000, 'Fiscal Federalism, EMU and Shock Absorption Mechanisms: A Guide to the Literature', *European Integration Online Papers* 4, http://eiop.or.at/eiop/texte/2000–004a.htm.

Peletier, B., R. Dur and O. Swank, 1999, 'Voting on the Budget Deficit: Comment', *American Economic Review* 89, 1377–81.

Persson, T. and G. Tabellini, 1996, 'Monetary Cohabitation in Europe', *American Economic Review*, Papers and Proceedings 86, 111–16.

Pina, A. M., 1999, 'Can Conservatism Be Counterproductive? Delegation and Fiscal Policy in a Monetary Union', *Manchester School* 67, Supplement, 88–115.

Rodrik, D., 1998, 'Why Do More Open Economies Have Bigger Governments?', *Journal of Political Economy* 106, 997–1032.

Rogoff, K., 1985a, 'The Optimal Degree of Commitment to an Intermediate Monetary Target', *Quarterly Journal of Economics* 100, 1169–90.

1985b, 'Can International Monetary Policy Cooperation Be Counter-productive?', *Journal of International Economics* 18, 199–217.

Rose, A. and E. Van Wincoop, 2001, 'National Money as a Barrier to International Trade: The Real Case For Currency Union', *American Economic Review* 91, 386–90.

Sala-i-Martin, X. and J. Sachs, 1992, 'Fiscal Federalism and Optimum Currency Areas: Evidence for Europe from the United States', in M. B. Canzoneri, V. U. Grilli and P. Masson (eds.), *Establishing a Central Bank: Issues in Europe and Lessons from the U.S.*, Cambridge: Cambridge University Press, pp. 195–219.

Sargent, T. and N. Wallace, 1981, 'Some Unpleasant Monetarist Arithmetic', Federal Reserve Bank of Minneapolis, *Quarterly Review* (Fall), 1–17.

Sims, C., 1994, 'A Simple Model for Study of the Determination of the Price Level and the Interaction of Monetary and Fiscal Policy', *Economic Theory* 4, 381–99.

1999, 'The Precarious Fiscal Foundations of EMU', *De Economist* 147, 415–36.

Svensson, L. E. O., 1997, 'Optimal Inflation Targets, Conservative Central Banks, and Linear Inflation Contracts', *American Economic Review* 87, 98–114.

Tabellini, G., 1986, 'Money, Debt and Deficits in a Dynamic Game', *Journal of Economic Dynamics and Control* 10, 427–42.

Ter-Minassian, T. (ed.), 1997, *Fiscal Federalism in Theory and Practice*, Washington, DC: International Monetary Fund.

Turnovsky, S., 1988, 'The Gains from Fiscal Cooperation in the Two-Commodity Real Trade Model', *Journal of International Economics* 25, 111–127.

Van Aarle, B., A. L. Bovenberg and M. Raith, 1997, 'Is there a Tragedy of a Common Central Bank? A Dynamic Analysis', *Journal of Economic Dynamics and Control* 21, 417–47.

Van Aarle, B. and F. Huart, 1999, 'Monetary and Fiscal Unification in the EU: A Stylized Analysis', *Journal of Economics and Business* 51, 49–66.

von Hagen, J., 1993, 'Monetary Policy Coordination in the European Monetary System', in M. Fratianni and D. Salvatore (eds.), 'Monetary Policy in Developed Economies', *Handbook of Comparative Economic Policies*, vol. 3, Westport: Greenwood Press, pp. 509–60.

1999a, 'Tumbling Giant: Germany's Experience with the Maastricht Fiscal Criteria', Working Paper no. B-5, ZEI, Bonn.

1999b, 'A Fiscal Insurance for the EMU?', in R. M. W. J. Beetsma and C. Oudshoorn (eds.), 'Tools for Regional Stabilisation', Discussion Paper no. 9903, Dutch Ministry of Economic Affairs.

von Hagen, J. and G. W. Hammond, 1998, 'Regional Insurance against Asymmetric Shocks: An Empirical Study for the European Community', *The Manchester School* 66, 331–53.

von Hagen, J., A. Hughes-Hallett and R. Strauch, 2001, 'Budgetary Consolidation in EMU', *Economic Papers* 148, Brussels: European Commission.

von Hagen, J. and S. Mundshenck, 2001, 'The Functioning of Economic Policy Coordination', Working Paper no. B-08, ZEI, Bonn.

Walsh, C. E., 1995, 'Optimal Contracts for Central Bankers', *American Economic Review* 85, 150–67.

Willett, T. D., 1999, 'A Political Economy Analysis of the Maastricht and Stability Pact Fiscal Criteria', in A. Hughes-Hallett, M. M. Hutchison and S. E. Hougaard Jensen (eds.), *Fiscal Aspects of European Monetary Integration*, Cambridge: Cambridge University Press, pp. 37–66.

Woodford, M., 1995, 'Price Level Determinacy without Control of a Monetary Aggregate', *Carnegie-Rochester Conference Series on Public Policy* 43, 1–46.

1998, 'Control of the Public Debt: A Requirement for Price Stability?', in G. Calvo and M. King (eds.), *The debt burden and its consequences for monetary policy*, IEA Conference Volume no. 118, New York: St Martin's Press, pp. 117–54.

Wyplosz, C., 1999a, 'Towards a More Perfect EMU', Discussion Paper no. 2252, CEPR, London.

1999b, 'Macroeconomic Policies in the EMU: Strategies and Institutions', Working Paper no. B11, ZEI, Bonn.

Yosha, O. and B. E. Sorensen, 1998, 'International Risk Sharing and European Monetary Unification', *Journal of International Economics* 45, 211–38.

6   Independent or coordinated? Monetary and fiscal policy in EMU

Luca Lambertini and Riccardo Rovelli

1   Introduction

> *In the third stage of EMU, Member States shall avoid excessive general government deficits: this is a clear Treaty obligation. The European Council underlines the importance of safeguarding sound government finances as a means of strengthening the conditions for price stability and for strong sustainable growth conducive to employment creation. It is also necessary to ensure that national budgetary policies support stability-oriented monetary policies. Adherence to the objective of sound budgetary positions close to balance or in surplus will allow all Member States to deal with normal cyclical fluctuations while keeping the government deficit within the reference value of 3% of GDP.*
>
> (Resolution of the European Council on the Stability and Growth Pact, adopted at Amsterdam, June 1997).[1]

The purpose of this chapter is to examine the relations between monetary and fiscal policies in the context of the European Economic and Monetary Union (EMU). The quotation reported above makes three points which are relevant in this respect: national budgetary policies should (i) be inspired by the commitment to respect the medium-term budgetary objective of 'close to balance or in surplus'; (ii) 'support stability-oriented monetary policies'; and (iii) be able to 'deal with normal cyclical fluctuations while keeping the government deficit within the reference value of 3% of GDP'. The Broad Economic Policy Guidelines (BEPG), which the European Council is required to formulate in terms of Article 99 of the Treaty of Maastricht,[2] is the official document by means of which member states effectively coordinate their economic policies.

We thank Roel Beetsma, Alessandro Missale, Guido Tabellini and the audience at the EMU Macroeconomics Institutions Conference (University of Milano Bicocca, 20–22 September, 2001) for useful comments and discussion. The usual disclaimer applies.
[1] http://europa.eu.int/abc/doc/off/bull/en/9706/i1027.htm.
[2] We follow the current numbering of the articles in the Treaty, in the updated version of 1 September 1999, amended after the Treaty of Amsterdam.

On matters of fiscal policy, the Treaty of Maastricht was essentially concerned only with ensuring fiscal discipline, so as to prevent threats to monetary stability. We believe that the new formulation of the objectives and constraints of fiscal policy, which has been adopted after the Treaty of Amsterdam, goes well beyond the simple emphasis of the Treaty of Maastricht. Moreover, we also think that this formulation poses a challenge to a recent but widespread tradition in economic modelling, which has been used to argue in favour of central bank independence (CBI). Within this tradition, the only challenge from fiscal policy to CBI appears when an 'indisciplined' fiscal policy, possibly unsustainable in the long run, forces the central bank to give up its independence and monetise the fiscal debt (Sargent and Wallace 1981). In fact, we argue below that even perfectly sustainable (in the long run) fiscal policies may undermine the policy stance adopted by the monetary authority. For instance a (relatively) more expansive fiscal policy (even within the 3% reference value) will have an expansionary effect on aggregate demand and consequently also on the rate of inflation. Thus, a more expansive (but perfectly sustainable and 'disciplined') fiscal policy could potentially undermine the stance of monetary policy in the pursuit of price stability.

If our argument is correct, then it follows not only that monetary policy should be governed by an independent authority, but also that national budgetary policies should be coordinated with it.[3] This argument is compatible with the Treaty of Maastricht, but clearly goes beyond it. Moreover, in order to formulate this argument precisely, an appropriate analytical framework would be required. Another question, which should also be addressed in this framework, is whether the 'division of labour' between monetary and fiscal policies, which is envisaged by the Stability and Growth Pact, is optimal from the point of view of the member countries of EMU.

Our aim here is to propose a framework within which these questions can be formally addressed. In fact, given the advanced status of institutional developments in the European Union (EU), it is surprising that such a framework has not yet been shared by a larger body of literature. To underline this point, in this introduction we first compare the status of mainstream thinking on monetary policy at the dawn of the EMU (which we identify as the drafting of the Treaty of Maastricht, in 1991) with current developments on the effectiveness of monetary policy in controlling prices and – in the meantime – in affecting aggregate demand. The main evolution in this area may be synthesised as the demise of the Lucas supply function, consequent to the adoption of a hypothesis of short-run price rigidity. We dramatise this evolution by telling the story of

---

[3] Tabellini (1986) makes a similar point in a different setup, i.e. in the context of a differential game between fiscal and monetary authorities, where the target variable is the time-path of the government debt.

when Rip van Winkle, a character well known to all the macroeconomists of the same generation of one of the two co-authors, went to sleep for a second time in 1991,[4] to awake only at the beginning of the new millennium.

1991

When Rip van Winkle went to sleep for the second time at the end of 1991, he thought his ideas about macroeconomics and monetary policy were, broadly speaking, reasonably clear. The first thing he was sure of was that monetary policy should be primarily focused on price stability. The thought that this important prescription had at last been acknowledged by economists and politicians alike, and that it had been embodied in such an important piece of constitutional architecture as the Treaty of Maastricht, satisfied him. Moreover, Rip was aware that most economists would also suggest that, to back up such an important statement, it would have been useful, if not strictly necessary, to enclose a strong statement on central bank independence. This indeed had been written in clear letters also in the Treaty of Maastricht. Rip was also aware, however, that the reasons why economists and politicians both agreed on this point would often be different. Economists on average wanted a conservative central bank, that would surely refrain from too much output stabilisation. Politicians instead (at least when sat at the constitutional drawing table, far removed from their constituencies) thought that it was a good thing to keep the central bankers removed from the tempting sirens of fiscal accommodation. To this purpose, indeed, it was the politicians who put several specific clauses in the Treaty, although Rip was well aware that, according to some economists (for instance, to Buiter, Corsetti and Roubini 1993) some of those clauses were perhaps too strict, either because they gave too much leeway to the ECB, or because they did not leave enough room for fiscal stabilisation (a task which, in a monetary union with decentralised fiscal authorities and a ridiculously small central budget, should naturally be assigned to national fiscal authorities).

Another thing about which Rip was convinced was that, if monetary policy was to have real effects, it would have to be only in the short run, and only through price (or inflation) surprises. When he went to sleep, the expectations-augmented Phillips curve, restated (that is, micro-founded) as the Lucas supply function, was all the rage in upbeat macroeconomics textbooks, and together with it went the nice corollary that any rule-based (that is, systematic) monetary policy would be ineffective. Also, having read several papers by Barro and Gordon and others, Rip was convinced that, if you left central bankers to run

---

[4] An account of Rip's first awakening as a macroeconomist, discovering the challenges that the natural rate of unemployment and rational expectations posed to the role of monetary policy, is given by Gordon (1976).

things their way, most of them would have spent most of their time trying to fool people with inflation surprises. Of course, Rip agreed that people were smart enough not to let themselves be fooled more than a few times in a row. But for some reason most economists, and Rip was one of them, thought that central bankers had never learned that old saying or, to put it more technically – which nevertheless amounts to the same thing – thought that a central banker would continue to design ad infinitum the same, one-period-ahead optimal (time-inconsistent) plans, as if they were faced by memoryless, atomistic agents.[5]

The world about which Rip was sure he knew enough monetary economics could thus be described by two simple equations:

aggregate supply: $y = y^* + a[\pi - E(\pi)] + \zeta_1$ (6.1)

aggregate demand: $m - p = ky + \zeta_2,$ (6.2)

where y is the log level of aggregate demand, y^* its natural (full-employment) level; m the log of the money stock, p the log of the price level, π the rate of inflation, $E(\cdot)$ the expectations operator, a, k positive parameters and ζ_1, ζ_2 i.i.d shocks. Thinking of policy issues, there was not much one could do, at the macro level, to affect output by means of systematic policy actions. The analysis of macroeconomic policies apparently had turned into a pretty unexciting field and, with this scenario in his mind, Rip went back to sleep.

2001

When Rip woke up again, it was a new century and a new millennium. One of the first things he became aware of was that events had indeed followed the course foreseen by the Treaty of Maastricht, and that the European Economic and Monetary Union had become real. Rip was pleased, although he did not quite understand why some countries had chosen to stay out of it, and why the euro was losing so much value against the dollar, but noticing that prices and public finances were, after all, quite stable and under control, he thought that the simple normative macroeconomic statements of one decade ago had fared remarkably well. So Rip decided that he should not waste too much time on monetary issues, and that there were certainly more interesting or exciting issues to experience and explore, and that he should become acquainted with the new features and attractions of living in the new millennium.

One day, casually, Rip found himself reading what at first looked like a very awkward debate. The press reported that the European Commission, and soon

---

[5] When he woke up ten years later, Rip was surprised to learn (Blinder 2000) how dramatically inaccurate that statement had been. In fact, Blinder reported that (i) most central bankers believe that their credibility is required to keep inflation down; and (ii) the way to acquire credibility is mostly by reputation, that is by having lived up to one's words in the past. So perhaps also central bankers can learn, observed Rip.

thereafter the Council of Ministers, had taken the unusual step of making a formal recommendation against one country, Ireland, which was accused of pursuing fiscal policies not coordinated with the rest of the EU. But, to Rip's surprise, Ireland was running a fiscal surplus of about 4% of its GDP, and also its debt level, below 40%, was one of the safest in the Union. 'Ireland is well within the Maastricht guidelines,' cried Rip, 'so what is the matter?' This sparked his curiosity. One of the things Rip liked most about the new millennium was, of course, the internet. He promptly logged on, and started searching his way around some official documents. He found a few that only served to arouse his curiosity further:

Exhibit 1 (The European Commission on fiscal–monetary inter-relations)

Contrary to the fears of many observers during the policy controversies at the beginning of 1999, the cyclical downturn did not trigger a general move towards expansionary fiscal policies which could have implied a loss of credibility of the commitment to budgetary discipline. This contributed to the credibility of the whole EMU stability-oriented policy framework. As a result, monetary policy could be eased in the course of 1999 so as to support growth without jeopardizing price stability in the euro area. (European Commission, 'Public Finances in EMU 2000', *European Economy* 3 (2000), 35)

Exhibit 2 (The European Commission on fiscal policy subordination to the goal of monetary policy)

Budgetary policies should continue to be geared to the achievement of public finances close to balance or in surplus, so as to support the price-stability orientation of monetary policy, and thereby to foster continued economic growth and employment creation. (Issue paper on the Broad Economic Policy Guidelines 2001, March 2001)

Exhibit 3 (The European Commission on Ireland's fiscal indiscipline)

The budget for 2001 will give a further substantial boost to demand in Ireland and its possible supply effects are likely to be small in the short term. It will therefore aggravate overheating and inflationary pressures and widen the positive output gap. (European Council Recommendation of 26/02/2001)[6]

Rip started to worry: was old fashioned Keynesianism back? Anyway, with fiscal authorities, that could not be too much of a surprise. But what does the European Central Bank think? Do the official statements of the ECB reflect

---

[6] http://ue.eu.int/emu/convergence/irl/IR-RECOMMENDATION2001.pdf.

the same position as that of the European Council? Rip looked for some more evidence.

Exhibit 4 (The European Central Bank on the AS–AD explanation of inflation)

In order to assess risks to price stability, it is important to know whether shocks originate on the supply or the demand side, have an external or domestic origin or are temporary or permanent . . . In line with standard models of the business cycle, this analysis is often centred on the effects of the interplay between supply and demand and/or cost pressures on pricing behaviour in the goods, services and labour markets. (ECB, 'The Two Pillars of the ECB's Monetary Policy Strategy', *Monthly Bulletin* November 2000, 43)

Exhibit 5 (The European Central Bank on inflationary fiscal policy, I)

Fiscal budgets are on average still not close to balance or in surplus and debt ratios are high. A proper response by fiscal policies at this stage would help to curb the emergence of inflation expectations which could otherwise affect the medium-term inflation outlook. (ECB, 'Two Pillars', 26)

Exhibit 6 (The European Central Bank on inflationary fiscal policy, II)

The expansionary fiscal policies planned for this year [2001] in a number of euro area countries are not conducive to containing aggregate demand and inflationary pressures. Particularly in the countries experiencing high economic growth rates, inflationary pressures will receive an additional stimulus from expansionary fiscal policies. (*ECB Annual Report 2000*, p. 47)

To say the least, Rip was puzzled. It's all about aggregate demand management, he thought. But where is the (expectations augmented) Phillips curve? Had he been awakened now in a world where Robert E. Lucas had never been alive? Back on the net, he was relieved to find that Lucas had been awarded the 1995 Nobel Prize in Economics. Relieved but still puzzled: they gave him the Nobel and then forgot about all his work? He went to search for Lucas' Nobel Lecture. It was a fascinating reading, deep and intellectually intriguing and technically accomplished. Also a pleasure to read. Towards the end of the paper, however, Rip stumbled:

Estimates . . . indicated that only small fractions of output variability can be accounted for by unexpected price movements. Though the evidence seems to show that monetary surprises have real effects, they do not seem to be transmitted through price surprises, as in Lucas (1972). (Lucas 1996, p. 679)

Oh gosh!, thought Rip, then something has changed in the macro foundations of monetary economics. Rip slowly became aware that, precisely in the era when central banks had been most willing and able to conquer inflation, the macroeconomics of temporary price rigidity was back in fashion. He sought human advice, a little chat with his friends over a glass of beer. Friends told him of the renaissance of neo-Keynesian macroeconomics and that many macro models were now embodying an assumption about prices (or inflation) being rigid, or predetermined in the short run. They also gave him several papers to read. After a little study, Rip thought that he had familiarised himself with the new literature. In particular, he borrowed from a paper of Svensson's (1997) two often-recurring equations, which he thought neatly formalised the aggregate observable implications of the new approach. Although he was well aware that assumptions about lags were quite crucial, Rip decided that he wanted to concentrate his thoughts on a simple, timeless structure. Thus he simplified Svensson's equations to:

$$\text{aggregate demand: } y = y^* - \alpha(i - \pi^* - \bar{r}) + \varepsilon_1 \qquad (6.3)$$

$$\text{aggregate supply: } \pi = \pi^* + \beta(y - y^*) + \varepsilon_2, \qquad (6.4)$$

where i is a short rate of interest, π^* is the target level of inflation (and also its expected value, in the absence of shocks), $\bar{r}$ is the equilibrium level of the short real rate of interest, α, β are two positive parameters and ε_1, ε_2 are two i.i.d shocks. Along with these came a third equation, which was in fact the first-order condition out of the minimisation of a loss function of a central bank. This equation was generically referred to as an optimal Taylor rule, similar in its reduced form to the ad hoc rules proposed in Taylor (1993). It was indeed an interest rate setting equation showing that the real short-run rate of interest should positively respond to both the *output gap* $(y - y^*)$ and the *inflation gap* $(\pi - \pi^*)$. 'And where is money?' Rip asked himself. So he learned that indeed the new fashion (Clarida, Galí and Gertler 2000) was to describe all monetary policy strategies, also those pursued by almost-monetarist central banks, using those interest rate rules, even outside an optimising framework. 'But where is money?' asked Rip again. To his relief, he discovered that money could still be in the picture, although somewhat in the background (Woodford 1997).

That same night, Rip set at his desk with a few papers in front of him. He was thinking about the issue of coordinating demand management. It was slowly becoming clear to him that indeed, if you accept the principle that monetary policy affects aggregate demand directly and more quickly than it affects inflation, then the issue of coordinating monetary and fiscal policies was not a trivial one at all. All that policy debate, all those claims about the need to coordinate, after all, were not at all inappropriate! Still, Rip began to be puzzled about a new issue. He felt he needed a model to analyse the whole question. But he did not recall having seen, in the past, any model suitable for the problem at hand.[7] And clearly the newspaper clippings he had collected (although some of those had actually been authored by respected economists) showed that only the surface of the whole issue was being openly discussed. Had all the economists been taken by surprise? Going back to more academic readings, Rip found, in a recent article by Taylor (2000) two almost identical policy rules: one for monetary policy – an ordinary Taylor rule – and one for the fiscal deficit. Both, however, shared almost the same functional form and right-hand-side arguments: the output gap and the inflation gap. So if they are both reacting to the output gap, thought Rip, shouldn't they coordinate? Rip realised that perhaps the EU Commission was trying to prevent the ECB and the fiscal authorities from putting too much stimulus into the economy at once. If this were the case, then they should have a model to explain this! And even if no one has done it yet, it should be easy to formulate such a model, thought Rip. So he went back to his two equations, and did a simple change to the AD:[8]

$$\text{AD with fiscal impulse: } y = y^* - \alpha(i - \pi^* - \bar{r}) + \eta f + \varepsilon_1, \qquad (6.5)$$

where f is a measure of the fiscal impulse, i.e. the ratio between the government deficit ($f > 0$) or surplus and GDP, and η is a positive parameter.[9] Now I shall solve the model of equations (6.4) and (6.5), thought Rip, and obtain optimal policy rules for fiscal and monetary authorities. He tried to do so, but soon encountered a problem. Indeed he could write down two structural equations and two policy instruments, and also two loss functions, but that was not enough. In fact, both instruments acted upon aggregate demand, so in fact they could not be treated as separate instruments: they were like the same instrument in the hands of two different policymakers. So Rip thought a bit more. He sketched a few equations, compared them, and then jotted down the following outline of

---

[7] Searching through the more recent literature, however, Rip did find some useful papers. See a brief review in section 2.1 below.

[8] After writing this down, Rip shouted: 'But this is Pangloss!' We thought this to be a reference to the famous character in a novel by the French philosopher, Voltaire. However, one referee kindly pointed out to us that most probably this was a reference to a paper by the contemporary Dutch economist, Buiter (1980, eq. 5).

[9] Rip also found this formulation to be coherent with a recent, authoritative survey of monetary policy issues in the USA by Benjamin Friedman (2000, p. 1): 'Monetary policy is one of the two principal means (the other being fiscal policy) by which government authorities in a market economy regularly influence the pace and direction of overall economic activity, importantly including not only the level of aggregate output and employment but also the general rate at which prices rise or fall. Indeed, the predominant trend over the last half century has been to place increasing emphasis on monetary policy (and correspondingly less on fiscal policy) for these purposes.'

things to be done:

Section 2: Objective functions of the monetary and fiscal authorities.
Sections 3–4: Monetary and fiscal policy with decentralised fiscal authorities.
Section 5: Conclusions and implications for policy analysis.

Rip added a few words and hints next to each section title. He thought it all looked neat and easy, and that anybody who had gotten to that point could easily wrap things up. He felt he had suggested the right framework to analyse the issue, and his intuition told him that a nice solution was waiting to be unfolded. But he was happy with that, and decided he did not want to be bothered any more with too many equations. He put his notes in an envelope, mailed it to us and went back to sleep. We continue in his tracks, beginning in the following section.

2   The objective functions of monetary and fiscal authorities

In this chapter we want to model the strategic interaction of three types of policymakers: the European Commission and the European Council, which for our analytical purpose will be identified as a single agent (EC), the European Central Bank (ECB) and the national governments, which act as the decentralised fiscal authorities (FA).

The ECB sets the monetary policy stance, and both its independence and mandate are clearly defined in the Treaty of Maastricht, as we discussed in the introduction. Since the mandate of the ECB is clearly lexicographic,[10] we assume that its main goal is to stabilise inflation around a chosen target value. Note that this does not preclude output stabilisation, to the extent that this is an intermediate step for controlling the inflationary pressures that might follow from shocks to aggregate demand (see Svensson 1997). However we assume that the ECB is not concerned with the level of demand per se in its loss function. Moreover, it has often been observed both in theory[11] and in empirical work that central banks are also motivated by a desire to reduce the volatility of the (nominal or real) rates of interest[12]: this argument has been advanced in reference to the Fed but clearly, given the experience of its first three years of operation, it applies even more strongly to the ECB. Also, this is consistent with the ECB's own view that it should aim to maintain price stability 'over the medium term'.

---

[10] The mandate is precisely defined in Article 105 of the Treaty Establishing the European Community.

[11] For instance Walsh (1998, ch. 10) surveys some motives why the central bank might attach a positive value to interest rate smoothing.

[12] The inclusion of a term in the volatility of interest rates in regression equations is also required to account for the observed persistence or graduality in the setting of the Federal Funds rate. See Favero and Rovelli (2003).

As regards the EC, the authorities in Brussels have very limited direct budgetary power, as the size of the EC budget is constrained within 1.27% of the aggregate GDP. However, the procedures and penalties instituted with the Stability and Growth Pact allow the EC to set and control the behaviour of national FA. Moreover, as the mandate of the ECB is derived from the Treaty Establishing the European Community, we also assume that the EC authorities act as the principal of the ECB. Hence, we shall assume that the EC sets its guidelines for fiscal policy taking into account a 'social welfare function' defined for the Community as a whole, and thus including the preference for price stability as well as for output stabilisation in each member country.[13]

For the FA, it is natural to assume that each member country is mainly concerned with domestic output stabilisation. It is also plausible to assume that, in this respect, national FA will not fully internalise the spillovers of each country's fiscal stance on the aggregate demand and inflation rate of the EC. Thus it will be natural to assume that the weight on inflation stabilisation adopted by national FA is smaller than that of the EC, or (to simplify matters) zero.[14] Moreover, each FA will also be concerned with the level of its own expenditures. This assumption reflects two facts: (i) a higher level of fiscal expansion implies a higher crowding out of private expenditures, and this is perceived to be costly; (ii) the Stability Pact requires that the fiscal stance is on average neutral ($f = 0$), so that departures from a balanced budget should only be small and temporary. To take into account the second interpretation, we prefer to include into the loss function the deviations from the balanced budget, f.[15,16] Accordingly, we may thus postulate the following loss functions:

$$\text{ECB: } L_M \equiv (\pi - \pi^*)^2 + \mu(r - \bar{r})^2; \tag{6.6}$$

$$\text{FA of country j: } L_{Fj} \equiv (y_j - y_j^*)^2 + \gamma f_j^2, \quad j = 1, \ldots, n; \tag{6.7}$$

$$\text{EC (social loss function): } L_S = \sum_{j=1}^{n} L_{Fj} + L_M, \tag{6.8}$$

---

[13] This assumption is generally accepted by the literature in this field (see the survey in the next subsection). Also notice that, for simplicity, we do not distinguish here between membership of the EU and of EMU.

[14] One way to make this assumption more plausible is to assume that inflation is the same both at the national and at the EMU-wide level.

[15] Banerjee (2001) assumes that the weight on inflation in the loss function of the FA is not greater than for the ECB. Gatti and Van Wijnbergen (2002) and Buti, Roeger and In't Veld (2001) instead assume that the national FA are not concerned with inflation. All these papers, and also Beetsma and Bovenberg (2001), assume that the FA are also concerned with stabilising either the level of public expenditures or the cyclically adjusted budget balance. Our formulation (6.7) is the same as in Buti, Roeger and In't Veld (2001).

[16] This assumption also implies that there will not be a sequence of government deficits, potentially generating an excessive accumulation of government debt, such as to pose a threat to the independence of monetary policy, as in Sargent and Wallace (1981).

where r is the current short-run real rate of interest and μ, γ are positive parameters. The formulation of the social loss function assumes that the output and inflation terms share the same weight. While this is arbitrary (but not unrealistic), it avoids introducing an additional weighting parameter. It will become clear below that no qualitative result depends critically on this assumption.[17]

On the basis of the loss functions (6.6)–(6.8) we can now study the interactions of the three types of policymakers from their respective points of view:

1. Given that the ECB is committed to stabilising inflation over the medium term, as implied in (6.6), is it preferable from this point of view that the stance of fiscal policy at the national level is set on the basis of the social loss function (6.8), or would the ECB prefer instead that national FA look only at their domestic conditions, i.e. aim at minimising (6.7)?

2. From the viewpoint of the EC (that is, of social welfare for the EU as a whole), and given that the ECB has received a specific mandate, is it better to direct the national FA[18] to minimise the social loss function, L_S, or instead to concentrate on the more narrowly defined task of stabilising domestic output, i.e. of minimising L_{Fj}?

3. Finally, from the point of view of national FA, if it turns out that the EC directs them to minimise L_S, is this compatible with their structure of incentives? Or might it be possible that they would not want to cooperate with the BEPG and instead want to stabilise only their domestic output?

Before we proceed, we may notice that the problem examined from the viewpoint of the EC (point 2 above) is analogous to the delegation problem examined by Vickers (1985) and, in the context of central banking, by Rogoff (1985). Just as it may be optimal, in order to minimise the social loss function, to choose a central banker who places more emphasis on inflation stabilisation that does society as a whole (is more *conservative*, in the terminology of Rogoff), we pose here a symmetric question: given that the EC has chosen an utterly conservative central banker (as the ECB places no weight on output stabilisation), could it be then optimal that, conditional on this choice, fiscal policy is assigned to a policymaker which places more weight on output stabilisation than society as a whole?[19] As we shall see, it turns out that, under the assumption that

---

[17] Similarly, the social loss function could easily be generalised to allow for different (strictly positive) country weights.

[18] The Broad Economic Policy Guidelines, which the EC sets according to Article 99 of the Treaty of Maastricht, are the institutional counterpart of these directives from the centre to the periphery.

[19] Note that our problem is different from Rogoff's in several aspects. In particular, we assume that all policymakers are pursuing feasible targets (that is, no one is trying to push output beyond the natural or full-employment level). Also, we assume here that policymakers' preferences cannot be chosen (by the principal) along a continuum: all the principal can do is to assign a mandate to concentrate on one or more objectives, without relative weights between alternative targets being either one or zero. We think that this restriction on the space of parameters corresponds more closely to actual policymaking procedures, at least when optimal contracts cannot be enforced.

stabilisation policy is feasible, the answer to this question cannot be unqualified, but will always be conditional on the cyclical turnout of the economy, that is on the specific analysis of demand and supply shocks.

In the next section we analyse the setting of the policy instruments and the resulting equilibria. Before doing so, however, we briefly compare our approach to others which have been proposed in the recent literature on EMU.

2.1   Review of the literature on fiscal and monetary policy coordination

The twin issues of macroeconomic policy coordination within one country and cooperation across countries have had a central place in the literature on the design of macroeconomic policies. However, only recently have these issues begun to be debated in reference to EMU. As remarked in the introduction, this is surprising given that EMU provides a very relevant and challenging case study, and that the debate on other economically relevant aspects of the Treaty of Maastricht has been otherwise intense.

With reference to the earlier, pre-EMU literature, several approaches may be relevant to the issues which arise with EMU, and in particular to the approach adopted in this chapter:

(1) Tabellini (1986) is to our knowledge the first paper to analyse the coordination of monetary policy (MP) and fiscal policy (FP) in the context of a differential game modelled for a single country, where the target variable is the path of government debt across time. He shows that policy coordination increases the speed of convergence to the steady state and leads the economy closer to the planned target as compared to the outcome of the non-cooperative game.

(2) Turnovsky and d'Orey (1986), following Hamada (1976), analyse the issue of MP coordination across countries. Their model features two identical open economies, hit by aggregate demand and supply shocks. Central banks have identical, linear quadratic preferences in output and inflation. In a static framework, they compare Nash, Stackelberg and cooperative equilibria, and find that the benefits from cooperation are likely to be quite small. This conclusion is reversed by Turnovsky, Basar and d'Orey (1988), who analyse a dynamic version of the same model. In this framework, gains from cooperation may become quite relevant.

(3) The literature on discretionary monetary policy regimes in closed economies, originating with Barro and Gordon (1983), generally neglects the issue of the interaction between monetary and fiscal policies. However, the normative conclusions originating from this literature have helped to shape the strong status of independence assigned to the ECB in the context of EMU.

(4) The literature on the monetary implications of fiscal (in)discipline, which originates with Sargent and Wallace (1981) emphasises that, to the extent that the path of a government's fiscal deficit is predetermined and unsustainable, then monetary policy and the price level are no longer exogenous to it. A similar point arises in the context of the 'Fiscal Theory of the Price Level' (Woodford 1995). However, in these frameworks the goals of fiscal policy are not explicitly discussed, and in particular they do not include macro stabilisation. Nevertheless, the scenario analysed by Sargent and Wallace has surely been influential in motivating the emphasis on fiscal discipline as a prerequisite for monetary stability, which has been placed in the Treaty of Maastricht and, in particular, on the design of the criteria for admission to the third phase of EMU.

Turning now to the more recent, post-EMU (more precisely, post-Treaty of Maastricht) literature, the issue of monetary–fiscal policy coordination has recently been analysed by a number of papers, with an explicit reference to EMU.[20] That is, these papers have generally assumed a framework characterised by a centralised monetary authority together with decentralised, national fiscal authorities. We distinguish in particular two groups of papers:

(5) Some authors have chosen to model the behaviour of the fiscal and/or monetary authorities as targeting time-inconsistent goals. For instance, Catenaro (1999) and Banerjee (2001) analyse the issue of coordination between policymakers, in the context of EMU, assuming that the central bank adopts a time-inconsistent behaviour. Beetsma and Bovenberg (2001) also analyse the case when both monetary and fiscal authorities in EMU are unable to commit to their policy targets and nominal wages are predetermined. They analyse under which conditions this leads to a 'wasteful strategic accumulation of government debt'. In particular they argue that, in the absence of an explicit commitment by fiscal authorities, ex-post coordination at the fiscal level may actually be harmful. Dixit and Lambertini (2001a, b) assume that both fiscal and monetary authorities act according to time-inconsistent rules and discuss how different coordination mechanisms may or may not alleviate the undesirable consequences of non-coordinated behaviour. For the reasons which we have discussed at length in the introduction, and in particular since we assume that the constraints on the discretionary behaviour of both fiscal and monetary authorities are effective in the context of EMU, we do not pursue this line of analysis in the present study. See Beetsma and Debrun (chapter 5 in this volume) for a full review of all this literature.

(6) Adopting a different policy focus, Buti, Roeger and In't Veld (2001) analyse the interaction of monetary and fiscal authorities in a framework quite similar to the one to be developed below, but assume a single fiscal authority (which can be rationalised, with reference to EMU, assuming perfect

---

[20] See also footnote 15.

symmetry and cooperation among all countries). Assuming that fiscal authorities do not care for inflation, they find that cooperation is desirable, in particular when the economies are hit by a supply shock. In a related, more general framework Van Aarle, Engwerda and Plasmans (2001) analyse two countries, with decentralised fiscal authorities and a centralised monetary authority. Their basic framework is very similar – also for the static specification of the various loss functions – to the one which we propose below, except that they also include a 'spillover' competitiveness term between the two countries. In addition, they analyse – by means of numerical simulations – the equilibrium strategies which arise in continuous time over an infinite horizon. The cases they consider include: non cooperation between the three authorities; full cooperation; coalition between the two fiscal authorities only; coalition between one fiscal authority and the monetary authority. These setups are examined under assumptions of both symmetry and asymmetry between the two countries involved. Their main finding is that cooperation is efficient for fiscal authorities in that a common stance against the ECB produces a Pareto improvement. This may not hold at the equilibrium of the fully cooperative (that is, including the ECB) game.

3   Monetary and fiscal policy with decentralised fiscal authorities

In this section we study the problem of coordination between fiscal and monetary authorities in a monetary union, composed of two equal-sized national economies and decentralised (at the national level) FA. To simplify the exposition and the notation, we assume the two economies to be identical and in particular we neglect the possibility of asymmetric shocks affecting either economy. We also redefine: $\bar{r} + \pi^* = \pi^*$. We shall examine the case where the three authorities set their respective instruments (i, f_j, f_k) simultaneously and compute the resulting Nash equilibria.[21]

Appropriately substituting the aggregate demand and supply equations into (6.6), the ECB shall choose the level of i so as to minimise:

$$L_M = \{\beta[\eta(f_j + f_k) + \varepsilon_1 - \alpha(i - \pi^*)] + \varepsilon_2\}^2 + \mu(i - \pi^*)^2. \quad (6.9)$$

Similarly, FA j and k are interested in the level of (domestic) aggregate demand, i.e. will set f_j in order to minimise:

$$L_{Fj} = \left[\eta f_j + \frac{\varepsilon_1}{2} - \alpha(i - \pi^*)\right]^2 + \gamma f_j^2, \quad (6.10)$$

---

[21] The assumption of symmetric demand shocks across counties suffices to prove that there exists an incentive to deviate from the EC directives. The introduction of idiosyncratic shocks would only make things worse, evidencing the incentive to deviate unilaterally.

and similarly for f_k. The first step to solve the model is now to compute each policymaker's best reply function, assuming as given the choice of the other authority. In particular, and following the discussion in section 2, we shall assume that national FA are either following a directive from the EC to minimise L_S, or instead to minimise L_{Fj}.[22]

$$\text{ECB}: i = \pi^* + \frac{\alpha\beta}{\alpha^2\beta^2 + \mu}\{\beta[\eta(f_j + f_k) + \varepsilon_1] + \varepsilon_2\} \qquad (6.11)$$

$$\text{FA using } L_{Fj}: f_j = \frac{\eta}{2(\eta^2 + \gamma)}[2\alpha(i - \pi^*) - \varepsilon_1] \qquad (6.12)$$

$$\text{FA using } L_S: f_j = \frac{\eta\{2\alpha(i - \pi^*) - \varepsilon_1 - 2\beta[\varepsilon_2 + \beta(\varepsilon_1 + \eta f_k - \alpha(i - \pi^*))]\}}{2[(1 + \beta^2)\eta^2 + \gamma]}. \qquad (6.13)$$

Note that, as should be expected, each authority manoeuvres its policy instrument in a restrictive way (higher i, lower f) in response to an expansionary (> 0) shock to aggregate demand (ε_1) or supply (ε_2).

3.1   Case I: both governments use L_{Fj}

In this sub-section, we analyse the case when the EC directs national FA to minimise L_{Fj}. To clarify, we stress that this case does *not* contradict the earlier assumption that the EC aims at minimising the social loss function L_S (6.8). Instead, we are modelling the case when, given that the EC wants to minimise L_S, and that it has already assigned to one agent, the ECB, a mandate to minimise L_M, it finds it (*second best*) optimal to assign to a second group of agents (the national FA) the mandate to minimise L_{Fj}. Hence in this case we study the Nash equilibrium which results from the interaction of the two sets of best reply functions (6.11)–(6.12),[23] that is:

$$f_j^{NF} = \frac{\eta[\alpha^2\beta(\beta\varepsilon_1 + 2\varepsilon_2) - \mu\varepsilon_1]}{2[\mu(\gamma + \eta^2) - \alpha^2\beta^2(\eta^2 - \gamma)]} \qquad (6.14)$$

$$i^{NF} = \pi^* + \frac{\alpha\beta[\beta\gamma\varepsilon_1 + \varepsilon_2(\gamma + \eta^2)]}{\mu(\gamma + \eta^2) - \alpha^2\beta^2(\eta^2 - \gamma)}. \qquad (6.15)$$

---

[22] Since we are assuming identical countries subject to identical monetary policy and exogenous shocks, we shall from now derive explicit solutions only for country j.

[23] Note that this case is observationally and conceptually equivalent to that of the national FA *cooperating* to minimise the sum: $L_{Fj} + L_{Fk}$. The reason why the Nash solution in this case is not different from the case of collusion between the two FA is that we neglect by assumption the existence of spillover effects between countries.

The Nash equilibrium strategies $\{f_j^{NF}, i^{NF}\}$ can be plugged into L_{Fj}, and L_M, which simplify as follows:

$$L_{Fj}^F = \frac{\gamma(\gamma + \eta^2)\{(\alpha^2\beta^2 - \mu)\varepsilon_1 + 2\alpha^2\beta\varepsilon_2\}^2}{4[\alpha^2\beta^2(\eta^2 - \gamma) - \mu(\gamma + \eta^2)]^2} \tag{6.16}$$

$$L_M^F = \frac{\mu(\alpha^2\beta^2 + \mu)[\beta\varepsilon_1\gamma + \varepsilon_2(\gamma + \eta^2)]}{[\alpha^2\beta^2(\eta^2 - \gamma) - \mu(\gamma + \eta^2)]^2}. \tag{6.17}$$

In this case, the associated social loss can be computed naturally from the sum $L_S^F = L_M^F + \sum_j L_{Fj}^F$ (see (6.8)), which we do not write down in full for the sake of brevity.

3.2   Case II: both governments use L_S

In this subsection we consider the case when the two national FA determine their respective fiscal stances from the the direct minimisation of L_S. That is, the EC asks them to share the aggregate, union-wide set of preferences. The Nash equilibrium computed from the two relevant reply functions (6.11) and (6.13) is then:

$$f_j^{NS} = \frac{\eta[\varepsilon_1(\alpha^2\beta^2 - \mu(1 + 2\beta^2)) + 2\beta\varepsilon_2(\alpha^2 - \mu)]}{2[\mu(\gamma + \eta^2(1 + 2\beta^2)) - \alpha^2\beta^2(\eta^2 - \gamma)]} \tag{6.18}$$

$$i^{NS} = \pi^* + \frac{\alpha\beta[\beta\gamma\varepsilon_1 + \varepsilon_2(\gamma + \eta^2)]}{\mu[\gamma + \eta^2(1 + 2\beta^2)] - \alpha^2\beta^2(\eta^2 - \gamma)}. \tag{6.19}$$

Using $\{f_j^{NS}, i^{NS}\}$, we obtain the equilibrium expressions for L_{Fj}^S, L_M^S and L_S^S, which are omitted for brevity.

4   Comparative statics

Now we can comparatively assess the results which we have obtained in the two preceding subsections. For the central bank, we observe that:

$$L_M^S - L_M^F \propto \alpha^2\beta^2(\eta^2 - \gamma) - \mu[\gamma + \eta^2(1 + \beta^2)], \tag{6.20}$$

entailing that:

Proposition 1 $L_M^S < L_M^F$ for all $\mu > \dfrac{\alpha^2\beta^2(\eta^2 - \gamma)}{\gamma + \eta^2(1 + \beta^2)}$.

Note in particular that $L_M^S < L_M^F$ for all $\mu \geq 0$ if $\gamma > \eta^2$. The interpretation of this result is that the central bank prefers the fiscal stance of national governments to be set according to the minimisation of L_S (that is, taking into account

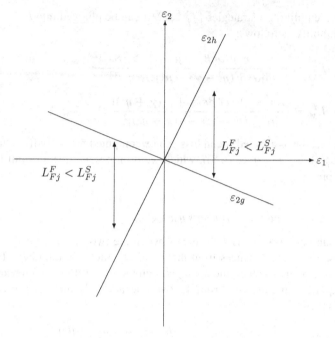

Figure 6.1 Incentives of national fiscal authorities

the welfare of the community as a whole), whenever the use of the monetary instrument is costly enough. Let us now turn to the viewpoint on the national FA. We notice that $L_{Fj}^S = L_{Fj}^F$ at

$$\varepsilon_{2g} = -\frac{\beta\gamma\varepsilon_1}{\eta^2 + \gamma} \tag{6.21}$$

and

$$\varepsilon_{2h} = \alpha^2\beta\gamma\varepsilon_1\{\alpha^2\beta^2[2\alpha^2\beta^2(\eta^2 - \gamma) - \mu(\eta^2(4 + 3\beta^2) + \beta^2\gamma)]$$
$$+ \mu^2(\eta^2 + \gamma)[2(1 + \beta^2) + \mu]\}/\{\alpha^2\beta^2[\alpha^2(\alpha^2\beta^2(4\gamma(\gamma - \eta^2)$$
$$+ \mu(6\eta^2\gamma - \eta^2 - \gamma^2)) + 4\gamma\mu(\gamma + \eta^2)) + 2\mu^2(\eta^4 - \gamma^2)] - \mu^3(\gamma + \eta^2)\}. \tag{6.22}$$

On these bases, the following can be easily established:

Lemma 1 $L_{Fj}^S > L_{Fj}^F$ *for all* $\varepsilon_2 \in (\min\{\varepsilon_{2g}, \varepsilon_{2h}\}, \max\{\varepsilon_{2g}, \varepsilon_{2h}\})$.

Note that $\min\{\varepsilon_{2g}, \varepsilon_{2h}\} = \varepsilon_{2g}$ for all $\varepsilon_1 > 0$, while $\min\{\varepsilon_{2g}, \varepsilon_{2h}\} = \varepsilon_{2h}$ for all $\varepsilon_1 < 0$. If $\varepsilon_1 = 0$, $\varepsilon_{2g} = \varepsilon_{2h} = 0$. This situation is illustrated in figure 6.1, where we consider a set of parameters and demand shocks such that ε_{2h} is upward sloping.

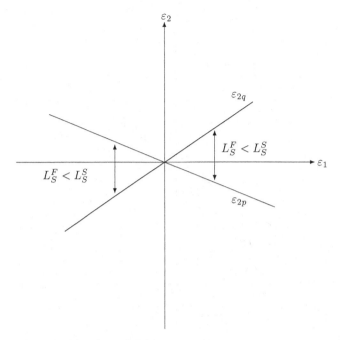

Figure 6.2 Incentives of the EC

Now we consider the point of view of the EC, as to whether it should direct national FA to set f_j according to the minimisation of either L_{Fj} or L_S. We have that $L_S^F - L_S^S = 0$ at:

$$\varepsilon_{2p} = -\frac{\beta\gamma\varepsilon_1}{\eta^2 + \gamma} \tag{6.23}$$

$$
\begin{aligned}
\varepsilon_{2q} &= \beta\gamma\varepsilon_1\{\alpha^2\beta^2[2\alpha^4\beta^2(\eta^2 + \gamma) - \alpha^2\mu(4\eta^2 + \beta^2(\eta^2 + \gamma)) \\
&\quad + 2\mu^2(\eta^2(1 - \beta^2) - \gamma)] + 2\alpha^2\mu(\eta^2 + \gamma) - \mu^3[\gamma + \eta^2(1 + 2\beta^2)]\}/ \\
&\quad \{\alpha^2\beta^2[4\alpha^4\beta^2(\eta^2 - \gamma) + \alpha^2\eta^2\mu(3\beta^2(2\alpha^2\beta^2\gamma - \eta^2) + 4\gamma) \\
&\quad + \alpha^2\gamma^2\mu(4 + \beta^2) + \mu^2(2 + \mu)(\eta^2 + \gamma)(\eta^2 + \gamma + 2\beta^2\eta^2)]\}. \tag{6.24}
\end{aligned}
$$

On these bases, the following can be easily established:

Lemma 2 $L_S^S > L_S^F$ for all $\varepsilon_2 \in (\min\{\varepsilon_{2p}, \varepsilon_{2q}\}, \max\{\varepsilon_{2p}, \varepsilon_{2q}\})$.

Note that $\min\{\varepsilon_{2p}, \varepsilon_{2q}\} = \varepsilon_{2p}$ for all $\varepsilon_1 > 0$, while $\min\{\varepsilon_{2p}, \varepsilon_{2q}\} = \varepsilon_{2q}$ for all $\varepsilon_1 < 0$. If $\varepsilon_1 = 0$, $\varepsilon_{2p} = \varepsilon_{2q} = 0$. This situation is illustrated in figure 6.2, where again we consider the case where ε_{2q} is upward sloping.

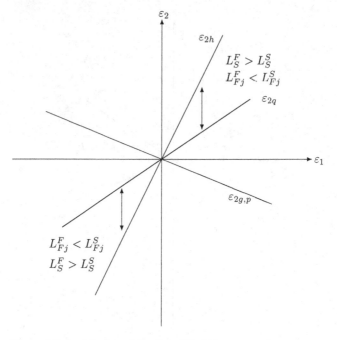

Figure 6.3 Socially harmful national deviations

Moreover, $\varepsilon_{2g} = \varepsilon_{2p}$ and

$$\varepsilon_{2h} \gtreqless \varepsilon_{2q} \text{ as } \varepsilon_1 \gtreqless 0. \qquad (6.25)$$

Thus, we observe that the region where $L_S^S > L_S^F$ is a subset of the region where $L_{Fj}^S > L_{Fj}^F$. This, in combination with Lemmata 1–2, leads us to the main result:

Proposition 2 *National FA will simultaneously deviate from the EC directive, i.e. from union-wide welfare maximisation, for all*

$$\varepsilon_2 \in (\min\{\varepsilon_{2h}, \varepsilon_{2q}\}, \max\{\varepsilon_{2h}, \varepsilon_{2q}\}) \qquad (6.26)$$

The region where there exists an incentive for every country in the union to deviate from union-wide welfare maximisation is illustrated in figure 6.3.

As a corollary to the above proposition, we may observe from equation (6.21)–(6.24) that: (i)

$$\lim_{\mu \to 0} \varepsilon_{2q} = \lim_{\mu \to 0} \varepsilon_{2h} = -\frac{\beta \varepsilon_1}{2} \qquad (6.27)$$

and: (ii) if $\varepsilon_1 = 0$, then also $\varepsilon_{2g} = \varepsilon_{2p} = \varepsilon_{2h} = \varepsilon_{2q} = 0$.

This leads us to the following:

Corollary 1 *For $\varepsilon_1 \neq 0$, national and union-wide incentives will always coincide if and only if the use of the monetary instrument is costless.*

Corollary 2 *In the absence of aggregate demand shocks ($\varepsilon_1 = 0$), there would be no source of potential conflict between national FA and the EC.*

Finally, using (6.14) and (6.18), we can also establish our final result:

Proposition 3 $f_j^{NF} > f_j^{NS}$ *for all $\varepsilon_2 > \varepsilon_{2g}$, when $\varepsilon_1 > 0$, while $f_j^{NF} < f_j^{NS}$ for all $\varepsilon_2 > \varepsilon_{2g}$, when $\varepsilon_1 < 0$.*

The interpretation of this result is that, when the AD shock is positive and the AS shock is also positive and large enough (that is, above the boundary common to cases I and II) then the national FA will deviate from union-wide welfare maximisation and pursue a *less restrictive* fiscal policy. The opposite holds when the AD shock is negative and the AS shock is also negative and large enough in absolute terms (below the boundary common to cases I and II): then the national government will choose a more restrictive fiscal stance than would be recommended by union-wide welfare maximisation.

To conclude, note that our interpretation of the role of fiscal policy in the context of macro stabilisation is consistent with the operation of automatic stabilisers: that is, one could design fiscal stabilisers that generate the same fiscal impulse as it is implied by either (6.14) or (6.18). Thus our model does not imply or require that fiscal policy is set in a discretionary way. Finally, note that the assumption of only *symmetric* demand shocks is crucial in determining the fact that national FA will both want either to cooperate or not with the EC. It is straightforward to show that if we were to introduce the possibility of asymmetric shocks, this conclusion would no longer hold; the incentive to deviate from the EC directives could then become unilateral.

5   Conclusions and implications for policy analysis

We have analysed the incentives for the coordination of macroeconomic policies in a monetary union with two fiscal authorities and a common central bank. Under the natural (in the context of EMU) assumption that the ECB has been given a mandate to minimise deviations from price stability (that is, from an inflation target), we find that, in realistic situations where the use of the monetary instrument entails a cost, the central bank prefers that national fiscal authorities cooperate in minimising a union-wide welfare function, which includes price stability among its arguments: that is, it is better from the perspective of the central bank that the fiscal stance is set taking into account the goal of monetary policy – instead of concentrating only on output stabilisation. EC authorities and national FA, instead, may have conflicting incentives. These will arise, depending upon the relative size of aggregate shocks, even in the absence of asymmetric shocks and of aggregate demand spillovers between countries. In particular, we find that when both aggregate demand and supply shocks are positive (resp. negative) and the latter are large enough in absolute terms, then national FA will pursue a more expansionary (resp. contractionary) fiscal policy than would be desirable from the point of view of the EC (that is, of social welfare). For instance, this might be the case of the too expansionary (according to the EC authorities) fiscal stance adopted by the Irish government in the budget for 2001.

This brings us to the potential normative implications of our analysis, re-garding the adoption of an appropriate institutional setup for EMU. Our results imply that, if the EC authorities (that is the European Commission and the European Council) should pursue a social welfare function defined over ag-gregate output and inflation, then it may be necessary to endow them with appropriate enforcement devices with respect to the fiscal policy stance of indi-vidual member countries. Whether these devices will be activated in any given period will depend upon the cyclical configuration of aggregate shocks to output and inflation. Since this conclusion has been obtained in the context of a static model without assuming any incentive to adopt a time-inconsistent behaviour on the part of any authority, we believe that it is also likely to hold in more general policy setups. We have not discussed whether the specific provisions envisaged in the Stability and Growth Pact are optimal in terms of our model; however, our conclusions strongly support the idea that the setting of fiscal policies by member countries needs to be disciplined, and in some instances possibly overruled, by the EC authorities. If this discipline were not enforced, then the volatility of inflation around its target might become excessive, and interest rates too volatile.

REFERENCES

Banerjee, G., 2001, 'Rules and Discretion with Common Central Bank and Separate Fiscal Authorities', *Journal of Economics and Business* 53, 45–68.

Barro, R. J. and D. B. Gordon, 1983, 'A Positive Theory of Monetary Policy in a Natural Rate Model', *Journal of Political Economy* 91, 589–610.

Beetsma, R. and A. L. Bovenberg, 2001, 'Structural Distortions and Decentralised Fiscal Policies in EMU', CEPR Discussion Paper no. 2851.

Beetsma, R. and X. Debrun, 2003, 'The Interaction between Monetary and Fiscal Policies in a Monetary Union: A Review of Recent Literature', chapter 5 in this volume.

Blinder, A., 2000, 'Central Bank Credibility: Why Do We Care? How Do We Build It?', *American Economic Review* 90, 1421–31.

Buiter, W., 1980, 'The Macroeconomics of Dr. Pangloss. A Critical Survey of the New Classical Macroeconomics', *Economic Journal* 90, 34–50.

Buiter, W., G. Corsetti and N. Roubini, 1993, 'Excessive Deficits: Sense and Nonsense in the Treaty of Maastricht', *Economic Policy* 16, 57–100.

Buti, M., W. Roeger and J. In't Veld, 2001, 'Stabilising Output and Inflation: Policy Conflicts and Co-operation under a Stability Pact', *Journal of Common Market Studies* 39, 801–28.

Catenaro, M., 1999, 'A Case for Fiscal Policy Co-ordination in Europe', Working Paper no. 23, Department of Political Economy, University of Milano-Bicocca.

Clarida R., J. Galí and M. Gertler, 2000, 'Monetary Policy Rules and Macroeconomic Stability: Evidence and Some Theory', *Quarterly Journal of Economics* 115, 147–80.

Dixit, A. and L. Lambertini, 2001a, 'Monetary–Fiscal Policy Interactions and Commitment versus Discretion in a Monetary Union', *European Economic Review* 45, 977–87.

    2001b, 'Fiscal Discretion Destroys Monetary Commitment', mimeo, Princeton University/UCLA.

Favero, C. A. and R. Rovelli, 2003, 'Macroeconomic Stability and the Preferences of the Fed. A Formal Analysis, 1961–98', *Journal of Money, Credit and Banking*.

Friedman, B. M., 2000, 'Monetary Policy', NBER Working Paper no. 8057.

Gatti, D. and C. Van Wijnbergen, 2002, 'Co-ordinating Fiscal Authorites in the Euro Zone: A key Role for the ECB', *Oxford Economic Papers* 54(1), 56–71.

Goodfriend M., 1987, 'Interest Rate Smoothing and Price Level Trend-Stationarity', *Journal of Monetary Economics* 19, 335–48.

Gordon, R. J., 1976, 'Recent Developments in the Theory of Inflation and Unemployment', *Journal of Monetary Economics* 2, 185–219.

Hamada, K., 1976, 'A Strategic Analysis of Monetary Interdependence', *Journal of Political Economy* 84, 677–700.

Lucas, R. E., 1972, 'Expectations and the Neutrality of Money', *Journal of Economic Theory* 4, 103–24.

    1996, 'Nobel Lecture: Monetary Neutrality', *Journal of Political Economy* 104, 661–82.

Rogoff, K., 1985, 'The Optimal Degree of Committment to an Intermediate Monetary Target', *Quarterly Journal of Economics* 100, 1169–89.

Sargent, T. J., and Wallace, N., 1981, 'Some Unpleasant Monetarist Arithmetic', Federal Reserve Bank of Minneapolis *Quarterly Review* (Fall), 1–17.

Svensson, L., 1997, 'Inflation Forecast Targeting: Implementing and Monitoring Inflation Targets', *European Economic Review* 41, 1111–46.

Tabellini, G., 1986, 'Money, Debt and Deficits in a Dynamic Game', *Journal of Economic Dynamics and Control* 10, 427–42.

Taylor, J. B., 1993, 'Discretion versus Policy Rules in Practice', *Carnegie-Rochester Conference Series on Public Policy*, 39, 195–214.

    2000, 'Reassessing Discretionary Fiscal Policy', *Journal of Economic Perspectives* 14, 21–36.

Turnovsky, S. J., T. Basar and V. d'Orey, 1988, 'Dynamic Strategic Monetary Policies and Coordination in Interdependent Economies', *American Economic Review* 78, 341–61.

Turnovsky, S. J. and V. d'Orey, 1986, 'Monetary Policies in Interdependent Economies with Stochastic Disturbances: A Strategic Approach', *Economic Journal* 96, 696–721.

Van Aarle, B., J. Engwerda and J. Plasmans, 2001, 'Monetary and Fiscal Policy Interaction in the EMU: A Dynamic Game Approach', CESifo Working Paper no. 437.

Vickers, J., 1985, 'Delegation and the Theory of the Firm', *Economic Journal*, 95, supplement, 138–47.

Walsh, C. E., 1998, *Monetary Theory and Policy*, Cambridge, MA: MIT Press.

Woodford, M., 1995, 'Price-Level Determinacy Without Control of a Monetary Aggregate', *Carnegie Rochester Conference Series on Public Policy* 43, 1–46.

1997, 'Doing Without Money: Controlling Inflation in a Post-Monetary World', NBER Working Paper no. 6188.

7 Interaction of fiscal policies in the euro area: how much pressure on the ECB?

Luca Onorante

1 Introduction

Since the Helsinki European Council of December 1999, a process of increased coordination of fiscal policies in the area of the euro seems to be on its way. In this chapter I examine this process from the point of view of the independence of the European Central Bank (ECB).

The interaction of the governments and the ECB is addressed in a game theoretical framework. First, the conditions under which the national governments are able to put pressure on the ECB are made explicit. Then the main question is addressed: would greater fiscal coordination reduce or increase the capacity of the monetary authority to target long-run inflation?

Formal and informal, discretional (positive) and rule-based (negative) coordination and their interactions are examined as possible solutions of the game. I conclude that the main point is not how much fiscal coordination there is, but the form it takes. It turns out that a mix of informal fiscal coordination and binding rules is the one that best preserves the independence of the ECB.

In the present chapter I try to determine which kind of coordination would allow the ECB to pursue its statutory goal of price stability. I start from the definition of 'best environment' as the one in which the ECB does not need to intervene to counteract exogenous or policy induced shocks. In such an ideal world, fiscal policy stabilises national output and unemployment while the central bank takes care of the common price stability.

In a world hit by shocks, governments tend to act in order to stabilise the domestic economy. In doing so, it is natural for them to take into account the foreseeable reaction of their central bank.[1] While this strategic interaction has been described in the case of one country, the possible outcome of the interplay

The author thanks Mike Artis and Pierpaolo Battigalli for supervision, Mirko Wiederholt for an enlightening intuition, Matthias Rau for his comments, and Anna Sanz de Galdeano for reading and correcting the very first version of the paper. All mistakes are mine.

[1] In many European countries governments did not just take into account the reaction of their monetary authority to fiscal policy, but went as far as directly influencing monetary policy by forcing the central bank to monetise the national debt. Such direct pressure is nowadays explicitly ruled out by the statute of the ECB.

of multiple fiscal authorities with a common central bank is not yet completely understood. In what follows I address this issue, and try to answer the following questions: which is the degree of fiscal coordination that best relieves the ECB from short-run stabilisation and allows it to concentrate on long-run inflation targeting? And should this coordination be based on binding rules (negative coordination) or discretional common decisions (positive coordination), or both?

1.1   The short story of European fiscal coordination

The current policy framework of the EMU. The current framework presents a strong and unique asymmetry between the management of fiscal and monetary policies. The single monetary policy is run by a unique decisionmaker (the European Central Bank) with a clear 'primary objective' (price stability); by contrast, fiscal policies remain in the hands of the member states, with no objective specified by the Treaty. The only instrument of positive coordination of fiscal policies is the Broad Economic Policy Guidelines (BEPG), non-binding recommendations prepared each year by the Commission and adopted by the ECOFIN Council. On the negative coordination side, the Stability and Growth Pact (SGP) is backed by sanctions in the case of 'excessive deficits'. The SGP allows the ECB to 'play on the safe side' by putting a strict limit on the discretionary power of national governments to conduct an independent fiscal policy.

The prospective scenarios. The Helsinki European Council of December 1999 adopted the conclusions of an ECOFIN Council report pleading for a strenghtening of economic policy coordination during Stage Three of Economic and Monetary Union (EMU). Broadly speaking, increased coordination should include (i) greater sharing of information among the member states, (ii) more positive coordination, and (iii) a progressive reduction of the importance of negative (rule-based) coordination.

The principle of informing the other members of the euro area and the Commission before adopting an economic policy measure should form part of a set of 'rules of conduct' elaborated by the Commission in consultation with the ECB. Furthermore, regular meetings would be held between the ECB President, the President of the Eurogroup and the representative of the Commission in the Council of Governors of the ECB.

While a literal interpretation of the Treaties impedes the formation of a formal governing body exclusively dedicated to fiscal coordination among the euro countries, it would certainly be possible to increase the powers of the Eurogroup within the Economic and Financial Committee, by transforming it into a permanent working party and increasing the frequency of its meetings.

Short of a Treaty change, the formal power of the Eurogroup could also be strengthened to the extent allowed by the 'closer cooperation' clauses.[2]

Note, however, that reinforced cooperation would not, even in the opinion of the Commission, determine the end of negative coordination (SPG), but only a diminution of its importance.

The terms of the debate. Like any other central bank, the ECB faces the conflicting objectives of long-run price stability and short-run stabilisation of the economy in the presence of shocks. But unlike any other central bank, the ECB does not face a single fiscal authority but twelve different ones. In such an unprecedented framework, the consequences in terms of pressure on the ECB are difficult to assess, and there is no unanimity of opinion. It is, then, not surprising that the Helsinki Council has revived the existing debate about coordination of fiscal policies, and that no agreement exists.

The first supporter of strong fiscal coordination is the European Commission. The advantage of coordination would be that active fiscal policy is recovered for stabilisation. Also, it is perceived by some that there is a need for fiscal coordination to ensure credibility of long-term commitments to macroeconomic stability.

On the other hand, a consistent section of the economics profession tends to be sceptical about the need for such a move. Many economists think that coordinated fiscal policies would place a greater burden on the monetary authority. A more intense coordination could lead to 'Keynesian style' fine-tuning of fiscal policies across the member states, and this would force the ECB to intervene in the policy mix and to pay too much attention to cyclical stabilisation, neglecting the objective of long-run price stabilisation.

The reported declarations by members of the board of directors of the ECB seem to proceed along both lines of reasoning: on the one hand, a stronger coordination between euro countries could be a potential threat to the independence of the ECB; on the other, it could reduce the level of political uncertainty resulting from a situation where economic policies are pursued independently by a large number of institutions. On this point even the ECB does not seem to dislike the idea of a 'credible interlocutor'.

It is the argument of this chapter that this question can be addressed only by analysing the strategic interaction of the various policymakers. Section 2 describes the model and clarifies the hypotheses that underline the idea of 'fiscal policies putting pressure on the ECB', finally providing a closed-form solution for the model. Section 3 examines the consequences of different levels of positive and negative coordination and their interactions. The results are

---

[2] The reinforced cooperation procedures are based on Articles 43, 44 and 45 of the Treaty of the Union and Article 11 of the EC Treaty.

also illustrated via a simulation of a monetary union of twelve countries whose weights are equal to those in the EMU. The conclusions follow. A mathematical appendix provides a more complete characterisation of the results.

Some literature. The issue of coordination in a monetary union is explicitly addressed in Dixit and Lambertini (2000), Bosca and Orts (1991), Van Aarle and Huart (1997), Beetsma and Bovenberg (1995) and in a game theory framework by Diaz-Roldan (2000). Gatti and Van Wijnbergen (2002) examine the conditions for fiscal restraint to emerge as a Nash equilibrium in the game between fiscal authorities in a monetary union. Bayoumi and Eichengreen (1993) and the texts of the Optimum Currency Areas in their bibliography are a good starting point for the analysis of the shocks that may hit a monetary union. The conclusions of this chapter regarding the rigidity of the SGP are similar to those in Eichengreen (1997). The legal framework in which coordination must arise is in the Treaty of Maastricht, discussed in Buiter, Corsetti and Roubini (1993), von Hagen and Eichengreen (1996), and of course, in Commission of the European Communities (1991). For fiscal federalism see Oates (1972), Tanzi (1996), Walsh (1992) and Pisani-Ferry (1991).

2   The model

In a simple monetary union hit by exogenous shocks, the single central bank and N national fiscal authorities interact to achieve low inflation and full employment. The interaction between the agents is modelled with a game theory model solvable by backward induction, in which the national governments are able to put pressure on the ECB by running their fiscal policies after an economic shock. The focus is on stabilisation after a shock, not on reputational issues of the players, therefore the game is static.

The preferences of national governments differ from those of the central bank because of the greater weight put on smoothing unemployment.[3] The governments in all participating countries have identical preferences. The model is one of short horizon, therefore the effect of fiscal and monetary policy on inflation and unemployment is described by two simple demand equations with fixed expectations of the public.

To keep notation simple, only two governments are explicitly represented. Government j can be seen as the weighted average of all other participating countries as seen by government i. This simplification does not alter the symmetric equilibrium of the model.

---

[3] Given the short-term characteristics of the model a greater weight on unemployment can also be interpreted as a greater *speed* of desired adjustment.

In the first section the game is described and solved for the general case. The equilibrium conditions are then used in the second part to analyse some different scenarios.

The first-best monetary policy. The ECB has two conflicting objectives: long-run inflation targeting (primary objective) and short-run stabilisation of the euro area. The more the ECB can neglect stabilisation, the better it can concentrate on the other goal. For this reason it is enough to model explicitly the short-run preferences for stabilisation. These preferences should be interpreted as the trade-off between inflation and unemployment that the ECB considers consistent with long-run price stability. The optimal 'working environment' for the ECB is then the one in which it does not have to intervene to correct what are, in terms of its preferences, 'errors of the national governments'. More specifically:

- It does not need to intervene to offset the inflationary effects of excessive government expenditure, where 'excessive expenditure' is expenditure that implies more inflation than the ECB would like, given the exogenous shock.
- It does not need to intervene because of lack of action by national governments. This may seem unlikely in the model, because the preferences of the national fiscal authorities are relatively more concerned about unemployment, but this eventuality may arise in presence of inflexible constraints to fiscal policy such as the ones implemented in the SGP. It will be shown that in some circumstances these constraints can prevent the member states from coping with asymmetric shocks[4] and put the burden of intervention onto the ECB.

The meaning of 'pressure on the ECB'. The generic worry that governments can influence the ECB 'hides' many other assumptions which need to be made explicit in order to check their likelihood. Briefly, these hypotheses are:

1. Backward induction: governments must be able to form expectations about the reaction of the ECB and take them into account when formulating fiscal policy. In the jargon of game theory, the governments 'move first'.
2. The ECB can have preferences that are quite conservative, but they must also to some extent include unemployment. When the ECB is committed to the exclusive targeting of prices[5] there is no scope for putting pressure on it because there is no trade-off between prices and unemployment in its best

---

[4] A relevant problem is whether the shocks come from outside or inside the monetary union. It is assumed here that there is consensus among the players on the relevant variables to watch, and the preferences of the players are expressed in terms of these variables. This is not an essential feature of the model and the problem is therefore assumed away, focusing attention only on the interaction of the players.

[5] Other solutions may exist. For instance, the Reserve Bank of New Zealand excludes from targeted inflation the effect of government sales taxes. This can be seen as an attempt to limit the influence of the government.

response. The two first years of EMU have clearly shown that employment is a relevant variable in the ECB policy decisions.[6]

3. The national fiscal authorities are relatively more concerned about increases in unemployment than the ECB. Absent this 'inflation bias' the problem of pressure on the ECB does not exist. It has been correctly stated that the case for fiscal coordination (and more generally for macroeconomic coordination) is weak when the ECB and the fiscal authorities 'keep their house in order' acting independently. On closer examination, the absence of inflation bias is not realistic. The expression 'keep their house in order' does not only imply that the fiscal authorities do not deviate from 'prudent' behaviour because of short-run political incentives; it also amounts to assuming that national governments show the same lack of concern about unemployment as does a conservative central bank. This assumption does not seem to be observed in practice in EU countries.[7] In the rest of the chapter, governments have an inflation bias.

4. Monetary policy is assumed to be relatively more efficient in controlling prices than fiscal policies.[8] This simply means that the institution relatively more concerned about prices (the ECB) has been assigned the instrument that best controls inflation. A situation of misallocation of instruments would lead to the absence of equilibrium.

Other hypotheses of the model are there simply to improve clarity and tractability.

The game aims at describing the interaction among public agents in responding to shocks. Each economy is then described by the same two simple equations of prices and unemployment. The interesting time horizon being the very short period, the expectations of the public are kept fixed. Finally, I want to concentrate on the effects of monetary policy and monetary externalities, therefore I neglect the direct fiscal externalities and assume that different countries are linked only by the common monetary policy: in other words, each national fiscal policy has direct effects in the domestic market only, and indirect effects abroad through monetary policy. The minimisation of these indirect effects is a central theme of the present work.

---

[6] Employment could be included as a predictor of future inflation. In this case it would appear as if the ECB were concerned about employment.

[7] Note that greater concern about unemployment by the fiscal authorities does not necessarily arise only from corruption or political cycles; while the ECB has a mandate oriented towards price stability, national governments are elected and their preferences should reflect those of the population.

[8] In reality it is enough that governments believe this when they move, but this would complicate the description of the game. While hypothesis 4 is different from the more commonly used Phillips curve, it can easily be shown that the latter would give no incentive to the fiscal authorities to put pressure on the ECB. While this case is perfectly possible, most economists seem to believe that this pressure is a real possibility.

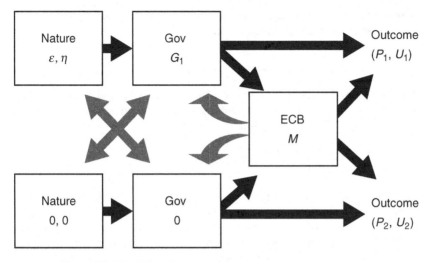

Figure 7.1 The order of moves

The sequence of moves. At the beginning of the game the market is in *equilibrium*, where equilibrium is defined as the situation where all agents (*ECB* and *Gs*) are playing their best responses, the common target values for prices and unemployment are met and there is no shock. The moves are as follows: first, national markets are hit by independent shocks to prices and/or to employment; second, national governments use the fiscal lever; and finally, the central bank sets the monetary policy. The structure of agents' preferences is common knowledge, therefore the game permits backward induction, i.e. the national governments take into account the foreseeable reaction of the central bank while setting their optimal policies.

The order of the moves (see figure 7.1) has been chosen to reflect both the capacity to influence each other that is observed in real world and (as argued in the previous section) the only interesting case. In the first two years of EMU, the policy of the ECB has been attentive to both inflation and unemployment levels, while the influence of the ECB on member states was limited to speeches, with the SGP as the only binding outcome. If the ECB is not uniquely committed to price stability it is reasonable to assume that, as long as governments have some freedom in the use of fiscal policy, they can take into account the possible reaction of the ECB.[9] The order of play then reflects the relations of power among agents. A second interpretation could be that the ECB is 'faster to react', in the sense that it can change policy much more frequently than national governments can; this greater flexibility allows the ECB to follow any change

[9] The SGP is a (very imprecise) way to take away such freedom from the governments.

in fiscal policies with an appropriate response. Under this interpretation, the order of players reflects a sequence in time.

2.1   The national markets

All national markets are identical in structure, but may have different inflation and unemployment levels and different sizes. Each of them is affected by public policies in the following stylised way[10]:

$$P = p_m M + p_g G + \varepsilon \tag{7.1}$$

$$U = -u_m M - u_g G + \eta, \tag{7.2}$$

where P, U, M, G indicate the deviations of prices, unemployment, money supply, fiscal expenditure from target values, and ε and η are i.i.d. shocks to prices and to unemployment. The target values are common to the ECB and the national governments, but the former is less inclined to short-run output stabilisation (hypothesis 3). All other letters are positive parameters.

Hypothesis 4 implies:

$$\frac{p_m}{u_m} > \frac{p_g}{u_g}$$

This condition simply states that monetary policy has a comparative advantage in controlling prices, and fiscal and monetary instruments have been correctly allocated.

2.2   The ECB

In models solvable by backward induction it is often convenient to start from the player who moves last, in this case the central bank (*ECB*). The reason is that the strategy of the ECB is taken into account by the governments (G), while the play of G is already known to the ECB when it moves.

The ECB runs the monetary policy for the whole union. The monetary policy is common and has symmetrical effects in all countries (given that they have identical structures).

The preferences of the ECB are defined over union aggregates:

$$L_{ECB}(M, G, \varepsilon, \eta) = [P(M, G, \varepsilon)]^2 + \beta [U(M, G, \eta)]^2, \tag{7.3}$$

where the variables without a subscript are the weighted average of the N participating countries:

$$M = \sum_{i=1}^{N} \lambda_i M_i$$

---

[10] It is important to notice that no single inflation level across the union is imposed.

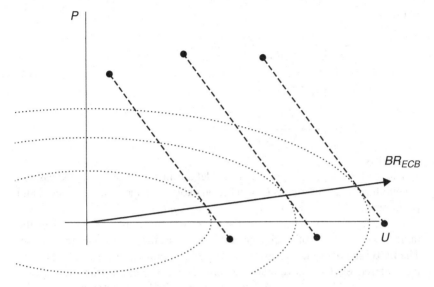

Figure 7.2 Preferences and best response of ECB

$$G = \sum_{i=1}^{N} \lambda_i G_i$$

$$\varepsilon = \sum_{i=1}^{N} \lambda_i \varepsilon_i$$

$$\eta = \sum_{i=1}^{N} \lambda_i \eta_i,$$

with

$$\sum_{i=1}^{N} \lambda_i = 1.$$

The parameter β expresses the relative aversion of the ECB to inflation and unemployment.

The best response of the ECB (BR_{ECB} in figure 7.2) can be expressed as follows (see appendix):

$$M(G, \varepsilon, \eta) = -\mu_g \left(\sum_{i=1}^{N} \lambda_i G_i \right) - \mu_e \left(\sum_{i=1}^{N} \lambda_i \varepsilon_i \right) + \mu_h \left(\sum_{i=1}^{N} \lambda_i \eta_i \right).$$

Or, in a condensed representation:

$$M(G, \varepsilon, \eta) = -\mu_g G - \mu_e \varepsilon + \mu_h \eta$$

with

$$\mu_g = - \left[\frac{1}{p_m^2 + \beta u_m^2} \right] (-\beta u_m u_g - p_g p_m)$$

$$\mu_e = - \left[\frac{1}{p_m^2 + \beta u_m^2} \right] (-p_m)$$

$$\mu_h = + \left[\frac{1}{p_m^2 + \beta u_m^2} \right] \beta u_m$$

all positive.

The best strategy of the ECB is to deflate in response to an increase of expenditure by governments (G) and to an exogenous increase of prices ε, and to support employment when a negative shock η hits it.

The term in square brackets is the reciprocal of the responsiveness of the target variables to a policy change and determines the size of the intervention. The ECB intervenes according to the slope of its Phillips curve (u_m/p_m) and to the preferences β. Observe that when only one or some countries of weight λ_i are hit by a shock or adopt a policy change, the ECB will move proportionally from the perceived situation to its *BR* line. This implies that each government faces a backward-induction 'budget constraint' that does not coincide with the best response of ECB unless $\lambda_i = 1$. As an example, the locus of equilibria chosen by a backward inducting government is pictured in figure 7.3 for $\lambda = \{0, 1/2, 1\}$.

2.3   *The governments*

In this section the best response function of the national governments is calculated in the most general framework. This will lead to some cumbersome notation, but it has the advantage of encompassing all the other situations as special cases.

In the general situation (symmetric information) each government is not constrained in the choice of its fiscal stance and is aware of the structure of the model and of the actions of nature (the shocks in all participating countries). Thus, each government is able to form expectations about the actions of its peers and (by backward induction) about the action of the ECB,[11] and acts accordingly.

The loss function of each government i is

$$L_{Gi}(M_i, G_i, \varepsilon_i, \eta_i) = [P_i(M_i, G_i, \varepsilon_i)]^2 + \alpha [U_i(M_i, G_i, \eta_i)]^2 \quad (7.4)$$

---

[11] The action of ECB is the only variable of interest for the government because it affects the payoff of its strategy, while the fiscal policies of the other countries do not have direct domestic effects but only indirect externalities coming from the reaction of the ECB.

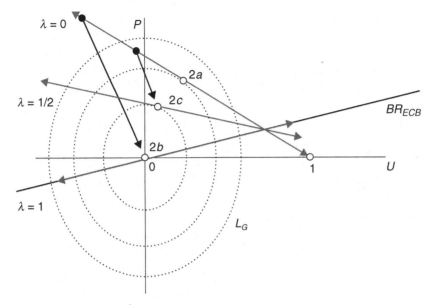

Figure 7.3 Size and possible equilibria

and (hypothesis 3) the government cares about unemployment more than the ECB, therefore $\alpha > \beta$.

Solving the FOC for G_i (in appendix), one obtains the best response function (BR_G in figure 7.4) of government i:

$$G_i(\eta_i, \eta_j, \varepsilon_i, \varepsilon_j, G_j) =$$

$$\Omega * \begin{Bmatrix} + [(-\lambda_i p_m \mu_h)(-\lambda_i p_m \mu_g + p_g) - \alpha(\lambda_i u_m \mu_g - u_g)(1 - \lambda_i u_m \mu_h)]\eta_i \\ + [(-\lambda_j p_m \mu_h)(-\lambda_i p_m \mu_g + p_g) - \alpha(\lambda_i u_m \mu_g - u_g)(-\lambda_j u_m \mu_h)]\eta_j \\ - [(1 - \lambda_i p_m \mu_e)(-\lambda_i p_m \mu_g + p_g) - \alpha(\lambda_i u_m \mu_g - u_g)(-\lambda_i u_m \mu_e)]\varepsilon_i \\ - [(-\lambda_j p_m \mu_e)(-\lambda_i p_m \mu_g + p_g) - \alpha(\lambda_i u_m \mu_g - u_g)(-\lambda_j u_m \mu_e)]\varepsilon_j \\ + [(p_m \mu_g \lambda_j)(-\lambda_i p_m \mu_g + p_g) + \alpha(\lambda_i u_m \mu_g - u_g)(-u_m \mu_g \lambda_j)]G_j \end{Bmatrix}$$

with

$$\Omega = \left[\frac{1}{(\lambda_i u_m \mu_g - u_g)^2 \alpha + (-\lambda_i p_m \mu_g + p_g)^2} \right].$$

Fortunately, this will be the most complicated expression in the chapter. In order to grasp the intuition one has to remember that the reaction of the ECB is automatically taken into account in the expression above, while those of the other players are not (and they explicitly appear as arguments). This difference in treatment is due to the fact that the governments move simultaneously.

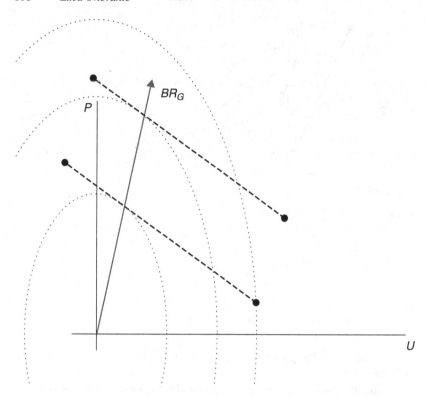

Figure 7.4 Preferences and best response of the governments

One extreme case ($\alpha = 0$) is ruled out by hypotheses 2 and 3, but it is useful to consider it for the purpose of exposition. If G_i cares only about inflation (that is, if it is even more conservative than the ECB) a fiscal restriction will follow a shock to domestic or foreign unemployment because the comparatively 'weak' ECB is going to allow some more inflation. The same is true after a domestic price shock only partially offset by the ECB. A fiscal expansion follows a foreign price shock simply because the ECB restriction is not welcome.

A government concerned only about the internal level of employment ($\alpha \to \infty$) always increases spending after a shock to unemployment. This reaction is somewhat smoothed because the government knows that the ECB will take part of the burden of the intervention ($1 - \lambda_i u_m \mu_h$). If the shock arises in another country, the expected monetary expansion of the ECB ($-\lambda_j u_m \mu_h$) leads to fiscal consolidation. The same is true (with different signs, because the expected reaction of the ECB goes in the other direction) for a shock to prices; the ECB will restrict the quantity of money, and this calls for fiscal expansion.

Finally, a shorter notation is introduced for the complex expenditure function of the generic government i: this function represents the best response of a government free to act, aware of the fact that the ECB will act next and informed about the shocks in all participating countries.

$$G_i = (\gamma_e \varepsilon_i + \gamma_h \eta_i) + \left(\gamma_e^f \varepsilon_j + \gamma_h^f \eta_j\right) + \gamma_g G_j, \tag{7.5}$$

with $\gamma_e < 0$, $\gamma_h > 0$, $\gamma_e^f > 0$, $\gamma_h^f < 0$ and $0 < \gamma_g < 1$ under the hypotheses of the model. The sign of the coefficients is derived analytically in the appendix.

The coefficient γ_g is the indirect externality reaction to the fiscal expansion of other members. In the appendix it is shown that hypothesis 4 implies that this parameter can take values between 0 and 1 (not included).[12] This condition ensures the existence of the subgame perfect equilibrium.[13]

3   Five possible scenarios

The proposals for coordination are of two kinds: positive coordination and negative coordination. Positive coordination consists of regular meetings in which the policy responses are coordinated on a case-by-case basis; negative coordination consists of rules laid down at the beginning and then followed throughout. By applying restrictions to the general model solved in section 2, we can analyse the following scenarios, ranked from minimal to maximal positive coordination and contrasted with negative coordination:

• No coordination and autonomous fiscal policies. The fiscal authorities in the different countries are free to fit their policies to their country's specific needs, and no interaction (neither informal nor formal) is relevant.

• Positive coordination via sharing of information (informal cooperation). A loose form of cooperation among fiscal authorities could take the form of periodic informal meetings. Such meetings would foster information exchange, without committing any of the participants to specific policies. The Euro-12 group seems to be a good example of such an institution.

• Positive coordination through formal mechanisms. In the context of increased cooperation, for example within a reinforced version of the BEPG (Broad Economic Policy Guidelines), there could be formal meetings in which the fiscal stance of the participating countries would be decided. The decisions taken in these meetings would then be binding for all euro members.

• Negative coordination: SGP.

---

[12] In the game the coefficient γ_g represents the (negative) reaction of G_i to the (negative) reaction of *ECB* to the variation in G_j. This is sometimes referred to as a 'domino effect' of fiscal policies.

[13] Technically, one has a Nash equilibium of a reduced form game between governments, with the reaction function of the ECB factored into their objective function. This corresponds to the subgame perfect equilibrium of the original game.

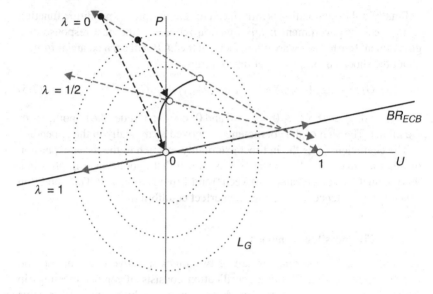

Figure 7.5 No coordination

- Negative coordination: an ECB-based, alternative SGP. If the ECB has to be free from pressure, it must be able to impose its preferences on the national member states. The proposal is that the 'alternative SGP' should be based on the declared preferences of the ECB, and the member states should comply with those requirements as they do with the current SGP. Such an arrangement would bring the ECB out of its role of Stackelberg follower and allow it to neglect most of the stabilisation issue.

  The current framework of the EMU includes the SGP and positive informal cooperation.

3.1   No coordination

When no coordination is possible and the exchange of information is scarce, no government is able to forecast the policies of the others.

In our model this implies that each government takes the a priori expected value of the shocks for the others, that is zero. Also, when the shocks are not known abroad, all the participating governments can only assume that the others will be inactive. This leads to a very simple behaviour: each government reacts as if it was the only one hit by a shock.

An asymmetric shock with no coordination. The outcome of a shock in country *i* when there is no coordination or exchange of information (figure 7.5) is

$$G_i = (\gamma_e \varepsilon_i + \gamma_h \eta_i)$$

$$P_i = p_m M(\lambda_i G_i, \lambda_i \varepsilon_i, \lambda_i \eta_i) + p_g G_i + \varepsilon_i$$
$$= (p_g \gamma_h + p_m \mu_h \lambda_i - \lambda_i p_m \mu_g \gamma_h)\eta_i + (1 + p_g \gamma_h - p_m \mu_e \lambda_i - \lambda_i p_m \mu_g \gamma_h)\varepsilon_i$$

$$U_i = -u_m M(\lambda_i G_i, \lambda_i \varepsilon_i, \lambda_i \eta_i) - u_g G_i + \eta_i$$
$$= (u_m \mu_g \lambda_i \gamma_h + 1 - u_m \mu_h \lambda_i - u_g \gamma_h)\eta_i + (u_m \mu_g \lambda_i \gamma_e - u_g \gamma_e + u_m \mu_e \lambda_i)\varepsilon_i$$

$$G_j = 0$$

$$P_j = p_m M(\lambda_i G_i, \lambda_i \varepsilon_i, \lambda_i \eta_i)$$
$$= (-\lambda_i p_m \mu_g \gamma_h + p_m \mu_h \lambda_i)\eta_i + (-p_m \mu_g \lambda_i \gamma_e - p_m \mu_e \lambda_i)\varepsilon_i$$

$$U_j = -u_m M(\lambda_i G_i, \lambda_i \varepsilon_i, \lambda_i \eta_i)$$
$$= (u_m \mu_g \lambda_i \gamma_h - u_m \mu_h \lambda_i)\eta_i + (u_m \mu_g \lambda_i \gamma_e + u_m \mu_e \lambda_i)\varepsilon_i$$

$$M^0 = M(\lambda_i G_i, \lambda_i \varepsilon_i, \lambda_i \eta_i)$$
$$= (-\mu_g \lambda_i \gamma_h + \mu_h \lambda_i)\eta_i + (-\mu_g \lambda_i \gamma_e - \mu_e \lambda_i)\varepsilon_i.$$

Prices and unemployment outcomes for the union are the weighted average of national values with weights λ_i and $\lambda_j = (1 - \lambda_i)$.

In case of an asymmetric shock in country i, both prices or unemployment rise after intervention of the players[14]; the solution for both $\varepsilon_i > 0$, $\eta_i > 0$ is, for every $\lambda \in (0,1)$,[15] $(P > 0, P_i > 0, P_j < 0; U > 0, U_j > 0; M^0 < 0)$. One should remark that the sign is not uniquely determined for U_i. This is not surprising: figure 7.5 shows that U_i can be either positive or negative depending on the value of λ_i. Our computer simulations show, however, that for realistic values of the parameters it takes a value of λ_i very close to 1 for u_i to have negative values.[16]

3.2   Positive coordination

In its strictest definition, positive coordination implies the implementation of a fiscal policy for the EU as a whole by a collegial 'decisionmaking body', whose decisions would be binding for all. This is the typical mode of operation of the common monetary policy in the ECB Council, and it has been suggested as a long-term objective for coordination in the framework of the 'closer cooperation' clauses.

---

[14] Prices are totally smoothed if $\lambda_i = 1$, which can be interpreted as the one-country case or a totally common shock. When $\lambda_i = 0$ the result is (trivially) zero as well.

[15] Once again $\lambda_i = 1$ and $\lambda_i = 0$ imply that the shocks have no effect on prices and unemployment.

[16] In computer simulations with $p_m = 2$, $p_g = u_g = u_m = 1$, $a = 1.25$, $\beta = 0.75$ it takes a value as big as $\lambda_i = 0.85$ to have a negative U_i as consequence of a shock in either η_i or ε_i. The biggest country in Europe is Germany, whose share in the EU GDP is only slightly above 30%.

As stated before, the likely scenario for the very short term seems to be limited to a greater sharing of information in the search for decisions based on consensus. This is the weakest form of positive coordination, and is analysed first.

3.2.1   Informal cooperation   It has been proposed that cooperation could be informal, in respect of the existing treaties that impede formal coordination among a subgroup of EU members. This informal cooperation could, for example, increase the sharing of information about the situation in the different countries, without reaching the point of harmonisation of policies.[17] In this section it will be clear that, even though the sharing of information is generally perceived to be a positive factor among economists, this need not be the case in a strategic environment.

A shock with informal cooperation. The new equilibrium following a shock will be the Nash equilibrium of the reduced form game, where the BR lines of the two governments intersect. The complete expression of the Nash equilibrium is reported in the appendix. After an asymmetric shock in country i, the outcome for country i is:

$$G_i = \frac{(\gamma_e \varepsilon_i + \gamma_h \eta_i) + \gamma_g \left(\gamma_e^f \varepsilon_i + \gamma_h^f \eta_i \right)}{1 - \gamma_g^2}$$

$$P_i = \left(p_m \lambda_i \mu_h + \frac{p_g \left(\gamma_h + \gamma_g \gamma_h^f \right) - p_m \mu_g \left[\left(\lambda_i \gamma_h + \lambda_j \gamma_h^f \right) + \left(\lambda_i \gamma_h^f + \lambda_j \gamma_h \right) \gamma_g \right]}{1 - \gamma_g^2} \right) \eta_i$$

$$+ \left(1 - p_m \lambda_i \mu_e + \frac{p_g \left(\gamma_e + \gamma_g \gamma_e^f \right) - p_m \mu_g \left[\left(\lambda_i \gamma_e + \lambda_j \gamma_e^f \right) + \left(\lambda_j \gamma_e + \lambda_i \gamma_e^f \right) \gamma_g \right]}{1 - \gamma_g^2} \right) \varepsilon_i$$

$$U_i = \left(u_m \lambda_i \mu_e + \frac{u_m \mu_g \left[\left(\lambda_i \gamma_e + \lambda_j \gamma_e^f \right) + \left(\lambda_j \gamma_e + \lambda_i \gamma_e^f \right) \gamma_g \right] - u_g \left(\gamma_e + \gamma_g \gamma_e^f \right)}{1 - \gamma_g^2} \right) \varepsilon_i$$

$$\left(1 - u_m \lambda_i \mu_h + \frac{u_m \mu_g \left[\left(\lambda_i \gamma_h + \lambda_j \gamma_h^f \right) + \left(\lambda_i \gamma_h^f + \lambda_j \gamma_h \right) \gamma_g \right] - u_g \left(\gamma_h + \gamma_g \gamma_h^f \right)}{1 - \gamma_g^2} \right) \eta_i$$

and for country j:

$$G_j = \frac{\left(\gamma_e^f \varepsilon_i + \gamma_h^f \eta_i \right) + \gamma_g \left(\gamma_e \varepsilon_i + \gamma_h \eta_i \right)}{1 - \gamma_g^2}$$

---

[17] The macroeconomic data are usually collected by independent statistical agencies, and become known to the public at a later stage (ex-post check). It is therefore assumed that the data are truthfully revealed to the partners.

$$P_j = \left(\frac{p_g\left(\gamma_e^f + \gamma_g\gamma_e\right) - p_m\mu_g\left[\left(\lambda_i\gamma_e + \lambda_j\gamma_e^f\right) + \left(\lambda_j\gamma_e + \lambda_i\gamma_e^f\right)\gamma_g\right]}{1 - \gamma_g^2} - p_m\lambda_i\mu_e \right)\varepsilon_i$$

$$+ \left(p_m\lambda_i\mu_h + \frac{p_g\left(\gamma_h^f + \gamma_g\gamma_h\right) - p_m\mu_g\left[\left(\lambda_i\gamma_h + \lambda_j\gamma_h^f\right) + \left(\lambda_i\gamma_h^f + \lambda_j\gamma_h\right)\gamma_g\right]}{1 - \gamma_g^2} \right)\eta_i$$

$$U_j = \left(\frac{u_m\mu_g\left[\left(\lambda_i\gamma_e + \lambda_j\gamma_e^f\right) + \left(\lambda_j\gamma_e + \lambda_i\gamma_e^f\right)\gamma_g\right] - u_g\left(\gamma_e^f + \gamma_g\gamma_e\right)}{1 - \gamma_g^2} + u_m\lambda_i\mu_e \right)\varepsilon_i$$

$$+ \left(\frac{u_m\mu_g\left[\left(\lambda_i\gamma_h + \lambda_j\gamma_h^f\right) + \left(\lambda_i\gamma_h^f + \lambda_j\gamma_h\right)\gamma_g\right] - u_g\left(\gamma_h^f + \gamma_g\gamma_h\right)}{1 - \gamma_g^2} - u_m\lambda_i\mu_h \right)\eta_i$$

and for the common monetary policy:

$$M^N = M(\lambda_i G_i + \lambda_j G_j, \lambda_i\varepsilon_i, \lambda_i\eta_i)$$

$$= \left(-\frac{1}{1 - \gamma_g^2}\left(\left(\lambda_i\gamma_h^f + \lambda_j\gamma_h\right)\gamma_g + \lambda_i\gamma_h + \lambda_j\gamma_h^f\right)\mu_g + \mu_h\lambda_i \right)\eta_i$$

$$+ \left(-\frac{1}{1 - \gamma_g^2}\left(\left(\lambda_j\gamma_e + \lambda_i\gamma_e^f\right)\gamma_g + \lambda_i\gamma_e + \lambda_j\gamma_e^f\right)\mu_g - \mu_e\lambda_i \right)\varepsilon_i.$$

This result can be compared with the one of no cooperation. In the previous case, the initial response to the shock ($\gamma_e\varepsilon + \gamma_h\eta$) was also the final outcome. Here, the initial shock 'spreads around' through monetary externalities. First, each government is informed about the shocks occurring abroad, and takes them into account ($\gamma_e^f\varepsilon_j + \gamma_h^f\eta_j$); then, the reaction of the partners is also considered (square brackets). Finally, the whole numerator is multiplied by $1/(1 - \gamma_g^2)$ because of the interaction of players.

The ECB intervention can also be compared with the one of the preceding case (no exchange of information). For example, in the case of an asymmetric unemployment shock in i the difference in intervention is

$$M^N - M^0 = -\frac{1}{1 - \gamma_g^2}\mu_g\left(\left(\lambda_i\gamma_h^f + \lambda_j\gamma_h\right)\gamma_g + \lambda_i\gamma_h\gamma_g^2 + \lambda_j\gamma_h^f\right)\eta_i,$$

which can be shown to be positive for $\lambda_i \in (0,1)$ by substituting in the definitions. A similar conclusion applies to an inflation shock in i. When the different governments are aware of each other's moves but they cannot coordinate, the ECB is forced to show more activism.

The signs of the variables in equilibrium are not unique as in the first case, and depend on λ_j. Substitution in the definition leads to the following signs: for $\lambda_i \in (0,1)$ we have ($P_i > 0, P_j < 0; U_j > 0; M^N < M^0 < 0$). If the country is the smaller one, $\lambda_i \in (0,1/2)$, then ($P > 0; U > 0, U_i > 0$), for bigger values of λ_i

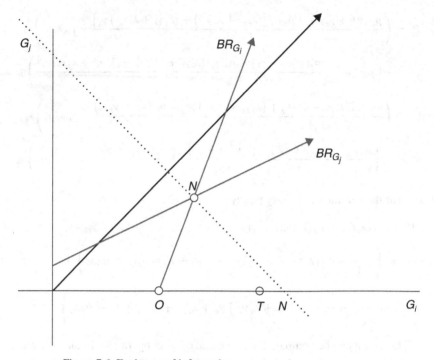

Figure 7.6 Exchange of information

it is true that ($P < 0$; $U < 0$). As in the previous case, U_i remains indeterminate although generally positive.

A graphic comparison. The example of an asymmetric shock in country i is shown in figure 7.6. The difference in overall fiscal expansion can be seen by tracing a diagonal line that reports the total expansion on the G_i axis: the distance between the quantities (O) and the point (N) is the increase in expenditure above the non-cooperation case, which would be realised if the interaction terms (γ_g, γ_e^f and γ_h^f) were zero. The interaction between the two Gs is due to the fact that country j observes the shock in i and anticipates the ECB restriction to the fiscal expansion in i, therefore j expands in order to offset it. This in turn is anticipated by i, and the fiscal expansion is amplified, and so on. The result is an increase in expenditure in the case of either an exogenous increase in prices or unemployment.

3.2.2   Formal coordination   In the context of formal fiscal coordination, the fiscal authorities 'act as if they were one', observe the average shocks to the whole union and compute the optimal policy response as if they were a single government.[18] Total coordination leads to exactly the same outcome as the one-country case, where the shocks are completely smoothed at the union level. As before, the complete characterisation of the solution is in the appendix. The outcome of an asymmetric shock in country i is:

$$G^T = \lambda_i \left(\tilde{\gamma}_e \varepsilon_i + \tilde{\gamma}_h \eta_i \right)$$

$$P = p_m M + p_g G + \lambda_i \varepsilon_i = 0$$

$$U = -u_m M - u_g G + \lambda_i \eta_i = 0$$

$$G_i = \lambda_i G^T$$

$$P_i = -p_g \lambda_j \lambda_i \left(\tilde{\gamma}_e \varepsilon_i + \tilde{\gamma}_h \eta_i \right) + \lambda_j \varepsilon_i$$

$$U_i = u_g \lambda_j \lambda_i \left(\tilde{\gamma}_e \varepsilon_i + \tilde{\gamma}_h \eta_i \right) + \lambda_j \eta_i$$

$$G_j = \lambda_j G^T$$

$$P_j = -p_g \lambda_i^2 \left(\tilde{\gamma}_e \varepsilon_i + \tilde{\gamma}_h \eta_i \right) - \lambda_i \varepsilon_i$$

$$U_j = u_g \lambda_i^2 \left(\tilde{\gamma}_e \varepsilon_i + \tilde{\gamma}_h \eta_i \right) - \lambda_i \eta_i$$

$$M^T = (-\mu_g \tilde{\gamma}_h + \mu_h) \lambda_i \eta_i + \left(-\mu_g \tilde{\gamma}_e - \mu_e \right) \lambda_i \varepsilon_i,$$

where $\tilde{\gamma}_e$, $\tilde{\gamma}_h$ are the closed-economy equivalents of γ_e and γ_h.[19]

Following either a symmetric shock or an asymmetric shock in country i, prices or unemployment remain unaltered at the aggregate level. After a price shock ($\varepsilon_i > 0$), for every $\lambda_i \in (0,1)$, then ($P = 0$, $P_i > 0$, $P_j < 0$; $U = U_i = U_j = 0$; $M^T < 0$). After an increase in unemployment ($\eta_i > 0$), for every $\lambda_i \in (0,1)$, then ($P = P_i = P_j = 0$; $U = 0$, $U_i > 0$, $U_j < 0$; $M^T < 0$). In both cases, the shock is partially translated to the other country, while the consequences on the other variable are neutralised.

The involvement of the ECB in the stabilisation is of the same order of magnitude as in the case of informal cooperation. The total smoothing of disturbances is due to the fact that now the response of the ECB is completely internalised, and therefore the joint fiscal authority can decide on which point of the ECB BR line it wants to be positioned. Figure 7.7 shows that the only point in which the *BR* lines of government and ECB intersect is the origin.

Subgame perfect equilibrium and Nash equilibrium. One obvious objection would be that the backward-induction story is not really credible in this case, because a reinforced Eurogroup would evolve as something similar to

[18] The weights used to calculate the aggregate shocks are assumed to be the same as the ECB uses when it has to compute its policy response; this assumption is not unrealistic (the weights could be the national GDPs for example) and allows for a clearer exposition, but it is in no way essential.

[19] The closed economy equivalents can be calculated by setting λ_i to unity. Their analytical expression is $\tilde{\gamma}_e = \frac{[-p_g]}{u_g^2 \alpha + p_g^2}$, $\tilde{\gamma}_h = \frac{\alpha u_g}{u_g^2 \alpha + p_g^2}$.

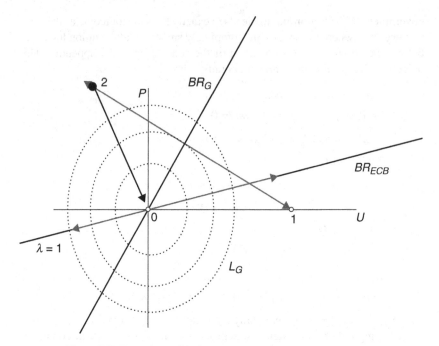

Figure 7.7 Formal coordination

an equal interlocutor to the ECB. As a matter of fact, when the decision about fiscal policy is taken 'as if' there was a single authority, the backward-induction solution always coincides with the Nash equilibrium between governments and the ECB. In this simple game it does not make a difference whether the ECB moves last (subgame perfect equilibrium) or at the same time (Nash equilibrium), because in both cases the final outcome is total smoothing of shocks, at the only place where the two *BR* lines intersect. For the one country case (or the Eurogroup case) the 'order of the moves' is irrelevant.

3.3   Negative coordination

Negative coordination denotes commonly agreed rules to prevent fiscal policy from overburdening monetary policy. Currently, the Stability and Growth Pact prevents the emergence of large public deficits and the resulting threat to price stability. In the following section the implemented SGP will be compared with a different one to show that it is far from being optimal, both from the point of view of stabilisation and from the point of view of the ECB.

3.3.1   The Stability and Growth Pact (SGP)   The SGP implies that the level of fiscal expansion is bounded above by a fixed level, say by $\bar{G}$ for the whole

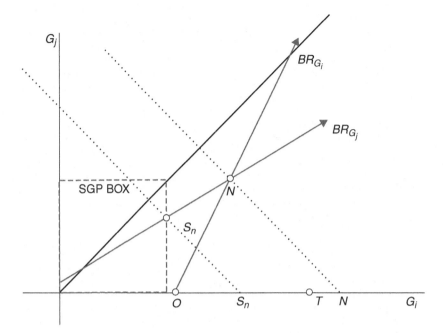

Figure 7.8 Rationale for the SGP

union. When the constraint is not binding the solution is one of those described above. Given that the governments are relatively more concerned about unemployment than the ECB, the result of letting them act freely would always be a restrictive policy by the ECB. The rationale of the SGP is to limit the potential involvement of the ECB in short-run smoothing by putting a cap on the fiscal expansion that governments can undertake. In the case of no cooperation,[20]

$$G_i = \min[(\gamma_e \varepsilon_i + \gamma_h \eta_i), \bar{G}]$$

$$G_j = \min[(\gamma_e \varepsilon_j + \gamma_h \eta_j), \bar{G}]$$

$$M^S = -\mu_g(\lambda_i G_i + \lambda_j G_j) - \mu_e(\lambda_i \varepsilon_i + \lambda_j \varepsilon_j) + \mu_h(\lambda_i \eta_i + \lambda_j \eta_j)$$

$$\geq -\mu_g \bar{G} - \mu_e(\lambda_i \varepsilon_i + \lambda_j \varepsilon_j) + \mu_h(\lambda_i \eta_i + \lambda_j \eta_j)$$

Figure 7.8 shows the rationale for the SGP. After a shock in i that leads to O, the interaction among governments would produce N as final outcome. If the SGP limits the expansion of each of them, the total fiscal expansion is limited

[20] The case of informal cooperation is not analytically expounded because the argument follows exactly the same line. The only difference is that the cap on the deficit is more useful because it has the additional effect of limiting the strategic escalation of deficits typical of the Nash equilibrium.

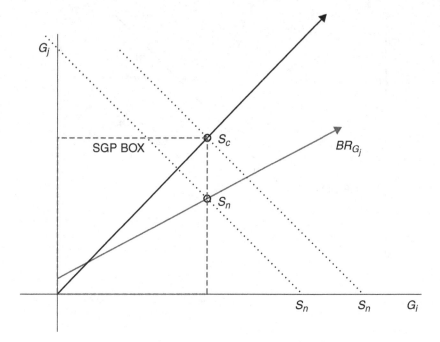

Figure 7.9 SGP and formal cooperation

to S_n (the maximum permitted by the Pact for country i, the best response to i for country j).

Interaction with positive coordination. An important point to stress is that negative coordination (upper bounds to fiscal expansion, as in the SGP) becomes less effective if coupled with *formal* positive coordination. This means that the SGP could be formally maintained but would lose some of its potential should the member states move to a formalised process of fiscal coordination.

The expected value of the restriction of the SGP is a measure of the potential protection that the ECB can receive from the constraints of the Pact. In the appendix it is proved that this value is lower when formal coordination is put into place. The reason is that, in the absence of formal cooperation, the limit binds every country separately, while in formal coordination the pact controls only the overall quantity G^T. When the policies are commonly run, all the countries run the same (percentage) deficit, no matter what their private shock might be, and all hit the constraint at the same time or not at all. In other words, the fiscal authorities borrow from each other the unused margins of freedom (see figure 7.9).

These results are shown analytically in the appendix. Here it is important to notice that the result is extremely general: the power of a negative constraint

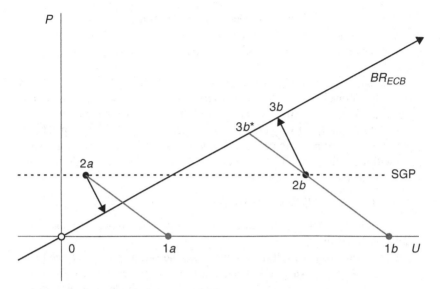

Figure 7.10 Is the SGP too rigid?

like the SGP is always and considerably weakened when the fiscal authorities can act together ($S_c > S_n$ always). Positive formal coordination weakens de facto the existing negative coordination.

Perverse effects of the SGP. The SGP could (surprisingly) also lead to a greater activism of the ECB: in the case of a major unemployment shock, the ECB could have incentives to increase the quantity of money in the presence of insufficient fiscal reaction. Figure 7.10 shows that in presence of a strong disturbance in unemployment the ECB could decide to increase the quantity of money ($2b \rightarrow 3b$) because the SGP constrains the national governments. The figure also shows that the fixed cap to fiscal expenditure implemented in the SGP favours those countries that have been hit by a light disturbance over those that really would need to use the fiscal lever even according to the conservative judgement of the ECB. While the more 'lucky' countries hit by a small shock are allowed to provoke 'unnecessary' inflation ($2a$), those in real need are forced to wait at ($2b$) for an intervention ($2b \rightarrow 3b$) of the ECB. Such intervention cannot be given for granted, because it depends on the overall situation in the union; furthermore, it would be costly because the monetary stance has more effect on prices than on unemployment. Point ($3b$) has more inflation and more unemployment than ($3b^*$).

Given the experience of the national governments before Maastricht became binding, it is certain that the fiscal discipline imposed by the SGP contributes to limiting the extent of short-run interventions by the ECB. Still, it appears to be an extremely rigid device, first because it imposes arbitrary limits, and then because it has the unpleasant consequence of allowing unnecessary expansion by some while impeding intervention where this would be necessary.

3.3.2   Comparing the SGP with a 'flexible SGP'   The SGP can be compared with a similar one based on different criteria. Suppose that the ECB communicates its preferences in terms of 'maximum inflation allowed for each variation in unemployment' (β). Every member state is then constrained to adopt a fiscal policy that, according to the commonly agreed model, keeps the target variables within the limits announced by the Central Bank. In other words, the limit ($G_i = \bar{G}$) on fiscal expansions is replaced by

$$\hat{G}_i \quad \text{s.t.} \quad [P_i(G_i, \varepsilon_i, \eta_i) = \beta \cdot U_i(G_i, \varepsilon_i, \eta_i)] \quad \forall i$$

The Excessive Deficit Procedure can be applied to non-complying states exactly as in the current SGP.

The resulting policies follow directly from the setup and do not need calculations. Take as an example a shock that increases prices or unemployment. The national governments, being more prone to accommodate shocks, always use the whole discretionary margin allowed by the Pact. By doing this, they perfectly substitute the ECB in the short-run stabilisation function. The ECB then does not need to react to inflationary pressures and is able to concentrate on the long-run stability of prices.

From the point of view of equity, this criterion also has the advantage of allowing those countries that are hit by bigger shocks a larger margin of intervention. On the other hand, there is no monetary spillover that can possibly amplify the effects of the original shock and the responses of the governments; the propagation of shocks of the Nash equilibrium is stopped at the first stage (see figure 7.11).

3.4   The interaction of positive and negative coordination

In the following section a simulation illustrates how elements of positive and negative coordination interact.

A monetary union of twelve countries is simulated. The countries have weights that corresponds to the GDPs of the countries that participate in the EMU. As in the theoretical part, I focus on the monetary externalities, therefore all the countries have the same structure ($p_m = 2$, $p_g = u_g = u_m = 1$) that respects the required hypothesis of allocation of instruments.

For each country and each period I create a shock to prices and one to employment. All the shocks are drawn from a standardised normal distribution and they are i.i.d. A series of Monte Carlo experiments is then run in order to see which framework imposes on the ECB the larger quantity of short-term

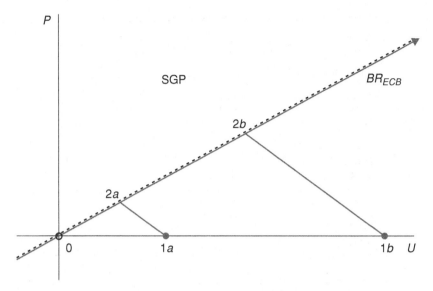

Figure 7.11 A flexible SGP

stabilising interventions. The results are summarised in table 7.1, where the
different levels of positive coordination (rows) interact with more or less binding
SGP fixed limits. For every combination the mean and variance of the fiscal
activism of a country with weight 0.17 (which in the EMU would correspond to
Italy) are reported. In the following row the activism of the ECB is described.
Finally, where applicable I report the percentage of cases in which the SGP
actually constrained the fiscal policy of the country.

The main problem is when the ECB feels it has to intervene (to abandon its
long-run policy) to counter what it perceives to be excessive inflation in the
union. A more detailed report (on restrictive monetary policy only) is presented
in table 7.2. The same table (in graphical form) also appears in the conclusions
(figure 7.12).

The first observation is that the theoretical case of no cooperation, no information produces very small fiscal responses compared to the others. In this case
the SGP does not have a role, and one can see that setting the ceiling $\bar{G}$ at 2 and
then at 1 changes the outcome very little.

The second row describes informal cooperation; in the absence of SGP, the
fiscal expansion implies an involvement of the ECB in short-run stabilisation
that is not only one order of magnitude bigger than the no-cooperation case, but
also bigger than the case of formal coordination. On the other hand, the SGP
effectively constrains the deficit of the member countries in a way that limits
the involvement of the central bank (from 289 to 96 in the table 7.2).

Table 7.1. *Effect of positive interventions on SGP limits*

	No SGP		SGP 2		SGP 1	
Coordination	Exp	Var	Exp	Var	Exp	Var
None						
Fiscal	0.02	0.05	−0.01	0.50	−0.08	0.47
Monetary	0	0	0	0	0.01	0
% Cut	−		0.4%		6.7%	
Nash						
Fiscal	0	1.65	−0.10	1.38	−0.31	0.96
Monetary	0	0.50	0.07	0.39	0.21	0.24
% Cut	−		3.5%		25.0%	
Formal						
Fiscal	−0.01	0.87	0	0.97	−0.09	0.74
Monetary	0	0.34	0	0.37	0.06	0.31
% Cut	−		3.2%		15.6%	

Table 7.2. *The overall size of the ECB restrictions in 1000 trials*

	Size of negative interventions		
Coordination	No SGP	SGP2	SGP1
None	19	21	15
Nash	289	231	96
Formal	251	240	210

The SGP becomes almost irrelevant when the countries can act as if they were one; the ceiling $\bar{G}$ limits the involvement of the ECB from 251 to 210 and cannot do better, because the fiscal authorities are now able to coordinate in a way that allows them to take full advantage of the freedom to spend left by the Pact.

4   Conclusions

In the preceding pages the question of which form of fiscal coordination would imply the least stabilising effort by the ECB has been addressed. From the analytical development of the game, it appears that two main forces enter into play:

- On the one hand, the awareness of the interplay of fiscal policies and monetary policies by the players can lead to quite complex interactions which result in the multiplication of the initial disturbances and to their propagation

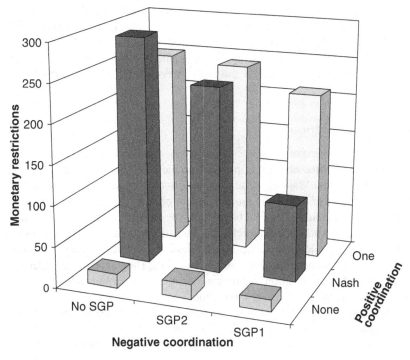

Figure 7.12 Monetary restrictions

to the whole union through monetary externalities. Information without co-ordination leads to policy-induced instability.
- On the other hand, complete coordination would internalise such effects and avoid propagations, while giving back to the fiscal authorities at least one degree of freedom in fiscal policy to counteract common disturbances. The game outlined the risk that complete coordination may weaken the SGP.
- In the case of formal coordination, both the backward-inducting and the Nash equilibrium imply pressure on the ECB and the complete smoothing of shocks. This result contradicts the common wisdom that policy coordination comprising both fiscal and monetary authorities would imply a lot of pressure on the ECB, while formal fiscal coordination alone would not.

Negative coordination is somewhat simpler, and the rules of the game are decided once and for all, therefore it is easier to apply. For these reasons it has probably been chosen to ensure limited liability of the ECB in a strategic context which was not (and probably still isn't) completely understood. The simulations underline both the importance of negative coordination and the danger that an excessive positive coordination could make it ineffective; as can be seen, the SGP is effective in reducing the involvement of the ECB, *unless* the fiscal decisions are formally coordinated.

The present limits stated in the SGP seem somewhat inflexible; to the extent that the SGP is designed to limit the liability of the ECB, it should be also designed according to the preferences of the ECB itself. A simple example showed that more flexibility can be granted in such a way to obtain at the same time more stabilisation and more independence of the Central Bank (figure 7.12).

4.1   Possible extensions

The goal of this chapter was to outline a very specific mechanism that may determine an unforeseen level of pressure on the ECB, along with a wider use of fiscal policy, should stronger fiscal coordination be implemented in the EMU. Many extensions of the model are possible in order to make it more realistic. The first and obvious one would be to allow for different preferences not only on smoothing, but also on the target level of unemployment. Direct externalities of fiscal policy could be also implemented, and their effect would smooth the sceptical conclusions about positive coordination. They have been neglected here for clarity of exposition and because their effect somehow adds up to the one described, without a strong interaction between the two.

Adding structural differences in national markets is probably the most interesting extension. This will be the object of a forthcoming paper, in which these differences are built-in in the form of a third category of players, worker's unions.

Many other extensions have been suggested, but they are better dealt with separately.

Appendix

First order condition for the ECB   By total differentiation of the FOC derived from (7.3), the locus of the optimal response of the ECB is described by:

$$\left(\sum_{i=1}^{N} \lambda_i P_i \right) = -\beta \frac{\frac{\partial u}{\partial m}}{\frac{\partial p}{\partial m}} \left(\sum_{i=1}^{N} \lambda_i U_i \right). \tag{7.6}$$

Given that the ECB is the last player, $\frac{\partial u}{\partial m} / \frac{\partial p}{\partial m}$ is simply $\frac{-u_m}{p_m}$.

First order condition for government G_i   The differentiation of the first order condition

$$(+p_g - \lambda_i(p_m\mu_g))[p_m M(G, \varepsilon, \eta) + p_g G_i + \varepsilon_i]$$
$$= -\alpha(\lambda_i(u_m\mu_g) - u_g)(-u_m M(G, \varepsilon, \eta) - u_g G_i + \eta_i)$$

for each of the governments leads to:

$$P_i = -\alpha \frac{\frac{\partial u_i}{\partial g_i}}{\frac{\partial p_i}{\partial g_i}} U_i. \tag{7.7}$$

From the definitions of P, U and $M(\cdot)$, and using backward induction:

$$\frac{\partial p_i}{\partial g_i} = \frac{\partial}{\partial g_i}(p_m M(G, \varepsilon, \eta) + p_g G_i + \varepsilon_i) = +p_g - \lambda_i p_m \mu_g$$

$$\frac{\partial u_i}{\partial g_i} = \frac{\partial}{\partial g_i}(-u_m M(G, \varepsilon, \eta) - u_g G_i + \eta_i) = \lambda_i u_m \mu_g - u_g$$

The symmetric Nash equilibrium

$$G_i = \frac{(\gamma_e \varepsilon_i + \gamma_h \eta_i) + \left(\gamma_e^f \varepsilon_j + \gamma_h^f \eta_j\right) + \gamma_g\left[(\gamma_e \varepsilon_j + \gamma_h \eta_j) + \left(\gamma_e^f \varepsilon_i + \gamma_h^f \eta_i\right)\right]}{1 - \gamma_g^2}$$

$$G_j = \frac{(\gamma_e \varepsilon_j + \gamma_h \eta_j) + \left(\gamma_e^f \varepsilon_i + \gamma_h^f \eta_i\right) + \gamma_g\left[(\gamma_e \varepsilon_i + \gamma_h \eta_i) + \left(\gamma_e^f \varepsilon_j + \gamma_h^f \eta_j\right)\right]}{1 - \gamma_g^2}$$

$$M = M(\lambda_i G_i + \lambda_j G_j, \lambda_i \varepsilon_i + \lambda_j \varepsilon_j, \lambda_i \eta_i + \lambda_j \eta_j)$$

$$= \left(-\frac{1}{1-\gamma_g^2}\left((\lambda_i \gamma_h + \lambda_j \gamma_h^f)\gamma_g + \lambda_i \gamma_h^f + \lambda_j \gamma_h)\mu_g + \mu_h \lambda_j\right)\eta_j$$

$$+ \left(-\frac{1}{1-\gamma_g^2}\left((\lambda_i \gamma_h^f + \lambda_j \gamma_h)\gamma_g + \lambda_i \gamma_h + \lambda_j \gamma_h^f)\mu_g + \mu_h \lambda_i\right)\eta_i$$

$$+ \left(-\frac{1}{1-\gamma_g^2}\left((\lambda_i \gamma_e + \lambda_j \gamma_e^f)\gamma_g + \lambda_j \gamma_e + \lambda_i \gamma_e^f)\mu_g - \mu_e \lambda_j\right)\varepsilon_j$$

$$+ \left(-\frac{1}{1-\gamma_g^2}\left((\lambda_j \gamma_e + \lambda_i \gamma_e^f)\gamma_g + \lambda_i \gamma_e + \lambda_j \gamma_e^f)\mu_g - \mu_e \lambda_i\right)\varepsilon_i.$$

Formal coordination

$$G^T = \tilde{\gamma}_e(\lambda_i \varepsilon_i + \lambda_j \varepsilon_j) + \tilde{\gamma}_h(\lambda_i \eta_i + \lambda_j \eta_j)$$

$$M^T = (-\mu_g \tilde{\gamma}_h + \mu_h)(\lambda_i \eta_i + \lambda_j \eta_j) - (\mu_e + \mu_g \tilde{\gamma}_e)(\lambda_i \varepsilon_i + \lambda_j \varepsilon_j)$$

$$P = p_m M + p_g G + (\lambda_i \varepsilon_i + \lambda_j \varepsilon_j) = 0$$

$$U = -u_m M - u_g G + (\lambda_i \eta_i + \lambda_j \eta_j) = 0$$

$$G_i = \lambda_i G^T$$

$$P_i = -p_g \lambda_j[\tilde{\gamma}_e(\lambda_i \varepsilon_i + \lambda_j \varepsilon_j) + \tilde{\gamma}_h(\lambda_i \eta_i + \lambda_j \eta_j)] + \varepsilon_i - (\lambda_i \varepsilon_i + \lambda_j \varepsilon_j)$$

$$U_i = u_g \lambda_j [\tilde{\gamma}_e(\lambda_i \varepsilon_i + \lambda_j \varepsilon_j) + \tilde{\gamma}_h(\lambda_i \eta_i + \lambda_j \eta_j)] + \eta_i - (\lambda_i \eta_i + \lambda_j \eta_j)$$

$$G_j = \lambda_j G^T$$

$$P_j = -p_g \lambda_i [\tilde{\gamma}_e(\lambda_i \varepsilon_i + \lambda_j \varepsilon_j) + \tilde{\gamma}_h(\lambda_i \eta_i + \lambda_j \eta_j)] + \varepsilon_j - (\lambda_i \varepsilon_i + \lambda_j \varepsilon_j)$$

$$U_j = u_g \lambda_i [\tilde{\gamma}_e(\lambda_i \varepsilon_i + \lambda_j \varepsilon_j) + \tilde{\gamma}_h(\lambda_i \eta_i + \lambda_j \eta_j)] + \eta_j - (\lambda_i \eta_i + \lambda_j \eta_j).$$

5.1   Calculation of some signs

These signs are important in that they allow more complex calculations later.

Some basic identities. The first equation is just a different version of the hypothesis $\frac{p_m}{u_m} > \frac{p_g}{u_g}$; when $z = 0$ the relation holds with equality, when z is positive the hypothesis is true with strict inequality. The other identities are the same seen before.

$$p_m = (1 + z)u_m \frac{p_g}{u_g}$$

$$\mu_g = -\left[\frac{1}{p_m^2 + \beta u_m^2}\right](-\beta u_m u_g - p_g p_m)$$

$$\mu_e = -\left[\frac{1}{p_m^2 + \beta u_m^2}\right](-p_m)$$

$$\mu_h = +\left[\frac{1}{p_m^2 + \beta u_m^2}\right]\beta u_m$$

$$\lambda_j = 1 - \lambda_i.$$

Effect of expenditure on prices. Sign $(-\lambda_i p_m \mu_g + p_g) =$ sign $-p_g \frac{\lambda_i u_g^2 \beta + \lambda_i p_g^2 + 2\lambda_i p_g^2 z + \lambda_i z \beta u_g^2 + \lambda_i p_g^2 z^2 - p_g^2 - 2p_g^2 z - p_g^2 z^2 - \beta u_g^2}{p_g^2 + 2p_g^2 z + p_g^2 z^2 + \beta u_g^2}$.

The numerator of the fraction is $(\beta u_g^2 + p_g^2 + 2p_g^2 z + z\beta u_g^2 + p_g^2 z^2)(\lambda_i - 1)$ always negative. Therefore the coefficient is always positive.

Effect of expenditure on unemployment. Sign $(\lambda_i u_m \mu_g - u_g) =$ sign $-u_g \frac{-\lambda_i u_g^2 \beta - \lambda_i p_g^2 - \lambda_i p_g^2 z + p_g^2 + 2p_g^2 z + p_g^2 z^2 + \beta u_g^2}{p_g^2 + 2p_g^2 z + p_g^2 z^2 + \beta u_g^2}$.

The numerator is equal to $(1 - \lambda_i)(u_g^2 \beta + p_g^2 + p_g^2 z) + p_g^2 z + p_g^2 z^2$ always positive. Therefore the coefficient is negative.

A shock to unemployment less the intervention of the ECB. Sign $(1 - \lambda_i u_m \mu_h) = (1 - \lambda_i)\beta u_g^2 + p_g^2 + 2p_g^2 z + p_g^2 z^2$ is always positive.

A shock to prices less the intervention of the ECB. Sign $(1 - \lambda_i p_m \mu_e) =$ sign $(1 - \lambda_i p_m \mu_e) =$ sign $-\frac{-p_g^2 - 2p_g^2 z - p_g^2 z^2 - \beta u_g^2 + \lambda_i p_g^2 + 2\lambda_i p_g^2 z + \lambda_i p_g^2 z^2}{p_g^2 + 2p_g^2 z + p_g^2 z^2 + \beta u_g^2}$.

The numerator of the fraction is $(p_g^2 + 2p_g^2 z + p_g^2 z^2)(\lambda_i - 1) - \beta u_g^2$ always negative. Therefore the coefficient is always positive.

5.2 Coefficients of government reaction function when the allocation of instruments is indifferent

$$G_i = (\gamma_e \varepsilon_i + \gamma_h \eta_i) + \left(\gamma_e^f \varepsilon_j + \gamma_h^f \eta_j\right) + \gamma_g G_j.$$

Sign of the coefficient of η_i. The parameter is always positive:
Sign $(-\lambda_i p_m \mu_h)(-\lambda_i p_m \mu_g + p_g) - \alpha(\lambda_i u_m \mu_g - u_g)(1 - \lambda_i u_m \mu_h) =$ sign
$-(-\lambda_i p_g^2 \beta + p_g^2 \alpha - \alpha \lambda_i u_g^2 \beta + \alpha \beta u_g^2)(-1 + \lambda_i)\frac{u_g}{p_g^2 + \beta u_g^2}$. Knowing that
$(-\lambda_i p_g^2 \beta + p_g^2 \alpha - \alpha \lambda_i u_g^2 \beta + \alpha \beta u_g^2) = (1 - \lambda_i)\alpha \beta u_g^2 + p_g^2(\alpha - \lambda_i \beta) > 0$ is
true, the whole parameter is positive.

Sign of the coefficient of η_j. The parameter is always negative:
$(-\lambda_j p_m \mu_h)(-\lambda_i p_m \mu_g + p_g) - \alpha(\lambda_i u_m \mu_g - u_g)(-\lambda_j u_m \mu_h) = (p_g^2 + \alpha u_g^2)$
$(\lambda_i - 1)\beta u_g \frac{\lambda_j}{p_g^2 + \beta u_g^2} < 0$ always.

Sign of the coefficient of ε_i. The sign of the coefficient of ε_i depends on the
size of the expected reaction of the ECB to the shock ε_i, that is on λ_i. When
the size of the country is small enough the sign is negative:
Sign $-[(1 - \lambda_i p_m \mu_e)(-\lambda_i p_m \mu_g + p_g) - \alpha(\lambda_i u_m \mu_g - u_g)(-\lambda_i u_m \mu_e)] =$
sign $-(-p_g^2 - \beta u_g^2 + \lambda_i p_g^2 + \alpha \lambda_i u_g^2)(-1 + \lambda_i)\frac{p_g}{p_g^2 + \beta u_g^2} =$
sign $(-p_g^2 - \beta u_g^2 + \lambda_i p_g^2 + \alpha \lambda_i u_g^2) = (p_g^2 + \alpha u_g^2)\lambda_i - (p_g^2 + \beta u_g^2)$ negative
when λ_i is small enough (unless λ_i is very close to one).

Sign of the coefficient of ε_j. The parameter is always positive:
$-[(-\lambda_j p_m \mu_e)(-\lambda_i p_m \mu_g + p_g) - \alpha(\lambda_i u_m \mu_g - u_g)(-\lambda_j u_m \mu_e)] =$
$-(p_g^2 + \alpha u_g^2)(\lambda_i - 1)p_g \frac{\lambda_j}{p_g^2 + \beta u_g^2} > 0$ always positive.

Sign of the coefficient of G_j. The parameter is always positive:
Sign $+[(p_m \mu_g \lambda_j)(-\lambda_i p_m \mu_g + p_g) + \alpha(\lambda_i u_m \mu_g - u_g)(-u_m \mu_g \lambda_j)] =$
$-(p_g^2 + \alpha u_g^2)(\lambda_i - 1)\lambda_j > 0$ always positive.

The coefficient of G_j is less than one if $z > 0$. The coefficient of G_j is less than
one if and only if the expression below is negative:

$$[(p_m \mu_g \lambda_j)(-\lambda_i p_m \mu_g + p_g) + \alpha(\lambda_i u_m \mu_g - u_g)(-u_m \mu_g \lambda_j)]$$
$$- \left((\lambda_i u_m \mu_g - u_g)^2 \alpha + (-\lambda_i p_m \mu_g + p_g)^2\right).$$

The λs sum to one, so the expression can be rewritten as

$$(-(\lambda_i u_m \mu_g - u_g)(u_m \mu_g - u_g))\alpha + (-\lambda_i p_m \mu_g + p_g)(p_m \mu_g - p_g)$$

or

$$\left(\lambda_i \beta u_g^2 + \lambda_i p_g^2 + \lambda_i z p_g^2 - p_g^2 - 2z p_g^2 - z^2 p_g^2 - \beta u_g^2\right)$$
$$= z p_g^2 (1 + z) \frac{\alpha u_g^2 + p_g^2}{\left(p_g^2 + 2z p_g^2 + z^2 p_g^2 + \beta u_g^2\right)^2}.$$

When the zeta is zero (the condition on instruments holds only with equality) the whole expression is zero and the coefficient is exactly one. No Nash equilibrium exists.

When zeta is positive, then the relevant term for the sign is

$$\left(\lambda_i \beta u_g^2 + \lambda_i p_g^2 + \lambda_i z p_g^2 - p_g^2 - 2z p_g^2 - z^2 p_g^2 - \beta u_g^2\right)$$
$$= -z^2 p_g^2 + \left(-2p_g^2 + \lambda_i p_g^2\right) z + \left(\beta u_g^2 + p_g^2\right)(\lambda_i - 1).$$

This part has a negative sign, therefore the coefficient is strictly less than one, and the Nash equilibrium exists in the case of positive informal cooperation.

5.3   *Positive formal coordination weakens the SGP*

This appendix shows that negative coordination (upper bounds to fiscal expansion, as in the SGP) becomes less effective if coupled with formal positive coordination.

Suppose the union-wide limit to the deficit is $\bar{G}$, and call the actual deficits G_i and G_j. The density function of (G_i, G_j) is $f(G_i, G_j)$.

In absence of formal cooperation (no cooperation or simple exchange of information) the limit binds every country separately, therefore the national caps are $(\lambda_i \bar{G}, \lambda_j \bar{G})$. The restriction imputable to the operation of the SGP is $\left(G_i - \lambda_i \bar{G}\right)$ if $G_i > \lambda_i \bar{G}$ $\left(G_j - \lambda_j \bar{G}\right)$ if $G_j > \lambda_j \bar{G}$.

When there is formal coordination, the pact only controls the overall quantity G^T. This can be seen by observing that in formal coordination $G_i = \lambda_i G^T$ and $G_j = \lambda_j G^T$ always, therefore when $G^T \leq \bar{G}$ it is also verified that $G_i \leq \lambda_i \bar{G}$ and $G_j \leq \lambda_j \bar{G}$.

The restriction imputable to the operation of the SGP is then $\left(G_i + G_j - \bar{G}\right)$ if $G_i + G_j \geq \bar{G}$.

The expected value of the restriction of the SGP is a measure of the potential protection that the ECB can receive from the constraints of the Pact. This value is lower when formal coordination is put into place.

To show this, the space (G_i, G_j) is partitioned in

$$C = \{(G_i, G_j) : G_i + G_j \leq \bar{G}\},$$
$$A = \{(G_i, G_j) : G_i > \lambda_i \bar{G}\},$$
$$B = \{(G_i, G_j) : G_j > \lambda_j \bar{G}\}$$
$$D = A \setminus C$$
$$E = C \setminus B$$
$$F = A \cup B$$
$$G = C \setminus A$$
$$H = B \setminus C$$

Then the expected value of the restriction imposed by the Pact is

$$E_{No}(G_i + G_j - \bar{G}) = \int_{D \cup E \cup F} (G_i - \lambda_i \bar{G}) \cdot f() dG_i dG_j$$

$$+ \int_{F \cup G \cup H} (G_j - \lambda_j \bar{G}) \cdot f() dG_i dG_j$$

$$E_{Formal}(G_i + G_j - \bar{G}) = \int_{E \cup F \cup G} (G_i + G_j - \bar{G}) \cdot f() dG_i dG_j$$

$$= \int_{E \cup F \cup G} [(G_i - \lambda_i \bar{G}) + (G_j - \lambda_j \bar{G})] \cdot f() dG_i dG_j$$

$$E_{No} - E_{Formal} = \int_D (G_i - \lambda_i \bar{G}) \cdot f() dG_i dG_j + \int_H (G_j - \lambda_j \bar{G}) \cdot f() dG_i dG_j$$

$$- \int_E (G_j - \lambda_j \bar{G}) \cdot f() dG_i dG_j - \int_G (G_i - \lambda_i \bar{G}) \cdot f() dG_i dG_j.$$

All integrals in the last expression are positive, excepted those defined over E and G and the one defined over F, which is zero. Then the sum is always positive.

REFERENCES

Bayoumi, T. and B. Eichengreen, 1993, 'Shocking Aspects of European Monetary Union', in F. Torres and F. Giavazzi (eds.), *Adjustment and Growth in the European Monetary Union*, Cambridge: Cambridge University Press, pp. 193–229.

Beetsma, R. and L. Bovenberg, 1995, 'Monetary Union with Fiscal Coordination May Discipline Policymakers', Discussion Paper, CentER, Tilburg University.

Bosca, J. E. and V. Orts, 1991, 'La coordinacion de politicas fiscales en el marco de una Union Economica y Monetaria', Working Paper no. EC 90–06, Instituto Valenciano de Investigaciones economicas, Valencia.

Buiter, W., G. Corsetti and N. Roubini, 1993, 'Excessive Deficits: Sense and Nonsense in the Treaty of Maastricht', *Economic Policy* 16, 57–100.

Commission of the European Communities, 1991, 'The Economics of EMU,' *European Economy*, Special Issue no. 1.

Diaz-Roldan, C., 2000, 'Coordination of Fiscal Policies in a Monetary Union', Working Paper no. 2000/03, Department of Economics, Universidad Publica de Navarra, Pamplona.

Dixit, A. and L. Lambertini, 2000, 'Fiscal Discretion Destroys Monetary Commitment', working paper, UCLA.

Eichengreen, B., 1997, 'Saving Europe's Automatic Stabiliser', *National Institute Economic Review* 159 (January), 92–8.

Gatti, D. and C. Van Wijnbergen, 2002, 'Co-ordinating Fiscal Authorities in the Eurozone. A Key Role for the ECB', *Oxford Economic Papers* 54, 56–71.

Maastricht Treaty, 1991, Treaty on Economic and Monetary Union, Luxembourg: Office for Official Publications of the European Communities.

Oates, W., 1972, *Fiscal Federalism*, New York: Harcourt Brace Jovanovich.

Pisani-Ferry, J., 1991, 'Maintaining a Coherent Macro-economic Policy in a Highly Decentralised Federal State: The Experience of the EC', Paper presented at the OECD Seminar on Fiscal Federalism in Economies in Transition, 2–3 April 1991.

Tanzi, V., 1996, 'Fiscal Federalism and Decentralisation: A Review of Some Efficiency and Macroeconomic Aspects', in *Annual World Bank Conference on Development Economics, 1995*, Washington, DC: World Bank, pp. 295–316.

Van Aarle B. and F. Huart, 1997, 'Monetary and Fiscal Unification in the EU: A Stylized Analysis', Working Paper no. 149, Centre for Economic Studies, University of Munich.

von Hagen, J. and B. Eichengreen, 1996, 'Fiscal Restraints, Federalism and European Monetary Union: Is the Excessive Deficit Procedure Counterproductive?', *American Economic Review* 86, 134–8.

Walsh, C., 1992, 'Fiscal Federalism: An Overview of Issues and a Discussion of Their Relevance to the European Community', Federalism Research Centre Discussion Paper no. 12, ANU.

8   The macroeconomic impact of different speeds of debt stabilisation in EMU

Campbell Leith and Simon Wren-Lewis

The potential importance of fiscal policy in influencing inflation has recently been highlighted, following Woodford (1998); under the heading of the 'Fiscal Theory of the Price Level' (FTPL). The Fiscal Theory has also been extended to consider the case of independent fiscal authorities operating under a common monetary authority (see Woodford 1998; Dupor 2000; Bergin 2000; Sims 1997).

The fiscal theory essentially characterises two regimes – one where the fiscal authorities act prudently, government debt does not constitute an element of net wealth and monetary policy is free to target inflation, and another, where fiscal insolvency requires surprise inflation to deflate the nominal value of government debt. In Leith and Wren-Lewis (2001) we relax a number of assumptions underlying the Fiscal Theory of the price level by considering a two-country model in continuous time with overlapping generations of consumers supplying labour to imperfectly competitive firms which can only adjust their prices infrequently. Policy is described by simple linear feedback rules. We find that there are two stable policy regimes similar to those in the Fiscal Theory: one where the government follows a rule which stabilises its debt and monetary policy is 'active' in the sense of Leeper (1991) and another where an imprudent government requires monetary policy to be 'passive'. However, unlike the Fiscal Theory, both monetary and fiscal policy affect inflation in both regimes. We also obtain the result that it is theoretically possible for one fiscal authority to partially compensate for some degree of lax fiscal policy on the part of another monetary union member, without implying an indefinite transfer of wealth from the citizens of that economy to the other.[1]

In this chapter we extend this work by developing a two-country open economy model in discrete time, where again each country has overlapping generations of non-Ricardian consumers who supply labour to imperfectly

We would like to thank Hubert Kempf, Massimiliano Rigon and Luca Sala for helpful comments on an earlier version. Campbell Leith would like to thank MURST (contract No. 9913572993/003) for financial support during the preliminary work on this chapter, which was then completed with the financial support of the ESRC (Grant No.L138251050), for which we are also grateful.
[1] The possibility that governments may borrow indefinitely from each other, which is explored in the literature, is discussed below.

191

competitive firms which can only change their prices infrequently. We examine the case where the two countries have formed a monetary union, but where the fiscal authorities remain independent. We allow for a richer menu of monetary and fiscal policy interaction by dropping the assumption of lump sum taxation and allowing the fiscal authorities to vary both tax rates (which are distortionary) and government spending (which feeds directly into aggregate demand). We restrict ourselves to considering only the policy regime in which the fiscal authorities act to stabilise their own debt, and where monetary policy is active, as this appears to characterise EMU under the Stability and Growth Pact. We then examine, through a series of policy simulations, how asymmetries in the fiscal policy responses to debt disequilibrium can affect the European Central Bank's ability to control inflation. We assume that each fiscal authority stabilises its own debt sufficiently to allow an active monetary policy regime, but ask what is the appropriate speed of debt stabilisation, and whether stabilisation that is too slow or too fast in one country will significantly influence the other.

The structure of the chapter is as follows. Section 1 outlines the model and section 2 examines the steady state of the model and linearises the non-linear model around this steady state. Section 3 then calibrates the model, before assessing the implications of (1) varying the speed of fiscal adjustment to debt disequilibrium, (2) asymmetric responses in fiscal policy to disequilibrium in the debt levels of the independent fiscal authorities and (3) asymmetries in the extent of nominal inertia across EU member states in the face of various symmetric and asymmetric shocks. Section 4 concludes.

1   The model

Our model consists of two countries operating under a monetary union, where a single monetary authority targets average consumer price inflation across the union, but each country's fiscal authorities are free to pursue independent fiscal policies. Within each country, overlapping generations of consumers supply labour to imperfectly competitive firms. Consumers in each country do not expect to live for ever, and there are no bequests in the model, so the conditions underpinning pure Ricardian equivalence do not hold. As a result the government's liabilities (consisting of money and bonds) constitute an element of net wealth and will, therefore, affect the real interest rate observed in the model. We also assume that the imperfectly competitive firms in each economy can only reset prices at random intervals, as under Calvo (1983) contracting. The combination of non-Ricardian consumers and nominal inertia implies that monetary and fiscal policies interact and that both can have real effects on the economy. We now proceed to outline the model in more detail, considering first the problem facing individual consumers, before aggregating across all consumers. We then turn to the pricing/output decisions of our representative firm before detailing the linearisation of the model required to render it suitable for numerical simulation.

1.1   The consumer's problem

The utility of a typical home consumer, i, is increased through consumption of a basket of consumption goods, c_s^i, holding real money balances, $\frac{M_s^i}{P_s}$, and suffers disutility from providing labour services, N_s^i. Consumers also face a constant probability of death $(1 - \gamma)$, which allows us to write the consumer's certainty equivalent utility function as,

$$E_t U_t^i = \sum_{s=0}^{\infty} (\gamma\beta)^s \left[\ln\left(c_s^i\right) + \chi \ln\left(\frac{M_s^i}{P_s}\right) - \frac{\kappa}{2}\left(N_s^i\right)^2 \right]. \tag{8.1}$$

This specification of utility is identical to that found in Obsfeldt and Rogoff (1995). The basket of consumption goods is defined by the following CES index applied across home and foreign goods,

$$c_s^i = \left[\int_0^1 c_s^i(z)^{\frac{\theta-1}{\theta}} dz \right]^{\frac{\theta}{\theta-1}}. \tag{8.2}$$

Similarly, the consumer price index is given by,

$$P_s = \left[\int_0^1 p(z)^{1-\theta} dz \right]^{\frac{1}{1-\theta}}. \tag{8.3}$$

Since there are assumed to be no impediments to trade, the law of one price holds for each individual good, so that the home price index can be re-written as

$$P_s = \left[\int_0^n p_s(z)^{1-\theta} dz + \int_n^1 (\bar{\varepsilon} p_s^*(z))^{1-\theta} dz \right]^{\frac{1}{1-\theta}}, \tag{8.4}$$

where $p(z)$ is the home currency price of good z, $p^*(z)$ is the foreign currency price of good z and $\bar{\varepsilon}$ is the nominal exchange rate, which is fixed under monetary union.

The consumer can hold her financial wealth in the form of domestic government bonds, D, foreign bonds, F, and money balances, M. Since there is a common monetary policy, domestic and foreign bonds earn the same nominal return, i_t, and domestic consumers receive a share in the profits of domestic firms. It is assumed that the consumer receives a premium from perfectly competitive insurance companies in return for their financial assets should they die.

This effectively raises the rate of return from holding financial assets by $\frac{1}{\gamma}$. The consumer also receives labour income of $W_t N_t^i$ and a share of the profits from all the imperfectly competitive firms in the economy, π_t.[2] The consumer's labour and profit income is taxed at a rate τ_t. Therefore, the consumer's budget constraint, in nominal terms, is given by

$$D_t^i = \frac{(1 + i_{t-1})}{\gamma} D_{t-1} + \frac{M_{t-1}^i}{\gamma} - M_t^i + (1 - \tau_t)\left(W_t N_t^i + \pi_t\right)$$

$$- c_t^i P_t - \bar{\varepsilon} F_t^i + \bar{\varepsilon} F_{t-1}^i \frac{(1 + i_{t-1})}{\gamma}. \tag{8.5}$$

Deflating the flow constraint by P_t

$$\frac{D_t^i}{P_t} = \frac{(1 + r_{t-1})}{\gamma}\left(1 - \phi + \phi \frac{P_t^e}{P_t}\right)\frac{D_{t-1}^i}{P_{t-1}} + \frac{M_{t-1}^i}{P_{t-1}\gamma}\frac{P_{t-1}}{P_t} - \frac{M_t^i}{P_t}$$

$$+ (1 - \tau_t)\left(\frac{W_t}{P_t} N_t^i + \frac{\pi_t}{P_t}\right) - c_t^i - \frac{\bar{\varepsilon} F_t^i}{P_t}$$

$$+ \frac{\bar{\varepsilon} F_{t-1}^i}{P_{t-1}}\frac{(1 + r_{t-1})}{\gamma}\left(1 - \phi^* + \phi^* \frac{P_t^e}{P_t}\right), \tag{8.6}$$

where r_t is the ex-ante real interest rate. The parameters ϕ and ϕ^* measure the proportion of domestic and foreign bonds, respectively, which are nominal. Therefore, when $\phi = \phi^* = 0$ all financial wealth is fully indexed such that the ex-post real interest rate enjoyed by holders of the financial asset is equivalent to the ex-ante real interest rate they expected. When $\phi = \phi^* = 1$ all debt is nominal and surprise inflation can erode the real value of nominal financial wealth by decreasing the ex-post real interest rate relative to the ex-ante rate as under the FTPL. In our policy simulations we shall assume that the economy was initially in steady state before an unanticipated shock moved the economy away from this steady state. We shall then track the response of the economy to this shock under different descriptions of monetary and fiscal policy. As a result, when the shock hits the economy it is possible for ex-ante real rates to differ from ex-post real rates. However, for the remainder of the simulation, owing to the pooling of risks due to finite lives and stochastic price setting, the economy behaves as if it is operating under perfect foresight. Therefore we can drop the distinction between ex-ante and ex-post real rates in periods other than the initial period, t, in which the shock hits. The consumer then has to

---

[2] By assuming that all consumers enjoy profits from all the firms in the economy this effectively pools the risk due to stochastic price setting, so that firms can ignore the risk aversion of consumers and will simply discount their profits at the risk free rate of interest.

maximise utility, (8.1), subject to her budget constraint, (8.5), along with the usual solvency conditions. The various first order conditions this implies are given below.

Firstly, there is the usual consumption Euler equation

$$c_{t+1}^i = \beta(1 + r_t)c_t^i. \tag{8.7}$$

The optimisation also yields a money demand equation

$$\frac{M_t^i}{P_t} = \chi c_t^i \frac{(1 + i_t)}{i_t}, \tag{8.8}$$

where the demand for money balances is increasing in the level of consumption, but decreasing in the nominal interest rate, which represents the opportunity costs of holding financial wealth in the form of money rather than bonds. The individual's optimal labour supply decision will satisfy

$$N_t^i = (1 - \tau_t)\frac{W_t}{P_t}\frac{1}{c_t^i \kappa} \tag{8.9}$$

such that it is increasing in real wages, but decreasing in consumption as workers attempt to substitute leisure for consumption.

Utilising the money demand equation (8.8), defining the consumer's portfolio of real financial assets as, $a_t^i = \frac{D_t^i}{P_t} + \frac{M_t^i}{P_t} + \frac{\tilde{\epsilon} F_t^i}{P_t}$, and iterating the flow budget constraint (8.6) forward allows us to write the consumer's intertemporal budget constraint as

$$\frac{(1 + r_{t-1})}{\gamma}\left(1 - \phi + \phi\frac{P_t^e}{P_t}\right)a_{t-1}^i = -(1 - \tau_t)\left(\frac{W_t}{P_t}N_t^i + \frac{\pi_t}{P_t}\right)$$

$$- \sum_{s=1}^{\infty} \frac{\gamma^s(1 - \tau_{t+s})\left(\frac{W_{t+s}}{P_{t+s}}N_{t+s}^i + \frac{\pi_{t+s}}{P_{t+s}}\right)}{\prod_{j=1}^{s}(1 + r_{t+j-1})}$$

$$+ (1 + \chi)c_t^i + \sum_{s=1}^{\infty} \frac{\gamma^s(1 + \chi)c_{t+s}^i}{\prod_{j=1}^{s}(1 + r_{t+j-1})}$$

$$+ \frac{1}{\gamma}\frac{M_{t-1}^i}{P_{t-1}}\left(\frac{P_{t-1}}{P_t}i_{t-1}\right). \tag{8.10}$$

Similarly, integrating the consumption Euler equation forward and substituting into the intertemporal budget constraint gives the consumer's consumption function

$$c_t^i = \frac{1 - \gamma\beta}{1 + \chi}$$

$$\times \begin{pmatrix} (1 - \tau_t)\left(\frac{W_t}{P_t}N_t^i + \frac{\pi_t}{P_t}\right) + \sum_{s=1}^{\infty} \frac{\gamma^s(1 - \tau_{t+s})\left(\frac{W_{t+s}}{P_{t+s}}N_{t+s}^i + \frac{\pi_{t+s}}{P_{t+s}}\right)}{\prod_{j=1}^{s}(1 + r_{t+j-1})} \\ + \frac{(1 + r_{t-1})}{\gamma}\left(1 - \phi + \phi\frac{P_t^e}{P_t}\right)a_{t-1}^i - \frac{1}{\gamma}\frac{M_{t-1}^i}{P_{t-1}}\left(\frac{P_{t-1}}{P_t}i_{t-1}\right) \end{pmatrix}.$$

$$(8.11)$$

1.1.1   Aggregating across individual consumers   By assuming that each cohort is of size 1 when born, a cohort of age s will have a size γ^s. Therefore the total size of the population is $\sum_{s=0}^{\infty} \gamma^s = \frac{1}{1-\gamma}$. We will also assume that the probability of death and initial cohort size are identical across the two countries. As a result, by examining average per capita values of variables we can still compare aggregate levels of variables across countries. Therefore the relationship between aggregate per capita labour supply and consumption in all cohorts[3] is given as,

$$N_t = (1 - \gamma)\sum_{i=0}^{\infty} \gamma^i (1 - \tau_t)\frac{W_t}{P_t}\frac{1}{c_t^i \kappa} \tag{8.12}$$

While the money demand equation is given by,

$$\frac{M_t}{P_t} = \chi c_t \frac{(1 + i_t)}{i_t} \tag{8.13}$$

The aggregate (per capita) consumption equation is,

$$c_t = \frac{1 - \gamma\beta}{1 + \chi}\begin{pmatrix} y_t(1 - \tau_t) + \sum_{s=1}^{\infty} \frac{\gamma^s y_{t+s}(1 - \tau_{t+s})}{\prod_{j=1}^{s}(1 + r_{t+j-1})} \\ + (1 + r_{t-1})\left(1 - \phi + \phi\frac{P_t^e}{P_t}\right)a_{t-1} - \frac{M_{t-1}}{P_{t-1}}\left(\frac{P_{t-1}}{P_t}i_{t-1}\right) \end{pmatrix}$$

$$(8.14)$$

---

[3] Here the non-linear nature of the labour supply decisions does not permit us to define aggregate labour supply purely in terms of other aggregate variables. However, upon log-linearisation full aggregation will be possible.

where we have used the national accounting identity to replace wage and profit income with output, y_t. Notice that future labour and profit income is discounted at an interest rate which is marked up by a factor which reflects the probability of death. This mark-up is critical in overturning the results of the standard Ricardian experiment of deficit financed tax cuts in our model. Consumers discount the future tax increases that a tax cut-induced deficit implies more heavily than the deficit accumulates interest. As a result a tax cut increases discounted human wealth and thereby, ceteris paribus, increases consumption.

In the foreign country there will be corresponding equations for labour supply,

$$N_t^* = (1 - \gamma) \sum_{i=0}^{\infty} c_t^{i*} \gamma^i \left((1 - \tau_t^*) \frac{W_t^*}{P_t^*} \frac{1}{c_t^{i*} \kappa} \right)^{\frac{1}{\mu - 1}}, \qquad (8.15)$$

money demand,

$$\frac{M_t^*}{P_t^*} = \chi c_t^* \frac{(1 + i_t^*)}{i_t^*} \qquad (8.16)$$

and consumption,

$$c_t^* = \frac{1 - \gamma \beta}{1 + \chi} \left(\begin{array}{l} (1 - \tau_t^*) \left(\frac{W_t^*}{P_t^*} N_t^* + \frac{\pi_t^*}{P_t^*} \right) + \sum_{s=1}^{\infty} \frac{\gamma^s (1 - \tau_t^*) \left(\frac{W_{t+s}^*}{P_{t+s}^*} N_{t+s}^* + \frac{\pi_{t+s}^*}{P_{t+s}^*} \right)}{\prod_{j=1}^{s} (1 + r_{t+j-1}^*)} \\ + (1 + r_{t-1}^*) \left(1 - \phi^* + \phi^* \frac{P_t^{*e}}{P_t^*} \right) a_{t-1}^* - \frac{M_{t-1}^*}{P_{t-1}^*} \left(\frac{P_{t-1}^*}{P_t^*} i_{t-1}^* \right) \end{array} \right), \qquad (8.17)$$

where $a_{t-1}^* = \dfrac{D_{t-1}^* + \frac{F_{t-1}^*}{\bar{\varepsilon}} + M_{t-1}^*}{P_{t-1}^*}$.

1.2   The firm's problem

We now turn the problem facing the firm. As consumers are able to pool the risks associated with asymmetric price setting on the part of individual firms, the representative firm's objective is to maximise the discounted value of its profits using the risk-free interest rate. Therefore we define the real profits of the home firm, producing good z, as

$$\frac{\pi(z)_t}{P_t} = \frac{p(z)_t}{P_t} y(z)_t - \frac{W_t}{P_t} N(z)_t. \qquad (8.18)$$

In the absence of capital and without any constraints on price setting the firm would simply maximise profits in each period in a static manner. However, we assume that firms are subject to the constraints implied by Calvo contracts, i.e. in each period only a proportion of firms $(1 - \alpha)$ are able to change prices and each firm does not know if it will be part of that group. As a result there is an intertemporal dimension to the firm's pricing/output decision. Suppose the firm is able to change its price this period, then its objective function for determining that optimal price is given by,

$$
V(z)_t = \frac{p(z)_t}{P_t} y(z)_t - \frac{W_t}{P_t} N(z)_t + \sum_{s=1}^{\infty} \alpha^s \frac{\dfrac{p(z)_{t+s}}{P_{t+s}} y(z)_{t+s} - \dfrac{W_{t+s}}{P_{t+s}} N(z)_{t+s}}{\displaystyle\prod_{j=1}^{s} (1 + r_{t+j-1})}.
$$

(8.19)

For simplicity it is assumed that the firm's production technology is linear, $y(z)_t = N(z)_t$. The CES form of the utility function implies that the ith home consumer's demand for product z is given by

$$
c(z)_t^i = \left(\frac{p(z)_t}{P_t} \right)^{-\theta} c_t^i
$$

(8.20)

while the ith foreign consumer will demand

$$
c(z)_t^{*i} = \left(\frac{p(z)_t}{\bar{\varepsilon} P_t^*} \right)^{-\theta} c_t^{*i}.
$$

(8.21)

Integrating demands across consumers, noting that PPP holds for the aggregate consumer price levels and assuming that the home government allocates its spending in the same pattern as home consumers implies that world demand for product z is given by,

$$
y(z)_t = \left(\frac{p(z)_t}{P_t} \right)^{-\theta} (c_t + g_t + c_t^* + g_t^*),
$$

(8.22)

where $y(z)$, c, c^*, g, and g^* are defined as real per capita variables. The firm's (per capita) demand for labour will be equivalent to equation (8.22).

Utilising the home and foreign demands for product z allows us to rewrite the firm's objective function as

$$
\begin{aligned}
V(z)_t = {} & \left(\frac{p(z)_t}{P_t} \right)^{-\theta} \left(\frac{p(z)_t}{P_t} - \frac{W_t}{P_t} \right) (c_t + g_t + c_t^* + g_t^*) \\
& + \sum_{s=1}^{\infty} \alpha^s \frac{\left(\dfrac{p(z)_t}{P_{t+s}} \right)^{-\theta} \left(\dfrac{p(z)_t}{P_{t+s}} - \dfrac{W_{t+s}}{P_{t+s}} \right) (c_{t+s} + g_{t+s} + c_{t+s}^* + g_{t+s}^*)}{\displaystyle\prod_{j=1}^{s} (1 + r_{t+j-1})}.
\end{aligned}
$$

(8.23)

The optimal price implied by the maximisation of this objective function is therefore given by,

$$
p(z)_t = \frac{\left[\begin{array}{l} \left(\theta\left(\frac{1}{P_t}\right)^{1-\theta} W_t\right)(c_t + g_t + c_t^* + g_t^*) \\[2mm] + \displaystyle\sum_{s=1}^{\infty} \alpha^s \frac{\left(\theta\left(\frac{1}{P_{t+s}}\right)^{1-\theta} W_{t+s}\right)(c_{t+s}+g_{t+s}+c_{t+s}^*+g_{t+s}^*)}{\displaystyle\prod_{j=1}^{s}(1+r_{t+j-1})} \end{array}\right]}{\left[\begin{array}{l} \displaystyle\sum_{s=1}^{\infty} \alpha^s \frac{\left((\theta-1)\left(\frac{1}{P_{t+s}}\right)^{1-\theta}\right)(c_{t+s}+g_{t+s}+c_{t+s}^*+g_{t+s}^*)}{\displaystyle\prod_{j=1}^{s}(1+r_{t+j-1})} \\[2mm] + \left((\theta-1)\left(\frac{1}{P_t}\right)^{1-\theta}\right)(c_t + g_t + c_t^* + g_t^*) \end{array}\right]} .
\tag{8.24}
$$

The pricing behaviour implied by this optimisation will give rise to an open economy version of the standard new Keynesian Phillips curve (see Goodfriend and King 1997 for a discussion) following linearisation (see below).

1.2.1 Aggregating across firms The home output price index, $p(h)$ is defined as

$$
p(h)_t = \left[\alpha p(h)_{t-1}^{1-\theta} + (1-\alpha)\tilde{p}_t^{1-\theta}\right]^{\frac{1}{1-\theta}} ,
\tag{8.25}
$$

where $\tilde{p}_t$ is the price set in accordance with equation (8.24) by those home producers that were able to change prices in that period, while average home output (relative to home population) is given by

$$
y(h)_t = \left(\frac{p(h)_t}{P_t}\right)^{-\theta}(c_t + g_t) + \left(\frac{p(h)_t}{\bar{\varepsilon} P_t^*}\right)^{-\theta}(c_t^* + g_t^*)
\tag{8.26}
$$

and the aggregate consumer price level is given by

$$
P_t = \left[n\left(\alpha p(h)_{t-1}^{1-\theta} + (1-\alpha)\tilde{p}_t^{1-\theta}\right) \right.
$$
$$
\left. + (1-n)(\bar{\varepsilon})^{1-\theta}\left(\alpha p(f)_{t-1}^{1-\theta} + (1-\alpha)\tilde{p}_t^{*1-\theta}\right)\right]^{\frac{1}{1-\theta}} .
\tag{8.27}
$$

Given the linear production technology, per capita demand for labour is obtained by summing across the n home firms,

$$
N_t = n\left(\frac{p(h)_t}{P_t}\right)^{-\theta}(c_t + g_t) + n\left(\frac{p(h)_t}{\bar{\varepsilon} P_t^*}\right)^{-\theta}(c_t^* + g_t^*).
\tag{8.28}
$$

1.3   The government

Finally, we consider the governments of both economies. The home government's budget constraint, in nominal terms, is given by

$$
D_t + F_t^* = (1 + i_{t-1})(D_{t-1} + F_{t-1}^*) + M_{t-1} - M_t + G_t - \tau_t Y_t,
\tag{8.29}
$$

that is domestic government bonds are held either by home consumers (D_t) or by foreign consumers (F_t^*). The government finances spending by issuing money and taxing home output at the rate τ_t.

The corresponding foreign government's budget constraint is given by

$$D_t^* + F_t = (1 + i_{t-1})(D_{t-1}^* + F_{t-1}) + M_{t-1}^*$$
$$-M_t^* + G_t^* - \tau_t^* Y_t^*, \tag{8.30}$$

where the interest paid on this debt may or may not be indexed to inflation. We shall discuss the formulation of both monetary and fiscal policy below.

1.4   Global market clearing conditions

In our two-country model there are also global market clearing conditions for the goods and asset markets. In the goods market it implies the following condition

$$\frac{p(h)_t}{P_t} y_t + \frac{p(f)_t}{P_t^*} y_t^* = c_t + g_t + c_t^* + g_t^*, \tag{8.31}$$

while equilibrium in the asset market implies that the sum of private financial assets in the two economies equals the sum of public liabilities,

$$a_t + a_t^* = l_t + l_t^*. \tag{8.32}$$

In both cases the usual closed economy identities do not hold, as one economy can be a net exporter to the other and can also hold net foreign financial assets.

2   Linearising the model around a symmetric steady state

In order to get the model into a tractable form for conducting policy simulations we need to linearise it (the infinite forward-looking summations implied by the firm's pricing decisions cannot be dealt with in a non-linear framework, even if we undertake numerical simulations). In this section we detail the steady state of our model, before log-linearising the dynamic equations around this steady state.

2.1   The symmetrical steady state of the model

In this section we derive the steady state of our model, as this will be the base around which we log-linearise our model before conducting a number of numerical policy simulations. The optimal price in steady state, which is the same as that which would be set under flexible prices, is given by

$$\bar{p}(h) = \frac{\theta}{\theta - 1} \bar{W} \tag{8.33}$$

As $\theta \to \infty$ the firms in the economy lose market power and tend towards a state of perfect competition. Combining this with the labour supply condition (8.12), the linear production function and the national accounting identity in a symmetrical steady-state, $y = c + g$, yields the following equilibrium output,

$$\bar{y} = \bar{N} = \frac{\bar{g} + \sqrt{\bar{g}^2 + \frac{4(\theta - 1)(1 - \bar{\tau})}{\theta \kappa}}}{2}. \tag{8.34}$$

To highlight the suboptimal level of output arising due to tax distortions and imperfect competition, consider a benevolent social planner who maximises individual utility by choosing c (taking g as given) in the following objective function

$$\ln(c) - \frac{\kappa}{2}(c + g)^2. \tag{8.35}$$

This yields a higher steady-state output level which removes the distortions due to imperfect competition and non-lump-sum taxation,

$$\bar{y}^* = \frac{\bar{g} + \sqrt{\bar{g}^2 + \frac{4}{\kappa}}}{2}. \tag{8.36}$$

If we normalise the fixed nominal exchange rate to one, the steady-state consumption function becomes

$$\bar{c} = \frac{1 - \gamma\beta}{1 + \chi}\left(\bar{y}(1 - \bar{\tau})\left(\frac{1 + \bar{r}}{1 + \bar{r} - \gamma}\right) + (1 + \bar{r})\left(\frac{\bar{D} + \bar{F}}{\bar{P}}\right) + \frac{\bar{M}}{\bar{P}}\right), \tag{8.37}$$

the domestic government's budget constraint in steady-state is

$$\frac{\bar{D} + \bar{F}^*}{\bar{P}} = \frac{\bar{\tau}\bar{y} - \bar{g}}{\bar{r}} \tag{8.38}$$

and money demand is given by

$$\bar{m} = \chi\bar{c}\frac{(1 + \bar{r})}{\bar{r}}. \tag{8.39}$$

Note that in this symmetrical equilibrium, with PPP due to free trade, it will also be the case that the real value of debt held overseas will be the same in both countries, $\frac{\bar{F}^*}{\bar{P}} = \frac{\bar{F}}{\bar{P}}$. This fact, combined with equations (8.34)–(8.39), will determine the steady-state value of real assets in the model, along with the equilibrium real interest rate. Since consumers are not infinitely lived, the real interest rate is not identical to consumers' rate of time preference, but will be affected by the outstanding stock of government liabilities, since these liabilities constitute consumers' net wealth.

2.2   Linearising the model around the steady state

We now proceed to log-linearise the model around this symmetrical steady state. To illustrate this consider the labour supply equation

$$N_t = (1 - \gamma) \sum_{i=0}^{\infty} \gamma^i (1 - \tau_t) \frac{W_t}{P_t} \frac{1}{c_t^i \kappa}. \tag{8.40}$$

Log-differentiation of this expression yields

$$\hat{N}_t = \hat{w}_t - \hat{c}_t - \frac{\bar{\tau}}{1 - \bar{\tau}} \hat{\tau}_t, \tag{8.41}$$

where a hatted variable denotes the percentage deviation from steady state, $\hat{X}_t = \frac{dX_t|_{X=\bar{X}}}{\bar{X}}$. This approach can be applied to all the equations in our model.

Next, consider the expression for the log-linearised optimal price set by a home firm

$$\left(\frac{1 + \bar{r}}{1 + \bar{r} - \alpha} \right) \hat{\tilde{p}}_t = \hat{P}_t + \hat{w}_t + \sum_{s=1}^{\infty} \left(\frac{\alpha}{1 + \bar{r}} \right)^s [\hat{P}_{t+s} + \hat{w}_{t+s}]. \tag{8.42}$$

Substituting for the log-linearised definition of consumer prices, $\hat{P}_t = \frac{1}{2} \hat{p}(h)_t + \frac{1}{2} (\hat{p}(f)_t)$, and quasi-differencing yields

$$\left(\frac{\alpha}{\alpha - \bar{r} - 1} \right) \hat{\tilde{p}}_{t+1} = \left(\frac{1 + \bar{r}}{1 + \bar{r} - \alpha} \right) \hat{\tilde{p}}_t - \frac{1}{2} \hat{P}(h)_t - \frac{1}{2} \hat{p}(f)_t - \hat{w}_t. \tag{8.43}$$

Using the equation governing the evolution of domestic output prices

$$\hat{p}(h)_t = \alpha \hat{p}(h)_{t-1} + (1 - \alpha) \hat{\tilde{p}}_t \tag{8.44}$$

we can rearrange this in terms of newly set prices and substitute back into equation (8.43) to obtain the Phillips curve

$$\hat{\pi}(h)_{t+1} = (1 + \bar{r}) \hat{\pi}(h)_t + \frac{(1 + \bar{r} - \alpha)(1 - \alpha)}{\alpha}$$
$$\times \left(\frac{1}{2} \hat{p}(h)_t - \frac{1}{2} \hat{p}(f)_t - \hat{w}_t \right). \tag{8.45}$$

Substituting the linearised labour supply function into this expression yields

$$\hat{\pi}(h)_{t+1} = (1 + \bar{r}) \hat{\pi}(h)_t + \frac{(1 + \bar{r} - \alpha)(1 - \alpha)}{\alpha}$$
$$\times \left(\frac{1}{2} \hat{p}(h)_t - \frac{1}{2} \hat{p}(f)_t - \hat{c}_t - \hat{y}_t - \frac{\bar{\tau}}{1 - \bar{\tau}} \hat{\tau}_t \right). \tag{8.46}$$

This is the same as the usual New Keynesian Phillips curve, except that there now exists a terms-of-trade effect in addition to the usual aggregate demand effect. There is also a distinction between the inflationary impact of an increase in consumption (which will raise both $\hat{c}_t$ and $\hat{y}_t$, ceteris paribus) and an increase in exports or government spending (which will raise $\hat{y}_t$ alone, ceteris paribus) which is not present in the usual New Keynesian Phillips curve. The reason for this distinction is that workers need to be compensated in the form of higher wages to supply the higher output, but in the case of an increase in consumption workers require additional compensation as they have an increased desire to substitute leisure for consumption. This distinction will turn out to be critical in defining the fiscal policy response required to eliminate the inflationary consequences of debt disequilibrium following a shock. Finally, increasing taxation will be inflationary owing to the detrimental effects this has on labour supply. A similar expression can be derived in terms of foreign output prices:

$$\hat{\pi}(f)_{t+1} = (1 + \bar{r})\hat{\pi}(f)_t + \frac{(1 + \bar{r} - \alpha)(1 - \alpha)}{\alpha}$$

$$\times \left(\frac{1}{2}\hat{p}(f)_t - \frac{1}{2}\hat{p}(h)_t - \hat{c}_t^* - \hat{y}_t^* - \frac{\bar{\tau}^*}{1 - \bar{\tau}^*}\hat{\tau}_t^* \right). \tag{8.47}$$

Now consider the domestic government's flow budget constraint in real terms:

$$l_t = (1 + r_{t-1})\left(1 - \phi + \phi\frac{P_t^e}{P_t}\right)l_{t-1} - \left(1 + r_{t-1} - \frac{P_{t-1}}{P_t}\right)m_{t-1} + g_t - \tau_t y_t, \tag{8.48}$$

where $l_t = \frac{D_t + F_t^* + M_t}{P_t}$. Log-linearising yields

$$\hat{l}_t = (1 + \bar{r})\hat{l}_{t-1} + (1 + \bar{r})\phi(\hat{P}_t^e - \hat{P}_t) + \left(\bar{r} - \frac{\bar{m}}{\bar{l}}\bar{r}\right)\hat{r}_{t-1}$$

$$- \bar{r}\frac{\bar{m}}{\bar{l}}\hat{m}_{t-1} - \frac{\bar{m}}{\bar{l}}(\hat{P}_t - \hat{P}_{t-1}) + \frac{\bar{g}}{\bar{l}}\hat{g}_t - \frac{\bar{\tau}\bar{y}}{\bar{l}}(\hat{y}_t + \hat{\tau}_t) \tag{8.49}$$

and, for the foreign government,

$$\hat{l}_t^* = (1 + \bar{r})\hat{l}_{t-1}^* + (1 + \bar{r})\phi(\hat{P}_t^e - \hat{P}_t) + \left(\bar{r} - \frac{\bar{m}}{\bar{l}}\bar{r}\right)\hat{r}_{t-1}$$

$$- \bar{r}\frac{\bar{m}}{\bar{l}}\hat{m}_{t-1}^* - \frac{\bar{m}}{\bar{l}}(\hat{P}_t^* - \hat{P}_{t-1}^*) + \frac{\bar{g}}{\bar{l}}\hat{g}_t^* - \frac{\bar{\tau}\bar{y}}{\bar{l}}(\hat{y}_t^* + \hat{\tau}_t^*), \tag{8.50}$$

where use was made of the fact that real interest rates (defined as nominal rates relative to consumer price inflation) are the same across all countries under EMU given the free trade in consumer goods.

Now we turn to the consumption function, (8.11), where log-linearisation yields

$$\hat{c}_t = \frac{(1-\nu\beta)}{1+\chi}\left[\frac{\bar{h}}{\bar{c}}\hat{h}_t + (1+\bar{r})\frac{\bar{a}}{\bar{c}}\left(\hat{a}_{t-1} + \phi\left(\hat{P}_t^e - \hat{P}_t\right)\right)\right.$$
$$\left. + \frac{\bar{a}\bar{r}}{\bar{c}}\hat{r}_{t-1} - \frac{\bar{r}\bar{m}}{\bar{c}}(\hat{m}_t - \hat{r}_t)\right],$$

(8.51)

where $\hat{h}_t$ is discounted human wealth, after tax, which evolves according to

$$\hat{h}_t = \frac{\gamma}{1+\bar{r}}\hat{h}_{t+1} - \frac{\gamma\bar{r}}{(1+\bar{r})^2}\hat{r}_t + (1-\bar{\tau})\frac{\bar{y}}{\bar{h}}\hat{y}_t - \frac{\bar{\tau}\bar{y}}{\bar{h}}\hat{\tau}_t.$$

(8.52)

There are similar linearised equations for foreign consumption

$$\hat{c}_t^* = \left(\frac{1-\nu\beta}{1+\chi}\right)\left[\frac{\bar{h}}{\bar{c}}\hat{h}_t^* + (1+\bar{r})\frac{\bar{a}}{\bar{c}}\left(\hat{a}_{t-1}^* + \phi^*\left(\hat{P}_t^{e*} - \hat{P}_t^*\right)\right)\right.$$
$$\left. + \frac{\bar{a}\bar{r}}{\bar{c}}\hat{r}_{t-1}^* - \frac{\bar{r}\bar{m}}{\bar{c}}(\hat{m}_t - \hat{r}_t)\right],$$

(8.53)

with an associated definition of human wealth

$$\hat{h}_t^* = \frac{\gamma}{1+\bar{r}}\hat{h}_{t+1}^* - \frac{\gamma\bar{r}}{(1+\bar{r})^2}\hat{r}_t^* + (1-\bar{\tau}^*)\frac{\bar{y}^*}{\bar{h}^*}\hat{y}_t^* - \frac{\bar{y}^*\bar{\tau}^*}{\bar{h}^*}\hat{\tau}_t^*. \quad (8.54)$$

Since this is an open economy, the government's budget constraint is not synonymous with those of consumers, whose holdings of financial wealth evolve according to

$$\hat{a}_t = (1+\bar{r})\hat{a}_{t-1} + (1+\bar{r})\phi\left(\hat{P}_t^e - \hat{P}_t\right) + \left(\bar{r} - \frac{\bar{m}}{\bar{a}}\bar{r}\right)\hat{r}_{t-1}$$
$$- \bar{r}\frac{\bar{m}}{\bar{a}}\hat{m}_{t-1} - \frac{\bar{m}}{\bar{a}}(\hat{P}_t - \hat{P}_{t-1}) + (1-\bar{\tau})\frac{\bar{y}}{\bar{a}}\hat{y}_t - \frac{\bar{c}}{\bar{a}}\hat{c}_t - \frac{\bar{\tau}\bar{y}}{\bar{a}}\hat{\tau}_t,$$

(8.55)

while in the foreign economy the evolution of private holdings of financial wealth follows

$$\hat{a}_t^* = (1+\bar{r})\hat{a}_{t-1}^* + (1+\bar{r})\phi^*\left(\hat{P}_t^e - \hat{P}_t\right) + \left(\bar{r} - \frac{\bar{m}}{\bar{a}}\bar{r}\right)\hat{r}_{t-1}$$
$$- \bar{r}\frac{\bar{m}}{\bar{a}}\hat{m}_{t-1} - \frac{\bar{m}}{\bar{a}}(\hat{P}_t - \hat{P}_{t-1}) + (1-\bar{\tau}^*)\frac{\bar{y}^*}{\bar{a}^*}\hat{y}_t^* - \frac{\bar{c}^*}{\bar{a}^*}\hat{c}_t^* - \frac{\bar{\tau}^*\bar{y}^*}{\bar{a}^*}\hat{\tau}_t^*.$$

(8.56)

The output of firms in the domestic economy is governed by the linearised version of equation (8.22)

$$\hat{y}_t = -\theta(\hat{P}(h)_t - \hat{P}(f)_t)$$
$$+ \frac{1}{2}\left[\frac{\bar{c}}{\bar{y}}\hat{c}_t + \frac{\bar{c}}{\bar{y}}\hat{c}_t^* + \left(1 - \frac{\bar{c}}{\bar{y}}\right)\hat{g}_t + \left(1 - \frac{\bar{c}}{\bar{y}}\right)\hat{g}_t^*\right] \tag{8.57}$$

and for foreign firms

$$\hat{y}_t^* = \theta(\hat{p}(h)_t - \hat{p}(f)_t)$$
$$+ \frac{1}{2}\left[\frac{\bar{c}}{\bar{y}}\hat{c}_t + \frac{\bar{c}}{\bar{y}}\hat{c}_t^* + \left(1 - \frac{\bar{c}}{\bar{y}}\right)\hat{g}_t + \left(1 - \frac{\bar{c}}{\bar{y}}\right)\hat{g}_t^*\right]. \tag{8.58}$$

There are also the two global market-clearing conditions. Firstly, for goods across the two economies,

$$\hat{y}_t + \hat{y}_t^* = \frac{\bar{c}}{\bar{y}}\hat{c}_t + \frac{\bar{c}}{\bar{y}}\hat{c}_t^* + \left(1 - \frac{\bar{c}}{\bar{y}}\right)\hat{g}_t + \left(1 - \frac{\bar{c}}{\bar{y}}\right)\hat{g}_t^* \tag{8.59}$$

and, secondly, for assets across the two economies,

$$\hat{l}_t + \hat{l}_t^* = \hat{a}_t^* + \hat{a}_t. \tag{8.60}$$

2.2.1   Describing monetary and fiscal policy   All that remains is to complete our description of monetary and fiscal policy. Our model contains a number of features which suggest goals for policymakers – for example, the distortions due to imperfect competition and taxation create incentives for policymakers to boost output above its steady-state level, while the nominal inertia generated by overlapping Calvo contracts suggests that a low (ideally zero) and constant rate of inflation is optimal for minimising the distortions the mispricing of these contracts can generate (see Goodfriend and King 1997 for a discussion of this point). Therefore, in describing monetary policy we assume that the independent ECB ignores the inflationary bias created by the distortions described above and implements its mandate to pursue its inflation target by following a simple interest rate rule. Specifically, we assume that the common monetary policy involves setting real interest rates to target the average rate of output price inflation across the two economies, so that,

$$r_t = \bar{r} + m\pi_t \tag{8.61}$$

and the target for inflation, consistent with minimising the distortions due to mispricing, is zero. Log-linearising this Taylor-type rule for monetary policy gives,

$$\hat{r}_t = \frac{m}{\bar{r}}\left(\frac{1}{2}\hat{\pi}(h)_t + \frac{1}{2}\hat{\pi}(f)_t\right). \tag{8.62}$$

In contrast, the fiscal authorities set the values of their tax instruments $\hat{t}_t$ and $\hat{g}_t$ independently – although one authority may seek to adjust policy in light of the policy actions of the other. Here there are a number of factors motivating the behaviour of these fiscal policymakers. For example the distortionary nature of taxation in this model gives them an incentive to smooth taxes as in Barro (1979). The institutional constraint implied by the Pact for Stability and Growth also implies that such fiscal authorities will be forced to use these fiscal policy instruments to rein in 'excessive' levels of deficits and government debt as defined by the pact. Since the model of tax smoothing applies over an infinite horizon, the short-run deficits it could imply could easily conflict with the detail of the Stability Pact. Additionally, for reasons of credibility, governments may have to react to deficits more quickly than pure tax smoothing considerations would imply. At the same time, general models of optimal fiscal policy, with quadratic loss functions detailing the extent to which governments are constrained in their ability to raise taxation and cut government spending, typically generate simple linear feedback rules operating from debt to fiscal policy instruments (see Lockwood, Philippopoulos and Snell 1996, for example). We therefore assume that the home government adjusts the tax rate relative to its steady-state value in an attempt to stabilise the debt stock. This can be thought of as a rule of thumb capturing all the above factors and, in particular, enabling the fiscal authority to avoid the costs associated with breaching the constraints implied by the Pact for Stability and Growth. This gives rise to the following taxation feedback rule in the domestic economy:

$$\hat{t}_t = f\hat{l}_{t-1} \tag{8.63}$$

and

$$\hat{t}_t^* = f^*\hat{l}_{t-1}^* \tag{8.64}$$

in the foreign economy.

We also consider the case where the feedback rules operating on taxation are replaced with similar feedback rules operating on government spending in the domestic and foreign economies:

$$\hat{g}_t = -f\hat{l}_{t-1} \tag{8.65}$$

$$\hat{g}_t^* = -f^*\hat{l}_{t-1}^*. \tag{8.66}$$

In our analysis, we consider equilibria in which the debt of each fiscal authority is stable. In contrast, other authors (e.g. Bergin 2000; Woodford 1998) have allowed one fiscal authority to borrow indefinitely from the other, in which case it is only the aggregate budget constraint that matters. These alternative assumptions are discussed in Canzoneri, Cumby and Diba (2001).

Table 8.1. *Parameters and steady state*

Parameter	Value	Variable	Steady state value	% of annual GDP
θ	8	$\bar{y}$	1	100
β	$\frac{1}{1+0.007}$	$\bar{r}$	3% (annualised)	n.a.
γ	0.9915	$\bar{h}$	47.23	1181
τ	0.25	$\bar{a} = \bar{l}$	2.882	72.0
α	0.75	$\bar{c}$	0.772	77.2
κ	0.847	$\bar{g}$	0.228	22.8
χ	0	$\bar{m}$	0	0

This completes our description of the economy which consists of Phillips curve relationships for output prices in both economies (equations (8.46) and (8.47)), consumption (equations (8.51) and (8.53)) with the associated equations of motion for human wealth (equations (8.52) and (8.54)) and financial wealth (equations (8.55) and (8.56)). There are also equations describing the evolution of each government's liabilities (equations (8.49) and (8.50)) and the output in each economy (equations (8.57) and (8.58)). Finally, there are the global goods and asset market clearing conditions (equations (8.59) and (8.60)) as well as the policy rules describing the common monetary policy (equation (8.62)) and the fiscal feedback rules for taxation ((8.63) and (8.64)) and government spending ((8.65) and (8.66)).

3   Interactions between monetary and fiscal policy under EMU

In this section we begin by discussing our choice of parameters before assessing, through the use of simulations, the policy implications of different degrees of fiscal rectitude under a common monetary policy.

3.1   Calibration

In parameterising the model, we assume a quarterly data period, and the parameters we choose are given in table 8.1, along with the steady-state values these imply.

The value of the elasticity of demand facing our imperfectly competitive firms, θ, comes from the econometric work of Rotemberg and Woodford (1998). The quarterly discount factor of $\frac{1}{1+0.007}$ is slightly higher than that found in other studies (such as Kollman 1998 or Rotemberg and Woodford 1998, for example). The reason for this is that these studies assume infinitely lived consumers so that their assumed value of $\frac{1}{1+0.0075}$ is equivalent to an annual real interest rate of around 3%. Since the existence of finite lives in our model raises the real rate of interest above consumers' rate of time preference, this slightly lower rate of time preference is consistent with the same equilibrium real interest rate commonly found in the literature.

The γ parameter is the probability of survival for our consumers and it implies an average working life for consumers/workers in our model of thirty years. Arguably this is a not implausible measure of average time spent in employment, although it admittedly implies a high probability of death if the model is taken literally. Nevertheless, such a parameter value is necessary to generate a plausible steady-state value of government debt relative to GDP. This mark-up over a literal probability of death can be justified as reflecting uncertainty not formally captured in our model. For example, Faruqee, Laxton and Symansky (1997) show that not raising the probability of death in this way implies near-Ricardian consumption behaviour. They then show that extending the model to allow for non-monotonic lifetime earnings profiles effectively raises the interest rate mark-up in the equation for aggregate human wealth in a manner consistent with our calibrated parameter.

τ is our basic rate of income tax and is set at 25%. The κ parameter is chosen to normalise the level of output to 1 to ease comparison of the steady-state levels of other variables. The parameter α measures the probability that a firm will not be able to reset its price in the next quarter. Therefore, $\frac{1}{1-\alpha}$ measures the average length of time between price changes. A value of $3/4$ means that it takes, on average, one year for firms to reset prices. This figure is consistent with the econometric work, using euro-area data, of Gali, Gertler and López-Salido (2001) and Leith and Malley (2001).

Finally, we assume, that the parameter governing the importance of money in utility approaches zero, implying that the economy approaches its cashless limit as in Woodford (1995). This simplifies our analysis without distorting our results, and can be justified as seigniorage revenues are relatively unimportant for EMU.

The steady state these parameters imply are shown in the right-hand side of the table 8.1. The real interest rate has an annualised value of around 3%, and the steady-state ratio of debt to GDP is around 70%, which is consistent with the average level of debt in the euro area at the end of 2000 (ECB 2001)). The ratio of government spending to GDP of 23% is also typical of European economies if you eliminate transfers from the definition of government spending to be left with government consumption as defined in our model (see Galí 1994 for a comparison of this ratio across OECD economies).

All that remains is to choose the policy feedback parameters for the monetary and fiscal policy rules. We assume that the coefficient on excess inflation, m, is 0.5 as this is widely used in studies of interest rate reaction function (see Taylor 1993, for example), and is often a good guide to the actual conduct of monetary policy. Adopting a positive value for m implies that monetary policy is 'active' in the sense of Leeper (1991). In Leith and Wren-Lewis (2001) we show that an 'active' monetary policy of this sort must be supported by fiscal policies in which fiscal instruments are adjusted so as to stabilise the domestic stock of government debt in the long run. In that paper we also show that it is possible for a strong fiscal reaction to debt disequilibrium in one economy to compensate for a relatively weak fiscal response in the other.

We also identify a policy regime where the fiscal authorities do not act to stabilise their respective debt stocks, but require the monetary authorities to abandon their 'active' targeting of inflation and utilise their monetary instruments to ensure debt stability. While this policy regime may be of historical interest, we would argue that the current policy arrangements underpinning EMU put us clearly in the 'active' policy regime. The conditions implied by the Pact for Stability and Growth more than satisfy the fiscal solvency conditions identified in Leith and Wren-Lewis (2001). Leith and Wren-Lewis (2000) also clearly showed, in the closed economy context, that fiscal policies which support an 'active' monetary policy were preferable to using monetary policy to stabilise debt as this tended to prolong any disequilibrium following shocks to the economy. For these reasons we focus on the conduct of policy in a policy regime where monetary policy 'actively' targets inflation and fiscal policy will ensure fiscal solvency in the long run. However, as we show, this still leaves significant room for manoeuvre, as a far weaker response to fiscal disequilibrium than is implied by the Stability Pact would still be consistent with saddlepath stability in our dynamic model. Our next section therefore investigates the optimal speed of response to debt disequilibrium.

3.2   Simulations

In this section we examine simulations of the calibrated version of our model to consider how quickly the authorities in each country should stabilise debt. Is rapid fiscal feedback better than slow debt stabilisation? If one country stabilises at an inappropriate rate, how does this influence the other economy?

3.2.1   Symmetric economies, shocks and policies   We first consider the symmetric case, where both countries choose the same value for the f parameter. For a symmetric shock, the two-country model acts as a single economy. We then consider what happens if one country adopts fiscal feedback that is 'too slow', or if the countries' inflation responses differ. In each case we consider both feedback on government spending and through taxes, as their implications are quite different.

The first shock we consider is an autocorrelated consumption shock: there is a positive shift in consumption in the first period of 1%, which dies out in a uniform way over the next four periods. (Consumption remains endogenous throughout, so the rise in consumption in the first period may not be 1%, because of changes to wealth or interest rates, for example.)

In the case where fiscal feedback operates through government spending, there is a clear benchmark case for the value of the *f* parameter. In our model, the only dynamic variables whose current values influence the future are asset stocks. A consumption shock will result in changes in the level of personal financial wealth, which will influence consumption and labour supply after the shock has passed. The only other direct influence that changes in wealth will have is through fiscal feedback, where changes in government debt will influence government spending. If the inflationary impact of the latter exactly offsets the former, inflation will be unchanged after the consumption shock has passed.

However, inflation stabilisation is not equivalent to output stabilisation, because labour supply is endogenous. Workers demand higher wages when they are asked to supply additional labour to produce more output. However, when the source of demand for the higher output is their own consumption then they will also require further wage increases as they seek to substitute consumption of goods for leisure (see the Phillips curve which embodies this labour supply behaviour, equation (8.46)). Therefore, to stabilise inflation after the shock is over, any offsetting change in government spending has to exceed the change in consumption in order to eliminate the inflationary wage demands of workers.

From equation (8.51) we see that in the log-linearised model the direct impact of financial wealth on consumption is given by

$$\frac{(1 - v\beta)}{1 + \chi}(1 + \bar{r})\frac{\bar{a}}{\bar{c}}\hat{a}_{t-1}. \tag{8.67}$$

As noted above, any fall in government spending must exceed the increase in consumption to leave inflation unchanged. Our assumption of quadratic disutility of labour supply implies that the percentage reduction in output must equal the percentage rise in consumption to eliminate the inflationary impact of the disequilibrium in financial wealth (see equation 8.50). If we consider only the direct financial wealth effect (see equation (8.67)), then the value of the feedback parameter *f* which achieves this is

$$f = \frac{(1 - v\beta)}{1 + \chi}(1 + \bar{r})\frac{\bar{a}}{\bar{c}}\frac{\bar{y}}{\bar{g}}(1 + \bar{c}/\bar{y}). \tag{8.68}$$

Given that the steady-state values of model variables are a function of model parameters and the government's choice of tax rates and government spending, this expression reveals that the 'matching' parameter is also a non-linear function of these parameters and policy choices. However, evaluating this function using plausible parameter values confirms the intuition that when consumers are near Ricardian and policy choices in combination with model parameters

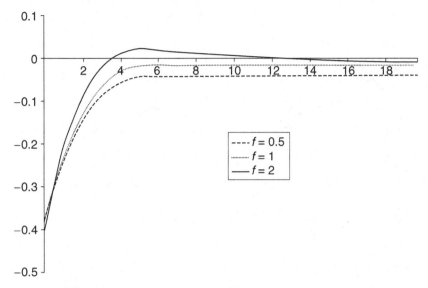

Figure 8.1 Autocorrelated consumption shock with fiscal feedback on government expenditure: government debt under alternative values of the f parameter

ensure that the equilibrium debt stock is not too large, then the value of f implied by this function is fairly small. In other words, when debt disequilibrium has little impact on consumption, then government spending does not need to be adjusted by much to offset the direct inflationary impact of debt disequilibrium.

This value of f is, however, only an upper bound on the matching parameter. As the change in government spending has to exceed the changes in consumption arising from changes in consumers' holding of financial wealth, output also changes and this feeds back onto consumption through human wealth. This is the indirect effect of debt disequilibrium on consumption and, via labour supply decisions, inflation. It turns out that, for our central parameter set, a value of f of 0.5 is close to the figure that allows fiscal policy to offset the effects of debt on inflation.[4] This implies a decrease in government spending of 0.5% for every 1% excess debt. We call this the 'matching case'. In an important sense, this is the only value of the feedback parameter which is consistent with the ECB's inflation target, because only with this degree of fiscal feedback will inflation be at target after any shock.

Figure 8.1 shows the path of government debt following this demand shock, and compares the matching case with two more aggressive fiscal stabilisation

---

[4] The value of the benchmark f was calculated numerically by grid search. In Leith and Wren-Lewis (2000) we calculate the benchmark value of f for our slightly simpler continuous time model analytically.

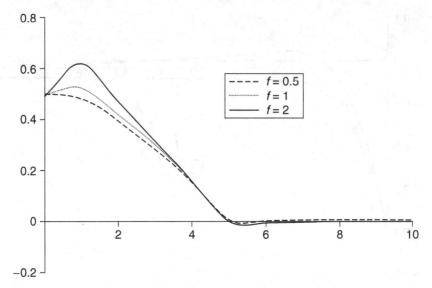

Figure 8.2 Autocorrelated consumption shock with fiscal feedback on government expenditure: output under alternative values of the f parameter

parameters, $f = 1$ and $f = 2$.[5] Under the more aggressive fiscal feedback regimes, debt is back to base after 20 periods (five years) and 12 periods (three years), respectively (with some overshooting when $f = 2$), whereas in the matching case debt disequilibrium takes around twenty years to disappear completely.

In all three simulations debt immediately falls, reflecting the direct impact of a surprise inflation on non-indexed debt. Although debt stays below base throughout when $f \leq 1$, reflecting lower savings corresponding to the positive consumption shock, the decline in savings is muted by additional income coming from higher interest rates on the existing debt stock. These effects are important: if the monetary policy response was more aggressive, or if the inflation response more rapid, or debt was indexed (see below), then it is quite possible for debt to rise after a period or two as higher debt interest payments dominate the evolution of government debt.

As we would expect, the most aggressive fiscal feedback leads to large short-term changes in government spending. Figure 8.2 plots output in these three simulations. After the initial period, output disequilibrium is significantly higher with aggressive feedback, because lower savings and debt generate higher levels

---

[5] In the figures all real variables are measured as percentage deviations from steady-state, while inflation is measured as a percentage.

Table 8.2. *Autocorrelated consumption shock with fiscal feedback on government expenditure: inflation (%, annual) under alternative values of the f parameter*

Period	1	2	3	4	5
$f = 0.5$	1.37	0.99	0.63	0.34	0.12
$f = 1$	1.39	1.01	0.64	0.34	0.12
$f = 2$	1.44	1.07	0.67	0.34	0.12

of public spending. (There is a one-period lag in fiscal feedback, so government spending does not change in the first period of the shock.)

Table 8.2 gives the change in inflation in these three cases over the first two years. The differences in inflation are smaller than figure 8.2 would suggest, for two reasons. First, the inflationary impact of higher government spending is half that of higher consumption, owing to the labour supply responses of workers (see discussion above). Second, under the more relaxed fiscal feedback, government spending and output are higher in the medium term. As inflation cumulates future excess demand with discounting, this has some impact on short-term inflation.

Although differences are small, inflation is higher with aggressive fiscal feedback, reflecting higher excess demand. The initial increase in output of around 0.5% is translated into an initial increase in the annual inflation rate of around 1.3%. Differences in inflation would be larger if monetary policy were less active. For example, if $m = 0.2$ rather than 0.5, then the impact figure for inflation would be 1.81% with $f = 2$, and 1.65% with $f = 0.5$.

Choosing the slower, matching feedback parameter therefore produces less output disequilibrium, slightly better inflation control in the short run, and eliminates inflation disequilibrium after the shock is over. The implication that the government's fiscal correction should be slow reflects the extent of consumption smoothing implied by our intertemporal model. It confirms and extends results obtained for a closed economy in Leith and Wren-Lewis (2000).

If fiscal feedback works through taxation rather than government spending, then there is no equivalent 'matching' case, because stabilisation works through consumption. Consumers will smooth the impact of tax changes, which means that these changes have little demand impact. However, in the model tax changes also influence labour supply, so that lower taxes will raise output and reduce inflation through this route. As a result, tax cuts aimed at restoring debt equilibrium will have a beneficial supply-side effect. As table 8.3 shows, more aggressive fiscal feedback produces lower inflation and higher output disequilibrium, but the differences are not large.

Table 8.3. *Autocorrelated consumption shock with fiscal feedback on taxation: inflation and output under alternative values of the f parameter*

Period	1	2	3	4	5	6
Inflation (%, annual)						
$f = 0.5$	1.33	0.93	0.60	0.31	0.11	0.00
$f = 1$	1.31	0.90	0.60	0.31	0.11	0.00
Output (%)						
$f = 0.5$	0.52	0.46	0.38	0.28	0.15	0.003
$f = 1$	0.53	0.46	0.38	0.28	0.15	0.003

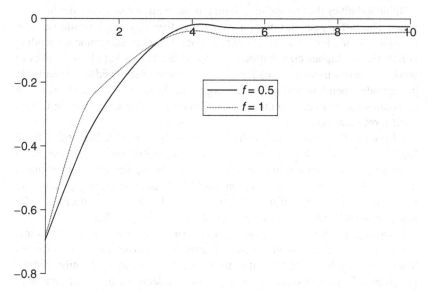

Figure 8.3 Inflation shock with fiscal feedback on government expenditure: government debt under alternative values of the *f* parameter

We now consider a supply shock, in the form of a one-year inflation shock, such that, ceteris paribus, inflation would be 1% higher in the first quarter, 0.75% in the second quarter etc. With non-indexed debt, this shock initially reduces the real value of debt (because of higher inflation), but subsequently debt is higher because of lower tax receipts and higher interest rates.

As debt falls initially, government spending initially rises, but then is cut in an effort to reduce higher debt. The more aggressive the fiscal feedback, the larger the initial rise, and subsequent reduction in government spending (figure 8.3). Figure 8.4 shows the consequences for output.

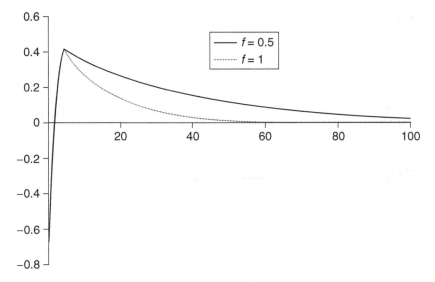

Figure 8.4 Inflation shock with fiscal feedback on government spending: output under alternative values of the f parameter

The more aggressive fiscal feedback initially reduces the fall in output, but after the first year output is lower. The net impact on inflation is small (as inflation depends on cumulated future excess demand), but it is marginally higher under the more aggressive feedback. On impact inflation is 0.71% higher when $f = 0.5$, but 0.73% higher if $f = 1$.

If feedback occurs through taxation, we get a similar pattern in tax rates (an initial cut, followed by subsequent increases), but consumers smooth their effect. The net result is that consumption and output disequilibrium is smaller when feedback is more aggressive, and so inflation is also slightly better initially (0.65% on impact when $f = 1$, and 0.67% when $f = 0.5$). However, inflation becomes slightly higher under the more aggressive fiscal policy after a few quarters, because higher taxes reduce labour supply, adding to inflationary pressures.

These results suggest that the optimal degree of fiscal feedback depends critically on whether feedback occurs through government spending or through taxes.[6] When taxes are used, there is a case for rapid feedback (as in the fiscal stability pact), although the benefits are minor. If debt stabilisation occurs through government spending, then disequilibrium after the shock is over is

---

[6] The dangers of rapid fiscal feedback through government spending were also emphasised in Leith and Wren-Lewis (2000), although the desirable properties of the 'matching' case were not examined. As that model contained a fixed level of labour supply, differences in fiscal feedback through taxation were less pronounced.

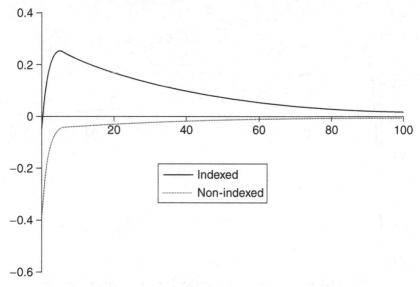

Figure 8.5 Autocorrelated consumption shock with fiscal feedback on government expenditure, $f = 0.5$: indexed and non-indexed government debt

minimised by choosing feedback that matches the response of consumers to changes in wealth, which probably implies slow fiscal feedback. The danger of rapid feedback is clearest following a demand shock, where the demand impact of fiscal correction intensifies the destabilising effects of the shock.

These conclusions are not critically dependent on our assumption that no debt is indexed. The path of debt following a consumption shock when all debt is indexed is shown in figure 8.5. We choose the 'matching' value of the feedback parameter.

When debt is indexed, its value is not automatically reduced by surprise inflation. On the other hand, higher interest rates increase debt interest payments, which adds to the debt stock, so that after the initial period debt is higher, despite the positive shock to savings. However, our earlier conclusions about the advantages of the matching case over faster fiscal feedback remain, because the matching parameter eliminates the inflation consequences of any debt disequilibrium, whatever its sign. In the case of an inflation shock, debt is now higher throughout as a result of higher interest rates. When fiscal feedback occurs through government spending, the larger fall in output under more aggressive fiscal feedback is brought forward. When taxes are used, inflation is still lower on impact when feedback is more aggressive, but the inflationary impact of higher tax rates noted above is also brought forward, so inflation is higher after the third quarter.

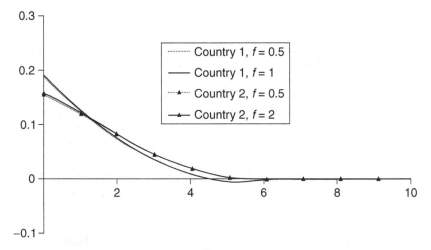

Figure 8.6 Asymmetric consumption shock with fiscal feedback on government spending: $f = 1$ and $f = 0.5$

3.2.2   Symmetric economies and policies, but asymmetric shocks   In our model the pattern of demand across goods is the same for both countries' consumers. As a result, an asymmetric demand shock (consumers save less in country one but not in country two) does not lead to any change in average preferences across individual goods. However, the shock involves not only an increase in consumers' demand for goods in country one, but also their demand for leisure. Therefore, while output rises in country two due to higher demand for their products, there is an offsetting fall in labour supply in country one, with the net result that output in country one hardly changes. At the same time the real exchange rate appreciates for country one to reduce global demand for their products in line with the reduced labour supply.

An asymmetric shock also means that consumers' wealth and government debt no longer move together. Consumers in country one finance their higher consumption mainly by borrowing from consumers in country two, rather than borrowing from their own government. In any one country, therefore, it no longer makes sense for fiscal feedback to try to match the response of consumers to changes in wealth, because debt and wealth follow quite different paths.

Figure 8.6 shows the impact of an asymmetric shock on inflation in both countries when government spending is used to stabilise debt. The impact of changing the degree of fiscal feedback is very small, as was the case for a symmetric shock. Once again, inflation is very slightly lower with slower fiscal feedback. Differences generated by alternative fiscal policies are dominated by differences between countries. In both cases, inflation is initially higher in country one (the source of the shock), but it also declines more rapidly there. The real exchange rate initially appreciates in country one, because output is higher in country two. A similar conclusion applies when feedback occurs through taxation, and for an asymmetric inflation shock.

3.2.3   Symmetric economies and shocks, but asymmetric policies   Suppose both countries face the same shock, but their speed of fiscal correction differs. This is a critical experiment in assessing the appropriateness of the fiscal stability pact. Implicit in the pact's formulation is the idea that lax fiscal control in one country could impose costs on the other, and could jeopardise the ability of the monetary authorities to control inflation. Our analysis in related work (Leith and Wren-Lewis 2001) showed that this was the case if one country applied little or no control over its public debt. However, does the same apply if debt control is slow rather than non-existent?

In the case of a demand shock and fiscal feedback through government spending, different speeds of adjustment have little differential effect on each country. In particular, the real exchange rate is unchanged. This is because government spending is spread equally across demand for each good, and consumers are indifferent between each country's debt. The only consequence of one country reducing its speed of fiscal feedback is that it lowers the average speed of correction for both countries. As we saw above, with this shock slow adjustment is preferable (the 'matching' case). As a result, the country adjusting quickly imposes costs (albeit small) on the country adjusting slowly! Much the same applies in the case of a supply shock.

When fiscal feedback occurs through taxation, then results are more interesting, because differences in taxation between countries generate differences in supply and the real exchange rate. In the case of a demand shock, debt falls and so the fiscal authorities reduce tax rates. Suppose feedback in country one is 'fast' ($f = 1$), and in country two 'slow' ($f = 0.5$). The more rapid fall in taxes in country one leads to greater labour supply in the short run, and higher output. To sell the additional output, country one's real exchange rate initially depreciates, but this is reversed after a few years when country two's taxes become lower relative to country one.

Slower adjustment in country two lowers the average speed of adjustment, and we saw in the case of symmetrical policies that it was preferable to adjust taxes quickly rather than slowly for a demand shock. As a result, slow adjustment in country two raises inflation in country one relative to the case where both countries adjust quickly. However, the differences are tiny: inflation at an annual rate is about 0.01% higher in country one as a result of slow adjustment in country two.

For a supply shock and feedback through taxes, it is clearest to look at the case of fully indexed debt, because then taxes rise throughout following the

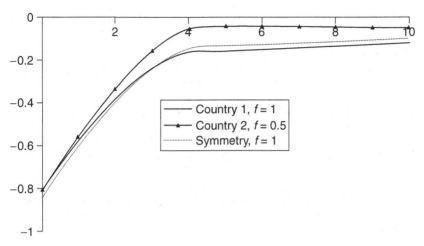

Figure 8.7 Output in country one following a symmetric inflation shock: tax feedback $f = 1, f = 0.5$ compared to $f = 1$ in both

increase in interest rates. (Recall that when debt is not indexed, taxes initially fall because inflation reduces the real value of debt.) As taxes rise more rapidly in country one compared to country two, then country one's labour supply falls by more and output is relatively lower in country one than in country two. However, consumption in country two is higher as a result of its slower fiscal reaction compared to the symmetric case, and this supports output in country one. As a result, slow adjustment in country two initially raises output in country one, but then output falls in country one relative to the symmetric policy case. The net impact on inflation in country one is therefore small: on impact it is 0.65% compared to 0.64% with symmetric policies. The figures are identical for country two.

For both countries, therefore, there is a very small cost in terms of higher inflation as a result of slower adjustment in country two. In terms of average inflation across both countries this is exactly what we would expect, given our results earlier: the interesting point is that the inflation experiences of both countries are very similar despite asymmetric policies (figure 8.7). In terms of output, country two clearly gains through slower fiscal adjustment, but country one is not obviously worse off than it would have been under symmetric policies. These results therefore provide some qualified support for the fiscal stability pact: there is a temptation to adjust slowly, the costs of which are spread across the union.

However, the support is qualified for many reasons. It does not apply if fiscal adjustment takes place through government spending – in this case the rapid fiscal adjustment implicit in the Pact appears unjustified. Benefits are only

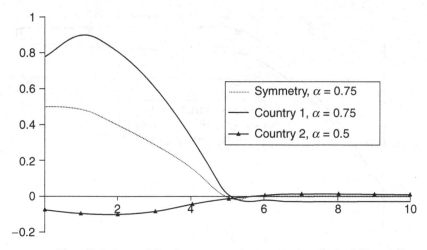

Figure 8.8 Output following a symmetric consumption shock: different inflation responsiveness between countries, with government spending feedback $f = 0.5$

noticeable for supply rather than demand shocks, and even then they are very small.

3.2.4   Asymmetric economies, symmetric policies and shocks   So far we have assumed that the two countries have an identical structure. One of the most frequently analysed cases where structure differs is where one country is more sluggish in its inflation response. Indeed governments in some countries in the EU have made a point of pressing their EU partners to undertake labour market and other structural reforms in an attempt to make markets there less rigid.

Consider the symmetrical demand shock analysed above, where fiscal feedback occurs through government spending, and we choose the matching value of $f (f = 0.5)$. Suppose price inertia in country two is less than in country one. In our model inertia in both goods and labour markets is captured by the alpha parameter. So far we have assumed $\alpha = 0.75$ in both countries, which implies that three-quarters of prices remain fixed each quarter. Suppose now that $\alpha = 0.5$ in country two, but remains at 0.75 in country one.

This difference in inflation responsiveness leads to quite different behaviour in each country, even though the shock is symmetric. Figure 8.8 looks at output in each country, and also plots the case where $\alpha = 0.75$ in both countries.

Inflation tends to increase more rapidly in country two, which leads to a depreciation in country one. As a result, output rises more rapidly in country one, but actually falls in country two. The differences in inflation between the

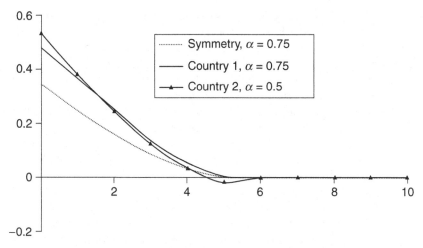

Figure 8.9 Autocorrelated consumption shock: inflation responses with different values of α, common government spending feedback $f = 0.5$

two countries are less marked, as figure 8.9 shows. The fact that differences in α influence output much more than inflation in part reflects the high demand elasticity we have assumed ($\theta = 8$). Small movements in the real exchange rate generate large differences in output.

The marked differences in output between the two countries lead to very different profiles in government debt. After inflation erodes debt in both countries, debt in country two is soon higher than base, while in country one it always stays below base. At first sight this might suggest that country two should reduce its debt disequilibrium more rapidly than country one. However, our results above suggest that rapid debt correction is not obviously desirable. This is confirmed by various simulation experiments not reported here: increasing the relative speed of fiscal feedback in country two does not lead to any clear benefits in terms of inflation or output for either country. One issue that would be worth pursuing in further research is whether asymmetric economic structures might generate a role for a countercyclical fiscal policy.

4   Conclusion

In this chapter we constructed a two-country model which contained a number of features which broke the distinction between Ricardian and non-Ricardian policies highlighted by the Fiscal Theory of the Price Level (Woodford 1998). Specifically, our two economies featured overlapping generations of consumers who did not expect to live for ever – as a result the government's liabilities (money and bonds) constitute an element of net wealth and their level will affect real interest rates in our economies. These consumers then supplied labour to imperfectly competitive firms who sold their output at home and abroad. These imperfectly competitive firms could adjust their prices only at random intervals. The combination of non-Ricardian consumers and the nominal inertia facing imperfectly competitive firms implied that both monetary and fiscal policy could have real and nominal effects in both countries.

Our policy simulations then analysed a situation where both countries had formed a currency union, where an independent central bank followed a common rule for monetary policy which sought to target the average rate of inflation across the two economies, but where the two fiscal authorities remained free to pursue independent fiscal policies. Through these simulations we sought to discover whether there is a case for rapid or slow stabilisation of debt stocks, and whether it might be justifiable to impose fast adjustment on both countries. We have shown that the answer depends critically on whether changes in spending or taxes are used to stabilise debt. If fiscal feedback occurs through government spending, then there is a strong case for choosing feedback that matches and offsets the private sector's response to additional debt. This matching case is likely to involve slow adjustment, and both countries have an incentive to adopt this policy. If feedback occurs through taxation, then there are circumstances where an individual country has an incentive to adjust slowly, with inflationary costs for the union, but these costs are small. Finally we show that the consequences of structural differences between countries may be much more significant than differences in fiscal policy.

REFERENCES

Barro, R. J., 1979, 'On the Determination of the Public Debt', *Journal of Political Economy* 87, 940–71.

Bergin, P. R., 2000, 'Fiscal Solvency and Price Level Determination in a Monetary Union', *Journal of Monetary Economics* 45, 37–53.

Calvo, G., 1983, 'Staggered Prices in a Utility Maximising Framework', *Journal of Monetary Economics* 12(3), 383–98.

Canzoneri, M. B., R. E. Cumby and B. T. Diba, 2001, 'Fiscal Discipline and Exchange Rate Systems', *Economic Journal* 474, 667–90.

Dupor, B., 2000, 'Exchange Rates and the Fiscal Theory of the Price Level', *Journal of Monetary Economics* 45, 613–30.

ECB, 2001, 'Euro Area Statistics', *Monthly Bulletin* August 2001, 1*–83*.

Faruqee, H., D. Laxton and S. Symansky, 1997, 'Government Debt, Life-Cycle Income, and Liquidity Constraints: Beyond Approximate Ricardian Equivalence', *IMF Staff Papers* 44(3), 374–82.

Galí, J., 1994, 'Government Size and Macroeconomic Stability', *European Economic Review* 28, 117–32.

Galí, J., M. Gertler and G. D. López-Salido, 2001, 'European Inflation Dynamics', *European Economic Review* 45, 1237–70.

Goodfriend, M. S. and R. G. King, 1997, 'The New Neoclassical Synthesis and the Role of Monetary Policy', in B. S. Bernanke and J. Rotemberg (eds.), *NBER Macroeconomics Annual 1997*, Cambridge, MA: MIT Press, pp. 231–82.

Kollman, R., 1998, 'International Financial Markets and G7 Business Cycles: A General Equilibrium Approach with Money and Nominal Rigidities', mimeo, University of Paris XII.

Leeper, E. M., 1991, 'Equilibria under "Active" and "Passive" Fiscal Policies', *Journal of Monetary Economics*. 27, 129–47.

Leith, C. and J. Malley, 2001, 'Estimated General Equilibrium Models for the Evaluation of Monetary Policy in the US and Europe', University of Glasgow Discussion Paper no. 2001-16.

Leith, C. and S. Wren-Lewis, 2000, 'Interactions between Monetary and Fiscal Policy Rules', *Economic Journal* 110, 93–108.

    2001, 'Compatability between Monetary and Fiscal Policy Under EMU', University of Glasgow Discussion Paper no. 2001-15.

Lockwood, B., A. Philippopoulos and A. Snell, 1996, 'Fiscal Policy, Public Debt Stabilisation and Politics: Theory and UK Evidence', *Economic Journal* 106, 894–911.

Obsfeldt, M. and K. Rogoff, 1995, 'Exchange Rate Dynamics Redux', *Journal of Political Economy* 103, 624–60.

Rotemberg, J. J. and M. Woodford, 1998, 'An Optimisation-Based Econometric Framework for the Evaluation of Monetary Policy: Expanded Version', NBER Technical Working Paper no. 233.

Sims, C. A., 1997, 'Fiscal Foundations of Price Stability in Open Economies', mimeo, Yale University.

Taylor, J., 1993, 'Discretion Versus Policy Rules in Practice', *Carnegie-Rochester Series on Public Policy* 39, 195–214.

Woodford, M., 1995, 'Price-Level Determinacy without Control of a Monetary Aggregate', *Carnegie-Rochester Conference Series on Public Policy* 43, 1–53.

    1998, 'Control of the Public Debt: A Requirement for Price Stability?' in G. Calvo and M. King (eds.), *The Debt Burden and Its Consequences for Monetary Policy*, New York: St Martin's Press, pp. 117–54.

9   Fiscal shocks and policy regimes in some OECD countries

Giuseppe De Arcangelis and Serena Lamartina

1   Introduction

The relevance of fiscal policy has been recently revived by both institutional decisions and recent empirical findings.

On the institutional ground, the celebrated Stability Pact represents the most important reference for all European governments. At the same time, the US government has been implementing fiscal policy measures that took into consideration the objective of the balanced budget. One question can then be raised: are governments surrendering an effective tool of macroeconomic stabilisation by obeying automatic rules like those of the Stability Pact or a general balanced-budget objective?

From the theoretical point of view, the literature on non-Keynesian effects of fiscal policy (initially inspired by Giavazzi and Pagano 1990) has shown that fiscal adjustments are able to bring about expansionary effects on the economy when they strongly affect private expectations. In particular, although fiscal policy may be restrictive in the traditional sense, when the fiscal restriction is implemented so as to credibly correct an intertemporal disequilibrium, private expectations may overturn the initial restrictive impact of fiscal contractions and induce an increase in economic activity.

Important case studies (such as Ireland, Denmark, Sweden, etc.) have also shown that these effects can actually occur and that they may depend on many different characteristics (for instance intensity and time length of the fiscal adjustment, etc.). One important element pointed out by Alesina and Perotti (1995, 1997) is the type of adjustment: whether the decrease in the stock of public debt is mainly conducted by means of decreasing expenditure or raising taxation; moreover, the decrease in public expenditure would have a different impact if done mainly by decreasing public transfers instead of other types of expenditure.

The authors would like to thank Carlo Favero, Chris Kamps and Carmine Trecroci for their useful comments, as well as all the participants at the section on Fiscal Policy at the European Economic Association meetings held in Lausanne, 28 August–1 September 2001, and at the conference 'EMU Macroeconomics Institutions' held in Milan-Bicocca, 20–22 September 2001. The views expressed herein are those of the authors and do not necessarily reflect those of the institutions to which they belong. The authors are fully responsible for errors and omissions.

In this chapter we want to tackle these issues from an empirical perspective. Our main objective is twofold. First, we want to discover which fiscal policy regime has characterised leading OECD countries in the past decades. By fiscal policy regime we mean some sensible rule according to which fiscal policy measures were decided. More exactly, it is interesting to check whether taxation decisions precede expenditure decisions or vice-versa. Moreover, given the political importance of expenditures on government wages and public transfers we test a policy regime that may combine taxation and other expenditure decisions in order to target such government spending. Finally, since in the residual spending are included interest payments on the public debt, some highly indebted countries (like Italy) may deem it more appropriate to target residual spending, hence changing taxation and expenditure on wages and transfers accordingly.

Once the fiscal policy regime has been identified, we then undertake a simulation analysis (second step of our investigation) to show the effects of fiscal policy shocks on economic activity and on other relevant macroeconomic aggregates.

Our work is highly inspired by the recent empirical literature on monetary policy. First, we use the same econometric technique (structural vector autoregression, SVAR), but opportunely adapted to the different characteristics of the policy tool in terms of temporal impact on economic aggregates. Second, we discuss the determination of policy regimes, as Bernanke and Mihov (1998) (and many others) have done, by proposing empirical tests to validate the parameter contraints implied by the different policy rules.

The structure of the chapter is as follows. Section 2 reviews some of the recent empirical literature on fiscal policy and in section 3 we describe how some fiscal variables behaved in the sample period of our analysis. Section 4 presents the empirical model, while estimation and simulation results are reported in section 5. Section 6 concludes and a data appendix follows.

2   Related literature

The bulk of the empirical literature on the macroeconomic effects of fiscal policy has developed only recently. Since the beginning of the 1990s, empirical contributions of fiscal policy have developed around two methodogical tools of investigation. The methodology that has had more success is that known as the 'ex-post approach'. The comparison of the macroeconomic and fiscal situation before, during and after an episode of fiscal consolidation allows a comprehensive study of the effects of a fiscal retrenchment on the level of economic activity and of its effectiveness in successfully reducing public debt. Owing to the extreme simplicity of the methodology and the possibility of analysing the behaviour of a large set of macroeconomic variables, this has been widely used in the empirical literature.

Since the second half of the 1990s a second line of research has emerged. Based on a more rigorous approach, it makes use of the VAR framework to estimate the responses of some relevant macroeconomic variables to fiscal shocks. The most advanced literature on this field allows the estimation of fiscal innovations through the identification of a SVAR model, thus avoiding the problem of arbitrarily choosing an indicator of the fiscal stance. Until now this methodology has been largely and successfully applied in the empirical monetary policy literature, while it has been used for fiscal policy exercises only in few recent works.

Given the importance of the ex-post approach in terms of number of empirical applications, in this section we will shortly discuss its main features and some relevant results emerging from the most significant contributions. This literature hinges on a common practice in conducting the analysis of fiscal consolidations. The procedure basically relies on the following three steps. At a first stage, relevant fiscal episodes are selected by means of a given rule. In practice, the indicator commonly used to capture the magnitude of fiscal adjustments is the Structural Primary Balance (SPB). The choice of this indicator derives from its independence of the cyclical fluctuations of output and from the non-inclusion of interest payments. Adjustments which result in a large reduction of the SPB/GDP ratio are identified as discretionary fiscal episodes. Once they have been selected, their main characteristics are studied in order to tell apart those that are more likely to be associated with a successful adjustment. A fiscal episode is defined a 'success' both if it induces an improvement in the economic activity ('macroeconomic success') and if it results in a large reduction of the debt/GDP ratio ('fiscal success'). Again, the identification of a fiscal success occurs by means of a rule, which usually relies on quantitative judgements on the debt/GDP ratio (e.g. the debt/GDP ratio must be 5% below the initial level three years after the adjustment).

The analysis of the main features of successful and expansive fiscal episodes has led to the identification of three major elements that might be relevant in the determination of a success. In two of the early empirical works of this kind, Giavazzi and Pagano (1990, 1996) highlighted the importance of the magnitude of fiscal adjustments in positively affecting the likelihood of a success. In particular, they found that fiscal retrenchments that induce a reduction of SPB/GDP by more than 5% are more likely to result in a success than fiscal episodes of smaller magnitude. Some other studies focus instead on the qualitative composition of a fiscal adjustment. McDermott and Wescott (1996), Alesina and Perotti (1997) and Alesina and Ardagna (1998) find that a consolidation implemented through a cut in public spending is more effective, on average, than one operated by an increase in taxation. Finally, Zaghini (1999) suggests that the persistence of the adjustment is a relevant characteristic in positively affecting the likelihood of both a successful reduction of public imbalances and an expansion of the economy.

The most recent empirical applications of fiscal policy use VAR models as a tool to investigate the impact of fiscal shocks on the economy. The first contributions to this literature are those by Ramey and Shapiro (1998), Edelberg, Eichenbaum and Fisher (1999) and Burnside, Eichenbaum and Fisher (1999, 2000). In these papers fiscal exogenous shocks are selected according to the so-called 'narrative approach' that consists of identifying the most relevant fiscal episodes through the reading and interpretation of historical documents. Then, a dummy variable, which takes value one at the start date of each selected episode, is introduced into a VAR model and the effect of a fiscal shock on several economic variables is studied. The results obtained in this way are compared with those stemming from the simulation of theoretical models.

The most advanced literature in this field avoids the problem of identifying fiscal exogenous shocks making use of subjective methods or judgements. Fiscal shocks are estimated after a structural VAR has been identified, i.e. after some restrictions are imposed on the system that describes the contemporaneous relationships among the variables in the VAR.

The most relevant work is that of Blanchard and Perotti (1999). They make use of institutional information on the tax and transfer system of the US economy to identify structural fiscal shocks and to estimate their impact on macroeconomic variables. The basic idea of their identification scheme is that a quarter (the periodicity used to estimate the model) is too short a period for economic variables to affect fiscal policy variables. Time is required for the policymaker to collect information about the state of the economy, to think about fiscal policy reactions and finally to implement them. Their model is composed of only three variables: government expenditure, tax revenue and the level of output. Tax revenue can be contemporaneously affected by output, but this would catch only automatic effects and not discretionary reactions of the policymaker. No feedback from economic activity to public spending is considered, while the economic activity is contemporaneously affected by unexpected changes in fiscal variables. The inclusion of taxation and spending in the model allows the authors to consider two possible ways in which the two items can affect each other. They consider both the case in which taxation decisions come first and spending follows, and the case in which taxation changes follow exogenous spending decisions. The authors estimate separately the two fiscal regimes but, owing to the lack of significance of both the coefficients that describe the two regimes, are unable to discriminate statistically between them. When the model is simulated to produce the impulse responses of the system to fiscal shocks (in turn, other macroeconomic variables are considered in place of the level of output), the economy shows Keynesian reactions to both kinds of shocks: an increase in taxation depresses both output and consumption, while a positive innovation in public expenditure produces positive effects on these variables.

Fatás and Mihov (2000) have proposed a variant of this model, which includes other variables. The identification scheme is basically the same, and no relevant differences emerge from the simulation exercises.

3   Recent trends of fiscal aggregates in four OECD countries

The role of fiscal policy has been changing over the last decades in all the industrialised countries. In the 1960s fiscal policy was considered an important stabilisation tool. But the attitude towards government deficits gradually changed in the 1980s owing to the rapid increase in public debt. As a consequence, in Europe strict official constraints on both deficit/GDP and debt/GDP ratios were imposed in the Maastricht Treaty (and now in the Stability and Growth Pact). In the USA fiscal imbalances decreased during the 1990s and have turned into surpluses in recent years.

We deem that not only deficits (or surpluses) are relevant, but also their *composition* and how the fiscal adjustment has been taking place. In particular, we want to concentrate on government expenditure and analyse the role of different components of total expenditure in determining fiscal policymaking.

Total government expenditure has been divided into government expenditure on wages and transfers and residual spending.[1] A detailed description of how the two components have been derived is presented in the data appendix. In our work we 'let the data speak' and see whether innovations on government expenditure on wages and transfers have preceded other fiscal policy decisions.

On average, during the period 1963–97 government expenditure on wages and transfers was the largest portion of total public expenditure for all the countries that we considered. The highest percentage is found in Italy, where around 70% of total public expenditure is on wages and transfers. France and Germany follows with around 66% of total expenditure. In the United States the figure falls to 59%.

A better picture of the increasing role of such expenditure for France, Germany, Italy and the USA is offered in figure 9.1. Public wages and transfers as a percentage of GDP have been rising since the 1960s in all countries (except for Germany in the 1990s): the three European countries showed an increase ranging from 23–24% in the 1960s up to 30–35% in the 1990s; even in the USA there is a positive change from 15–16% to over 20%.

Figure 9.2 shows that such an increase in spending occurred with an upward trend in fiscal pressure (i.e. the ratio of fiscal revenue to GDP). In all countries fiscal pressure has been rising monotonically in the last four decades, but with differing intensity. In Europe the largest increase occurred in Germany

---

[1] Interest payments on public debt have been included in residual spending since they are more 'endogenous' than wages and transfers and fiscal authorities cannot change them autonomously.

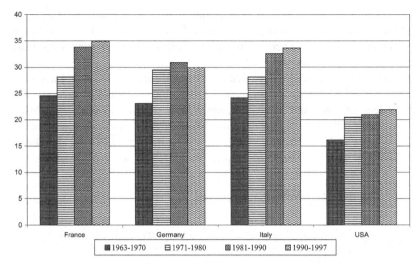

Figure 9.1 Weight of government expenditure on wages and transfers (as percentage of GDP) in some OECD countries

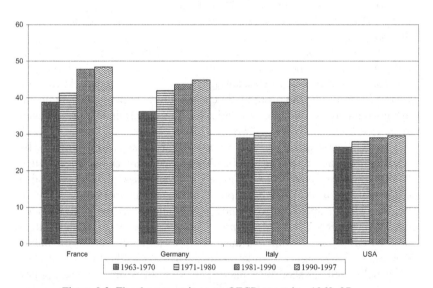

Figure 9.2 Fiscal pressure in some OECD countries, 1963–97

during the 1970s and in Italy and France during the 1980s; in all three European countries fiscal pressure was well above 40% at the end of the 1990s. In the US the increase over the period was much less sharp and the fiscal pressure has never been higher than 30%.

Does such an increase in government expenditure on wages and transfers correspond to fiscal regimes where decisions on those expenses preceded every other decision? Was that increase in expenditure to cause an increase in fiscal pressure, or did the decisions on taxes precede decisions on spending? In the empirical model presented below we try to tackle these questions and obtain the dynamic effect on output of different fiscal policy measures.

4   A model of fiscal policy regimes

The purpose of this paper is twofold. First, we want to focus on the type of fiscal policy regime that characterised the selected OECD countries in our sample. In other words, a fiscal policy regime is defined by the order of causality of fiscal decisions. For instance, two different regimes might be characterised by the fact that expenditure decisions precede tax measures and vice-versa.

Once the fiscal policy regime is established, the second aim is to use the estimated model for simulation to obtain the qualitative (and quantitative) responses of the main macroeconomic aggregates to the correctly identified fiscal policy shocks.

As discussed above, besides offering an endogenous determination of the fiscal policy regimes, the relevant contribution of this chapter is also to focus on the distinction between two main aggregates of government expenditure instead of considering the overall public expenditure. In particular, we distinguish government expenditure on salaries and transfers from all other types of expenditure.[2]

The current analysis is based on VAR econometrics and is highly inspired by the recent literature on monetary policy.[3] In particular, recent advances in that field have proposed analytical ways to check for monetary policy regimes that consider detailed institutional descriptions of the relevant markets.[4]

Similarly to that approach, we propose a distinction of the variables included in the VAR between *policy* and *non-policy* variables. We recall that the distinction is based on the capability of the authorities to directly affect the policy variables. In the mentioned works on monetary policy, the first set of variables usually includes short-term interest rates and bank reserves. Non-policy

---

[2] Besides the well-defined first type of expenditure, the residual expenditure is also relevant, especially in Europe. Indeed, residual expenditure includes interest payments on the public debt, which has been (and still is, for some highly indebted European countries) a considerable percentage of total government outlays.

[3] See Christiano, Eichenbaum and Evans (1998) for a detailed survey.

[4] See Bernanke and Mihov (1998) for an approach to monetary policy very close to the one taken in this chapter for fiscal policy.

variables include instead final objectives of monetary authorities that the policymaker cannot influence directly, such as output or the price level. Moreover, since monetary policy authorities are generally very quick to react to 'news' on the non-policy variables, it is commonly assumed that policy variables can react to innovations in the non-policy variables *within* the same sample period (say one month, when using monthly data); however, it takes more than one sample period to observe any reaction in the non-policy variables to innovations in the policy variables.

We deem that a similar distinction can also be proposed for the relationship between fiscal policy variables and relevant macroeconomic aggregates, although the temporal order of causality is different.[5] In particular, we distinguish between *fiscal policy* (FP) variables and *non-fiscal policy* (NFP) variables: the former are under the direct control of the government, whereas the latter must be taken into account by the authorities but are not able to respond to fiscal policy shocks within the sample period. A particular status is assigned to the output of the economy. Differently from monetary policy, output reacts contemporaneously (i.e., within the same sample period) to fiscal policy variables and shocks because some fiscal policy variables (like value-added government expenditure) are part of the total expenditure of the economy. On the other hand, the inside lag that characterises fiscal policy is very high and innovations in output are likely to take more than one sample period before they affect fiscal policy decisions (for instance, because it takes more than a quarter before fiscal measures are passed through Parliament or Congress with appropriate laws).[6] Hence, output is considered the most 'endogenous' variable of the model. The FP variables usually include the budget balance or some kind of disaggregation of its main items. The NFP group, instead, is composed of variables such as the price level and the short-term interest rate: they affect both FP variables and output, but are less likely to be affected (especially by FP variables) within the sample period considered.

In the next two sub-sections we present the econometric model to estimate and the identification restrictions of the SVAR, which follow the general lines described above and add economic content to the definition of the different fiscal policy regimes.

4.1   VAR structure and estimation

The estimation of a structural VAR (SVAR) involves two stages. In the first stage, the unrestricted VAR generates a vector of reduced-form residuals that cannot be economically interpreted. The second stage establishes a set of links

---

[5] This intuition is present in Blanchard and Perotti (1999), although in a smaller model.

[6] Of course, taxation is contemporaneously affected by output that affects the various tax bases; further discussion is provided in sub-section 4.1.

between reduced-form innovations and (economically meaningful) structural innovations. Since structural innovations are mutually uncorrelated, the links between reduced-form and structural innovations represent an explicit way of controlling for the contemporaneous correlations of the reduced-form residuals. These links are shaped according to plausible restrictions among the economic variables of the original VAR.

Let us collect all the economic variables in the vector x_t decomposed into three subvectors: $x_{NFP,t}$, which contains the NFP variables, $x_{FP,t}$ with the FP variables and, finally, the output of the economy, y_t.[7]

The NFP subvector contains (from top to bottom) the price level and the short-term interest rate. We assume that prices are sticky and react with at least one sample-period (i.e. one quarter) lag. The interest rate is necessary in our analysis since we want to model government outlays for interest payments on the public debt. Its role among the NFP variables can be justified either as a monetary instrument and by assuming that monetary policy decisions are taken independently of fiscal policy shocks and variables or, more generally, as a (weakly) exogenous variable for the fiscal policy regime.

Next, the FP vector contains all three fiscal aggregates: government expenditure for wages and transfers, other government expenditure and tax revenue.

In the first stage the estimation of the unrestricted VAR (given by (9.1)) generates three subvectors of innovations, one for NFP variables ($u_{NFP,t}$), one for FP variables ($u_{FP,t}$) and one for output ($u_{y,t}$):

$$\mathbf{R}(L) \begin{bmatrix} \mathbf{x}_{NFP,t} \\ \mathbf{x}_{FP,t} \\ y_t \end{bmatrix} = \begin{bmatrix} \mathbf{u}_{NFP,t} \\ \mathbf{u}_{FP,t} \\ u_{y,t} \end{bmatrix}, \tag{9.1}$$

where $\mathbf{R}(L)$ is a matrix of polynomials in the lag operator L and $\mathbf{R}(0) = \mathbf{I}$.

In the estimation of the orthogonalised, economically meaningful (structural) innovations in the second stage, a recursive causal block-order is assumed from the set of NFP variables to the set of both the FP variables and output. Moreover, the recursive causal order is also established for the NFP variables in $x_{NFP,t}$.[8]

In terms of the relationship between the fundamental innovations ($u_{NFP,t}$, $u_{FP,t}$ and $u_{y,t}$) and the structural innovations ($v_{NFP,t}$, $v_{FP,t}$ and $v_{y,t}$, which are all mutually and serially uncorrelated), this implies:

$$\begin{bmatrix} \mathbf{A}_{1,1} & 0 & 0 \\ \mathbf{A}_{2,1} & \mathbf{A}_{2,2} & 0 \\ \mathbf{a}_{3,1} & \mathbf{a}_{3,2} & 1 \end{bmatrix} \begin{bmatrix} \mathbf{u}_{NFP,t} \\ \mathbf{u}_{FP,t} \\ u_{y,t} \end{bmatrix} = \begin{bmatrix} \mathbf{B}_{1,1} & 0 & 0 \\ 0 & \mathbf{B}_{2,2} & 0 \\ 0 & 0 & b_{3,3} \end{bmatrix} \begin{bmatrix} \mathbf{v}_{NFP,t} \\ \mathbf{v}_{FP,t} \\ v_{y,t} \end{bmatrix} \tag{9.2}$$

---

[7] Bold lower-case (capital) letters indicate vectors (matrices).

[8] According to the definitions of our vectors, this means that the price level contemporaneously affects the short-term interest rate, but not vice-versa. Hence, the interest rate equation may be interpreted as a monetary rule that mainly focuses on inflation.

The shape of the matrices that link the NFP shocks are all known according to the definition of the NFP variables that we discussed above.[9] In addition, we assume that output reacts to all fundamental innovations (i.e., $\mathbf{a}_{3,1}$ and $\mathbf{a}_{3,2}$ are full vectors with no zero restrictions).

Hence, the core of our identification strategy are the matrices $\mathbf{A}_{2,2}$ and $\mathbf{B}_{2,2}$, which shape the relationships among the fiscal innovations and the fiscal shocks:

$$\mathbf{A}_{2,2}\mathbf{u}_{FP,t} = \mathbf{B}_{2,2}\mathbf{v}_{FP,t}. \tag{9.3}$$

The idea is that, in order to correctly identify a fiscal policy shock, it is necessary to propose different fiscal policy regimes, i.e. different sets of causal links among the fiscal variables that will identify the intentions of the fiscal authorities in terms of their 'operative objectives'.

These different intentions can be translated into appropriate constraints in the relationship between $\mathbf{u}_{FP,t}$ and $\mathbf{v}_{FP,t}$. Hence, the core of the analysis focuses on the shape that the matrices $\mathbf{A}_{2,2}$ and $\mathbf{B}_{2,2}$ must take according to the different intentions of the fiscal authorities. This entails setting linear constraints on the elements of those two matrices. A test for overidentifying restrictions can possibly be applied to check whether the constraints implied by the different regimes are rejected by the data. Impulse response functions of FP and NFP variables to fiscal shocks are used to check further whether the identified fiscal policy innovations can be plausibly qualified as such.[10]

4.2   What are fiscal policy variables?

Before proceeding to the identification of the fiscal regimes, it is important to better qualify the fiscal policy (FP) variables that we use in our analysis. This is particularly relevant because of the zero constraints that have been imposed in

---

[9] More exactly, $\mathbf{A}_{1,1}$ is lower triangular, $\mathbf{B}_{1,1}$ is diagonal and $\mathbf{A}_{2,1}$ is a full matrix.

[10] In this empirical approach to fiscal policy, non-stationarity of the data is not generally emphasised and cointegration analysis is not undertaken. A first justification is that the data may be *quasi-non-stationary*; in fact, the presence of unit roots in the time series cannot be tested with high power. Moreover, even though unit roots may characterise the data, Sims, Stock and Watson (1990) show that most traditional, standard asymptotic tests are still valid if the VAR is estimated in levels.

The neglecting of cointegration constraints is motivated by the following considerations. First, the analysis is generally focused on short-run constraints and the short-run dynamic response of the system. When cointegration constraints are excluded, this implies only that the *long-run* responses of some variables are not constrained and might follow a divergent path. However, the short-run analysis is still valid. Second, Sims, Stock and Watson(1990) proved that standard asymptotic inference is not affected even when the variables included in the VAR in levels are cointegrated. Finally, although FIML estimates are no longer efficient if cointegration constraints are not included, they still remain consistent. Hence, the lower efficiency in the estimates can be justified by the objective difficulty in the economic interpretation of some of the cointegration constraints showed by the data (in our study for some OECD countries we found four cointegrating vectors, which were very difficult to interpret and identify).

the system (9.2) More specifically, the block-recursive shape imposes that the FP variables do not react contemporaneously to output.

Among the FP variables we include two expenditure items and the tax revenue. The zero constraint of the effect of output on expenditure aggregates is justified by the inside lag of fiscal policy when taking decisions on the expenditure side. As already mentioned, this lag is due to the time needed to pass new laws.[11]

The same argument is more difficult to support for tax revenues. Indeed, output changes have an immediate effect on the tax bases and may induce automatic variations in the tax aggregate. Blanchard and Perotti (1999) compute the elasticity of the tax revenue to output and impose a coefficient equal to the estimated value. Here, we take a different approach and assert that the coefficient may be equal to either zero or one. In the former case we assume that the tax base may react immediately, but that it takes a quarter to affect the total tax revenue. In the latter case we consider the opposite case: tax base and tax revenue react immediately and equally in the same quarter. Of course, we will highlight the changes that such different assumptions on the contemporaneous reaction of the tax revenue to output may cause.

Among the two assumptions, the more plausible one is that the tax revenue reacts within the quarter. This choice implies that fiscal authorities are able to affect directly the ratio of tax revenue/output (i.e. an index of fiscal pressure). More technically, the structural innovations on the tax side can be recovered from innovations to the fiscal pressure.[12]

In the next section we examine in detail the links among the fiscal policy innovations that can identify four plausible fiscal policy regimes.

4.3   The fiscal policy regimes

The FP variables included in our VAR are: the government expenditure for wages and transfers (whose reduced-form innovation is g_w), other government expenditures (reduced-form innovation is g_r) and the tax revenue (reduced-form innovation is τ).[13]

We assume that there are no direct links among the fundamental innovations of each FP variable. Instead, the links among them are due to the structural

---

[11] Blanchard and Perotti (1999) impose the same constraint by imposing $b_1 = 0$ in their terminology.

[12] Within the VAR we have also estimated the coefficient that considers the influence of output on fiscal pressure: for all countries (except for the USA, for which we had problems of convergence) all the coefficients were highly non-significant. The inclusion of that additional coefficient to estimate, however, makes the system exactly identified and we lose the ability to check for the different regimes. Hence, we decided to set that coefficient to zero so as to carry out overidentifying tests.

[13] We omit the time t subscript for simplicity in this section since all the relationships are contemporaneous.

innovations identified by each FP variable. The links among the FP variables can be summarized in the following system (9.4) of equations:

$$g_w = \sigma_w v^w + \gamma_1 v^r + \gamma_2 v^\tau$$
$$g_r = \gamma_3 v^w + \sigma_r v^r + \gamma_4 v^\tau \qquad (9.4)$$
$$\tau = \phi_1 v^w + \phi_2 v^r + \sigma_\tau v^\tau$$

where v^ω, v^τ and v^τ are respectively the own, structural (i.e. mutually uncorrelated and economically meaningful) shocks to the two expenditure aggregates and the tax revenue.

The overall system is underidentified since the number of parameters to be estimated is higher than the number of degrees of freedom that the available covariances of the first stage allow. Some additional constraints are required to estimate the model and we propose four sets of restrictions in order to identify different fiscal policy regimes.

1. *T regime:* $\phi_1 = \phi_2 = \phi_1 = \gamma_1 = \gamma_3 = 0$. This regime is characterised by the (weak) exogeneity of the tax decisions that affect the expenditure decisions without being influenced in return. Moreover, the two expenditure aggregates are not correlated at the same time. Were this regime not rejected by the data, the tax-revenue structural innovations would be the fiscal policy shocks.

2. *G regime:* $\gamma_1 = \gamma_2 = \gamma_3 = \gamma_4 = 0$. On the contrary, in this case expenditure decisions are taken without any contemporaneous feedback from the tax revenue side, whereas tax decisions take into account the expenditure shocks. Both expenditure decisions are taken separately and there is no interaction between the two; they can both be considered fiscal policy shocks.

3. *GR regime:* $\phi_1 = \gamma_2 = \gamma_3 = \gamma_4 = 0$. This is a slight but significative variation of the previous (expenditure) regime where a central role is played by residual spending. Innovations to this latter expenditure are the fiscal policy shocks: both spending on wages and transfers and the tax revenue are adjusted according to the own shocks to residual spending. We ought to notice that the influence of the interest rate change on this part of total public spending is already taken into account since innovations in the interest rate enter the g_r equation via the coefficient which takes the place $(2,2)$ in the matrix $\mathbf{A}_{2,1}$. Shocks to this equation are own innovations that depend on the residual part.

4. *GW regime:* $\phi_2 = \gamma_1 = \gamma_2 = \gamma_4 = 0$. This latter regime is similar to the previous one, but it takes government expenditure on wages and transfers as the most exogenous component of fiscal policy. In other words, all the changes in the other expenditure component and taxes are adjusted so as to accommodate exogenous decisions on wages and transfers.

The first two regimes are not completely new in the literature. As quoted above, they were first proposed by Blanchard and Perotti (1999), although in a less extensive model. The GW regime, though, is proposed here for the first time and is basically justified by the fact that government expenditure on wages and transfers has been the object of a recent discussion on the way of implementing a fiscal retrenchment to reduce public debt. The GR regime is proposed for completeness.

Apart from the characteristic of the estimation, in the following section we test which of the proposed fiscal regimes is accepted by the data and present a simulation analysis on the responses of output to the identified fiscal shocks.

5   Empirical findings

The model has been estimated for four OECD countries (France, Germany, Italy and the USA) for the period 1960–97 (with slight differences amongst countries; see data appendix) by using quarterly data mostly derived from the OECD database.[14] In particular, the price level is the GDP deflator and the interest rate is the money market rate (except for Italy, for which we used a short-term government bond yield). Output is constant-price GDP. Output and the price level are taken as log transform.

The public finance data are still obtained by the OECD database for government statistics, where they are available only at current prices. The aggregates of government finance are all log-transformed. Just as monetary authorities are able to affect the nominal interest rate, fiscal authorities are able to change directly nominal government expenditure; hence, we decided not to correct the expenditure aggregates with any price deflator.[15]

The estimation lags have been selected according to the usual optimality criteria and are equal to three for Italy and US and four for France and Germany. Estimation is FIML and the standard errors of the impulse response functions are computed via the Delta method. As mentioned in the section 4.2, as the default model, we consider the contemporaneous one-to-one reaction of taxes to changes in GDP; the distinction between the two cases will be dealt with for the impulse response functions to tax innovations.

Table 9.1 shows the results of the overidentification test (likelihood-ratio, LR, test) for the four regimes and it shows a clear prevalence of fiscal regimes based on government expenditure rather than on tax revenue (more exactly, fiscal pressure). At the 5% probability level, the GR regime is not rejected for all countries. Moreover, the GW regime is still not rejected for both France and Italy, whereas an overall G regime cannot be rejected for the USA. Germany is the only country for which the GR regime is the only one 'accepted'. The USA is the only country for which no clear rejection of regimes occurs, especially

---

[14] A detailed description of the data set is presented in the data appendix.

[15] As in Blanchard and Perotti (1999), we used the GDP deflator to correct nominal government expenditure and continued with the analysis. No major differences were found in the impulse response functions and all the overidentifying tests concluded for the same fiscal regimes.

Table 9.1. *LR tests for the identification of fiscal regimes (probability values)*

Countries	T regime	G regime	GR regime	GW regime
France	6.70×10^{-15}	9.03×10^{-15}	0.409	0.334
Germany	7.03×10^{-8}	9.75×10^{-9}	0.408	0.014
Italy	0.006	0.006	0.262	0.852
USA	0.032	0.069	0.091	0.005

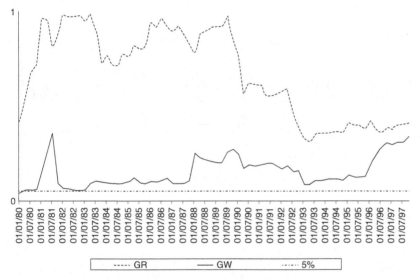

Figure 9.3 France: Probability values for the LR tests of the fiscal regimes, 1980Q1–1997Q4

between the G and the T regimes. Blanchard and Perotti (1999) cannot test for fiscal policy regimes since their system is exactly identified; they also say, however, that little correlation is present between the tax and the expenditure innovations, thus making the order of causality between tax and expenditure aggregates an unresolved issue. Our result of no clear distinction among fiscal regimes for the USA may be in line with what Blanchard and Perotti (1999) found.

How stable are the found fiscal regimes over time? In order to check for the possible change of fiscal regimes in our sample, we have computed the same overidentifying tests for all the successive samples starting in 1980Q1. The probability values of the most relevant regimes are reported in the figures 9.3–9.6. The results show for France and Italy that the validity of the GW and the

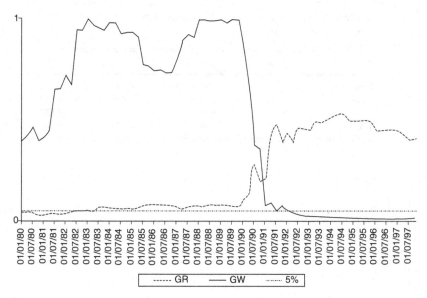

Figure 9.4 Germany: Probability values for the LR tests of the fiscal regimes, 1980Q1–1997Q4

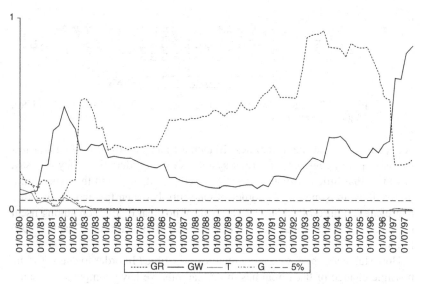

Figure 9.5 Italy: Probability values for the LR tests of the fiscal regimes, 1980Q1–1997Q4

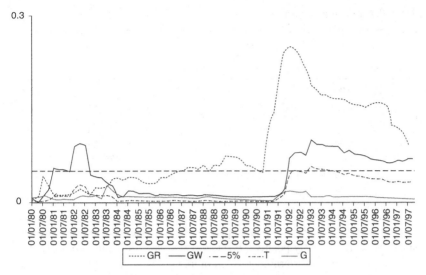

Figure 9.6 USA: Probability values for the LR tests of the fiscal regimes, 1980Q1–1997Q4

GR regimes is stable over all the subsamples. For the USA the GR regime is valid only starting from the end of the 1980s, whereas the overall G regime is valid from the beginning of the 1990s. Germany shows an interesting feature: up to 1991 the GW regime was not rejected even with a much higher probability level than the GR regime. The regime switch seems to occur at the unification period. Given these results, we report estimation and simulation only for the not-rejected regimes, excluding also the GW regime for Germany because it is rejected from 1991.

The estimates of the coefficients involved in system (9.4), together with that of the interest rate in the residual expenditure equation, are reported in table 9.2. We deem that 'virtuous' fiscal authorities decide on an increase in expenditure together with the corresponding financing measure, either by a decrease of some other type of expenditure and/or by an increase in taxes. In our framework we are able to evaluate whether any of the fiscal authorities were 'virtuous' by looking at the signs of estimated coefficients.

For instance, in France and Italy shocks to the two expenditure aggregates are positively correlated since both γ_1 and γ_3 are significantly positive, i.e. an increase in government wages and transfers occurs together with an increase in the residual spending. At the same time, no contemporaneous response is present in the tax revenue since ϕ_1 and ϕ_2 are not statistically significant. Hence, in France and Italy fiscal authorities did not link decisions on expenditure with those on the tax side.

Table 9.2. *Parameter estimates*

	France		Germany	Italy		USA	
Parameters	GR	GW	GR	GR	GW	G	GR
γ_1	0.0052^*	–	0.0083^*	0.0026^*	–		-0.0015
γ_3	–	0.0052^*	–	–	0.0029^*	–	–
ϕ_1	–	0.0005	–	–	-0.0015	-0.0019^{**}	–
ϕ_2	-0.0009	–	0.0041^*	-0.0006	–	0.0032^*	0.0030^*
$\eta_{gr,r}$	-0.0025		-0.0041^*	0.0021		-0.0065^*	

Note: * significant at the 5% level; ** significant at the 10% level.

The opposite conclusion is valid for the USA: a positive shock to government expenditure (especially the residual part) induces an increase in fiscal pressure since ϕ_2 is significantly positive. For Germany, we still obtain a positive correlation between the government expenditure aggregate (i.e. γ_1 is significantly positive), but we also have a positive increase in the fiscal pressure (i.e. ϕ_2 is significantly positive).

Among the other parameters of matrix **A**, it is important to consider the coefficient that describes the effect of a change in interest rates on the residual spending equation. From table 9.2, the reactivity of the residual government expenditure to nominal interest rate innovations (parameter $\eta_{gr,r}$) has the expected sign (although not significant) only for Italy, thus showing that an increase in the interest rate induces an increase in the residual spending. For all the other countries the sign is negative (even significantly for Germany and USA). The residual spending contains all the other government expenditures, which may overcome the effect of interest payments on public debt.

5.1   Impulse response analysis

Turning to the estimated impulse-response functions (IRFs), our attention will be mainly focused on the identified *fiscal policy shocks*, i.e. shocks to the type of spending that induces changes in the other fiscal aggregates. However, we will also show how output responds to other kinds of fiscal shocks (innovations to the tax revenue and to other aggregate expenditure that may not be identified as *the* fiscal policy shock). All the simulations consider an initial negative shock on public expenditure. In order to be able to compare the effects of fiscal shocks on output growth among countries, we normalise fiscal shocks by constructing responses to a 1% decrease in expenditure/GDP ratio. In other words, when considering the effects of, say, the shock to government expenditure on wages and transfers, we present the responses of output growth (in % per quarter),

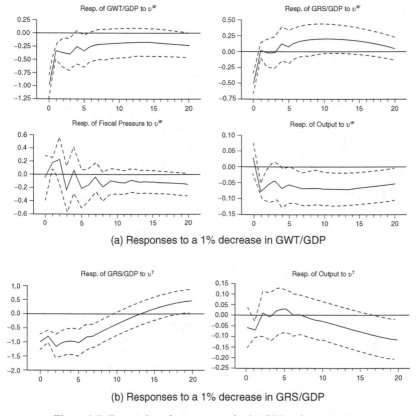

(a) Responses to a 1% decrease in GWT/GDP

(b) Responses to a 1% decrease in GRS/GDP

Figure 9.7 France: Impulse responses in the GW regime

the residual expenditure/GDP and tax revenue/GDP (%) when the government wages and transfers/GDP ratio decreases by 1% (i.e., say from 34% of GDP to 33%).[16]

Figures 9.7 and 9.8 refer to France and show the effects of fiscal-policy innovations on the expenditure side to the other fiscal variables and output.[17] Shocks

---

[16] Blanchard and Perotti (1999) show the dollar-to-dollar reaction of output to government expenditure and taxes. Here, we decided to consider a different normalisation for the shocks to highlight the effect on output growth and to consider the to-GDP ratios of government variables.

[17] The responses to all the other variables (i.e. price level and interest rate) are available from the authors upon request. Moreover, as in panels (b) of figure 9.7, for each country we report the effect of the innovation in the 'other' (with respect to the fiscal regime) government expenditure item (i.e., shock to residual spending (GRS) in the GW regime) only on own expenditure and output. In most cases the responses of the other variables are not very different from the responses to the shock on the expenditure item of the own regime (i.e., responses to the shock in government expenditure on wages and transfers in the GW regime).

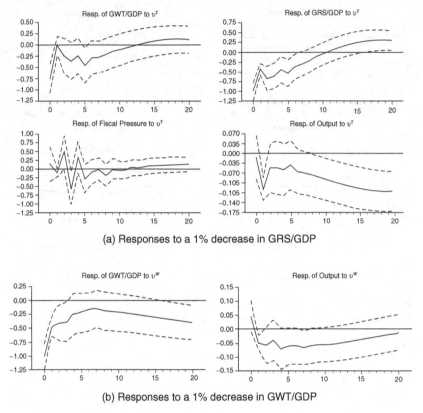

(a) Responses to a 1% decrease in GRS/GDP

(b) Responses to a 1% decrease in GWT/GDP

Figure 9.8 France: Impulse responses in the GR regime

to government spending on wages and transfers (GWT) have the strongest (and statistically significant)[18] effect on output under both the GW and GR regimes: after an initial positive (but not significant) reaction, output decreases by 0.05–0.1% in response to a 1% decrease in GWT/GDP. Under the GW regime, the response is very significant from the fourth quarter on; it is only just significant under the GR regime. Moreover, under the GR regime the decrease in output occurs together with a decrease in the price level below trend (not presented in our figures): this co-movement in prices and output (which is found also for other countries) shows that the system is moving along the AS curve and that we are correctly identifying AD shocks.

For Germany we show only the IRFs for the GR regime, since the overidentifying test and the relative stability analysis suggest it as the most recent and

---

[18] Significance is always referred to at a 5% probability level unless stated otherwise.

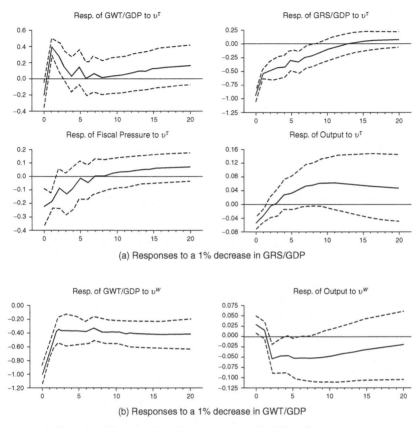

Figure 9.9 Germany: Impulse responses in the GR regime

probable fiscal regime. The shock in the residual government spending (GRS) – which lowers the GRS/GDP ratio by 1% – has an immediate effect on output: the initial decrease is significant and equal to 0.04–0.08%, but lasts for only three quarters (figure 9.9). A similar feature is shown by the shock on the GWT expenditure: output decreases by 0.05% after two quarters, but this decrease is no longer significant as of the sixth quarter.

In Italy too the spending aggregate on government wages and transfers has the strongest effect on output under both the valid regimes (GW and GR). Figures 9.10 and 9.11 both show a similar reaction of output, that permanently decreases by 0.1%. An initial negative shock on GRS lowers output significantly only in the first two quarters under both fiscal regimes.

Finally, in the USA we find a similar pattern as in Italy (Figures 9.12 and 9.13): an initial decreasing shock on GWT has a significantly negative effect on

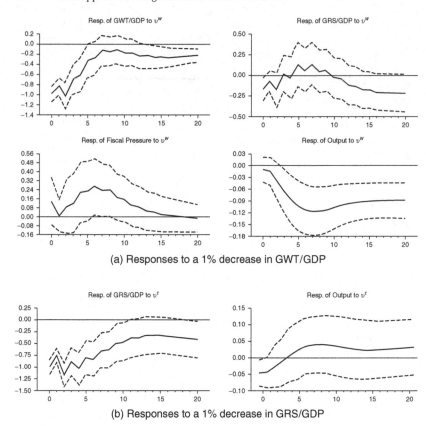

(a) Responses to a 1% decrease in GWT/GDP

(b) Responses to a 1% decrease in GRS/GDP

Figure 9.10 Italy: Impulse responses in the GW regime

output starting from the fourth quarter. Output decreases by (maximum) 0.1%
after the initial 1% fall in GWT/GDP. We observe only an initial (significant)
negative impact on output of the shock to GRS.

5.2   *Responses to a tax shock*

As mentioned above, we designed two different ways in which the tax revenue
can react to output: the tax revenue can react contemporaneously either one-to-
one or not at all. Up to now we have considered the first case (which is the most
plausible one). When analysing the effects of tax shocks, we deem it important
to include both polar cases in order to obtain the extremes of the likely response
of output to a tax decrease.

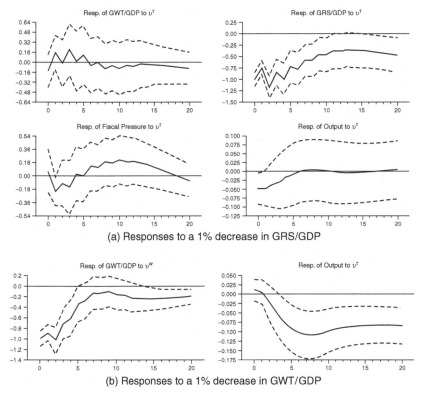

(a) Responses to a 1% decrease in GRS/GDP

(b) Responses to a 1% decrease in GWT/GDP

Figure 9.11 Italy: Impulse responses in the GR regime

Figures 9.14 to 9.17 show the effects of the tax shock that decreases fiscal pressure by 1 percentage point. The two panels of each figure show the two extremes, i.e. when the tax revenue reacts fully or not (immediately) at all.

The effects on GDP are more positive for all countries when the tax revenue reacts to output. In this case, in all countries except France, we observe a significant increase in output, even though with different characteristics. In Germany and Italy the increase in output is immediate and lasts significantly for many quarters (fifteen quarters in Germany and twelve in Italy, although at the 90% significance level in the latter country); the magnitude of this increase is 0.1% in Germany and 0.05–0.07% in Italy. In the USA, at impact the decrease in taxes has a surprisingly negative impact on output that becomes not significant after one quarter. This latter result may suggest that a further reduction in the tax revenue may not cause a positive effect on output since fiscal pressure is already low in the USA.

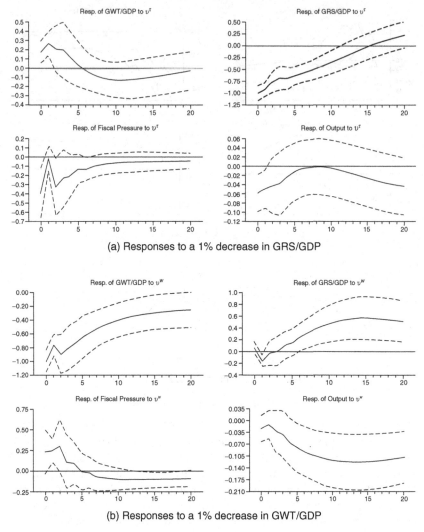

(a) Responses to a 1% decrease in GRS/GDP

(b) Responses to a 1% decrease in GWT/GDP

Figure 9.12 USA: Impulse responses in the GW regime

5.3   *Forecast error variance decomposition*

In order to measure the quantitative importance of the fiscal shocks in the dynamics of output, figures 9.18 and 9.19 report the forecast error variance decomposition (FEVD) of output in Germany and Italy, respectively. We do not show the FEVD graphs for the other countries since the fiscal shocks are only marginally significant there.

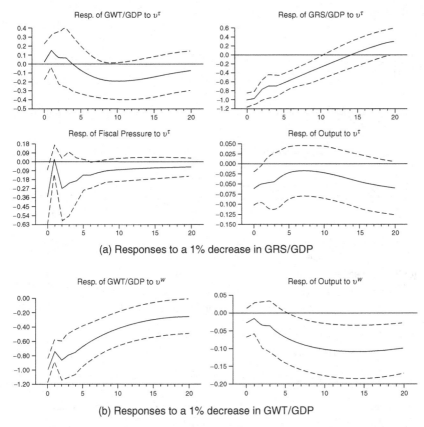

(a) Responses to a 1% decrease in GRS/GDP

(b) Responses to a 1% decrease in GWT/GDP

Figure 9.13 USA: Impulse responses in the GR regime

Germany and Italy are two interesting cases where different fiscal shocks play an important role for the output dynamics. In Germany the v^r and the v^τ shocks (i.e., respectively, the structural shock to residual government expenditure and the structural shock to the tax revenue) are the most important shocks. In particular, v^r is significant for the first six steps ahead and has a high weight immediately (over 20% of the forecast error variance of output is explained by the v^y shock), but rapidly decreases after two to three quarters. Instead v^τ (shock to fiscal pressure) is significant between the fourth and the tenth quarter with a weight around 10–17%. No significant weight is assigned to v^w. Most of the variability in the forecast error variance is explained by the innovation to output, but the overall importance of all fiscal shocks never decreases below 21%.

In Italy the importance of the fiscal shocks in the variability of the forecast error in output is reversed: shocks to GWT are more important in the medium

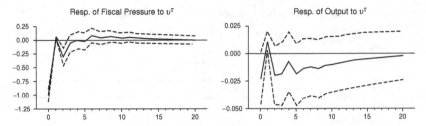

(a) Responses to a 1% decrease in (T/GDP) – one-to-one contemporaneous reaction of T to GDP

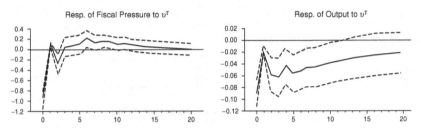

(b) Responses to a 1% decrease in (T/GDP) – no contemporaneous reaction of T to GDP

Figure 9.14 France: Impulse responses functions of output to innovations in fiscal pressure

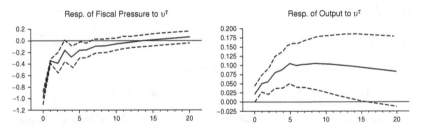

(a) Responses to a 1% decrease in (T/GDP) – one-to-one contemporaneous reaction of T to GDP

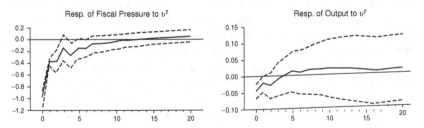

(b) Responses to a 1% decrease in (T/GDP) – no contemporaneous reaction of T to GDP

Figure 9.15 Germany: Impulse responses functions of output to innovations in fiscal pressure

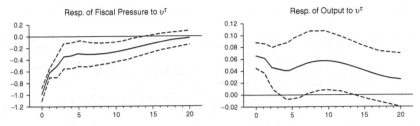

(a) Responses to a 1% decrease in (T/GDP) – one-to-one contemporaneous reaction of T to GDP

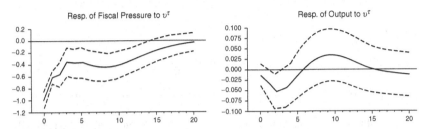

(b) Responses to a 1% decrease in (T/GDP) – no contemporaneous reaction of T to GDP

Figure 9.16 Italy: Impulse responses functions of output to innovations in fiscal pressure

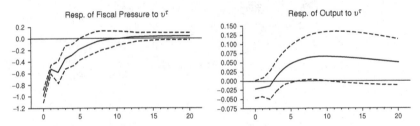

(a) Responses to a 1% decrease in (T/GDP) – one-to-one contemporaneous reaction of T to GDP

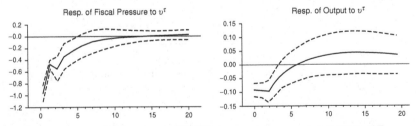

(b) Responses to a 1% decrease in (T/GDP) – no contemporaneous reaction of T to GDP

Figure 9.17 USA: Impulse responses functions of output to innovations in fiscal pressure

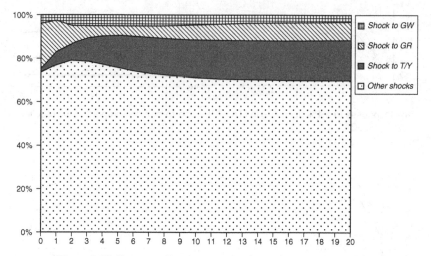

Figure 9.18 Germany: Forecast error variance decomposition of output (GR Regime)

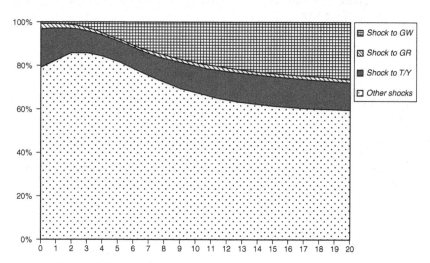

Figure 9.19 Italy: Forecast error variance decomposition of output (GW regime)

to long run, whereas shocks to fiscal pressure are relevant in the short run. In particular, ν^w (structural shock to government wages and transfers) is significant starting from the ninth step ahead and is able to explain up to 26% of the forecast error variance of output (at twenty-one steps ahead). Shocks to fiscal pressure (ν^τ) are instead significant up to the fourth step ahead ranging between 18% (first step) and 10% (fourth step).

6   Conclusions

Different ways of conducting fiscal policy can be described as *fiscal policy regimes*. In this chapter we have proposed an approach to test for these regimes with two main aims. First, by disentangling government expenditure on wages and transfers from total spending, we wanted to test in which countries decisions on such types of government expenditure precede all the other fiscal variables (i.e. residual expenditure and taxes). Second, we designed the structural VAR in such a way as to obtain an overidentified structural form so that each fiscal regime could be tested.

France and Italy are the two countries for which the GW fiscal regime cannot be rejected, i.e. where government expenditure on wages and transfers are decided 'before' the other fiscal variables. This means that in those countries innovations in government expenditure on wages and transfers may be considered primary fiscal shocks that induce structural variations in residual spending and fiscal pressure. Although such a regime is rejected in both Germany and the USA, structural innovations in government spending for wages and transfers still have the strongest effect on output there. Shocks to tax revenues have the expected sign on output: a decrease in tax revenues that reduces fiscal pressure causes an increase in output (except for France, where there is no effect on output) that may last up to fifteen quarters in (Germany). However, in all simulations the maximum impact of fiscal policy shocks is limited and an induced 1% change in government spending or fiscal pressure rarely has an impact on output over 0.1%. In no country does the shock to tax revenue have a long-run impact.

In terms of output dynamics, the results are country-specific. In Germany no role is played by the shock to government expenditure on wages and transfers in the forecast error variance of output. But in Italy such a shock is able to explain over one-fourth of the total variance in the forecast error of output. An important role is assigned to shocks to the tax revenue (between 10% and 18%).

Further work should be done to obtain the responses of other components of aggregate demand and to investigate different types of government expenditure (such as public investment).

7   Data appendix

All data, if not otherwise specified, come from the OECD Statistical Compendium. Data on public finance refer to general government. Most of the available data are at quarterly frequency but, since for some budget items series are released only biannually a simple procedure has been implemented to impute the six-monthly data to the single quarters.[19] In what follows, sources, codes and definitions of the original variables are reported.

OECD Business Sectoral Database

CGW = government consumption, wages
GDP = gross domestic product (market prices), value
GDPV = gross domestic product (market prices), volume
IG = fixed investment, government
PGDP = deflator for GDP at market prices, base year = 100
TIND = indirect taxes
TSUB = subsidies
TYB = direct Taxes, Business

OECD Economic Outlook

CGNW = government consumption, excluding wages
SSPG = social benefits paid by government
SSRG = social security contributions received by government
TRPG = other current transfers paid by government
TRRG = other current transfers received by government
TY = total direct taxes
YPEPG = property income paid by government
YPERG = property income received by government
YPG = current disbursement, government
YRG = current receipts, government

OECD Main Economic Indicators

126207D = call money rate, Germany
426227D = US dollar in London three-month, USA

---

[19] The procedure consists, firstly, in identifying for each biannual variable a quarterly series whose pattern could approximate that of the low-frequency series. Then, the biannual value is distributed among the quarters following the pattern of the related series.

IMF International Financial Statistics

line 61b = government bond yield, medium-term, Italy
line 60b = money market rate, France

Current revenue

The corresponding OECD variable, YRG, is available only at biannual frequency. It is the sum of YPERG, TIND, TY, SSRG and TRRG. Among these series, only TIND is available at quarterly frequency. OECD also releases quarterly series of the portion of TY related to firms (TYB), which, added to TIND, represents almost 40% of the total current revenue. Hence, the biannual series YRG has been distributed among the quarters following the pattern, in the same quarters, of the series obtained from the sum of TIND and TYB.

Total expenditure

OECD Database do not provide a series for this aggregate. A good approximation for it is given by the sum of the total current expenditure, YPG (available at biannual frequency) and the public investment spending, IG (quarterly). The series YPG can be obtained as:

$$YPG = CGW + CGNW + TSUB + SSPG + TRPG + YPEPG.$$

Since, among these series, only CGW and TSUB are available at quarterly frequency, and they are about one-third of the total current expenditure, the sum of the two series has been used to distribute the series YPG amongst the quarters. The resulting series has been added up to the IG series.

Transfers

We define transfers as the sum of subsidies (TSUB), social benefits paid by government (SSPG) and other current transfers paid by government (TRPG). Among these series, only TSUB is available at quarterly frequency. The sum of the biannual series SSPG and TRPG is more than one-third of total public expenditure. So, this sum has been attributed to the quarters on the basis of the pattern of the total expenditure variable. The resulting series has been summed up to the quarterly TSUB series.

Public wages

For this series we have used the OECD series CGW.

Interest rates

This variable should represent the actions of the monetary authority, so we use short-term interest rates where available, and three-month or medium-term interest rates otherwise. We used a medium-term interest rate for Italy, the call money rate for Germany, the money rate for France and the US Dollar in London three-month for the USA.

Prices

For all the countries we have considered the GDP deflator.

Countries and samples used for the estimation

France: 1963Q1–1997Q4
Germany: 1961Q1–1997Q4
Italy: 1960Q1–1997Q4
USA: 1961Q1–1997Q4

REFERENCES

Alesina, A. and S. Ardagna, 1998, 'Tales of Fiscal Adjustment', *Economic Policy* 27, 489–545.

Alesina, A. and R. Perotti, 1995, 'Fiscal Expansions and Adjustments in OECD Countries', *Economic Policy* 21, 205–47.

1997, 'Fiscal Adjustment in OECD Countries: Composition and Macroeconomic Effects', *IMF Staff Papers* 44, 210–48.

Bernanke, B. and I. Mihov, 1998, 'Measuring Monetary Policy', *Quarterly Journal of Economics* 113(3), 869–902.

Blanchard, O. J. and R. Perotti, 1999, 'An Empirical Characterization of the Dynamic Effects of Changes in Government Spending and Taxes on Output', NBER Working Paper, no. 7269.

Burnside, C., M. Eichembaum and J. Fisher, 1999, 'Assessing the Effects of Fiscal Shocks', mimeo, Northwestern University.

2000, 'Fiscal Shocks in an Efficiency Wage Model', NBER Working Paper no. 7515.

Christiano, L., M. Eichenbaum and C. Evans, 1998, 'Monetary Policy Shocks: What Have We Learnt and to What End?', NBER Working Paper no. 6400.

Edelberg, W., M. Eichembaum and J. Fisher, 1999, 'Understanding the Effect of a Shock to Government Purchases', *Review of Economics Dynamics* 2, 166–206.

Fatás, A. and I. Mihov, 2000, 'Measuring the Effects of Fiscal Policy' mimeo, INSEAD.

Giavazzi, F. and M. Pagano, 1990, 'Can Severe Fiscal Contractions be Expansionary? Tales of Two Small European Countries', in O. J. Blanchard and S. Fischer (eds.), *NBER Macroeconomics Annual*, 1990 Cambridge, MA: MIT Press, pp. 75–111.

1996, 'Non-Keynesian Effects of Fiscal Policy Changes: International Evidence and the Swedish Experience', *Swedish Economic Policy Review* 3, 67–103.

McDermott, C. J. and R. F. Wescott, 1996, 'An Empirical Analysis of Fiscal Adjustments', *IMF Staff Papers* 43, 725–53.

Ramey, V. A. and M. D. Shapiro, 1998, 'Costly Capital Reallocation and the Effects of Government Spending', *Carnegie-Rochester Conference Series on Public Policy* 48, 145–94.

Sims, C., J. Stock and M. W. Watson, 1990, 'Inference in Time Series Models with Some Unit Roots', *Econometrica* 58, 113–44.

Zaghini A., 1999, 'The Economic Policy of Fiscal Consolidation: The European Experience', Bank of Italy Discussion Paper no. 353.

10 Monetary and fiscal policy interactions over the cycle: some empirical evidence

V. Anton Muscatelli, Patrizio Tirelli and Carmine Trecroci

1 Introduction

The advent of EMU has raised a number of issues regarding the relative roles of fiscal and monetary policy. The Stability and Growth Pact (SGP henceforth) has imposed strict limits to countercyclical fiscal policies. Whilst the SGP is seen as a tool to avoid excessive debt accumulation (see Beetsma and Jensen 1999; Beetsma and Uhlig 1997), a number of authors (see Eichengreen and Wyplosz 1998, for example) fear that the SGP will hamper the operation of automatic stabilisers.

However, there is relatively scarce evidence on the interaction of fiscal and monetary policies. Whilst considerable attention has been given to the way in which monetary authorities respond to macroeconomic conditions,[1] much less empirical work has been done on fiscal policy.[2] Even less attention has recently been paid to the interdependence between fiscal and monetary policy at the empirical level. The only notable exceptions are the studies by Mélitz (1997, 2000), Wyplosz (1999) and von Hagen, Hughes Hallett and Strauch (2001). For instance, using pooled data for a number of OECD economies, Mélitz (1997) finds that fiscal and monetary policy tend to move in opposite directions to each other.[3] In other words, they are strategic substitutes. He also finds that a higher debt burden tends to trigger an adjustment process.

The present chapter extends this work in a number of directions. We use VAR models (both conventional and Bayesian VARs) to characterise fiscal–monetary interactions rather than estimating monetary and fiscal reaction functions using

The authors are grateful to participants at the conference on 'EMU Macroeconomic Institutions' held in Milan in September 2001, for comments on an earlier draft of this paper, and particularly to Giuseppe de Arcangelis, Roel Beetsma, Alex Cukierman and Jacques Melitz for helpful comments. We are also grateful to seminar participants at Mainz and Trento. The usual disclaimer applies.

[1] See for example Clarida, Galí and Gertler (1998, 2000), Muscatelli, Tirelli and Trecroci (2000, 2002a), Favero and Rovelli (1999).

[2] See Blanchard and Perotti (1999) and Fatás and Mihov (2000).

[3] Mélitz uses a short-term money market rate as the monetary instrument and the primary surplus as a percentage of potential output as the fiscal instrument.

single-equation methods. VAR studies of fiscal policy are relatively scarce. This may be due to the standard criticism that a government change may determine the expectation of a fiscal policy shift well before the new fiscal stance is detected in the VAR (see, for example, Mountford and Uhlig 2002). In our view, such a criticism is probably overstated. In fact, one should bear in mind that the specific features of a policy package are crucial in determining agents' reactions to fiscal legislation, whose details often remain uncertain until the legislative process has been completed. Moreover, our results show that the fiscal shocks identified in the VAR do have significant effects, while additional evidence discussed in Muscatelli, Tirelli and Trecroci (2002b) shows that fiscal and monetary shocks play a similar role in explaining the forecast error variance of business cycle fluctuations. The evidence collected in the present chapter sheds some light on the dynamic adjustment of output, inflation and monetary policy. This allows us to obtain a more complete picture of the dynamic interactions (including regime shifts) between these jointly endogenous variables, and to address a number of issues.

First, we examine whether the strategic substitutability result holds for individual OECD countries. Our focus is on some of the major G7 economies, and we estimate VAR models with both fiscal and monetary policy instruments to model the fiscal–monetary interactions. Our findings show that the result of strategic substitutability does not hold uniformly for all countries. Indeed, our results point to some interesting asymmetries in the responses of fiscal and monetary policy. Moreover, our approach enables us to examine the changes over time in the degree of strategic interaction between fiscal and monetary policy, as the relationship between the policy instruments may not be constant over time. In a number of countries in our sample the behaviour of monetary policy has changed markedly since the early 1980s, with fiscal policy in Europe becoming increasingly constrained by the process of nominal convergence. The SGP was the final element in this policy shift. Even in the USA, the debt-reduction measures of the 1990s represent a sea change in the conduct of fiscal policy. We thus analyse the extent to which the nature of fiscal–monetary interactions has changed by reporting VAR estimates for the latter part of our sample, and by computing some Bayesian VAR estimates. These show that, in some countries, the linkage between fiscal and monetary policy has shifted over time.

Second, we examine whether Mélitz's result that a high degree of indebtedness triggers an adjustment in fiscal policy is robust for individual countries, and whether it holds at all times. We find no evidence of a deficit feedback on past debt levels, with the exception of Germany.

Third, by using our VAR model of the fiscal–monetary interactions, we see whether, taking account of fiscal policy, we still get a plausible picture of how

(a) monetary policy reacts to output and inflation shocks; (b) output and inflation react to interest rate shocks. As we shall see, our VAR models seem to be broadly consistent with existing studies on monetary policy reaction functions.

Fourth, we examine how fiscal policies react to output and inflation shocks. Theoretical models are unambiguous about how fiscal stabilisation policies operate. Is the empirical evidence consistent with the prescriptions of these theoretical models?

Fifth, we examine how fiscal shocks are transmitted to the economy and whether output and inflation react as expected. We show that some differences emerge between countries, and that in some cases non-Keynesian effects tend to show up (see Giavazzi and Pagano 1990, 1996).

The rest of the chapter is structured as follows. In Section 2 we survey some of the existing literature on monetary–fiscal interactions and outline some of its key predictions. In Section 3 we outline our empirical methodology. In Section 4 we report and discuss our estimated models. Section 5 concludes and a data appendix follows.

2   Models of fiscal–monetary interactions

The nature of the interdependence between fiscal and monetary policy is a recurring theme in macroeconomics. The traditional analysis focuses on the optimal policy mix when both policy instruments are under the control of a single policymaker who aims at mutually inconsistent targets. In recent years, following the widespread shift to a separation of powers between fiscal authorities and independent central banks, theoretical research has turned to the analysis of fiscal–monetary policy interactions when the two policymakers' objectives differ.

An important issue has been whether fiscal discretion should be regarded as a threat to monetary policy commitment. The so-called Fiscal Theory of Price Level Determination rests on the assumption that price stability is unattainable unless intertemporal government solvency is guaranteed. This, in turn, implies that a rise in inflationary pressures calls for both an interest rate rise and the sterilisation of the ensuing higher debt-service payments. Dixit and Lambertini (2000, 2001) explore the relation between fiscal discretion and monetary commitment in a model where the central bank has only partial control over inflation, which is also directly affected by the fiscal policy stance.[4] Not surprisingly,

---

[4] Furthermore, conflicting objectives between the two policymakers, where the central bank tries to achieve output and inflation levels below the fiscal authority's targets, lead to highly suboptimal Nash equilibria where monetary policy is too contractionary and the fiscal stance is insufficiently expansionary.

these authors find that in this case fiscal discretion destroys monetary commitment. Dixit and Lambertini also show that a tendency towards substitutability emerges when fiscal policy tends to increase both output and inflation, whilst complementarity could emerge where fiscal expansions have non-Keynesian (contractionary) effects on output and inflation.

An intriguing contribution by Hughes Hallett and Viegi (2000) suggests that policy conflict may be endogenous to the choice of central bank preferences: a strong bias in favour of price stability may induce the election of fiscal policymakers who are more concerned about output.

Buti, Roeger and In't Veld (2001) suggest that the specific form of interdependence between fiscal and monetary policies, i.e. the alternative between strategic substitutability and complementarity, should not necessarily be interpreted in terms of conflict or cooperation, and might be shock-dependent. In their model the bank targets inflation and a nominal interest rate objective, whereas the fiscal authority pursues output and deficit targets. Supply shocks unambiguously induce conflicting policies, whereas the opposite holds true for demand shocks.

Empirical evidence, uniformly based on panel data analysis, is scarce and loosely related to the theoretical debate. Work by Mélitz (1997, 2000) and Wyplosz (1999) broadly supports the view that the two policies tend to move in opposite directions. By contrast, von Hagen, Hughes Hallett and Strauch (2001) find that the interdependence between the two policymakers is asymmetric: looser fiscal stances match monetary contractions, whereas monetary policies broadly accommodate fiscal expansions. Finally, from the early 1990s these authors detect smaller fiscal responses to both monetary shocks and cyclical conditions.

3   Empirical issues and the econometric methodology

Structural VAR techniques are now a customary tool in the study of monetary policy. They provide a simple and powerful way to describe the dynamic interactions between jointly endogenous variables. In fact, the lags associated with the formulation of budget policies, and those usually thought to characterise the macroeconomic effects of tax and spending decisions, make the VAR framework in principle better suited to analyse the process of fiscal transmission than in the case of monetary policy changes. VARs are particularly attractive in the context of economic policy analysis[5] because of their ability to encompass the identification of macroeconomic effects of policy decisions and the feedback

---

[5] See Canova (1995) for a survey, and Bernanke and Mihov (1998) for an often-cited application to the analysis of monetary policy.

reaction of policy authorities to the business cycle in a relatively intuitive estimation strategy. Of course, one of the strengths of VAR models (the limited need to rely on identifying restrictions) is also one of its weaknesses. There is no attempt, in just-identified VARs, to identify policymakers' preferences, or to estimate theory-based structural reaction functions. In practice the policy reactions estimated in a VAR model could be interpreted as reduced forms of forward-looking policy reaction functions and structural parameters of the underlying economy. The impulse responses would then be interpreted as responses to unanticipated shocks to the economy. However, we would make two points in this regard. First, in order to estimate structural reaction functions, one has to make some restrictive assumptions regarding the specification of the policy rules and impose (or assume) certain identifying restrictions. These modelling assumptions are likely to be controversial, especially as far as fiscal policy rules are concerned, as they are likely to be less robust and stable over time. Second, whilst a VAR does not allow one to focus on individual structural parameters of the policy reaction functions, it does nevertheless allow a general picture to emerge regarding the policy reactions which occurred, especially when the econometric evidence is backed up with reference to well-known policy events or policy regime changes. The estimation of a fully fledged structural model of fiscal and monetary reaction functions is beyond the scope of this chapter and will be considered in further work.

Indeed, as noted above, the use of VAR models to identify fiscal policy shocks and the effects of their transmission is still at a rather embryonic stage,[6] whereas the interplay between fiscal and monetary policy decisions and their macroeconomic effects are yet to be tackled, to our knowledge, in a dynamic, system-based approach.

In this chapter we apply two complementary VAR methodologies to a set of quarterly variables for five OECD countries: Germany, France, Italy, the United Kingdom, and the USA. First, we estimate and analyse a conventional structural VAR on a vector comprising the output gap (y_t), the inflation rate (π_t), a measure of fiscal stance (g_t) and the call money rate (r_t).

The measure of fiscal stance is constructed as the deviation of total deficit from a Hodrick–Prescott filtered trend (setting the HP factor at $\lambda = 1600$). Other studies (see Mélitz 1997, 2000; Wyplosz 1999) use the primary deficit. Our choice is motivated by the fact that primary deficit data are available only at low frequencies and would not allow us sufficient observations to estimate our VAR models. It may be argued that, owing to the contemporaneous effect of interest rate payments, total deficit measures provide a somewhat blurred

---

[6] Blanchard and Perotti (1999), Edelberg, Eichenbaum and Fisher (1998) and Fatás and Mihov (2000) are amongst the early contributions to this approach.

picture of the fiscal policymaker's true reactions to the business cycle. However, by filtering the deficit series, we are removing the long-run trend component in the deficit, which is driven by debt interest dynamics. This way, our FPI variable arguably captures short-run fiscal impulses and allows us to analyse countercyclical fiscal policy.[7] On the other hand, we cannot identify the primary deficit response to credibility shocks, which presumably affect the overall deficit through debt service payments. Nevertheless, our analysis of the fiscal response to inflation shocks does provide an indirect test of the fiscal theory of price level determination (see the discussion in the conclusions).

The optimal VAR order was selected according to results from the application of conventional information criteria (AIC, HQ, SC) and formal LR tests; the models we estimated were either VAR(2) or VAR(3). The structural parameters were recovered through the imposition of a recursive, Cholesky-type decomposition of the residual covariance matrix. The variable ordering chosen allows for contemporaneous effects of all variables on the monetary policy instrument, while the fiscal policy indicator is assumed not to react to interest-rate shocks within the quarter. The longest estimation sample starts from the early 1970s for the European countries and from the late 1950s for the USA. Clearly, the use of such a long span in a standard structural VAR approach has to take into account the possibility of structural changes and regime shifts over the sample. This is why we also illustrate estimates from subsample periods, in an attempt to capture differences between the last two decades and the preceding years.

Next, we pursue the attempt to identify regime changes further, by computing time-varying VAR estimates. Our approach follows the Bayesian route pioneered by Doan, Litterman and Sims (1984), which allows the parameters of the estimated VAR and of the impulse response function to evolve over time as more observations are added. This feature is particularly useful in our case, as regime shifts that took place over the sample might have not only modified the parameters of the functions we are about to study, but they might have done so in a gradual manner.

We now sketch the estimation procedure we followed. Let us start with a standard VAR (p):

$$X_t = c + \sum_{j=1}^{p} A_j X_{t-j} + \varepsilon_t, \qquad (10.1)$$

where X_t is an $n \times 1$ vector of endogenous variables, A_js are the $n \times n$ matrices of parameter coefficients and ε_t is an $n \times 1$ vector of disturbances, for

[7] Elsewhere we extend our investigation to construct quarterly series on the budget deficit – see Muscatelli, Tirelli and Trecroci (2002b).

which:

$$E\{\varepsilon_t\} = 0; \ E\{\varepsilon_t \varepsilon_t'\} = \Sigma; \ E\{\varepsilon_t \varepsilon_s'\} = 0, \forall t \neq s.$$

In what follows we use the same notation as in Lutkepohl (1991), and Hamilton (1994).[8] We thus rewrite the model in the following way:

$$X = AZ + U;$$
$$X = (X_{p+1} \ X_{p+2} \ldots X_T);$$
$$A = (c \ A_1 \ldots A_p); Z = (Z_p \ Z_{p+1} \ldots Z_{T-1}); \tag{10.2}$$

$$Z_t = \begin{pmatrix} 1 \\ X_{t-1} \\ X_{t-2} \\ \vdots \\ X_{t-p} \end{pmatrix}.$$

Assuming time-varying coefficients, equation j from the system in (10.1) can be written as

$$x_{t,j} = \mathbf{Z}' \begin{pmatrix} c_j \\ \beta_{j1}^1 \\ \vdots \\ \beta_{jn}^1 \\ \vdots \\ \beta_{j1}^p \\ \vdots \\ \beta_{jn}^p \end{pmatrix} + \varepsilon_{t,j} = \mathbf{Z}' \beta_t + \varepsilon_{t,j}, \tag{10.3}$$

where the β_ts are the elements of the VAR coefficient vector.

Doan, Litterman and Sims (1984) postulate a Bayesian prior distribution for the first-period value of the coefficient vector: $\beta_{11} \sim N(\bar{\beta}, \mathbf{P}_{1/0})$. The procedure we follow assumes that the VAR coefficients follow an AR(1) process; the transition equation of the system is therefore:

$$\beta_{1t} = (1 - \psi_1)\bar{\beta} + \psi_1 \beta_{1t-1} + \boldsymbol{\xi}_{1t}. \tag{10.4}$$

In the above equation, the parameter vector follows a simple autoregressive process, in which the weighting parameter ψ_1 determines the importance of the steady-state value for the coefficient vector. The disturbance term is uncorrelated with the disturbances in the original VAR: $\text{cov}(\xi_{1t}, \varepsilon_{1t}) = 0$, whereas the

---

[8] See also Kim and Nelson (1999).

expected value $\bar{\beta}$ consists of a vector of zeros with one as elements corresponding to the own variable at lag 1 ($Z_{1,t-1}$) for each equation. This prior holds that changes in the endogenous variable modelled are so difficult to forecast that the coefficient on its lagged value is likely to be near unity, while all other coefficients are assumed to be near zero. The prior distribution is independent across coefficients, so that the MSE of the state vector is a diagonal matrix.

The matrix $\mathbf{P}_{1|0}$ is given by:

$$\mathbf{P}_{1|0} = \begin{pmatrix} v\hat{t}_1^2 & \mathbf{0}' \\ \mathbf{0} & (G \otimes C) \end{pmatrix}, \tag{10.5}$$

where

$$G = \begin{pmatrix} \gamma^2 & 0 & 0 & \dots & 0 \\ 0 & \gamma^2/2 & 0 & \dots & 0 \\ 0 & 0 & \gamma^2/3 & \dots & 0 \\ \vdots & \vdots & \vdots & \dots & \vdots \\ 0 & 0 & 0 & \dots & \gamma^2/n \end{pmatrix} \tag{10.6}$$

$$C = \begin{pmatrix} 1 & 0 & 0 & \dots & 0 \\ 0 & w^2\hat{t}_1^2/\hat{t}_2^2 & 0 & \dots & 0 \\ 0 & 0 & w^2\hat{t}_1^2/\hat{t}_3^2 & \dots & 0 \\ \vdots & \vdots & \vdots & \dots & \vdots \\ 0 & 0 & 0 & \dots & w^2\hat{t}_1^2/\hat{t}_k^2 \end{pmatrix} \tag{10.7}$$

Q, the covariance matrix of ξ_{1t}, is given by: $Q = \psi_2 \mathbf{P}_{1|0}$.

Doan, Litterman and Sims (1984) suggest the use of a predefined set of values for the above parameters. The following assumptions are made: $\gamma^2 = 0.07$, $\omega^2 = 1/74$, $v = 630$, $\psi_1 = 0.999$, $\psi_2 = 10^{-7}$. In addition, $\hat{t}_i^2$ is the estimated variance of the residuals for a univariate AR(n) regression estimated for series i. Note that the assumption is that the coefficient vector β converges only very slowly towards the mean. The factor ψ defines the analyst's confidence that the first-order autoregressive coefficients β_{ii}^1 relating z_{it} to z_{it-1}, is near unity for all i; it is set sufficiently large to ensure that the prior expectation that the constant term is zero is given little weight; ω^2 is set low to ensure that lags of other variables z_{jt} ($j \neq i$) are less useful in forecasting z_{it} than own-lags. Doan, Litterman and Sims find that these values work well for typical time series.

This general time-varying estimation problem is solved by forecasting in each period the optimal state vector based on information available up to the previous period. Under the normality and independence assumptions about the disturbances, the computation of the state vector is simply obtained by applying the Kalman filter (Harvey 1989; Hamilton 1994). This allows us to obtain filtered estimates of the VAR parameters and the residual variance-covariance matrix for each observation in the sample. Orthogonalised impulse responses are finally computed according to the standard Cholesky decomposition, generating a set of different impulse responses for each observation of our sample.

4   Results

4.1   Standard SVAR, full sample estimates

The analysis carried out in this chapter focuses on impulse response functions.[9] Figures 10.1–10.5 show 95% confidence bands for the impulse responses computed from our structural VAR model estimated over the full sample.[10] Turning first to the strategic complementarity/substitutability issue, we see that the form of interdependence between the two instruments is asymmetric and differs across countries. In the USA and the UK interest rates fall significantly in the first quarter after the fiscal expansionary shock. In the cases of Italy, Germany and France there seems to be no clear monetary reaction, although in Germany there are some signs that monetary policy tends to offset fiscal policy shocks, as the impulse responses are nearly significant.

In contrast, fiscal policy tends to be a strategic substitute for monetary policy, with the exception of a temporary complementarity in the case of Germany and the USA after 1–2 quarters, subsequently reversed in the medium run. In the case of the UK the fiscal policy response is not significant.

We turn next to how the policy instruments react to the output gap and inflation. The monetary policy reactions to the inflation and output gap shocks have the predicted signs. In all cases interest rates respond positively to the inflation and output gap shocks, although there is a difference in the quantitative response, as one might expect from existing evidence on monetary reaction functions (see Rudebusch and Svensson 1999). In general, the response is stronger in countries like the USA and Germany.[11]

We find evidence of the usual price puzzle immediately following an interest rate shock.[12] By contrast, the interest rate shock triggers a fall in the output

---

[9] The decomposition of the forecast error variance of output gap shocks confirms, among other things, that a large role is played by both fiscal and monetary policies. This result, and additional evidence as to the relative importance of economic policy innovations in the stabilisation of macroeconomic fluctuations, are discussed in a companion paper (Muscatelli, Tirelli and Trecroci 2002b).

[10] All figures referred to in this chapter will be found following the data appendix, pp. 273–93.

[11] It should be recalled that these are full-sample estimates, and therefore include the somewhat more accommodating monetary policies implemented before 1980 (see Clarida, Galí and Gertler 1998, 1999; Muscatelli, Tirelli and Trecroci 2002a).

[12] The price puzzle could be removed by introducing a commodity price index, but this reduces our available sample considerably and affects the significance of our results.

gap. This evidence shows that the introduction of fiscal variables does not yield markedly different conclusions from the conventional VAR analysis conducted in terms of monetary policy only.

Fiscal policy reacts as expected to output gap shocks: the deficit falls after a short lag. In the UK and the USA the fiscal policy response is quantitatively larger than in France, Italy and Germany. The evidence on countercyclical responses to inflation is weaker and far less uniform (significant countercyclical responses are observed only in the USA and France). This mixed evidence on the response to inflation can be rationalised by assuming that fiscal responses are mostly driven by automatic stabilisers, which are triggered when output fluctuates, and much less so in the face of inflation shocks.

Fiscal shocks seem to have a standard expansionary impact on output in the case of the USA, and to a lesser extent the UK (the impulse response function is not significant in the latter case). Negative (non-Keynesian) impacts on the output gap are evident for other countries after 5–9 quarters, although these effects are not significant. The only exception is Germany at even longer horizons, where the impulse response function is almost significant at the 5% level. The impact of fiscal shocks on inflation, more conventionally Keynesian, is only significant in the case of Germany and, in the longer run, of the USA.

4.2   Robustness checks: identification and non-linearities

Although our impulse responses were obtained with a Cholesky decomposition, in fact the ordering seems to matter little to the results, which are reasonably robust. In fact, we computed some generalised impulse responses for the above VAR estimates (see Koop, Pesaran and Potter 1996) and obtained very similar response dynamics. These illustrate that the residual variance-covariance matrix is close to being diagonal, and orthogonalisation using a Cholesky decomposition does not produce markedly different results. In addition, we estimated the VAR models imposing a different ordering for the monetary and fiscal policy instruments where the short-term interest rate comes before the budget deficit – though both always follow output and inflation. Our results were broadly confirmed.[13] Hence in what follows we continue to present and discuss results obtained using the Cholesky decompositions with the ordering discussed in section 3.

Another, more subtle point,[14] concerns the possibility that the contemporaneous response of the deficit to a unit shock in the short-term interest rates may be different from zero, in contrast to what is assumed with a standard recursive triangularisation of the disturbance matrix. For instance, in the case

---

[13] The full results are available from the authors upon request.
[14] We thank Giuseppe De Arcangelis for raising this point.

of Italy, where outstanding debt has generally been high and mainly short-term, one might expect any change in the level of interest rates to have an immediate impact on debt service payments and hence on overall budget deficits. To check for this, we imposed several non-zero values for the contemporaneous reaction of Italian deficits to a 1% shock to interest rates. As shown in figure 10.6, even assuming an 8% immediate increase in the budget deficit, the conclusions we have drawn in the former section remain broadly unscathed. In detail, most impulse responses seem to gain some significance, without changing sign. Monetary policy responses to fiscal policy shocks appear almost significant (with a 5–6-quarter lag) and pulling in the same direction, whereas interest rates look slightly more effective in stabilising the cycle than before. The first finding is more evident when the model is estimated over the last two decades, whereas the second is more typically found over the 1970s–1980s sample.

Finally, we tested for the possibility of non-linear behaviour by the monetary and fiscal policy authorities. In particular, following Granger and Terasvirta (1993), we fitted the following models for the estimated residuals $\widehat{\varepsilon_t}$ of each policy function:

$$\widehat{\varepsilon_t} = \gamma_0' \nu_t + \gamma_1' \nu_t z_t + \gamma_2' \nu_t (z_t)^2 + \gamma_3' \nu_t (z_t)^3 \qquad (10.8)$$

where ν_t is the vector of the variables (except the policy instrument at hand) entering the original VAR models, and z_t is a transition variable that is assumed to be in turn either one of the other variables in the VAR model (output gap, inflation, the other policy instrument), or the lagged value of the instrument itself. The results of the tests for the Italian case, which prima facie is the most likely to be characterised by non-linearities in the behaviour of policy authorities, are displayed in table 10.1. These findings do show some signs of non-linear behaviour in the model, though the evidence is not clear-cut. Note from Table 10.2 that the null hypothesis $\gamma_1 = 0$ may be picking up some heteroscedasticity due to multiplicative terms in the regressors. The most relevant test of non-linear policy responses is $\gamma_1 = \gamma_2 = 0$, which picks up whether there is a policy response that depends in a non-linear way on the transition variable. This hypothesis is rejected at the 5% level only for the fiscal response, and even then the non-linearity is in terms of the lagged budget deficit, which suggests that the non-linearity is unlikely to affect any inference about the responses of fiscal policy to monetary shocks and vice-versa.

Moreover, we should point out that these tests for non-linearity are very general: they do not specify a precise form for the non-linear reaction under the alternative hypothesis. In other words, even when non-linear effects are detected, no obvious operational conclusion can be drawn about the features of the models we estimate. Given that the statistical test we implement has power against different kinds of non-linear models, and that its results do not

Table 10.1. *Italy, tests of non-linear policy responses*

Transition variable		Hypothesis testing	
Policies		$H_0 : \gamma_1 = 0$	$H_0 : \gamma_1 = \gamma_2 = 0$
Monetary	$z_t = y_t$	1.2985	2.1442*
	$z_t = \pi_t$	1.1656	1.9218*
	$z_t = r_{t-1}$	0.6674	0.7605
	$z_t = bd_t$	2.8207**	1.8046
Fiscal	$z_t = y_t$	0.4528	0.3139
	$z_t = \pi_t$	1.3712	0.7273
	$z_t = r_t$	2.4969*	1.6111
	$z_t = bd_{t-1}$	1.3807	4.5129***

Notes: The test $\gamma_1 = 0$ is distributed as an $F(3, 94)$ variate under H_0; the test $\gamma_1 = \gamma_2 = 0$ is instead distributed as an $F(6,94)$ variate under H_0. ***, **, and * indicate that the null is rejected, respectively, at the 1%, 5%, and 10% significance level.

unambiguously point to non-linearity, this lends support to our view that a linear model provides a useful characterisation of reality.

4.3 Subsample estimates

In this section we divide our full sample into two subperiods, pre- and post-1980. The choice of the subsamples is suggested by the break in monetary policy stance which was experienced by all these countries in the late 1970s or early 1980s (see Clarida, Galí and Gertler 1998). Thus, for the USA we consider a break around 1979Q4, which is usually seen as the point after which the Fed took a more decisive stance on inflation control. For the EU countries we break the sample around 1980Q1, with the exception of Italy. In 1981Q2 there were major reforms in Italy, separating the functions of the fiscal and monetary authorities and the operations of the Bank of Italy. The breakpoint is therefore set at 1982Q4. In the case of France, and Italy, the post-1983 period was then characterised by a gradual hardening of the ERM. In the UK, the post-1981Q2 period saw an end to the strict monetarist experiment, and the adoption of a more eclectic monetary policy regime.[15]

We first look again at the complementarity/substitutability issue. Table 10.2 summarises the results for the two subsamples, fully presented in figures 10.7a to 10.11. A (+) or (−) indicates respectively significant evidence of

---

[15] Although further policy breaks were to follow – e.g. the UK's entry to the ERM in 1990, its exit in 1992 (followed by the adoption of inflation targets), and the granting of instrument independence to the Bank of England in 1997.

Table 10.2. *Complementarity/substitutability in fiscal and monetary policy*

Country	pre-1980	post-1980
Fiscal policy reaction to monetary policy shock		
USA	+/−	0
UK	0	−
Germany	−	+
France	+	−
Italy	−	0
Monetary policy reaction to fiscal policy shock		
USA	+	+
UK	0	+
Germany	+	0
France	0	+
Italy	0	+

complementarity or substitutability in the reaction of the fiscal or monetary policy instrument to a shock in the other instrument.[16] A (0) indicates that there is no significant response detected from the impulse response function. A double sign indicates a non-monotonic response; i.e. +/− shows that there is complementarity after an initial lag, then followed by substitutability.

There are a number of points to note from table 10.2. There is strong evidence that post-1980 monetary policy is used as a complement to fiscal shocks, with the notable exception of Germany. In contrast, the evidence on fiscal policy is ambiguous. In Germany post-1980 there is a reversal to complementarity, whilst the opposite happened in the UK and France. In the case of Italy, the insignificant result for the 1980s might be explained by a fiscal strategy which was decoupled from the business cycle, both during the apparently unstoppable fiscal expansion of the 1980s and during the subsequent contraction in the 1990s. Our post-1980 estimates of the reaction of fiscal policy to monetary policy correspond then to the results of Mélitz (1997, 2000), and more closely to those of von Hagen, Hughes Hallett and Strauch (2001),[17] who find that fiscal policy has become less sensitive to the business cycle, in line with the process of nominal convergence and the imposition of the Maastricht criteria.

Turning to figures 10.7–10.11, we find little evidence in favour of Dixit and Lambertini's (2000, 2001) argument that the relationship between the two

---

[16] Thus, for instance, the (−) in the case of the fiscal reaction to monetary policy in France in the post-1980 results shows that FPI reacted with an expansion to an increase in the interest rate (i.e. a monetary contraction).

[17] Recall that von Hagen et al. find that whilst monetary contractions lead to fiscal policy expansions, fiscal expansions are accommodated by monetary policy over the sample period 1973–89.

policy instruments depends on the sign of the fiscal impact on inflation and output. In fact, fiscal policy does not appear to have a very significant impact on output and inflation. Even ignoring the significance of the impulse responses, we noted above that there is a tendency for more conventional Keynesian effects of fiscal policy in the UK and USA, and negative impacts on output in the other countries (particularly Italy and Germany post-1980). Whilst this might explain why monetary policy has become more complementary to fiscal policy post-1980 in Italy and France, it is difficult to rationalise the pattern in the other countries. In our view, a more consistent explanation is that a conventional Keynesian reaction to the output cycle seems to be the main driving factor behind fiscal policies, with a decreasing importance over time in Germany and Italy.

4.4   Debt dynamics and fiscal policy

We have also experimented with extensions to our VAR analysis to include debt adjustment. The purpose of this was to identify any feedback between the deficit and debt to GDP ratio.[18] We thus examined whether nominal debt and nominal GDP were cointegrated for the countries in our sample. Our results were generally disappointing. Cointegration was not found for any of the countries with the exception of Germany, where there was some evidence of feedback from the debt/GDP ratio to fiscal policy. To some extent this is not entirely surprising, as the sample includes periods over which the nominal debt/GDP ratio was trending in a number of countries, and these countries were not targeting a particular value of the debt/GDP ratio. These results are not reported here for reasons of space, but in further work we intend to explore whether the feedback effect can be detected over subsamples.

4.5   Bayesian VAR estimates

In this subsection we reconsider the issue of policy shifts, i.e. changes in the nature of the interdependence between the two policy instruments. Simple subsample estimates are a rough-and-ready indicator, whereas Bayesian estimates allow us to get far deeper insights. In fact we find that some of the conclusions we reached above must be at least qualified.

To illustrate how the Bayesian VAR analysis can capture shifts in the VAR's parameters, in figure 10.12 we analyse the French fiscal policy response to a shock in the output gap, showing four observations: 1985Q1, 1988Q1, 1990Q1 and 1996Q1. This exercise gives some intuition on how the working of automatic

---

[18] As discussed in the policy design context by Leith and Wren-Lewis (2000) and detected in empirical work by Mélitz (1997).

stabilisers and discretionary fiscal policy has varied over time. In 1985 and 1988 we detect an inverse response of the budget deficit to the output shock. However, since 1990 fiscal policy seems to have turned pro-cyclical. Such a shift could not be detected in the post-1980 impulse response functions depicted in figure 10.6.

For reasons of space, we focus only on some episodes where there appear to have been clear policy shifts in the relationship between fiscal and monetary policy. Figures 10.13 to 10.16 show some of these episodes. In figure 10.13 we show Bayesian VAR estimates for the response of fiscal policy to a unit shock in the monetary instrument in France. Recall that table 10.2 suggested that, post-1983, French fiscal policy had acted as a complement to fiscal policy. Figure 10.13 confirms this pattern, but provides a richer and more detailed picture. From the graphs, it is apparent that monetary policy complemented to fiscal policy in the 1980s, but became much less complementary post 1985, as the hard-ERM regime took hold. Indeed, there is clear-cut evidence that since 1995 monetary policy has again become a strategic substitute for fiscal policy. This evolution is confirmed by the estimates for four individual years: 1985, 1988, 1993 and 1997, which show the turning point.

Turning next to Italy, in figure 10.14 we show the fiscal policy reaction to monetary policy shocks. This had become insignificant post-1983 (table 10.2). Again, we see that a richer picture emerges. Up until the mid-1990s fiscal policy had reacted to interest rate increases with an expansion, with a lag of 7–8 quarters (i.e. fiscal policy was a strategic substitute, as reported in table 10.2). However, we detect a gradual policy change in the 1990s, i.e. the fiscal expansion becomes less and less significant, confirming conventional wisdom about what happened during the transition to EMU.

Figure 10.15 shows some results concerning the reaction of monetary policy to fiscal shocks in the UK. Post-1982 we had detected a strategic complementarity. However, the detailed impulse responses for 1981, 1985, 1992 and 1998 show that such a complementarity is significant only in the 1990s.[19]

Finally, figure 10.16 shows some estimates for the USA.[20] In the 1960s the complementary response of monetary policy to a fiscal shock was barely significant. From the mid-1970s onwards, however, monetary policy appears to complement fiscal policy, again confirming our earlier results.

In the case of Germany, our Bayesian VAR estimates did not capture any significant shifts in policy, despite the shifts detected by dividing the samples into two subsamples in the VARs reported in table 10.2. The most likely explanation for this is that the major policy changes in Germany came before or

---

[19] Other Bayesian VAR estimates, not reported here for reasons of space, show that fiscal policy has become more complementary to monetary policy in the 1990s.

[20] We also found that the fiscal responses to monetary policy were not significant, confirming the post-1980 results reported in table 10.2.

around 1980. Our Bayesian VAR estimates require a number of observations to initialise the estimation, and significant effects can be detected only after 1980. It appears that since this date little has changed in German policy.

5   Conclusions

The empirical analysis of the interdependence between monetary and fiscal policies, and of their interactions with key macroeconomic variables, is a largely unexplored field. This is despite the growing number of theoretical models that emphasise the role of fiscal rules in influencing monetary policy conduct and affecting business cycle fluctuations. To some extent, our findings are reassuring: the conventional wisdom on the transmission of monetary policy, received from traditional SVAR models, survives the introduction of a fiscal policy variable. On the other hand, we find that the output effects of fiscal shocks are ambiguous, that fiscal responses to inflation shocks are difficult to detect, and that the nature of interdependence between the two policy variables is highly unstable. None of these results is easily reconciled with popular models designed to explain fiscal policy rules. Moreover, our results indicate also that the fiscal deficit does not react significantly to an inflationary shock. This in turn implies the absence of fiscal dominance, as the fiscal authorities are willing to sterilise the increased debt service from the monetary response to the inflation shock.

Future work should extend Bayesian VAR estimates to model the evolving features of the deficit feedback onto past debt levels. It would also be useful to characterise more precisely shifts in policy regimes, to identify the fundamental driving forces behind the shifts in the interdependence between fiscal and monetary policy. This would enable us to test Buti, Roeger and In't Veld's (2001) hypothesis that the nature of the interdependence between fiscal and monetary policies depends on the nature of the shocks hitting the economy.

Finally, our models have focused on monetary and fiscal policy reactions to unanticipated policy shocks. A natural extension to this chapter would be to focus on quarterly measures of primary fiscal deficits and the systematic interactions between structural fiscal and monetary rules. This would allow us to analyse the extent of monetary–fiscal complementarity/substitutability in response to aggregate demand and supply shocks, which is the subject of further work (see Muscatelli, Tirelli and Trecroci, 2002b).

Data appendix

The data employed were quarterly observations, seasonally adjusted where available. The output gap is defined as the (log) difference between actual and potential output. Inflation is the 4-quarter (log) difference in the consumer price index and, in the US case, in the GDP price index. The monetary policy instrument considered was the Fed funds rate for the USA, and the respective call money rate for all other countries. The fiscal policy indicator was the total budget deficit, i.e. the difference between government current expenditures (consumption + investment) and tax receipts. A Hodrick–Prescott filter ($\lambda =$ 1600) was applied to the series to extract its trend.

The following is a short description of all variables' sources.

United States Bureau of Economic Analysis, NIPA tables. The data can be downloaded from www.bea.doc.gov/bea/dn/nipaweb/ AllTables.asp. The output gap is calculated as the (log) difference between real gross domestic product and real potential gross domestic product, in billions of chained 1996 dollars (source: US Congress, Congressional Budget Office). Inflation is the 4-quarter (log) difference in the gross domestic product chain-type price index, 1996 = 100, seasonally adjusted (source: US Department of Commerce, Bureau of Economic Analysis). The call money rate is the Federal funds' rate, obtained from IMF's IFS. The fiscal policy indicator was obtained from the sum of federal and state and local current surplus or deficit, billions of dollars, seasonally adjusted annual rate (source: National Income and Product Accounts Tables, tables 3.2 and 3.3).

Germany, France, United Kingdom and Italy (for output, inflation and interest rate data) IMF's *International Financial Statistics* (revenue, expenditure and lending minus repayment, call money rate, consumer price index and gross domestic product); *OECD Statistical Compendium* (output gap, semi-annual observations, linear interpolation was employed to construct the quarterly series).

Italy, budget series only The series from IFS lacks a number of observations around 1990. Consequently, a corresponding Bank of Italy's series was employed to integrate.

Figures

The plots in the following pages are 95% confidence bands of the impulse responses from a just-identified SVAR in the output gap (YGAP), inflation (INF), the deviations of the fiscal stance from its HP filtered trend (FPI), and the call money rate (CMR). Bootstrapping methods (500 simulations) were employed to determine 95% confidence bands around the orthogonalised response (Cholesky factorisation of the varcov matrix was applied). INF→YGAP, for instance, stands for impulse response of the output gap to a unit shock in the inflation rate.

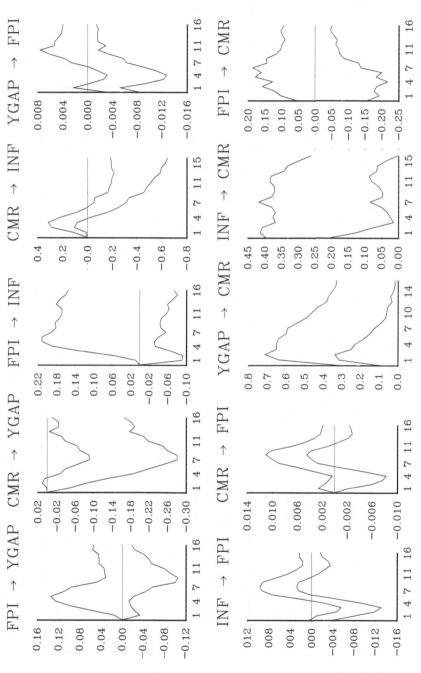

Figure 10.1 Impulse responses, France: 1973Q2–1998Q4

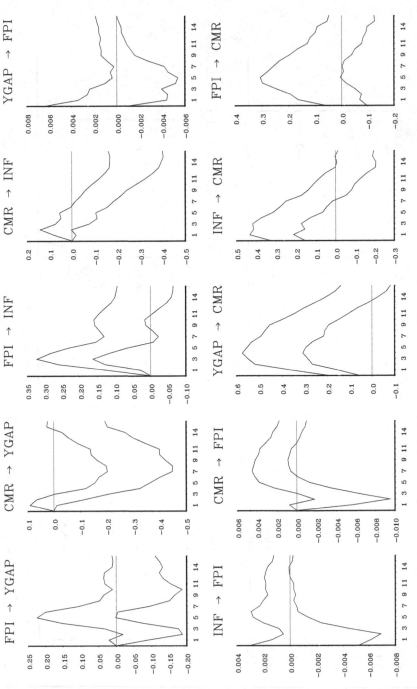

Figure 10.2 Impulse responses, Germany: 1971Q1–1998Q4

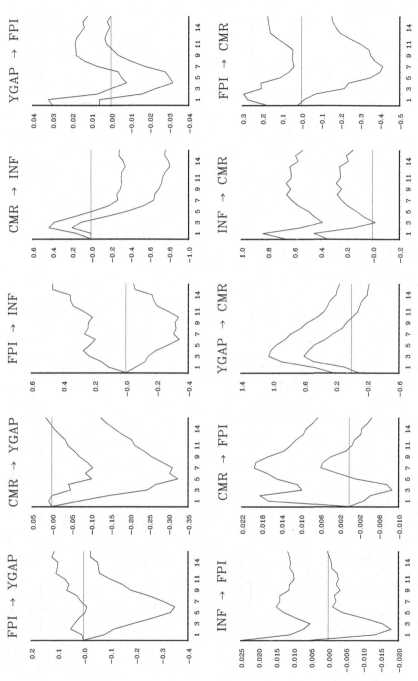

Figure 10.3 Impulse responses, Italy: 1971Q4–1998Q4

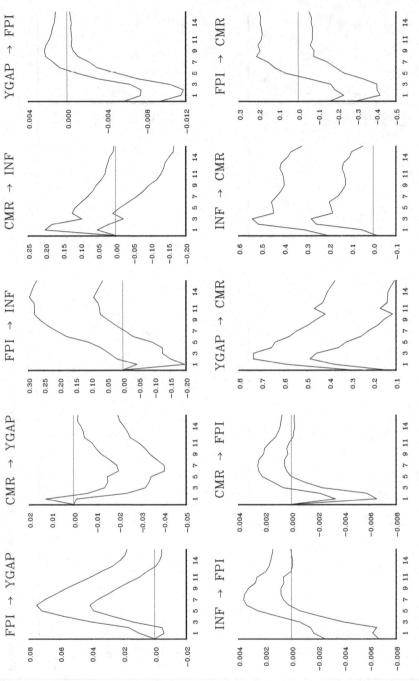

Figure 10.4 Impulse responses, USA: 1955Q1–1998Q4

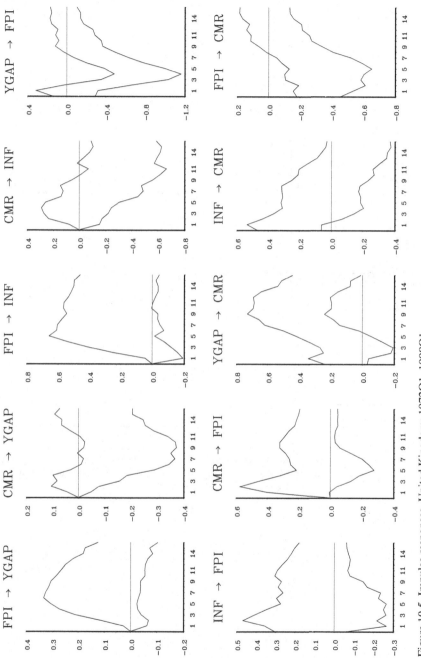

Figure 10.5 Impulse responses, United Kingdom: 1972Q1–1998Q1

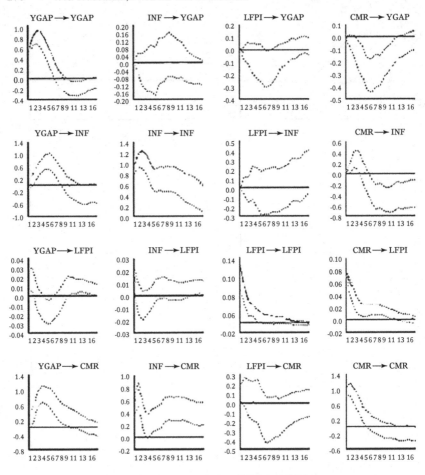

Figure 10.6 Impulse responses, Italy: 1971Q4–1998Q4
Note: It is assumed that a 1% change in interest rate has a contemporaneous impact of 8% on the size of the budget deficit.

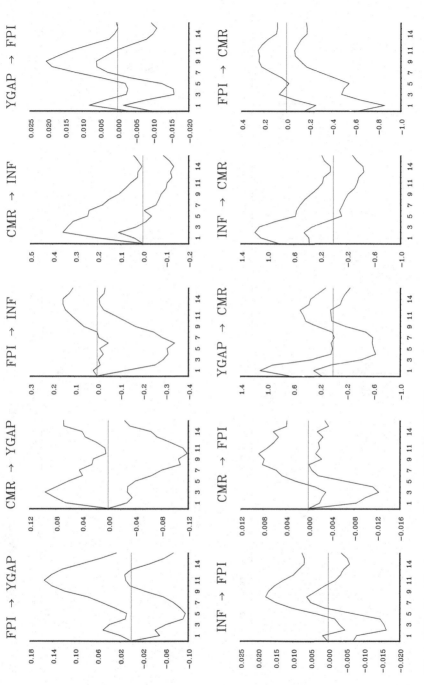

Figure 10.7a Impulse responses, France: 1973Q2–1982Q2

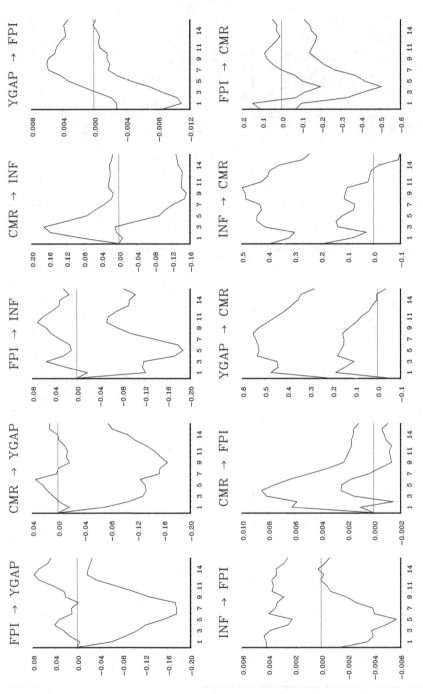

Figure 10.7b Impulse responses, France: 1980Q1–1998Q4

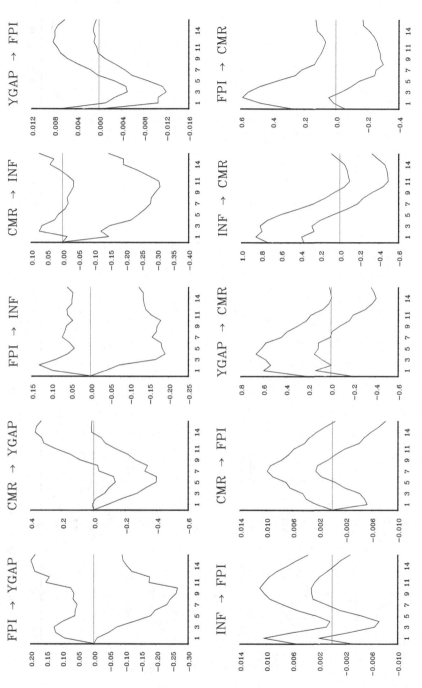

Figure 10.8a Impulse responses, Germany: 1971Q1–1982Q2

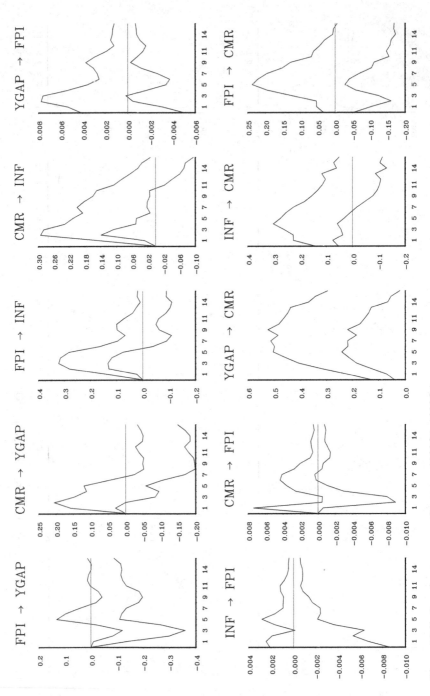

Figure 10.8b Impulse responses, Germany: 1980Q1–1998Q4

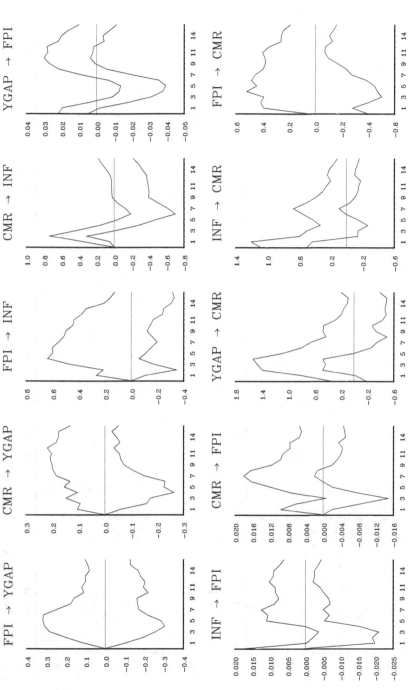

Figure 10.9a Impulse responses, Italy: 1971Q4–1982Q2

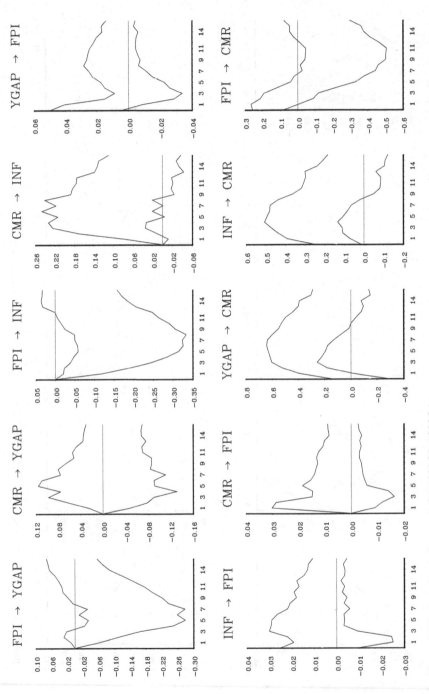

Figure 10.9b Impulse responses, Italy: 1983Q1–1998Q4

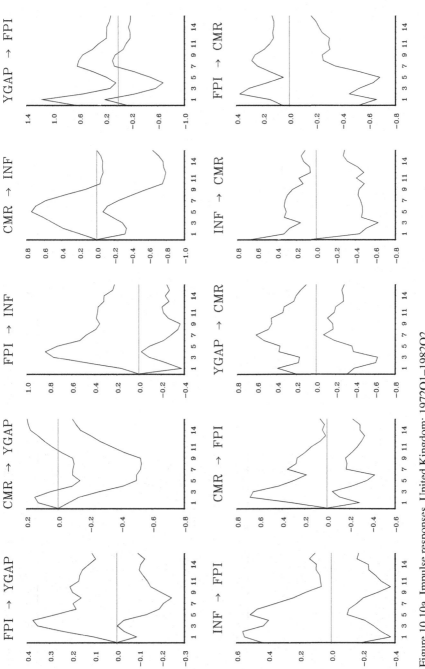

Figure 10.10a Impulse responses, United Kingdom: 1972Q1–1982Q2

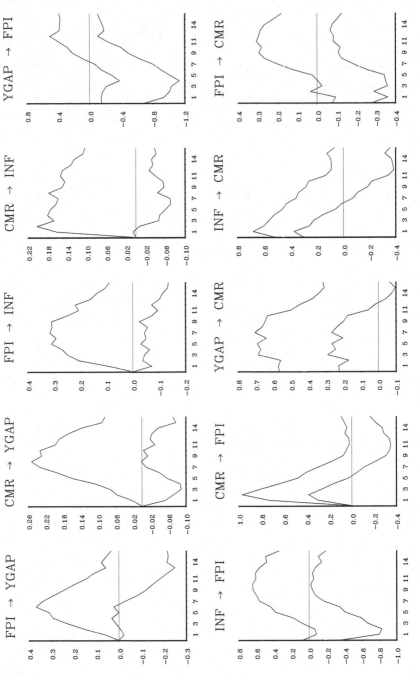

Figure 10.10b Impulse responses, United Kingdom: 1980Q1–1998Q4

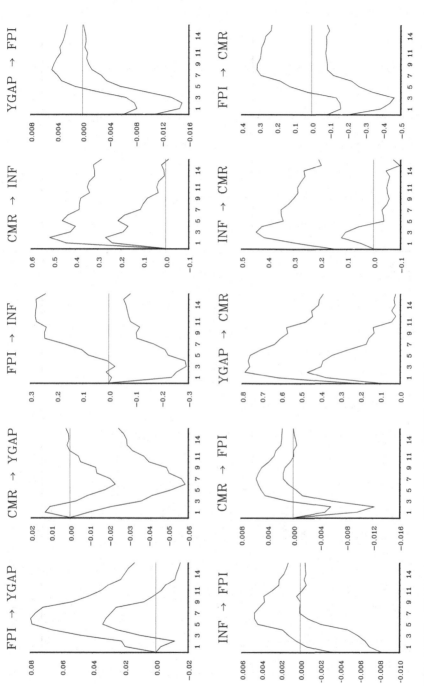

Figure 10.11a Impulse responses, United States: 1955Q1–1979Q4

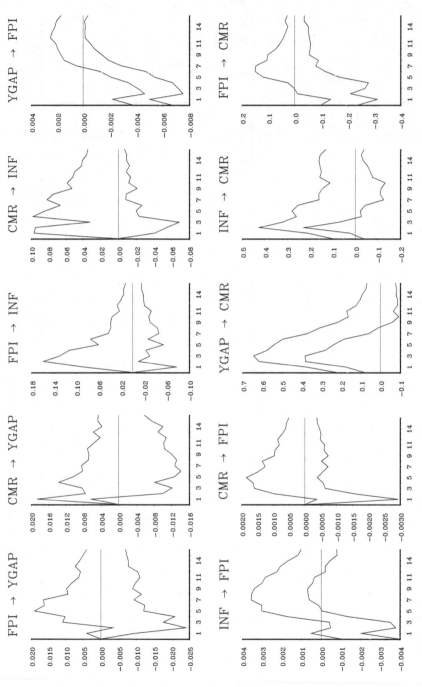

Figure 10.11b Impulse responses, United States: 1980Q1–1998Q4

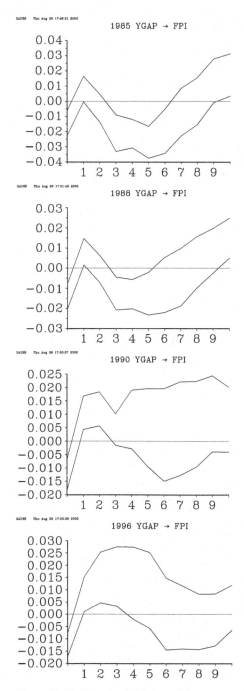

Figure 10.12 Bayesian VAR, impulse responses of the fiscal policy indicator
to a shock in the output gap, first quarters of various years, France, 1973Q2–
1998Q4

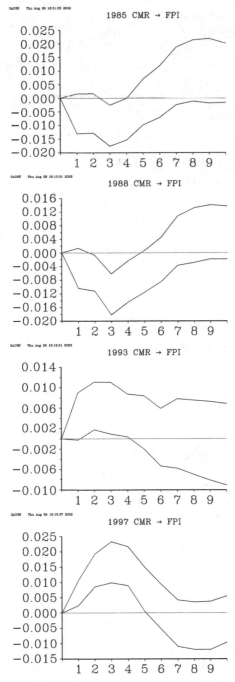

Figure 10.13 Bayesian VAR, impulse responses of the fiscal policy indicator to a shock in the call money rate, first quarters of various years, France, 1973Q2–1998Q4

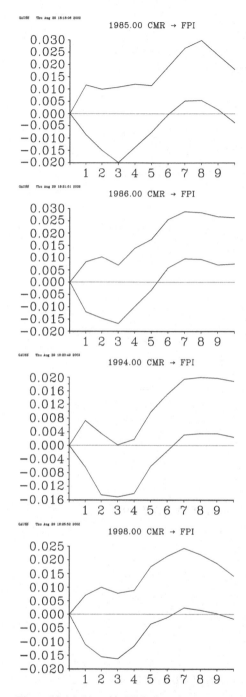

Figure 10.14 Bayesian VAR, impulse responses of the fiscal policy indicator to a shock in the call money rate, first quarters of various years, Italy, 1971Q4–1998Q4

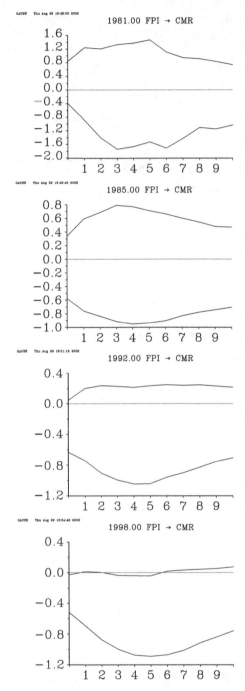

Figure 10.15 Bayesian VAR, impulse responses of the fiscal policy indicator to a shock in the call money rate, first quarters of various years, United Kingdom, 1972Q1–1998Q1

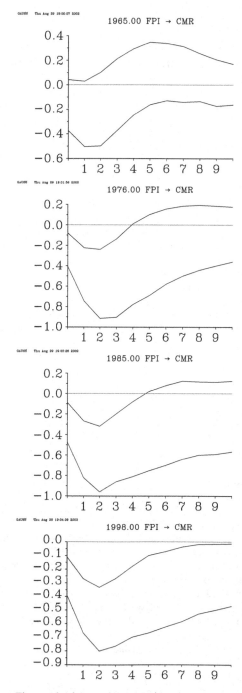

Figure 10.16 Bayesian VAR, impulse responses of the fiscal policy indicator to a shock in the call money rate, first quarters of various years, USA, 1957Q1– 1998Q4

REFERENCES

Alesina, A. and G. Tabellini, 1987, 'Rules and Discretion with Noncoordinated Monetary and Fiscal Policies', *Economic Inquiry* 25(4), 619–30.

Beetsma, R. M. W. J. and A. L. Bovenberg, 1998, 'Monetary Union without Fiscal Coordination May Discipline Policymakers', *Journal of International Economics* 45, 239–58.

Beetsma, R. M. W. J. and H. Jensen, 1999, 'Optimal Inflation Targets, "Conservative" Central Banks, and Linear Inflation Contracts: Comment', *American Economic Review* 89, 342–7.

Beetsma, R. M. W. J. and H. Uhlig, 1997, 'An Analysisis of the Stability and Growth Pact,' *Economic Journal* 109, 546–71.

Bernanke, B. S. and I. Mihov, 1998, 'Measuring Monetary Policy', *Quarterly Journal of Economics* 113(3), 869–902.

Blanchard, O. J. and R. Perotti, 2000, 'An Empirical Characterization of the Dynamic Effects of Changes in Government Spending and Taxes on Output', Working Paper, MIT, http://econ-www.mit.edu/faculty/blanchar/papers.htm.

2002, 'An Empirical Characterization of the Dynamic Effects of Changes in Government Spending and Taxes on Output', *Quarterly Journal of Economics* 117(4), 1329–68.

Buti, M., W. Roeger and J. In't Veld, 2001, 'Stabilising Output and Inflation in EMU: Policy Conflicts and Cooperation under the Stability Pact', *Journal of Common Market Studies* 39, 801–28.

Canova, F., 1995, 'Vector Autoregressive Models: Specification, Estimation, Inference and Forecasting', in M. H. Pesaran, and M. Wickens (eds.), *Handbook of Applied Econometrics: Macroeconomics*, Oxford: Blackwell, pp. 73–138.

Canzoneri, M. B., R. E. Cumby and B. T. Diba, 1998, 'Is the Price Level Determined by the Needs of Fiscal Solvency?', NBER Working Paper no. 6471.

Clarida, R., J. Galí and M. Gertler, 1998, 'Monetary Policy Rules in Practice: Some International Evidence', *European Economic Review* 42 (6), 1033–67.

1999, 'The Science of Monetary Policy: A New Keynesian Perspective', NBER Working Paper no. 7147.

2000, 'Monetary Policy Roles and Macroeconomic Stability: Evidence and Some Theory', *Quarterly Journal of Economics* 115(1), 147–80.

Dixit, A. and L. Lambertini, 2000, 'Fiscal Discretion Destroys Monetary Commitment', Working Paper, Princeton University and UCLA.

2001, 'Monetary–Fiscal Policy Interactions and Commitment Versus Discretion in a Monetary Union', Working Paper, Princeton University and UCLA.

Doan, T., R. Litterman and C. Sims, 1984, 'Forecasting and Conditional Projections Using Realist Priori Distributions', *Econometric Reviews* 3(1), 1–100.

Edelberg, W., M. Eichenbaum and J. D. M. Fisher, 1998, 'Understanding the Effects of a Shock to Government Purchases', NBER Working Paper no. 6737.

Eichengreen, B. and C. Wyplosz, 1998, 'The Stability Pact: More than a Minor Nuisance?', *Economic Policy* 26, 65–104.

Fatás, A. and I. Mihov, 2000, 'Fiscal Policy and Business Cycles: An Empirical Investigation, mimeo, INSEAD.

Favero, C. A. and R. Rovelli, 1999, 'Modelling and Identifying Central Banks' Preferences', CEPR Discussion Paper no. 2178.

Giavazzi, F. and M. Pagano, 1990, 'Can Severe Fiscal Contractions Be Expansionary?
Tales of Two Small European Countries', in O. J. Blanchard and S. Fischer (eds.),
NBER Macroeconomics Annual 1990, Cambridge, MA: MIT Press, pp. 75–111.

1996, 'Non-Keynesian Effects of Fiscal Policy Changes: International Evidence and
the Swedish Experience', *Swedish Economic Policy Review* 3(1), 67–103.

Giavazzi, F., T. Jappelli and M. Pagano, 2000, 'Searching for Non-linear Effects of Fiscal
Policy: Evidence from Industrial and Developing Countries', *European Economic
Review* 44(7), 1259–89.

Granger, C. W. J. and T. Terasvirta, 1993, *Modelling Non-linear Economic Relationships*,
Oxford: Oxford University Press.

Hamilton, J., 1994, *Time Series Analysis*, Princeton: Princeton University Press.

Harvey, A. C., 1989, *Forecasting, Structural Time Series Models and the Kalman Filter*,
Cambridge: Cambridge University Press.

HM Treasury, 2000, 'UK Policy Co-ordination: The Importance of Institutional Design',
available at http://www.hm-treasury.gov.uk/.

Hughes Hallet, A. and N. Viegi, 2000, 'Central Bank Independence, Political Uncertainty, and the Assignment of Instruments to Targets', mimeo, University of
Strathclyde.

Kim, C.-J. and C. R. Nelson, 1999, *State-Space Models with Regime Switching*, Cambridge, MA: MIT Press.

Koop, G., M. H. Pesaran and S. M. Potter, 1996, 'Impulse Response Analysis in Non-
linear Multivariate Models', *Journal of Econometrics* 74, 119–47.

Leith, C. and S. Wren-Lewis, 2000, 'Interactions between Monetary and Fiscal Policy
Rules', *Economic Journal* 110, C93–C108.

Lutkepohl, H., 1991, *Introduction to Multiple Time Series Analysis*, New York: Springer
Verlag.

Mélitz, J., 1997, 'Some Cross-Country Evidence about Debt, Deficits, and the Behaviour
of Monetary and Fiscal Authorities', CEPR Discussion Paper no. 1653.

2000, 'Some Cross-Country Evidence about Fiscal Policy Behaviour and Consequences for EMU', mimeo, CEPR.

Mountford, A. and H. Uhlig, 2002, 'What Are the Effects of Fiscal Policy Shocks?',
Tilburg University CentER Discussion Paper no. 2002-31.

Muscatelli, A., P. Tirelli and C. Trecroci, 2002a, 'Does Institutional Change Really
Matter? Inflation Targets, Central Bank Reform and Interest Rate Policy in the
OECD Countries', *The Manchester School* 70(4), 487–527.

2002b, 'Monetary and Fiscal Policy Interactions: Evidence Using Structural New
Keynesian Models', forthcoming, *Journal of Macroeconomics*, Special Issue on
5th Bundesbank Spring Conference.

Muscatelli, A. and C. Trecroci, 2000, 'Monetary Policy Rules, Policy Preferences, and
Uncertainty: Recent Empirical Evidence', *Journal of Economic Surveys* 14(5),
597–627.

Rudebusch, G. D. and L. E. O. Svensson, 1999, 'Policy Rules for Inflation Targeting',
in J. B. Taylor (ed.), *Monetary Policy Rules*, Chicago: University of Chicago Press,
pp. 203–46.

von Hagen, J., A. Hughes Hallett and R. Strauch, 2001, 'Budgetary Consolidation in EMU', *Economic Papers* 148, Brussels: European Commission.

Woodward, B., 2000, *Maestro: Greenspan's Fed and the American Boom*. New York: Simon and Schuster.

Wyplosz, C., 1999, 'Economic Policy Coordination in EMU: Strategies and Institutions', ZEI Policy Paper no. B11.

Part III

Labour markets

11 Monetary institutions, monetary union and unionised labour markets: some recent developments

Alex Cukierman

1 Introduction

This chapter is a selective survey of recent developments regarding the strategic interaction between labour unions and the monetary authority. Since Rogoff's (1985) influential work a basic tenet of the literature on strategic monetary policy with competitive labour markets is that, abstracting from stabilisation policy, the level of central bank conservativeness (CBC) affects inflation but not real variables. An important general message of the burgeoning literature on unionised labour markets and monetary institutions is that, when wage settlements are centralised within a small or moderate number of unions, CBC affects inflation *as well as* real variables like unemployment, output and real wages. This insight and the analytical frameworks that underlie it are particularly relevant for European economies in which the fraction of the labour force covered by collective agreements is large and in which wage-bargaining institutions are frequently rather centralised.

Most of the recent literature on the strategic interaction between the central bank (CB) and unions shares two basic presumptions. First, nominal wages are contractually fixed for a certain period of time, to which I shall refer as the 'contract period'. Second, monetary policy and prices can be adjusted during the contract period. Casual observation supports both presumptions. Union nominal wages are normally fixed for at least one year while prices and the money supply are usually adjusted at intervals that are shorter than one year. Those presumptions lead to the formulation of simple game theoretic models in which unions move first and set nominal wages while the CB moves second and chooses, depending on the model, the rate of inflation or the money supply. Third, union management likes higher real wages for its members but dislikes unemployment among them. Some of the recent literature also assumes that unions are averse to inflation.[1] This is motivated by the observation that, in many

Some of the main ideas in this paper were presented as a keynote lecture at the University of Milan-Bicocca conference on 'EMU Macroeconomic Institutions', 20–22 September, 2001.

[1] A non-exhaustive list includes Yashiv (1989), Cubitt (1992, 1995), Agell and Ysander (1993), Gylfason and Lindbeck (1994), Skott (1997), Jensen (1997), Grüner and Hefeker (1999), Cukierman and Lippi (1999, 2001), Guzzo and Velasco (1999) and Lawler (2000).

cases, the pensions of union workers are not indexed and that union members, like other individuals, generally dislike inflation. Fourth, as in the early Kydland and Prescott (1977) and Barro and Gordon (1983) (KPBG hereafter) literature and its spin-offs, the CB is assumed to possess a loss function that is quadratic in both inflation and unemployment.

For the sake of simplicity a good part of the recent literature investigates the strategic interaction between the labour market and the CB for the extreme case of a single, all encompassing, monopoly union. The more recent literature generally considers the case of several unions.[2] Following the lead of the KPBG-type models, much of the literature on unions and the CB assumes that the CB directly controls the rate of inflation.[3] More recent literature recognises that prices are set by firms and that the policy instrument of the monetary authority is the money supply. A basic consequence of this difference in modelling choices is that in the first group of models monetary policy affects the economy only via supply-side channels, whereas in the second group it affects it also through demand-side channels.[4]

This difference in modelling strategy leads to diametrically opposed conclusions about the real effects of CBC on the economy. In particular, papers which assume that the CB directly controls inflation and that unions are averse to inflation conclude that, by alleviating the inflationary fears of unions, more conservative central banks induce higher real wage demands and higher levels of unemployment. In the extreme case of a monopoly union this view implies that (abstracting from stabilisation policy) a populist or ultra liberal central bank that cares only about unemployment is best for a society that dislikes both inflation and unemploment (Skott 1997; Cukierman and Lippi 1999; Guzzo and Velasco 1999, 2002; Lawler 2000; Lippi 2002). On the other hand work by Soskice and Iversen (1998, 2000), which abstracts from unions' inflation aversion and postulates that the monetary authority controls the money supply, concludes that less accommodating central banks moderate unions' wage demands more by raising the fear of unemployment among their members. This view implies that both inflation and unemployment are lower under less accommodative central banks. Since the frameworks used by the two groups of papers differ in structure, and each group abstracts from some of the factors

---

[2] Papers by Cubitt (1992, 1995), Gylfason and Lindbeck (1994), Jensen (1997), Grüner and Hefeker (1999), and Lawler (2000) represent the labour market by a single monopoly union. Papers by Bleaney (1996), Forteza (1998), Skott (1997), Cukierman and Lippi (1999, 2001) and Guzzo and Velasco (1999) consider the case of many unions.

[3] Except for Cubitt (1992, 1995) all the papers mentioned in the previous footnote adopt this assumption.

[4] Papers by Cubitt (1992, 1995) Soskice and Iversen (1998, 2000), Bratsiotis and Martin (1999), Holden (2001) and Coricelli, Cukierman and Dalmazzo (2000, forthcoming) fall into the second class of models.

included in the analysis of the other group, it is hard to reach a verdict on this controversy from these papers alone.

Coricelli, Cukierman and Dalmazzo (2000) propose a framework that embeds these different mechanisms within a *unified* framework, making it possible to identify the conditions under which either one dominates. This framework features both supply-side and demand-side transmission channels of monetary policy. They find that, for realistic values of the relative aversion of unions to inflation and to unemployment, higher CBC reduces the bargaining power of unions and leads to lower levels of unemployment, real wages and inflation. The main features of this framework are as follows. Prices and wages are set, respectively, by monopolistically competitive firms and by labour unions. Prices are fully flexible and wages are contractually fixed. The CB affects the price level and employment *indirectly* via its choice of money supply. The game now has a third stage in which firms set prices so as to maximise their real profits. This is preceded by the choice of money supply in the second stage and by the choice of nominal wages in the first stage.

The creation, at the beginning of 1999, of the European Monetary Union (EMU) and of the European Central Bank (ECB) altered the strategic interaction between the monetary authority and labour unions in the EMU area. Before the creation of the ECB labour unions in each country interacted only with their own national CB. In some countries, such as Germany, the CB was setting monetary policy so as to attain its preferred level of domestic objectives. In other countries, such as Austria and Belgium, the CB conducted monetary policy so as to maintain a fixed parity with the Deutschmark (DM), importing the Bundesbank's monetary policy. After the creation of EMU the strategic interaction between labour unions and the CB obviously changed. In particular, each labour union became a smaller player relative to the CB of the monetary union. For labour unions of countries whose CB previously conducted an independent monetary policy, national monetary policy was replaced by that of the ECB. For labour unions of countries whose CB was previously pegging to the DM the monetary policy of the ECB replaced the peg. In addition, for some of the countries involved, the level of CBC went up while for other countries, like Germany and its monetary satelites, CBC went down. Some of the conceptual frameworks mentioned above have recently been adapted to investigate the long-run macroeconomic consequences of these changes in monetary institutions. Various aspects of those major institutional changes are analysed in Grüner and Hefeker (1999), Sibert and Sutherland (2000), Cukierman and Lippi (2001) and Coricelli, Cukierman and Dalmazzo (forthcoming). A broad survey of the issues and implications for the future appear in Calmfors (2001b).

The organisation of the chapter is as follows. Section 2 reviews baseline models of CB – labour union interaction in which the CB controls inflation directly. Section 3 reviews models of CB – labour union interaction in which the CB controls the money supply and the price level is determined by the individual pricing decisions of monopolistically competitive firms. An important difference between those two families of models is that in the first group monetary policy affects the economy only via supply. By contrast, in the second group monetary policy impacts the economy through *both* supply and demand channels. Section 4 discusses the recent controversy regarding whether, in the presence of large unions, the CB should be more, or less, inflation averse than society. It critically reviews the notion, discovered independently by Skott (1997), Cukierman and Lippi (1999), Guzzo and Velasco (1999) and Lawler (2000), that a populist CB is socially desirable and contrasts it with the view that a non-accomodating CB is socially desirable (due to Soskice and Iversen 1998, 2000). Section 5 reviews recent literature on the long-run macroeconomic consequences of the shift from national monetary policies to a monetary union (MU). This is followed by concluding remarks.

2   A baseline model: CB–labour unions interaction when the CB directly controls inflation

The objective of this section is to illustrate the basic forces operating in the presence of a, relatively simple, strategic interaction between unions and the CB in a precise but not too specific manner.[5] Although this requires a concrete model, many of the conclusions transcend the structure of the particular model, and when this is not the case the model provides a benchmark for qualification of the conclusions.

The economy consists of n independent unions and of a CB whose degree of CBC is characterised by a parameter I. The typical union likes high real wages and low unemployment for its members and also dislikes inflation to some extent. This is captured by the loss function

$$\Omega_j \equiv -2w_{rj} + Au_j^2 + B\pi^2,   \tag{11.1}$$

where u_j is the rate of unemployment among members of union j, $\pi \equiv p - p_{-1}$ is the rate of inflation (defined by the difference in the log of the price level) and A and B are positive parameters. The first two arguments reflect the union's sectoral interest and are conventional in the theory of trade union behaviour.[6] The third one reflects the union's aversion to inflation.

---

[5] This section draws on Cukierman and Lippi (1999). For proofs and additional detail the reader is referred to that paper.

[6] Those two arguments are standard in the theory of labour union behaviour (Oswald 1982). They can also be justified by political economy considerations internal to the union of the type discussed in Saint-Paul (2000).

The CB is concerned with aggregate unemployment (u) and price stability. More precisely, the objective of the CB is to minimise the loss function

$$\Gamma \equiv u^2 + I\pi^2,\tag{11.2}$$

where I is a measure of the relative inflation aversion of the CB. This parameter characterises the level of CB conservativeness (CBC). The basic institutional parameters highlighted by this framework are CBC as proxied by the parameter I, and the degree of centralisation of wage bargaining (CWB), characterised by $1/n$.

2.1   The labour market

Total labour supply in the economy is L. All labour is unionised and is evenly distributed over the n unions. Although the labour of any given union can be usefully employed in all industries, it is not perfectly substitutable for the labour of other unions. The notion underlying this specification is that labour is generally differentiated. Labour of a given union is supplied completely inelastically and is mobile across industries. The demand for the labour of workers in union j is given by

$$L_j^d = \left[\frac{a}{n}(d - w_{rj}) - \gamma(w_{rj} - \bar{w}_r)\right]L,\tag{11.3}$$

where L_j^d is demand for the labour of that union, w_{rj} is the (logarithm) of the real wage obtained by its members, $\bar{w}_r \equiv \sum_{j=1}^{n} \frac{w_{rj}}{n}$ is the (arithmetic) mean of w_{rj} over all unions in the economy and d, a and γ are positive parameters. This demand function states that the share (in total labour force) of labour demand facing union j is decreasing in its own real wage and increasing in the average real wage in the economy. This demand emanates, in general, from all industries, although the demand for the labour of a particular union may be dominated by the demands of a smaller number of industries. The specification of demand presumes that each worker is affiliated with only one union. Summing over unions, aggregate demand for labour in the economy is given by

$$L^d \equiv \sum_{j=1}^{n} L_j^d = a(d - \bar{w}_r)L.\tag{11.4}$$

Equation (11.4) states that aggregate demand for labour depends (negatively) *only* on the average real wage $\bar{w}_r$. In particular, aggregate demand for labour *does not* depend on the number of unions in the economy. Equation (11.3) implies that any union that sets its real wage equal to the average real wage in the economy obtains $1/n$ of aggregate labour demand for its members. When it sets the real wage above (below) the mean wage its total share of aggregate demand is lower (higher) than $1/n$. But, since labour is differentiated, deviations of the real wage of a particular union from the economy-wide average do not induce a total loss of demand or an infinite demand. For a given number of unions the parameter γ measures the degree of substitutability between the labour of different unions.

Equation (11.3) implies that the absolute value of the elasticity of labour demand facing union j, η_j, with respect to the (level of the) real wage set by the union is

$$\eta_j = \frac{a + \gamma(n-1)}{a(d - w_{rj}) - n\gamma(w_{rj} - \bar{w}_r)}. \tag{11.5}$$

This elasticity is increasing with the degree of decentralisation of wage bargaining as measured by n, provided w_{rj} does not deviate too much, in an upward direction, from the mean real wage.[7] Thus, equation (11.3) implies that, although *total* labour demand does not depend on the degree of centralisation of wage bargaining, the extent of wage competition among unions is larger when the labour force is spread over a larger number of bargaining units. This is the competition effect of more decentralisation discussed by Calmfors and Driffill (1988) and Calmfors (1993).

2.2   Equilibrium

The strategic interaction between labour unions and the CB is framed as a two-stage game solved by backward induction. In the second stage, the CB chooses inflation, taking the nominal wages previously set by all unions as given, so as to minimise its loss function. In the first stage each union chooses its nominal wage rate so as to maximise its objectives, taking the nominal wage chosen by all other unions and the subsequent central bank reaction as given. Labour unions are thus Stackelberg leaders vis-à-vis the CB. The solution for the reaction function of the CB is

$$\pi = \frac{a^2}{a^2 + I}(\bar{\phi} + E\pi), \quad \bar{\phi} \equiv \bar{w}_r - w_r^c. \tag{11.6}$$

where w_r^c is the competitive (identical across labour types or unions) real wage rate and $\bar{\phi}$ is the average real wage premium in excess of the competitive benchmark. The CB reaction function implies that the CB partially accommodates the wage premium as well as expected inflation. In particular, the more militant are unions on average (the higher $\bar{\phi}$), the higher is the rate of inflation produced by the CB. For given values of expected inflation and of unions' militancy, the extent of accommodation is larger the higher is the response of aggregate labour

---

[7] Details appear in footnote 14 of Cukierman and Lippi (1999).

demand to the average real wage, α, and the lower the conservativeness of the CB, I.

Minimisation with respect to the *nominal* wage, by each union, of the loss function in equation (11.1), taking into consideration the reaction of the (CB) in equation (11.6), leads to the following solution for the average real wage premium:[8]

$$\bar{\phi} = \frac{Z_w}{a\left\{AZ_u + B\frac{a}{I}(1 - Z_w)\right\}} = \phi_j, \quad \forall j's, \tag{11.7}$$

where

$$Z_w \equiv 1 - \frac{d\pi}{dw_j} = 1 - \frac{a^2}{(a^2 + I)n}, \quad Z_u \equiv aZ_w + \gamma(n - 1),$$

$$j = 1, \ldots, n. \tag{11.8}$$

This is also the wage premium of each individual union since the problem is symmetric. Since, from equations (11.8) $1 > Z_w > 0$, the real wage premium is always positive, reflecting the market power of unions. Z_w is the elasticity of a single union real wage with respect to its nominal wage, taking into consideration the reaction of the CB to the union's nominal wage choice. Since it is a measure of the overall effectiveness of changes in the nominal wage in bringing about changes in the union's real wage, I refer to it as an 'overall elasticity'. For finite values of CB conservativeness and of the number of unions this elasticity is positive but smaller than one. This implies that in order to raise its real wage by 1% the union has to raise its nominal wage rate by more than 1%. Z_u is the marginal impact of an increase in the union's nominal wage on the rate of unemployment among its members.[9] It is composed of two terms. The first, aZ_u, reflects the direct impact of an increase in the real wage of the union on unemployment among its members. The second, $\gamma(n - 1)$, is a substitution effect in labour demand. It reflects the impact of a decrease in the competitiveness of the union's labour when its relative wage goes up. The impact of this competition effect on unemployment among the union's members is larger the larger the substitution parameter, γ, and the larger the number of unions, n.

2.3   Factors affecting unions' bargaining power

The effective bargaining power of unions is conveniently summarised by the equilibrium expression for the wage premium in equation (11.7). The wage

---

[8] In solving this problem each union takes the *nominal* wages of other unions as given. Thus each union plays Nash with the other unions and acts as a Stackelberg leader with respect to the CB.

[9] It is also the overall elasticity of labour demand facing the union with respect to the union's nominal wage.

premium is lower, and employment higher, the higher the parameters A and B that characterise unions' aversion to unemployment and inflation, respectively. The higher A, the more unions care about unemployment among their members, which directly leads them to set lower real wages. The higher B, the more averse are unions to the inflationary response of the CB to the increase in unemployment triggered by their wage demands. Hence high aversion to either unemployment or inflation on the part of unions decreases their bargaining power and moderates their wage demands. The larger the degree of substitutability between different kinds of labour as measured by the parameter γ, the lower the bargaining power of unions and the lower, therefore, the wage premium.

It is easy to check, from equation (11.7), that, other things the same, the wage premium is an increasing function of the elasticity Z_w. The reason is that the marginal benefit to the union in terms of the real wage is higher, and the marginal cost in terms of inflation is lower, when Z_w is higher. On the other hand, given Z_w, the wage premium is lower the higher the elasticity Z_u. The reason, of course, is that the higher this elasticity, the higher the overall impact of an increase in the union's nominal wage on unemployment among its members.

The expression for Z_w in equation (11.8) reveals that the overall elasticity of a typical union's real wage with respect to its nominal counterpart is lower the smaller the number of unions and the more liberal is the CB (the lower I). The positive effect of n on real wages through Z_w reflects the strategic effect of a more decentralised labour market. At lower levels of CWB each union internalises a smaller portion of the inflationary response of the CB. As a consequence, the moderating effect, on real wages, of the central bank's expected inflationary reaction is weaker. This effect also appears in Guzzo and Velasco (1999), who refer to it as the 'internalisation' effect. At first blush it would therefore seem that the wage premium is lower the smaller is n and the more liberal the CB. But this neglects the fact that the wage premium also depends on n through the elasticity, Z_u, and that this elasticity increases with the number of unions. The positive relation between Z_u and n reflects the competition effect of a more decentralised system of wage bargaining. Notice that the marginal impact of an increase in the union's nominal wage on the rate of unemployment among its members is independent of CBC, I.

Depending on parameter values, and on the structure of the economy, the competition or internalisation effect may dominate over either parts of n or over the entire range of n. In the model of Cukierman and Lippi (1999) those two offsetting effects produce a Calmfors–Driffill relation between the wage premium and the degree of CWB, provided the inflation aversion of unions is larger than some threshold. The Calmfors–Driffill hypothesis maintains that at high levels of CWB the internalisation or strategic effect dominates; at low levels of centralisation the competition effect dominates, and at intermediate levels of centralisation those effects roughly offset each other. As a consequence, the wage premium attains a maximum at intermediate levels of CWB (Calmfors and Driffill 1988; Calmfors 1993). In the Guzzo and Velasco (1999) model, which starts from individual utility and a Dixit–Stiglitz production function, the interaction between the competition and the internalisation effect produces a reverse Calmfors–Driffill relation between the real wage and CWB. An important general implication of the recent literature is that the position and shape of the Calmfors–Driffill relation depends on CBC.

2.3.1   CBC and unions' bargaining power   A central implication of models with inflation averse unions in which the CB directly controls inflation is that a more conservative CB raises the bargaining power of unions and, with it, the wage premium. The mechanism responsible for this result is as follows. The more conservative the CB, the less it inflates in response to an increase in the nominal wage of an individual union. As a consequence, for a given increase in its nominal wage, the union gains more in terms of real wage and sustains a lower penalty in terms of inflation. Both factors push the union to set a higher real wage. This mechanism operates in all the models with inflation averse unions independently of whether they feature a single monopoly union or several unions.

But in the case of several unions there is an additional factor that operates in the same direction even if unions are indifferent to inflation (i.e. $B = 0$). In this case the basic trade-off faced by the individual union is between a higher wage and a lower level of competitiveness that leads to more unemployment among its members. At higher levels of CBC the marginal benefit of a higher nominal wage in terms of the real wage is higher since the elasticity Z_w is higher. But the marginal cost of this action, which depends on the *relative* wage of the union, is unaltered by CBC since, given nominal wages, relative wages are the same for all inflation rates. Hence, at higher levels of CBC the marginal benefit in terms of real wages is higher in comparison with the marginal cost in terms of unemployment, inducing the union to set a higher real wage. The positive effect of I on the real wage premium in this case can be demonstrated formally by letting $B = 0$ in equation (11.7), differentiating it with respect to I and observing that, provided there is more than one union, the derivative is positive. Cukierman and Lippi (1999) refer to this mechanism as a 'competition induced strategic non-neutrality'.[10] In essence it arises because the level of CBC alters the marginal trade-off between a higher real wage and competition over jobs at the level of the individual union.

---

[10] For a fuller discussion and a proof the reader is referred to proposition 5 of that paper.

2.4   *Unemployment, inflation and CWB*

Using equation (11.3) it can be shown that

$$u \equiv \frac{L - L^d}{L} = a\phi, \tag{11.9}$$

implying that unemployment is higher the higher the wage premium. Since, owing to the market power of unions, the equilibrium wage premium is positive, so is the 'natural' rate of unemployment. Since there is no uncertainty and expectations are rational, the rate of inflation is forecasted perfectly by unions at contracting time. Imposing the rational expectations condition that $\pi = E\pi$ in equation (11.6), the equilibrium expression for inflation is

$$\pi = \frac{a^2}{I}\phi, \tag{11.10}$$

which replicates the well known KPBG result that inflation is positive when the natural rate of unemployment (which is positive) is above the desired rate (zero, in our case). The root source of the bias here is the market power of unions. The bias is lower the higher is CBC, I, and the lower the market power of unions as characterised by ϕ (since all wage premia are identical in equilibrium the bar above ϕ has been omitted).

Equations (11.9) and (11.10) imply that unemployment and inflation bear the same qualitative relation to CWB as does the wage premium. For example, if the parameters are such that the wage premium is an inverted U function of CWB, inflation and unemployment will also be inverted U functions of CWB.

3   CB–labour union interaction in the presence of monopolistically competitive price setting firms

When the CB is assumed to control inflation directly, monetary policy affects the economy only by changing the real content of contractually fixed nominal wages through inflation. Frameworks that use this modelling strategy implicitly assume that monetary policy affects the economy *only* through supply by changing real wages and the quantity of labour demanded. As a consequence, the large family of models that utilises this assumption abstracts from traditional demand channels of monetary policy recently revived by advocates of the New Keynesian approach to monetary theory and policy.[11] This section reviews recent extensions of the baseline model that features *both* supply- and demand-driven transmission mechanisms of monetary policy. The extension introduces price setting, monopolistically competitive firms and recognizes that

[11] A survey of this approach appears in Clarida, Galí and Gertler (1999).

the monetary authority controls the money supply rather than inflation.[12] In this formulation product demand, and therefore the demand for labour, depend on real money balances. More precisely, given real money balances, each firm sets the price of its product so as to maximise its real profits. This determines the relative price of the firm, the demand for its product and the firm's derived demand for labour. As a consequence monetary policy affects employment and unemployment *also* by changing aggregate demand.

The strategic interaction between unions and the CB is represented, as in the baseline model, by a sequence of events in which unions move first, setting nominal wage contracts, and the CB moves second and chooses the money supply. But now there is a third stage in which each monopolistically competitive firm chooses its price, taking the previously detemined nominal wages and the money supply as given. Thus, wages are sticky but prices are fully flexible. A central new element of this framework in comparison to the baseline model is that, when it sets the nominal wage, the individual union takes into consideration the effect of the CB response *also* on the demand for the goods produced by the firms that utilise its labour.

In particular, when an individual union raises the nominal wage of its members, it triggers an increase in the relative prices of the goods of the firms that use the union's labour. This action has two consequences. First, the derived demand for labour of the affected firms goes down, increasing unemployment among the union's members. Second, inflation rises. The CB dislikes both the higher unemployment and the higher inflation. But it cannot fully offset both effects since it possesses only one instrument. Depending on its preferences, the CB decides to use monetary policy to counteract either the impact of the wage increase on inflation or its impact on unemployment. If the CB is highly conservative it reacts by contracting the money supply, thus aggravating the unemployment problem. If the CB is relatively liberal it reacts by expanding the money supply, thus aggravating the inflation problem. The union dislikes inflation as well as unemployment among its members. If it is relatively averse to unemployment, a higher level of CBC is associated with lower bargaining power for the union. If the union is relatively averse to inflation a lower level of CBC is associated with lower bargaining power for the union.

3.1   The model

The economy is composed of a continuum of monopolistically competitive firms and of n, equally sized, labour unions that organise the entire labour force. The firms are evenly distributed over the unit interval and their mass is one. Thus, each union covers the labour force of a fraction $1/n$ of the firms. A quantity

---

[12] This section draws on Coricelli, Cukierman and Dalmazzo (2000).

L_0 of workers, equal across firms, is attached to each firm but works only if the union in charge signs a labour contract with the firm. For convenience, and without loss of generality, the firms are indexed so that all firms whose labour force is represented by union i are located in the contiguous subinterval $(\frac{i}{n}, \frac{i+1}{n})$ of the unit interval, where $i = 0,1 \ldots, n - 1$. Each firm owns a production technology that exhibits decreasing returns to scale to labour input, and is given by

$$Y_{ij} = L_{ij}^{\alpha}, \quad \alpha, < 1, \tag{11.11}$$

where Y_{ij} and L_{ij} are output supply and labour input of firm j. The index i means that the labour force of the firm belongs to union i. Each firm faces a demand for its output given by

$$Y_{ij}^d = \left(\frac{P_{ij}}{P}\right)^{-\eta} \frac{M}{P}, \quad \eta > 1, \tag{11.12}$$

where P_{ij} and P are, respectively, the price of the individual firm and the general price level, M is the aggregate nominal money supply, and η is the (absolute value of the) elasticity of demand facing the individual firm with respect to its relative price. Equation (11.12) states that the demand facing the individual firm is increasing in real money balances and decreasing in the relative price of its product.[13] The general price level is defined as the integral, over the unit interval, of the (logarithms of) the prices of individual firms. It is convenient to write it as

$$p = \frac{1}{n} \sum_{i=0}^{n-1} \left(\frac{\int_{\frac{i}{n}}^{\frac{i+1}{n}} p_{ij}dj}{\int_{\frac{i}{n}}^{\frac{i+1}{n}} dj}\right) = \sum_{i=0}^{n-1} \int_{\frac{i}{n}}^{\frac{i+1}{n}} p_{ij}dj = \int_0^1 p_{ij}dj, \tag{11.13}$$

where p_{ij} is the logarithm of P_{ij} and p is the logarithm of P. This way of expressing the general price level facilitates the identification of the firms that are affected by an increase in the nominal wage rate set by union i.

The objective functions of unions and of the CB are the same as in the baseline model and are given respectively by equations (11.1) and (11.2).

---

[13] The demand function in equation (11.12) can be derived from a more basic formulation in which each individual chooses consumption so as to maximise his utility subject to his wealth constraint. Details appear in chapter 8 of Blanchard and Fischer (1989).

More broadly, as well as more realistically, the effect of real money balances on demand can be thought of as reflecting a whole variety of demand-induced effects of real balances on demand. Those include the well-known Keynes–Tobin effect of monetary expansion on demand via a lower interest rate, the Bernanke–Gertler credit channel, as well as the narrow Pigou–Patinkin real balance effect. When real balances go up they generally stimulate demand through all those channels. I will therefore sometimes refer to the total impact of real balances on demand as a 'generalised' real balance effect. Chapter 25 of Mishkin (2001) discusses the various channels through which monetary policy affects aggregate demand. A summary appears in figure 1 of that chapter.

3.2 Equilibrium

Equilibrium is characterised by backward induction. The firm's problem is solved first, then the CB problem and finally the union's wage decision.

3.2.1 Price setting by monopolistically competitive firms

Real profits of an individual firm are given by

$$
\Pi_{ij} = \frac{P_{ij}}{P} Y_{ij}^d - \frac{W_i}{P} L_{ij} = \left(\frac{P_{ij}}{P}\right)^{1-\eta} \frac{M}{P} - \frac{W_i}{P} \left[\left(\frac{P_{ij}}{P}\right)^{-\eta} \frac{M}{P}\right]^{\frac{1}{\alpha}},
$$

(11.14)

where the second equality is obtained by using (12), the demand facing the individual firm, and (11), the production function. In the third stage of the game, the firm takes P, M and the nominal wage, w_i, as given and chooses its own price, P_{ij}, so as to maximise real profits. Maximising with respect to P_{ij}, taking logarithms and rearranging yields

$$
p_{ij} - p = \theta + \frac{1}{\alpha + \eta(1-\alpha)}[\alpha(w_i - p) + (1-\alpha)(m - p)],
$$

(11.15)

where θ is a combination of the basic model's parameters and lower case letters stand for the logarithms of the corresponding upper case letters. Equation (11.15) states that the optimal relative price of a typical monopolistically competitive firm is higher the higher the real wage it pays and the higher are real money balances. The first element reflects the firm's reaction to labour costs and the second its reaction to the demand for its product. The firm's derived demand for labour can be obtained by equating the product demand (equation (11.12)) with the firm's supply (equation (11.11)). Taking logarithms and rearranging yields

$$
l_{ij}^d = \frac{1}{\alpha}[-\eta(p_{ij} - p) + (m - p)].
$$

(11.16)

Equation (11.16) states that the individual firm's derived demand for labour is an increasing function of real money balances and a decreasing function of its relative price. Using equation (11.15) in equation (11.16), the firm's demand for labour can be rewritten in the alternative form

$$
l_{ij}^d = \kappa + \frac{1}{\alpha + \eta(1-\alpha)}[-\eta(w_i - p) + (m - p)],
$$

(11.17)

where κ is a combination of the model's parameters. This form implies that when the union manages to raise the real wage, the firm's demand for labour goes down unless real money balances increase. This feature of labour demand plays a crucial role later.

3.2.2   Choice of money supply by the CB

The CB picks the money supply in the second stage so as to minimise its loss function (11.2), after observing nominal wages and anticipating the pricing and employment reaction of firms to its own choice (as given by equations (11.15) to (11.17)). Averaging equation (11.15) over firms and rearranging, yields

$$(m - p) = \rho - \frac{\alpha}{(1 - \alpha)}(w - p), \tag{11.18}$$

where ρ is a combination of the basic parameters of the model and p and w are respectively the logarithms of the average price and of the average nominal wage. Equation (11.18) states that, in the aggregate, there is an inverse *equilibrium* relation between the average real wage and real money balances. The equilibrium general rate of inflation can be obtained from equation (11.18) by rearranging and by substracting the (log of) the previous period, historically given, price level, p_{-1}:

$$\pi = p - p_{-1} = -(1 - \alpha)\rho + \alpha w + (1 - \alpha)m - p_{-1}. \tag{11.19}$$

Thus, except for a constant that depends on the basic parameters of the economy, the equilibrium price level is a weighted average of nominal wages and of the nominal money supply. Averaging equation (11.16) over firms yields the (log of the) average level of employment per firm:

$$l^d = \frac{1}{\alpha}(m - p). \tag{11.20}$$

Since the total mass of firms is one, l^d also coincides with aggregate demand for labour. In contrast with 'supply-side' models, where the CB picks inflation directly, equation (11.20) reflects the 'Keynesian' feature of the extended model, where monetary policy affects employment not only via supply but also through aggregate demand. Note that this Keynesian feature arises even though prices are completely flexible.

Let $l_0 \equiv \log[L_0]$ be the logarithm of labour supply per firm. The average rate of unemployment per firm, as well as the average economy-wide rate of unemployment, is therefore

$$u = l_0 - \frac{1}{\alpha}(m - p). \tag{11.21}$$

Taking the average nominal wage w as given, the CB chooses the nominal stock of money m so as to minimise its loss function. Substituting the expressions for inflation and unemployment (equations (11.19) and (11.21)) into the CB loss function in equation (11.2) and minimising with respect to m yields the reaction function

$$m = \mu + \frac{1 - \alpha(1 - \alpha)I}{1 + (1 - \alpha)^2 I} w, \tag{11.22}$$

where μ is a combination of the basic parameters of the model.

3.2.3   Wage setting by unions   Each union takes the nominal wages of other unions as given and chooses its own *nominal* wage so as to minimise the loss function in equation (11.1) while taking into consideration the effects of the reaction of the CB and of firms for the union's real wage, for unemployment among its members, and for the general rate of inflation. Coricelli, Cukierman and Dalmazzo (2000) show that the (common) real wage premium that emerges from the solution to this problem is given by

$$\phi \equiv w_r - w_r^c = \frac{(1 - \alpha)^2 Z_w}{(1 - \alpha)A Z_u + \frac{B}{I}(1 - Z_w)}, \tag{11.23}$$

where

$$1 - \frac{dp}{dw_i} \equiv Z_w = 1 - \frac{1}{n[1 + (1 - \alpha)^2 I]} > 0 \tag{11.24}$$

and

$$-\frac{dl_{ij}^d}{dw_i} = \frac{du_i}{dw_i} \equiv Z_u = \frac{1}{\alpha}\left[\eta\frac{d(p_i - p)}{dw_i} - \frac{d(m - p)}{dw_i}\right]$$

$$= \frac{1}{n}\left[\frac{\eta(n - 1)}{\alpha + \eta(1 - \alpha)} + \frac{(1 - \alpha)I}{1 + (1 - \alpha)^2 I}\right] > 0. \tag{11.25}$$

Notice that the wage premium is always non-negative and that it increases with Z_w and decreases with Z_u, A and B. As in the baseline model, Z_w is the overall elasticity of the union's *real* wage with respect to the nominal wage and is bounded between 0 and 1. Similarly, Z_u is the (absolute value of) the overall elasticity of employment among union members with respect to the union's nominal wage. It is also equal to the marginal impact of an increase in the union's nominal wage on the rate of unemployment among union members.[14] The overall elasticities, Z_w and Z_u, internalise the subsequent reactions of monetary policy and of prices to union i's wage decision.

It is instructive to compare and contrast the expression for the wage premium here and in the baseline model. As in the baseline model, the elasticity, Z_w, of

---

[14] To highlight the fact that, from a conceptual point of view, Z_w and Z_u are the same in the two models, I am using the same notation for them across models in spite of the fact that their particular functional forms vary across models.

the real wage with respect to the nominal wage is an increasing function of n and of I. An important difference between the models concerns the marginal impact, Z_u, of an increase in the union's nominal wage on unemployment among its members. In the present model, this marginal impact depends on CBC, I. By contrast, in the baseline model it does not. The reason is that the baseline model does not incorporate an aggregate demand channel of monetary policy on economic activity into the analysis, while the present model does. It is easily seen, from equation (11.25), that higher values of CBC are associated with higher values of Z_u, implying that, given Z_w, the wage premium is lower. Thus (given Z_w), the higher the level of CBC, the larger the union's cost, in terms of unemployment, of an increase in the nominal wage and the lower the bargaining power of the union. This non-neutrality is related to the effects of the CB response to an increase in the union's nominal wage on the demand for goods, and through it, on the demand for the union's labour. The direction and magnitude of this response depends on CBC.[15] The following subsection takes a deeper look at the consequences of this reponse.

3.3   Central bank conservativeness, accommodation and unions' bargaining power

Examination of the reaction function of the CB in equation (11.22) reveals that, depending on the degree of CBC, I, the CB either counteracts or accommodates an increase in nominal wages. If the CB is sufficiently conservative ($1 - \alpha$ $(1 - \alpha)I < 0$), a nominal wage increase triggers a tightening of the money supply. If the CB is relatively liberal ($1 - \alpha(1 - \alpha)I > 0$) it partially accommodates wage increases.

The intuition underlying this result is as follows. Firms respond to an increase in nominal wages by increasing their prices. This raises the rate of inflation and, for a given nominal money supply, reduces real money balances. The second effect reduces the derived demand for labour and pushes unemployment up. The upshot is that, in the absence of any reaction by the CB, an increase in the average level of nominal wages raises both inflation and unemployment. The response of the CB is designed to optimally spread the costs of those two 'bads' between the two components of its loss function. If it cares relatively more about price stability, the CB partially counteracts the effect of wage increases on inflation at the cost of even higher unemployment. If it cares relatively more about unemployment, the CB partially counteracts the adverse effect of higher wages on unemployment at the cost of even higher inflation.

---

[15] Several additional results concerning the effects of CWB, n, and of product markets' local monopoly power, η, on unions' bargaining power are implicit in the expressions for the wage premium in equations (11.23)–(11.25). For further details the reader is referred to Coricelli, Cukierman and Dalmazzo (2000).

Casual evidence about the industrial organisation of labour negotiations in Germany in the pre-EMU period as well as recent empirical evidence concerning monetary policy reaction functions supports the above mechanism. Studies of industrial relations in Germany such as Berghahn and Detlev (1987) and Streeck (1994) report that the Bundesbank often threatened to tighten monetary policy in response to excessive wage settlements. Hall (1994, p. 12) and Hall and Franzese (1998) note that, owing to the high level of independence of the Bundesbank, labour unions usually took this threat seriously but that, from time to time, the German CB actually tightened monetary policy in response to high wage settlements in order to maintain its credibility. This point of view is corroborated by empirical reaction functions from Cukierman, Rodriguez and Webb (1998) that provide estimates of the degree of monetary accommodation (characterised by the reaction of high-powered money growth to wage inflation) in a group of developed economies between the mid-1970s and the beginning of the 1990s. Cukierman et al. find that in countries with low effective CBC the coefficient of accommodation tends to be significantly positive; in countries with intermediate levels of CBC it is insignificantly different from zero; and in high CBC countries like Germany and Austria it is significantly negative. Those findings support a reaction function of the type that appears in equation (11.22). In countries with a highly independent and conservative CB, the monetary authority leans against inflationary wage increases by contracting money growth in response to wage inflation.

4   Should the central bank be more liberal or more conservative than society?

The answer to the question posed in the title of this section depends on the effects of CBC on unemployment and inflation. This largely depends, in turn, on whether a higher level of CBC raises or reduces the bargaining power of unions. The recent literature contains two opposing views on this issue. One is that, by raising the inflationary fears of unions, a more liberal CB (lower I) is more effective in deterring unions from raising wages. The other is that a less accommodating CB, by raising unions' fears about unemployment, is more effective in achieving this objective. The first view is expressed in, or implied by, the work of Skott (1997), Cukierman and Lippi (1999), Guzzo and Velasco (1999, 2002), Lawler (2000) and Lippi (2002). The second view is implied by the work of Soskice and Iversen (1998, 2000).

4.1   The populist central bank result

The first view above leads to the strong result that, in the case of a single, inflation averse, monopoly union, a populist or ultra-liberal CB that does not care at all about inflation ($I = 0$) is socially optimal. The framework is identical to that of Rogoff (1985), but without any shocks.[16] Society dislikes both inflation and unemployment, and assigns a positive relative weight S to the cost of inflation. The higher S, the more averse is society to inflation in comparison with unemployment.

When all the labour force is represented by a single monopoly union the union fully internalises the effect of its wage policy on the subsequent response of the money supply and of prices. Since the 'ultra-liberal' CB cares *only about unemployment* it produces very high inflation even when unemployment is mildly positive. Even if the union is only moderately averse to inflation (in the sense that B is small but strictly positive), it strongly dislikes such high inflation. Knowing that even the slightest level of unemployment will induce the CB to inflate at an extremely high rate, the union reduces the wage premium to zero in order to avoid this calamity. And, indeed, when the wage premium is zero, there is no unemployment and the CB has no reason to inflate. An ultra-liberal CB thus delivers both zero inflation and zero unemployment, maximising social welfare.

As soon as there is more than one union this result no longer necessarily holds, because the wage policy of each union is correctly perceived to have a smaller effect on CB policy than in the case of a monopoly union. As a consequence, deterrence through the inflation fears of unions is smaller and extreme populism need not be socially optimal. In addition, when it is recognised that the degree of wage indexation is endogenous, the social optimality of appointing a populist CB no longer holds, even for the extreme case of a monopoly union. The reason, as pointed out by Liviatan (2001), is that the union will defend itself against the extreme inflationary tendencies of such a bank by indexing wages and this will neutralise the moderating impact of the union's inflation fears on its real wage demands.

4.2   Deterrence through fear of unemployment versus deterrence through fear of inflation

Soskice and Iversen (1998, 2000) construct models in which the aggregate demand channel of monetary policy is incorporated explicitly. They show that a less accommodating CB, by raising the unions' fear of unemployment, reduces their bargaining power and, with it, the real wage. This begs the following question. What is the overall effect of CBC on the real wage, or the wage premium, when the deterrent effects of unions' fears of *both* inflation and unemployment are acknowledged. Since the papers that stress unions' inflation

---

[16] The absence of shocks implies that there is no motive for stabilisation policy. Lawler (2000) provides a discussion of optimal contracts for central bankers in the presence of such a motive for the case of a monopoly union.

aversion abstract from the effects of monetary policy via demand while the Soskice and Iversen (1998, 2000) papers abstract from the inflation aversion of unions, it is hard to judge from either group of papers which of those two deterring mechanisms is likely to dominate.

By incorporating unions' inflation aversion, aggregate demand and aggregate supply channels of monetary policy within a *single* framework, the model in Coricelli, Cukierman and Dalmazzo (2000), reviewed in section 3, makes it possible to evaluate the factors that determine the overall effect of CBC on the real wage, unemployment and inflation. This framework implies that the equilibrium relations between unemployment and inflation on one hand, and the wage premium on the other, are given by

$$u = \frac{1}{1 - \alpha} \phi \tag{11.26}$$

$$\pi = p - p_{-1} = \frac{1}{(1 - \alpha)^2 I} \phi. \tag{11.27}$$

Hence, given I, unemployment and inflation are increasing functions of the wage premium.

The main lessons from the analysis in that paper are as follows. If the relative aversion of unions to inflation versus unemployment is large (B/A is large), deterrence works mainly through the inflation fears of unions. In such cases relatively liberal central banks are better at moderating the real wage demands of unions so that the wage premium is lower the more liberal is the CB. This implies (from equation (11.26)) that unemployment is also lower under a relatively liberal CB. But, as can be seen from equation (11.27), the effect on inflation is generally ambiguous. Although a more liberal CB reduces the inflationary bias by lowering the wage premium and unemployment, it raises it directly since it cares less about the costs of inflation. Nonetheless, as pointed out by Guzzo and Velasco (2002), a CB that is more liberal than society may still be socially desirable in such a case.

When unions are relatively more averse to unemployment than to inflation (B/A is small) deterrence works mainly through the fears of unions about unemployment. Hence relatively more conservative central banks are more effective at reducing the bargaining power of unions, and with it the wage premium, unemployment and inflation. In such a case, a CB that is more conservative than society is socially desirable since it unambiguously reduces both inflation and unemployment. Since, as implied by equation (11.22), the degree of accommodation is a decreasing function of CBC, this case is consistent with the views expressed in Soskice and Iversen (1998, 2000).

Which of those two deterring mechanisms is likely to dominate in reality? Coricelli, Cukierman and Dalmazzo (2000) show that, for realistic values of B/A, a CB that is more conservative than society is socially optimal. In addition, their analysis suggests that the social optimality of a populist CB (for which $I = 0$) is likely to be an extreme special case that arises only when B/A is relatively large and wage bargaining is highly centralised (n is very small).

5   Strategic and related effects of a monetary union

The recent formation of the European Monetary Union (EMU) changed the nature of the strategic interaction between the CB and labour unions within the euro area. Before the formation of EMU labour unions within each country interacted only, or mainly, with the CB of their own country. With the creation of EMU, instead of facing its own national CB, each union now faces the European Central Bank (ECB). An important consequence of this institutional change is that the labour force of each union constitutes a smaller fraction of the total labour force in the euro area than was the case hitherto, under decentralised national monetary policies. An immediate consequence of this observation is that, under EMU, each individual union internalises the consequences of its wage policy on the reaction of the ECB to a lesser extent than before.

A seemingly general intuitive implication of this observation is that unions' wage demands are moderated by the anticipated reaction of the CB to a lesser extent under a monetary union (MU) than under national monetary policies (NMP). This argument appears to apply both in the case in which this moderation is attained mainly because of unions' fears of unemployment, as well as in the case in which it is achieved mainly through their inflationary fears. Soskice and Iversen (1998) focus on the first mechanism and Grüner and Hefeker (1999) and Cukierman and Lippi (2001) focus on the second. Grüner and Hefeker consider the case of a single union per country while Cukierman and Lippi allow countries to differ in centralisation of wage bargaining (CWB), in size and in the degree of substitutability between labour of different unions across countries (i.e., the parameter γ in equation (11.3) can vary across countries).

5.1   The strategic effect of replacing independent national monetary policies by a monetary union

With the formation of a MU each labour union becomes smaller relative to the monetary area in the sense that the impact of its wage policy on the area-wide average wage and unemployment becomes smaller. When the dominant moderating mechanism is via unions' fears of unemployment, the increase in the number of unions facing a single CB moderates the perceived adverse employment repercussions of an increase in a union's nominal wage and leads to higher nominal and real wages. Similarly, when the dominant moderating mechanism is via unions' inflation fears, the increase in the number of unions moderates the perceived inflationary repercussions of an increase in a single union's nominal wage and leads to higher wage premia.

It turns out that this basic intuition holds in some circumstances, but not in all. In particular, Cukierman and Lippi (2001) show, using the baseline model of section 2, that if union and CB preferences are identical across countries, and do not change with the establishment of a MU, then the wage premium in the MU is higher than under NMP at all levels of the common value of CWB. They refer to this outcome as the 'strategic effect' of a monetary union. We saw in section 2 that both unemployment and inflation are positively related to the wage premium.[17] Hence, in those circumstances, unemployment and inflation go up too when independent monetary policies are replaced by a MU.

This result needs to be qualified in several ways. First, it assumes that the level of CBC remains unaltered before and after the creation of a MU. If (as was the case with the creation of EMU) average CBC goes up with the creation of a MU there may be, depending on the level of CBC and on the relative aversion of unions to inflation and to unemployment, an offsetting or a reinforcing effect. We saw in section 3 that, if the inflation aversion of the CB is high relative to that of unions, an increase in CBC moderates real wages. Hence, in those circumstances, a higher level of CBC in the MU moderates the upward influence of the strategic effect on real wages, unemployment and inflation. Second, the strategic effect of a MU unambiguously raises the wage premium only if the parameters γ and n of the baseline model (section 2) are not too dissimilar across countries and provided the countries do not differ too much in size.

5.2   The strategic effect of replacing a German dominated ERM by a monetary union

For a substantial number of years prior to joining EMU some countries, such as Austria, the Netherlands and Belgium, were essentially pegging their currencies to the Deutschmark via the Exchange Rate Mechanism (ERM). Such countries did not conduct independent monetary policies even before the advent of EMU. Instead they subjugated their monetary policies to the objective of maintaining a fixed peg to the DM. For such countries the change in institutions brought about by the creation of EMU altered the strategic interaction between unions and the monetary authority in a somewhat different way.

The replacement by a MU of a system of unilaterally fixed pegs to the currency of a centre country that conducts an independent monetary policy is analysed in Grüner and Hefeker (1999) and Cukierman and Lippi (2001). The basic framework involves two players. First, a leader country that conducts monetary policy so as to minimise losses from domestic inflation and unemployment, to

---

[17] See equations (11.9) and (11.10) of the baseline model.

which I shall refer as Germany. The second is a group of follower countries that credibly subjugate their monetary policies to the objective of maintaining fixed pegs with respect to the German currency. The main result of both papers is that the replacement of a credible ERM by a MU should raise the wage premium in Germany and reduce it in the follower countries. The conception underlying this result is illustrated by means of the baseline model of section 2 under the assumption that all parameters are identical across countries.

Under this characterisation of the ERM, monetary policy in Germany in the pre-MU period is described by a NMP regime so that the equilibrium wage premium is still given by equation (11.7) of the baseline.model. The crucial difference introduced by the existence of a credible ERM in the pre-MU period concerns the unions of the countries that precommitted to follow German monetary policy. Domestic inflation is unrelated to the wage premia of those unions, because they know that domestic inflation is determined by the German CB, which looks *only* at developments in Germany. Hence, each union in a follower country perceives that its individual action has no impact on the rate of inflation, implying $Z_w = 1$. It follows that the wage premium in a follower country under the ERM is[18]

$$\bar{\phi}_f^{ERM} = \frac{1}{\alpha A \left[\alpha + \gamma(n-1)\right]},$$

(11.28)

which is larger than the premium obtained under NMP as given by equation (11.7).[19] The fact that under a credible ERM the unions in the follower countries do not internalise the impact of their actions on inflation eliminates a deterrent to high wage claims and therefore leads them to adopt a more aggressive wage strategy.

Under this characterisation, the creation of a MU should increase the wage premium of German unions and decrease the premia of unions in the follower countries. The reason is that the creation of a MU *reduces* the perceived impact of each individual German union on inflation whereas the opposite happens in the other countries, whose unions now correctly realise that their wage decisions have a non-zero impact on the inflationary reaction of the monetary union's CB. Again this conclusion requires appropriate qualifications when basic parameters differ markedly across countries.

5.3   Monetary union and labour market reform

The creation of a MU may alter policymakers' incentives to reform the labour market. This issue is relevant for Europe, where labour market rigidities are

---

[18] The subscript f designates a follower country's CB.

[19] This follows from the observation that the wage premium in equation (11.7) is increasing in Z_w.

considered by many as an important determinant of poor employment performance (Bean 1994; Nickell 1997). Calmfors (2001a) has argued that the creation of EMU may stimulate reforms in labour market institutions.

Sibert and Sutherland (2000) used a variant of the KPBG model to analyse this question. In their model monetary policy is discretionary and policymakers face an inflationary bias that is directly proportional to the rate of unemployment. Moreover, owing to international spillovers, inflation is higher when monetary policy is implemented in an uncoordinated manner (i.e. NMP) than in the MU. Policymakers have an incentive to reduce labour market distortions, because this lowers the equilibrium rates of unemployment and of inflation. A main point of their paper is that since, in their framework, inflation is lower in a MU than under NMP, the incentives to eliminate labour market distortions are lower in the MU than under NMP. But, as we saw above, the creation of a MU may actually reduce the discipline of wage setters. Holden (2001) argues on this basis that the incentive to coordinate wage setting (in order to recapture some of the gains from the lost discipline) is therefore stronger in a MU. In view of those conflicting conclusions the more general message is probably that, if a MU raises (reduces) real wages, the incentives for labour market reform are higher (lower) under a MU.

5.4   Open economy extensions

Most of the models reviewed in this survey are closed economy frameworks that abstract from foreign trade linkages. Open economy extensions in a two-country world have been studied by Coricelli, Cukierman and Dalmazzo (forthcoming), Chprits (2002), Knell (2001) and Cavallari (2002). Those papers are open economy extensions of the type of framework surveyed in section 3 in which prices are set by monopolistically competitive firms and in which the CB chooses the money supply.

The first paper analyses the effects of institutions on economic performance in a monetary union in the presence of a stabilisation policy. It relates average as well as country-specific economic performance within the monetary union to country size, number of unions, the degree of product differentiation on product markets, and CBC. Economic performance is characterised by unemployment, inflation, real wages and trade competitiveness. Both average and country-specific economic performance in the presence of (possibly) heterogeneous shocks and a unified stabilisation policy are evaluated.

Using a similar framework, Chprits (2002) re-examines the effects of replacing a 'German' dominated ERM by a monetary union when monetary authorities choose the money supply rather than the rate of inflation and prices are set by monopolistically competitive firms. She finds that, other things the same, replacement of a 'German' dominated ERM by a MU raises real wages in the follower country and reduces them in the leader country (Germany). The intuition underlying this result is that, under the ERM, the leader country sets its monetary policy without any regard for unemployment in the follower country and so does the follower country, since it is bound by the rules of the credible ERM. This imposes substantial wage discipline on the unions of the follower country. By contrast, since they realise that their CB does care to some extent about domestic unemployment, unions in the leader country demand higher real wages. Under a MU the CB cares to some extent about unemployment in both countries, but not as much about unemployment in the leader country as the leader's CB did under ERM. As a consequence real wages under a MU are higher in the follower country, and lower in the leader country than under the ERM.

The paper by Knell (2001) examines the robustness of several results surveyed here to the incorporation of foreign trade linkages. The paper shows that the domestic Calmfors–Driffill curve depends on the nature of both domestic and foreign institutions. It also provides a further qualification to the result in Grüner and Hefeker (1999) and in Cukierman and Lippi (2001) (subsection 5.2) by showing that, when open economy linkages are acknowledged, the replacement of an ERM by a MU does not always increase unemployment. The paper by Cavallari (2002) examines the consequences of a MU in an open economy framework in which the typical labour union tries to maximise the average welfare of its members.

6   Concluding remarks

The notion that monetary policy has real effects owing to some nominal rigidities has a long tradition in economics. The Keynesian notion that it is mainly the stickiness of *prices* that provides a lever for the real effects of monetary policy was seriously questionned during the 1970s and 1980s, particularly by economists with a classical orientation. Believers in price stickiness sometimes submit the existence of price lists that are revised at discrete dates as evidence in favour of price stickiness. This casual evidence has been criticised on the ground that, owing to the existence of discounts and producers' ability to adjust various qualitative dimensions of their products, prices are actually substantially more flexible than would appear to be the case from a price list. In spite of those arguments, macroeconomics witnessed a remarkable revival of sticky-price models during the second half of the 1990s. A survey of this approach appears in Clarida, Galí and Gertler (1999), and more recent theoretical foundations are developed in Woodford (forthcoming).[20]

By contrast, the literature surveyed in this chapter is built on the notion that nominal wages are sticky, or that they are, at least, substantially more

---

[20] See also Calvo (1983).

sticky than prices. Casual observation, as well as more systematic work, like that of Stigler and Kindhal (1970), supports the view that this is a realistic presumption. This notion dictates the timing structure of the models used to depict the stategic interaction between wage setters, the monetary authority and price setters. Since they are bound by nominal contracts that are normally in effect for at least a year, wage setters are assumed to move first and to remain committed to the contract nominal wage over the period of the game. To reflect the fact that monetary policy is more flexible than nominal wages, the CB is assumed to move after wage setters. In the wide subclass of models that postulate, for simplicity (following KPBG), that the monetary authority directly controls prices, this is a natural way to reflect the reasonable presumption that monetary policy and prices are both more flexible than wages.

In the subclass of models in which the CB chooses the money supply and prices are set by monopolistically competitive firms there are, a priori, two possible assumptions about the relative timing of moves between price setters and the choice of money supply by the CB. Assuming that price setters move first implies that prices are more sticky than monetary policy is, and assuming that the monetary authority moves first implies the opposite. Models with a New Keynesian orientation of the Clarida, Galí and Gertler (1999) type use the first assumption while the family of models with unions and price setting firms (see section 3) use the second assumption.

I believe that the second timing assumption is preferable for two reasons. First, as we saw above, the notion that wages are sticky is less controversial than the notion that prices are sticky. Second, given that there are sticky wages in the model, there is not much to be gained in terms of insights by introducing a second, and less probable, type of nominal stickiness. As a matter of fact it is likely that price stickiness in New Keynesian models is largely a reduced form proxy for the more substantial degree of wage stickiness observed in reality.

In the family of models reviewed in section 3 prices do not fully move when the money supply changes (see equation (11.19)). But this is not because it is costly to adjust prices. Instead, it is because it *does not pay* profit maximising firms to fully adjust their prices in line with the money supply as long as *nominal wages have not been adjusted.* The upshot is that monetary policy has real effects, even in the presence of fully flexible prices, owing to the existence of contractually fixed nominal wages.

REFERENCES

Agell, J. and B.-C. Ysander, 1993, 'Should Governments Learn to Live with Inflation? Comment', *American Economic Review* 83, 305–11.

Barro, R. J. and D. Gordon, 1983, 'A Positive Theory of Monetary Policy in a Natural Rate Model', *Journal of Political Economy* 91, 589–610.

Bean, C., 1994, 'European Unemployment: a Retrospective', *European Economic Review*, 38, 523–34.

Berghahn, V. and K. Detlev, 1987, *Industrial Relations in West Germany*, Oxford: Berg.

Blanchard, O. and S. Fischer, 1989, *Lectures in Macroeconomics*, Cambridge, MA: MIT Press.

Bleaney, M., 1996, 'Central Bank Independence, Wage-Bargaining Structure, and Macroeconomic Performance in OECD Countries', *Oxford Economic Papers* 48, 20–38.

Bratsiotis, G. and C. Martin, 1999, 'Stabilisation, Policy Targets and Unemployment in Imperfectly Competitive Economies', *Scandinavian Journal of Economics* 101, 241–56.

Calmfors, L., 1993, 'Centralisation of Wage Bargaining and Macroeconomic Performance – A Survey', *OECD Economic Studies* 21, 161–91.

2001a, 'Unemployment, Labor Market Reform and Monetary Union', *Journal of Labor Economics* 19(2), 265–89.

2001b, 'Wage and Wage-Bargaining Institutions in the EMU – A Survey of the Issues', *Empirica* 28, 325–51.

Calmfors, L. and J. Driffill, 1988, 'Bargaining Structure, Corporatism, and Macroeconomic Performance', *Economic Policy* 6, 14–61.

Calvo, G., 1983, 'Staggered Prices in a Utility Maximizing Framework', *Journal of Monetary Economics* 12(3), 383–98.

Cavallari, L., 2002, 'Inflationary Performance in a Monetary Union with Large Wage Setters', unpublished manuscript, University of Rome.

Chprits, E., 2002, 'Monetary Union versus Alternative Exchange Rate Regimes: Analysis of Economic Performance', MA thesis, Berglas School of Economics, Tel-Aviv University.

Clarida, R., J. Galí and M. Gertler, 1999, 'The Science of Monetary Policy: A New Keynesian Perspective', *Journal of Economic Literature* 37, 1661–707.

Coricelli, F., A. Cukierman and A. Dalmazzo, 2000, 'Monetary Institutions, Monopolistic Competition, Unionized Labor Markets and Economic Performance', CEPR Discussion Paper no. 2407. Abridged and revised version (May 2002) at http://www.tau.ac.il/~alexcuk/pdf/ccd-revej1.pdf

forthcoming, 'Economic Performance and Stabilisation Policy in a Monetary Union with Imperfect Labor and Goods Markets', in Sinn and Widgren (eds.), *Issues of Monetary Integration in Europe*, Cambridge, MA: MIT Press, also available at http://www.tau.ac.il/~alexcuk/pdf/ccdmu5-04a.pdf.

Cubitt R. P., 1992, 'Monetary Policy Games and Private Sector Precommitment', *Oxford Economic Papers* 44, 513–30.

1995, 'Corporatism, Monetary Policy and Economic Performance: A Simple Game Theoretic Analysis', *Scandinavian Journal of Economics*, 97(2), 245–59.

Cukierman, A. and F. Lippi, 1999, 'Central Bank Independence, Centralisation of Wage Bargaining, Inflation and Unemployment – Theory and Some Evidence', *European Economic Review* 43, 1395–434; also available at http://www.tau.ac.il/~alexcuk/pdf/Lippi1EER.pdf.

2001, 'Labour Markets and Monetary Union: A Strategic Analysis', *Economic Journal* 111, 541–65; also available at http://www.tau.ac.il/~alexcuk/pdf/LipiEMU799.pdf.

Cukierman, A., P. Rodriguez and S. Webb, 1998, 'Central Bank Autonomy and Exchange Rate Regimes – Their Effects on Monetary Accommodation and Activism', in

S. Eijffinger and H. Huizinga (eds.), *Positive Political Economy – Theory and Evidence*, Cambridge: Cambridge University Press, pp. 78–119.

Forteza, A., 1998, 'The Wage Bargaining Structure and the Inflationary Bias', *Journal of Macroeconomics* 20(3), 599–614.

Grüner, H. P. and C. Hefeker, 1999, 'How Will EMU Affect Inflation and Unemployment in Europe?', *Scandinavian Journal of Economics* 101(1), 33–47.

Guzzo, V. and A. Velasco, 1999, 'The Case for a Populist Central Bank', *European Economic Review* 43, 1317–44.

2002, 'Revisiting the Case for a Populist Central Banker: A Comment', *European Economic Review* 46, 613–21.

Gylfason, T. and A. Lindbeck, 1994, 'The Interaction of Monetary Policy and Wages', *Public Choice* 79, 33–46.

Hall, P. A., 1994, 'Central Bank Independence and Coordinated Wage Bargaining: Their Interaction in Germany and Europe', *German Politics and Society* 31, 1–23.

Hall, P. A. and R. J. Franzese Jr., 1998, 'Mixed Signals: Central Bank Independence, Coordinated Wage Bargaining, and European Monetary Union', *International Organization* 52(3), 505–35.

Holden, S., 2001, 'Monetary Regimes and the Coordination of Wage Setting', CESifo Working Paper no. 429, Munich.

Jensen, H., 1997, 'Monetary Policy Cooperation May Not Be Counterproductive', *Scandinavian Journal of Economics* 99, 73–80.

Knell, M., 2001, 'Wage Formation in Open Economies and the Role of Monetary and Wage-Setting Institutions', manuscript, Austrian National Bank, Economic Studies Division.

Kydland, F. E. and E. Prescott, 1977, 'Rules Rather than Discretion: The Inconsistency of Optimal Plans', *Journal of Political Economy* 85, 473–92.

Lawler, P., 2000, 'Centralised Wage Setting, Inflation Contracts, and the Optimal Choice of Central Banker', *Economic Journal* 110, 559–75.

Lippi, F., 2002, 'Revisiting the Case for a Populist Central Banker', *European Economic Review* 46, 601–12.

Liviatan, N., 2001, 'The Case Against a Populist Central Bank', manuscript, Bank of Israel.

Mishkin, F., 2001, *The Economics of Money, Banking, and Financial Markets*, New York: Addison-Wesley.

Nickell, S., 1997, 'Unemployment and Labor Market Rigidities: Europe Versus North America', *Journal of Economic Perspectives* 11(3), 55–74.

Oswald, A. J., 1982, 'The Microeconomic Theory of the Trade Union', *Economic Journal* 92, 576–95.

Rogoff, K., 1985, 'The Optimal Degree of Commitment to a Monetary Target', *Quarterly Journal of Economics* 100, 1169–90.

Saint-Paul, G., 2000, *The Political Economy of Labor Market Institutions*, Oxford: Oxford University Press.

Sibert, A. and A. Sutherland, 2000, 'Monetary Union and Labor Market Reform', *Journal of International Economics* 51, 421–35.

Skott, P., 1997, 'Stagflationary Consequences of Prudent Monetary Policy in a Unionized Economy', *Oxford Economic Papers* 49, 609–22.

Soskice, D. and T. Iversen, 1998, 'Multiple Wage-Bargaining Systems in the Single European Currency Area', *Oxford Review of Economic Policy* 14, 110–24.

2000, 'The Non Neutrality of Monetary Policy with Large Price or Wage Setters', *Quarterly Journal of Economics* 115, 265–84.

Stigler, G. J. and J. K. Kindhal, 1970, *The Behavior of Industrial Prices*, New York: Columbia University Press for NBER.

Streeck, W., 1994, 'Pay Restraint without Income Policy: Institutionalized Monetarism and Industrial Unionism in Germany', in R. Dore, R. Boyer and Z. Marn (eds.), *The Return of Income Policy*, London: Pinter.

Woodford, M., forthcoming, *Interest and Prices: Foundations of a Theory of Monetary Policy*, Princeton: Princeton University Press.

Yashiv, E., 1989, 'Inflation and the Role of Money Under Discretion and Rules', Working Paper no. 8–89, PSIE, MIT, November.

12 Inflationary performance in a monetary union with large wage setters

Lilia Cavallari

1 Introduction

In the literature on international monetary policy games, the switch from unco-ordinated national monetary policies to a monetary union is generally argued to lead to higher inflation. One reason why the formation of a monetary union is likely to raise inflation for a given level of employment is that the unified central bank's incentive to boost employment is no longer restrained by the cost of the exchange rate depreciation that follows unilateral monetary expansions (Rogoff 1985a). Higher inflation may then result as a consequence of rational agents anticipating the central bank's attempt to create surprise inflation.

A further channel leading to higher inflation has been recently stressed in the literature on strategic wage setting. Basically, it is argued that wage setters may be induced to behave more aggressively in a monetary union as they perceive an increase in their wages to have a smaller impact on the union-wide inflation rate relative to the one on their country-specific inflation rate.[1]

As the move to a monetary union alters the strategic environment faced by the central bank and labour unions, the incentives of *both* actors should be explicitly accounted for when analysing the macroeconomic impact of such a monetary policy regime shift.[2] In this chapter, we accomplish this task in a simple general-equilibrium setup in the tradition of the new open economy macroeconomics. Drawing on Cavallari (2001b), we model a two-region world

The present chapter benefited from comments by Lars Calmfors, Jürgen von Hagen and my discussant Fabrizio Coricelli. I would also like to thank participants in seminars at the Centre for European Integration Studies of the University of Bonn, the Institute for International Economic Studies of the University of Stockholm and at the conferences of the Royal Economic Society 2001 and 'EMU Macroeconomic Institutions'. Financial support from MURST is gratefully acknowledged.

[1] This point has been stressed by Zervoyanni (1997), Grüner and Hefeker (1999), Cukierman and Lippi (2001), Coricelli, Cukierman and Dalmazzo (2000b) and Soskice and Iversen (1998) among others.

[2] The impact of monetary unification on the nature of the game between monetary authorities and labour unions is analysed by Carmignani, Muscatelli and Tirelli (2001) and Rantala (2001).

economy characterised by unionised labour markets and imperfect competition in both the factor and goods markets.

While moving to a monetary union unambiguously increases the central bank's temptation to inflate, the model in this chapter shows that such a monetary policy regime shift may either favour or inhibit wage discipline. Wage setters are found to behave less aggressively in the monetary union relative to a regime of independent monetary policies, provided there are monopoly distortions in the labour market.

For an intuitive account of this result, consider the unions' perception of the inflationary consequences of their wage claims in the two monetary policy regimes. Under sovereign monetary policies, each union understands that the increase in its own wage raises domestic inflation to an extent that is larger the bigger the union and the lower the central bank's inflation aversion. When switching to a monetary union, the impact of domestic wages on the union-wide inflation rate is diluted, thereby reducing unions' inflation awareness. This has two contrasting effects on wage behaviour. On the one side, wage setters expect less competition from other unions and may then be induced to demand higher wages. On the other side, however, they also perceive their wage claims to affect negatively the real wage and aggregate demand, favouring wage restraint.

Our analysis further shows that, when the establishment of a monetary union leads to higher employment, this generally comes at the cost of higher inflation unless wage setting is fully centralised in the monetary union. International coordination in wage setting makes international monetary policy cooperation effective in reducing wage inflation at no employment costs, in contrast to what is claimed in Rogoff (1985a).[3] In our setup, wage centralisation in the monetary union may lead the economy to the first-best allocation, namely to an equilibrium with zero inflation and competitive output. This happens provided the central bank is not ultra-liberal, i.e. provided the common central bank cares about inflation. It is worth stressing that it does not matter how conservative the central bank is, even a very small aversion towards inflation on the part of the central bank is sufficient for the optimal monetary policy to be time-consistent.

Since the contributions by Velasco and Guzzo (1999) and Cukierman and Lippi (1999), it is well known that monetary institutions may permanently affect the trade-off between inflation and unemployment through strategic wage setting. The results in this chapter extend this insight to a particular monetary policy regime shift, by showing that the macroeconomic consequences of establishing a monetary union may depend in a non-linear way on wage bargaining institutions.[4]

---

[3] Unionisation and international monetary policy cooperation is discussed in Jensen (1997).

[4] The significance of unionised wage setting for the optimal design of central banking institutions in a closed economy is analysed by Lawler (2000) and Soskice and Iversen (2000).

Strategic interactions between the central bank and wage setters as those analysed in this chapter may play a role in the macroeconomic performance in the EMU, as several European countries are characterised by intermediate to high centralisation in wage bargaining.[5] Our results stress the harmful consequences of establishing the anti-inflation credentials of the European Central Bank (ECB) through the standard way of reputation building when labour markets are unionised and imperfectly competitive. In these circumstances, in fact, wage restraint may be favoured in the monetary union without any need to appoint an ultra-conservative central banker at the ECB and imparting a 'deflationary bias' in the conduct of European monetary policy. This, besides the usual costs in terms of employment, may turn out to threaten the ECB's anti-inflationary credibility.[6]

The analysis in this chapter is closely related to a contribution by Cukierman and Lippi (2001) on the implications of monetary unification for strategic wage behaviour. Three main distinguishing features characterise our approach. Firstly, we explicitly derive demands for both labour and goods from profit and utility maximisation, while Cukierman and Lippi adopt a partial equilibrium approach. Secondly, our framework encompasses trade across the countries in the monetary union and considers optimal price setting by monopolistic firms. Finally, we make a first step towards a welfare-based analysis of the strategic interaction between central banks and wage setters by specifying preferences for unions and the central bank that are consistent with the behavioural analysis. Building on our micro-founded framework, we are able to show that monetary unification may induce a more or less aggressive wage behaviour, while only the former effect may appear in the Cukierman-Lippi model.

The chapter is structured as follows. Section 2 models the two-country world economy. Section 3 describes the one-shot, three-stage game between the central bank, unions and firms in the two monetary policy regimes. In section 4, the equilibrium outcomes under independent monetary policies and a monetary union are compared in the case of uncoordinated national wage setting as well as under international wage centralisation.

2   The world economy

We model a world economy that consists of two equally sized regions, Home and Foreign. Home is inhabited by a continuum of agents $j \in (0, 1/2]$. Agents

---

[5] Calmfors (2001) provides a comprehensive survey of the literature on nominal wage bargaining within the EMU, focusing on the link between institutions and macroeconomic performance as well as on the likely effects of EMU on wage setting.

[6] This accords with the views expressed in Allsopp and Vines (1998) favouring the development of an appropriate reaction function rather than the establishment of a tough anti-inflationary reputation as the main task of the ECB. A similar conclusion is drawn by Bean (1998).

living in Foreign are indexed by $j \in [1/2,1)$. In our notation, foreign variables are denoted by an asterisk. Each country specialises in the production of a traded good that can be manufactured in a variety of brands indexed by $z \in (0,1)$. Labour is the only factor of production and is supplied in a variety of labour types defined in the interval $(0,1)$.

Workers in the home country are organised in $n > 1$ labour unions, each of size $1/n$, while in the foreign country there are $n^* > 1$ unions of size $1/n^*$. In this setup, the degree of wage centralisation is proportional to union size and is higher the smaller the number of unions that bargain independently in the economy.

2.1   Technology

Home's production function exhibits decreasing returns to scale relative to the labour input

$$Y = \left[\int_0^1 \ell_i^{\frac{\phi-1}{\phi}} \, di \right]^{\frac{\alpha\phi}{\phi-1}}, \tag{12.1}$$

where Y is output of the home good, ℓ_i is labour of type i, $\alpha < 1$ and the parameter $\phi > 1$ captures the degree of substitutability among different labour types.

Let W_i represent the nominal wage of worker i. Then the price index for labour inputs is defined as the minimal nominal cost of producing a unit of output

$$W = \left[\int_0^1 W_i^{1-\phi} \, di \right]^{\frac{1}{1-\phi}}. \tag{12.2}$$

Cost minimisation implies the following demand for each labour type i:

$$\ell_i = \left(\frac{W_i}{W} \right)^{-\phi} \left(\frac{W}{P\alpha} \right)^{-\frac{1}{1-\alpha}}. \tag{12.3}$$

2.2   Preferences of . . .

2.2.1   . . . consumers
Agents in the world economy consume the same basket of goods and derive utility from consumption and leisure:

$$U_j = \ln C_j - \frac{\kappa}{2}(\ln \ell_j)^2, \tag{12.4}$$

where the real consumption index C aggregates consumption of the domestic good, C_H, and the foreign good, C_F:

$$C = C_H^{\frac{1}{2}} C_F^{\frac{1}{2}} \tag{12.5}$$

Each good can appear in an infinite variety of imperfectly substitutable brands (or types), all of which are consumed in the world economy. We define the following consumption sub-indexes:

$$C_H = \left[\int_0^1 C_{Hz}^{(\frac{\theta-1}{\theta})} dz \right]^{\frac{\theta}{\theta-1}}$$

$$C_F = \left[\int_0^1 C_{Fz}^{(\frac{\theta-1}{\theta})} dz \right]^{\frac{\theta}{\theta-1}}, \tag{12.6}$$

where $\theta > 1$ captures the elasticity of substitution among different brands of home and foreign goods, while the elasticity of substitution between the home and foreign type of good is equal to one according to (12.5).

Given additive separable preferences and Cobb–Douglas consumption indexes, it is easy to show that each firm faces a demand for the brand it produces that depends on its relative price and on world consumption

$$Y_z = \frac{1}{2} \left(\frac{P_{Hz}}{P_H} \right)^{-\theta} (C + C^*), \tag{12.7}$$

where P_{Hz} is the price for a home good of type z and $P_H[\int_0^1 P_{ZH}^{(1-\theta)} dz]^{\frac{1}{1-\theta}}$ is the price index of domestic goods.

2.2.2 ... the central bank In the tradition of the literature on time inconsistency in monetary policy, we assume that the monetary authority dislikes inflation while caring about the real performance in the economy, which in our setup coincides with agents' utility. We consider two monetary regimes, namely a regime of independent, non-cooperative national monetary policies and a monetary union.

Under sovereign monetary policies, the domestic and foreign central banks aim at country-specific targets:

$$\Omega = 2 \int_0^{\frac{1}{2}} U_j dj - \frac{\beta}{2} \pi^2$$

$$\Omega^* = 2 \int_{\frac{1}{2}}^1 U_{j^*} dj^* - \frac{\beta}{2} \pi^{*2}, \tag{12.8}$$

where π and π^* are, respectively, the domestic and foreign inflation rates. The parameter β captures the weight of inflation relative to other policy targets and represents the central bank's degree of 'conservativeness' (Rogoff 1985b).

The common central bank similarly cares about the average utility of the agents in the monetary union while disliking union-wide inflation

$$\Omega^U = 2 \left[\int_0^{\frac{1}{2}} U_j dj + \int_{\frac{1}{2}}^1 U_j^* dj^* \right] - \frac{\beta}{2} \pi^2, \tag{12.9}$$

where we have used the fact that with the consumer price index (12.13) and an irrevocably fixed nominal exchange rate the inflation rates are equalised across countries. In specifying the central bank's preferences (12.8) and (12.9), we assume that monetary conservativeness does not vary, so as to focus on inflation targeting as the sole difference across monetary regimes.

2.2.3 . . . unions   In the theory of trade-union behaviour as surveyed by Oswald (1982), the unions' objective function depends on their sectorial interests, usually specified in terms of real wages and unemployment. In our micro-founded framework, this is equivalent to assuming that each domestic and foreign union is interested in the average utility of its own members

$$\Psi_i = n \int_{i-n^{-1}}^{i} U_j \mathrm{d}j$$

$$\Psi_i^* = n^* \int_{i-n^{*-1}}^{i} U_{j^*} \mathrm{d}j^*. \tag{12.10}$$

By relying on preferences that are consistent with the behavioural assumptions in the model, this specification provides a natural benchmark for welfare comparison across monetary regimes.

It is worth noticing that we abstract from inflation aversion on the part of unions so as to focus on the monetary policy regime shift as the sole incentive for wage restraint.[7]

2.3   Resource constraints

While markets are complete domestically (everyone owns an equal share of all domestic firms), there is no international equity trade. This assumption is benign since, given Cobb–Douglas preferences over domestic and foreign goods (12.5) and separable utility functions (12.4), international equity trade is redundant (Corsetti and Pesenti 2001).

Each agent in the economy needs cash in advance so as to pay for nominal expenses,

$$M_j \geqslant PC_j, \tag{12.11}$$

and faces the following budget constraint:

$$M_j + PC_j = M_j^0 + W\ell_j + D_j + T_j, \tag{12.12}$$

where M_j are money balances, D_j nominal aggregate profits, T_j nominal transfers from the government and P is the consumer price index. It is easy to show

---

[7] Soskice and Iversen (2001), Cukierman and Lippi (2001) and Grüner and Hefeker (1999) analyse the macroeconomic impact of monetary unification when unions are averse to inflation.

that:

$$P = P_H^{\frac{1}{2}} P_F^{\frac{1}{2}}, \tag{12.13}$$

where P_F is the domestic-currency price of the foreign good. It is worth stressing that the law of one price holds in our model, so that $P_F = \varepsilon P^*_F$, where ε is the nominal exchange rate in home currency and P^*_F the foreign-currency price of the foreign good.

The home government is assumed to rebate all seignorage revenue in the form of lump-sum transfers to households

$$\int_0^{\frac{1}{2}} M_j - M_j^0 \mathrm{d}j = \int_0^{\frac{1}{2}} T_j \mathrm{d}j. \tag{12.14}$$

Finally, the domestic goods market clears when

$$Y \geqslant \left(\frac{P}{P_H}\right) \frac{1}{2}(C + C^*), \tag{12.15}$$

where the law of one price and purchasing power parity are used in deriving the aggregate resource constraint (12.15).

A representation parallel to (12.1)–(12.15) exists for the Foreign economy.

2.4   A useful reduced form

As a first step in solving our model, we derive the domestic and foreign current account by integrating the agents' budget constraints (12.12) in, respectively, the interval $(0, \frac{1}{2}]$ and $[\frac{1}{2}, 1)$. Using the domestic aggregate resource constraint (12.15), the government budget constraint (12.14) and their foreign analogues into the resulting expressions, it is immediate to show that consumption is equalised across countries:

$$C = C^*. \tag{12.16}$$

This is not surprising, as full international risk sharing is a standard result within this class of models (Corsetti and Pesenti 2001). As the equilibrium current account is always balanced, the nominal exchange rate is proportional to nominal spending and coincides with relative money supply:

$$\varepsilon = \frac{PC}{P^*C^*} = \frac{M}{M^*}. \tag{12.17}$$

It is worth stressing that equations (12.15), (12.11) and (12.16) imply that aggregate demand is proportional to money supply, as one would expect in a framework with nominal rigidities:

$$Y = \frac{M}{P_H}$$

$$Y^* = \frac{M^*}{P_F^*}.$$
(12.18)

In each country, two reduced-form equations are needed in order to study the monetary policy game. The first is obtained by taking logarithms of labour demand (12.3), yielding

$$\ln \ell_i = -\phi (w_i - w) - \frac{1}{1 - \alpha} (w - p),$$
(12.19)

where w_i is the growth of the nominal wage of labour of type i, w is the aggregate nominal wage growth and p is (the log of) the consumer price index.[8]

Finally, (the log of) domestic real consumption c_i is obtained by substituting labour demand (12.3) into the individual budget constraint (12.12) and taking logarithms:

$$c_i = (1 - \phi)(w_i - w) - \frac{\alpha}{1 - \alpha} (w - p).$$
(12.20)

Two equations parallel to (12.19)–(12.20) hold for the foreign country.

3   Strategic monetary policy

We consider a one-shot, three-stage game between firms, monetary authorities and labour unions in a monetary union, U, and in a regime of sovereign national monetary policies, N.

In the first stage, each union sets the rate of growth of the nominal wage of its members in an uncoordinated way relative to both foreign and other domestic unions. Unions are Stackelberg leaders vis-à-vis the central bank while playing Nash relative to other unions. These rules of the game reflect the presence of nominal rigidities in labour markets.[9]

After wages are set, the common central bank chooses the union-wide money supply in an attempt to control inflation in the monetary union and

---

[8] By normalising the previous period nominal wage to unity, the current nominal wage can be expressed as

$$W_i = 1 + w_i,$$

where w_i is the percentage increase in the nominal wage of worker i. In the text, the following approximations are used: $\ln(W_i / W) = w_i - w$ and $\ln(W/P) = w - p$.

[9] Jerger (2002) provides an example of strategic nominal wage bargaining where unions act non-cooperatively relative to both other unions and the central bank.

distributes money symmetrically across regions. Sovereign central banks, instead, choose the country-specific money supply in the uncoordinated monetary policy regime.

In the last stage, taking the general price level as given, each firm sets the price of its own brand so as to maximise profits.[10] The backward solution of the game provides the general equilibrium of the economy.

3.1   Price setting

Profit maximisation implies that the price for brand z of the domestic and foreign good is proportional to, respectively, domestic and foreign real wages and real money balances:

$$p_{Hz} - p_H = \frac{\alpha}{1 + \theta - \alpha\theta}(w - p_H) + \frac{1 - \alpha}{1 + \theta - \alpha\theta}(m - p)$$

$$p_{Fz}^* - p_F^* = \frac{\alpha}{1 + \theta - \alpha\theta}(w^* - p_F^*) + \frac{1 - \alpha}{1 + \theta - \alpha\theta}(m^* - p^*). \qquad (12.21)$$

Each firm charges a higher price for its own brand following a rise in marginal costs or an increase in aggregate demand.

In a symmetric equilibrium, where $p_{Hz} = p_H$ and $P_{Fz}^* = p_F^*$ for all z, real money balances are negatively related to real aggregate wages:

$$m - p = \frac{-\alpha}{1 - \alpha}(w - p_H)$$

$$m^* - p^* = \frac{-\alpha}{1 - \alpha}(w^* - p_F^*). \qquad (12.22)$$

Recalling the definition of the consumer price index (12.13), and using the nominal exchange rate (12.17), equations (12.22) imply that the general price level in each country can be written in terms of domestic and foreign wages and money supplies:

$$p = \pi = \frac{\alpha}{2}(w + w^*) + \frac{2 - \alpha}{2}m - \frac{\alpha}{2}m^*$$

$$p^* = \pi^* = \frac{\alpha}{2}(w + w^*) + \frac{2 - \alpha}{2}m^* - \frac{\alpha}{2}m, \qquad (12.23)$$

where the first equalities follow after normalising the previous period price level to one.

---

[10] Coricelli, Cukierman and Dalmazzo (2000a) originally considered optimal price setting in the literature on nominal wage bargaining.

3.2   *Optimal monetary policy*

With independent monetary policy, the domestic central bank chooses domestic money supply so as to maximise (12.8) subject to (12.19) and (12.20) and taking into account optimal price setting by monopolistic firms (12.22) in the home country. This yields the reaction function

$$\frac{\alpha}{2} - \frac{(2-\alpha)}{(1-\alpha)}\kappa \int_0^{1/2} \ln \ell_j dj - \beta\pi\left(1 - \frac{\alpha}{2}\right) = 0. \tag{12.24}$$

An equation similar to (12.24) describes the behaviour of the foreign central bank. Using reduced-form employment (12.19) in (12.24), it is apparent that monetary authorities will raise inflation in an attempt to boost output – which is suboptimally low owing to monopolistic distortions – up to the point where the marginal benefit of doing so (the first two terms on the left-hand side of (12.24)) equals the marginal cost.

The reaction functions of the domestic and foreign central banks are common knowledge for wage-setters, who can easily calculate the inflationary impact of an increase in their nominal wage growth

$$\frac{\partial \pi}{\partial w_j} = \frac{\kappa}{n[\kappa + \beta(1-\alpha)^2]} \equiv s^N \in (0, 1)$$

$$\frac{\partial \pi^*}{\partial w_j^*} = \frac{\kappa}{n^*[\kappa + \beta(1-\alpha)^2]} \equiv s^{*N} \in (0, 1). \tag{12.25}$$

Unions' perception of the inflationary impact of an increase in the nominal wage of their members is positively related to union size ($1/n$ in our specification) and negatively related to monetary conservativeness. A very conservative central bank may even counteract wage pressure by restricting money supply, while a liberal central bank always accommodates it. This can easily be seen by taking the partial derivative of money supply in the reaction function (12.24) relative to the domestic wage. In so doing, we obtain

$$sign\left(\frac{\partial m}{\partial w}\right) = sign\left(\frac{\kappa(1-\alpha/2)}{\alpha/2(1-\alpha)^2} - \beta\right),$$

where it is apparent that a sufficiently conservative central bank, i.e. when $\beta > \kappa(1-\alpha/2)/\alpha/2(1-\alpha)^2$, contracts money supply in the wake of an increase in nominal wages.

In the monetary union, the common central bank chooses the union-wide money supply so as to maximise the utility of all agents in the union, (12.9), subject to (12.19), (12.20) and their foreign analogues, as well as taking into account optimal price setting by monopolistic firms (12.22) at home and abroad.

The central bank's optimal strategy is:

$$\frac{\alpha}{2} - 2\kappa \int_0^{1/2} \ln \ell_j dj - 2\kappa \int_{1/2}^1 \ln \ell_j^* dj^* - \pi \frac{(1-\alpha)\beta}{2} = 0.$$

(12.26)

As before, the common central bank balances marginal costs and benefits of raising union-wide inflation. However, while the marginal benefit of higher inflation (and output) does not change across monetary regimes, the cost of a 1% increase in union-wide inflation halves relative to the regime with sovereign monetary policies. This is due to the disappearance of exchange rate costs in the monetary union.

Building on (12.26), domestic and foreign unions calculate the union-wide inflationary impact of their wage claims

$$\frac{\partial \pi}{\partial w_j} = \frac{\kappa}{n[2\kappa + \beta (1-\alpha)^2]} \equiv s^U$$

$$\frac{\partial \pi}{\partial w_j^*} = \frac{\kappa}{n^*[2\kappa + \beta (1-\alpha)^2]} \equiv s^{*U}.$$

(12.27)

Comparing (12.25) and (12.27), it appears that the move from sovereign monetary policies to the monetary union reduces the perception on the part of unions of the inflationary consequences of their wage claims. This is due to the weaker bargaining position of unions vis-à-vis the common central bank. It is worth stressing that unions' inflation awareness reduces in the monetary union despite the higher incentive to raise inflation and accommodate wage pressure of the common central bank relative to sovereign monetary authorities.

3.3   Wage setting

Under simultaneous bargaining, each union sets the rate of growth of the nominal wage of its members so as to maximise (12.10) subject to (12.19), (12.20), the central bank's reaction function in the appropriate monetary policy regime, i.e. (12.24) or (12.26), and taking as given the nominal wages set by other unions at home and abroad. The optimal non-cooperative strategy of the domestic union i is

$$\alpha(1 - s^r - \xi^r) + \xi^r \kappa \ln \ell_i = 0,$$

(12.28)

where ξ^r is the elasticity of labour demand to the nominal wage of union i in the monetary policy regime $r = U, N$:

$$\xi^r \equiv -\frac{d \ln \ell_i}{d \ln w_i} = \phi \left(1 - \frac{1}{n}\right) + \frac{1}{1-\alpha}\left(\frac{1}{n} - s^r\right).$$

(12.29)

An analogous equation describes the behaviour of the foreign union. A unitary increase in the nominal wage of union i has two contrasting effects on its members' utility. On one side, utility decreases since consumption reduces (this is captured by the term in brackets in (12.28)), while on the other side the increase in leisure raises utility.[11] Each union's optimal nominal wage is then set so as to balance these costs and benefits.

Drawing on the constant relation between increases in nominal and real relative wages, $dw_i/d \ln (W_i/P) = 1/(1 - s^r)$, we can cast the first order condition (12.28) in terms of the real effects of the union's nominal wage, obtaining

$$\ln \ell_i = \frac{\alpha}{\kappa} \left(1 - \frac{1}{\eta^r} \right), \tag{12.30}$$

where $\eta^r \equiv \xi^r/(1 - s^r)$ is the elasticity of the demand for labour of type i to the real relative wage in regime r. Using (12.29) and (12.25) or (12.27) when appropriate, the elasticity of labour demand to the real wage in the two monetary regimes can be easily expressed in terms of the model's parameters:

$$\eta^N = \frac{\phi \left(1 - \frac{1}{n} \right) + \frac{1}{1-\alpha} \left(\frac{1}{n} - \frac{\kappa}{n[\kappa+\beta(1-\alpha)^2]} \right)}{1 - \frac{\kappa}{n[\kappa+\beta(1-\alpha)^2]}}$$

$$\eta^U = \frac{\phi \left(1 - \frac{1}{n} \right) + \frac{1}{1-\alpha} \left(\frac{1}{n} - \frac{\kappa}{n[2\kappa+\beta(1-\alpha)^2]} \right)}{1 - \frac{\kappa}{n[2\kappa+\beta(1-\alpha)^2]}} \tag{12.31}$$

Interpreting equation (12.30), it appears that unions are induced to raise nominal wages when they expect this to have small consequences for employment, namely when the elasticity of labour demand is low. The move from sovereign monetary policy to a monetary union may change the incentives for wage restraint by affecting the perception on the part of unions of the inflationary consequences of their wage hikes.

As discussed above, the monetary regime shift reduces unions' inflation awareness. This, in turn, has two opposing effects on strategic wage behaviour. On the one side, each union expects an increase in the nominal wage of its members to lead to a higher increase in the real aggregate wage and hence a larger contraction of aggregate demand. The employment consequences of wage aggressiveness are high in this case, favouring wage restraint.[12]

On the other side, however, when unions perceive the inflationary impact of their wages to be small, they also expect the real wage of other unions to

---

[11] The overall effect of the increase in the nominal wage of union i on consumption is negative, since the effect of the increase in the real wage $(1- s)$ is smaller than the reduction in labour demand (ξ).

[12] This is akin to the adverse output effect discussed in Lippi (1999).

decrease to a lesser extent, which in turn implies that the shift of labour demand towards cheaper labour types is small. The adverse competition effect favours wage aggressiveness.[13]

Which of these two contrasting effects prevails depends on monopoly distortions in labour markets. Comparing the elasticity of labour demand across monetary regimes, it appears that the move to a monetary union favours wage restraint whenever monopoly distortions are not too low. Using (12.31), it is easy to show that

$$\eta^U - \eta^N \geq 0 \text{ iff } \phi \leq \frac{1}{1-\alpha}.$$

4   Macroeconomic performance and the monetary policy regime

Under uncoordinated national monetary policies, the domestic and foreign inflation rates can be obtained by combining the respective unions' equilibrium strategies (12.28) in a symmetric equilibrium, $\ell_i = \ell$, with the central bank's reaction function (12.24), which yields the area-wide average inflation rate

$$\pi^N = \frac{\alpha}{2(1-\alpha)\beta} \left(\frac{1}{\eta^N} + \frac{1}{\eta^{*N}} \right). \tag{12.32}$$

For the well-known reason discussed in Kydland and Prescott (1977) and Barro and Gordon (1983), equilibrium inflation is suboptimally positive. Other than on central bank's inflation aversion, β, the economy's inflationary bias depends on labour market features as synthesised in the elasticities η^N and η^{*N}. Using (12.31) it is easy to verify that inflation is higher the less substitutable the different types of labour and the more decentralised the wage bargaining structure.[14]

A similar procedure that combines (12.28) and (12.26) yields the equilibrium inflation rate in the monetary union

$$\pi^U = \frac{\alpha}{(1-\alpha)\beta} \left(\frac{1}{\eta^U} + \frac{1}{\eta^{*U}} \right). \tag{12.33}$$

Employment in the two monetary regimes is given by equation (12.30) evaluated in a symmetric equilibrium where $\ell_i = \ell$

Comparing the macroeconomic performance in the two monetary regimes using equations (12.32), (12.33) and (12.30), it appears that in the absence of

---

[13] A lower incentive for wage restraint is a common result in the literature. Alternative mechanisms leading to wage aggressiveness in the monetary union are discussed, among others, by Grüner and Hefeker (1999), Cukierman and Lippi (2001), Soskice and Iversen (2001) and Coricelli, Cukierman and Dalmazzo (2000b).

[14] This accords with the analysis in Cubitt (1995) and Calmfors and Driffil (1998).

strategic effects – namely, when $\eta^U = \eta^N$ and $\eta^{*U} = \eta^{*N}$ – inflation under sovereign monetary policies is unambiguously lower than in a monetary union for a given level of employment. The reason the move to a monetary union raises inflation is the stronger incentive of the common central bank to resort to surprise inflation relative to national central banks (Rogoff 1985a).[15] This matches with the empirical regularity documented by Romer (1993) showing that open economies display lower inflation in a broad cross-section of countries.[16]

When wage setters are large, however, the move to a monetary union also affects wage behaviour and, as our analysis above shows, it does so in a way that crucially depends on monopoly distortions in labour markets. When labour types are poor substitutes for each other, i.e. when the adverse competition effect is low, the establishment of a monetary union favours wage restraint, the more so the more liberal is the central bank. In our setup, however, wage discipline is unable to compensate for the increase in the union-wide inflationary bias due to central bank behaviour. Higher employment can be obtained solely at the cost of higher inflation.

4.1   *International wage coordination*

It is useful to investigate in which circumstances wage restraint in the monetary union is sufficiently strong to reduce inflation at no employment cost. A natural candidate is the case of union-wide wage coordination, where wage discipline is at its best. Intuitively, a coordinated increase in nominal wages in the monetary union reduces union-wide aggregate demand, which in turn decreases union-wide employment. The perception of heavy employment consequences of wage pressure disciplines wage behaviour.[17]

A more formal argument in favour of international wage coordination in the monetary union can be provided by considering a supranational union that sets domestic and foreign nominal wages so as to maximise the utility of the population in the monetary union. In our setup, this is equivalent to assuming that there is a single monopoly union, namely that $n = n^* = 1$. It is worth noticing that regions in the monetary union are perfectly symmetric in this case, which in turn implies that in equilibrium domestic and foreign wages are equalised.

[15] As apparent in (12.24) and (12.26), the central bank's incentive to inflate is negatively related to the economy's degree of trade openness. In our setup, the degree of openness is $1/2$ under independent monetary policies, while the monetary union is a closed economy.

[16] See also Lane (1997) and Campillo and Miron (1997), among others. Cavallari (2001a) investigates the link between inflation and openness when wage setters are large.

[17] As recently stressed in the literature on nominal wage bargaining, monetary unification is likely to alter the structure of wage setting across member countries. Calmfors (2001), for example, argues in favour of less centralisation in wage setting as a result of monetary unification. Holden (1999), instead, stresses the gains to wage centralisation in a monetary union.

Two features characterise the strategic behaviour of the supranational union relative to large non-coordinated unions. The first is the perception of the inflationary consequences of an increase in the union-wide nominal wage. Taking the partial derivative of inflation in the monetary reaction function (12.26) relative to the aggregate union-wide wage, we obtain

$$s^W = \frac{\kappa}{[\kappa + \beta(1-\alpha)^2]}. \tag{12.34}$$

Comparing (12.25) and (12.34), it is easy to verify that the supranational union fully internalises the impact of wage claims on the union-wide inflation rate and perceives higher inflationary consequences of wage pressure relative to unions that act in a non-cooperative way. In contrast to the case with large but uncoordinated unions, however, inflation awareness unambiguously disciplines the behaviour of the monopoly union.

Secondly, the optimal choice of the union-wide wage is such that:

$$\kappa \int_0^1 \ln \ell_j \, dj - \alpha = 0. \tag{12.35}$$

Evaluating (12.35) in a symmetric equilibrium, we obtain:

$$\ln \ell_i = \ln \ell = \frac{\alpha}{\kappa}. \tag{12.36}$$

The equation above says that the supranational union sets the union-wide nominal wage so as to restore the perfectly competitive level of employment, namely that which prevails when the elasticity of labour demand to the real wage is infinite.

Plugging (12.36) into the monetary reaction function in the monetary union (12.26) gives an equilibrium inflation rate equal to zero:

$$\beta(1-\alpha)\pi = 0. \tag{12.37}$$

International wage coordination in the monetary union is able to restore the first-best allocation provided the common central bank cares about inflation, namely provided β is positive. It does not matter how conservative the central bank is, even a tiny aversion towards inflation on the part of the central bank is sufficient for the optimal monetary strategy to be time-consistent. This result is due to the symbiosis of wage and monetary policies when the supranational union and the common central bank have the same objectives.[18] Since both players are interested in the utility of the population in the monetary union, the competitive standard is the bliss point for both of them. In the absence of shocks, once the bliss level of employment is reached, the central bank has no incentive

---

[18] A similar result is achieved in the strategic interaction between monetary and fiscal policies (Dixit and Lambertini 2003).

to raise inflation and sets money supply so as to deliver zero inflation. Should the central bank be 'ultra-liberal', i.e. β is equal to zero, then the equilibrium inflation rate would be indeterminate.

Our results suggest that the union-wide macroeconomic performance may be improved in terms of *both* inflation and employment when wages are internationally coordinated. Provided the common central bank is not ultra-liberal, the first-best allocation can be attained with employment at the competitive standard and zero inflation.

REFERENCES

Allsopp, C. J. and D. Vines, 1998, 'The Assessment: Macroeconomic Policy after EMU', *Oxford Review of Economic Policy*, 14(3), 1–23.

Barro, R. and D. Gordon,1983, 'A Positive Theory of Monetary Policy in a Natural Rate Model', *Journal of Political Economy* 91, 589–610.

Bean, C. R., 1998, 'The New UK Monetary Arrangements: A View from the Literature', *Economic Journal* 108, 1795–809.

Calmfors, L., 2001, 'Wages and Wage Bargaining Institutions in EMU: A Survey', *Empirica* 28(4), 325–51.

Calmfors, L. and J. Driffill, 1998, 'Bargaining Structure, Corporativism and Macroeconomic Performance', *Economic Policy* 6, 14–61.

Campillo, M. and J. Miron, 1997, 'Why Does Inflation Differ Across Countries?' in C. Romer and D. Romer (eds.), *Reducing Inflation: Motivation and Strategy*, Chicago: Chicago University Press, pp. 335–570.

Carmignani, F., A. Muscatelli and P. Tirelli, 2001, 'Who's Afraid of the Big Bad Central Bank? Union-Firm-Central Bank Interactions and Inflation in a Monetary Union', mimeo, University of Milan La Bicocca.

Cavallari, L., 2001a, 'Inflation and Openness with Non-atomistic Wage-Setters', *Scottish Journal of Political Economy* 48(2), 210–25.

2001b, 'Macroeconomic Performance in a Monetary Union with Large Wage Setters', *Empirica* 28(4), 419–33.

Coricelli, F., A. Cukierman and A. Dalmazzo, 2000a, 'Monetary Institutions, Monopolistic Competition, Unionized Labor Markets and Economic Performance', CEPR Discussion Paper no. 2407.

2000b, 'Economic Performance and Stabilisation Policy in a Monetary Union with Imperfect Labor and Goods Markets', CEPR Discussion Paper no. 2745.

Corsetti, G. and P. Pesenti, 2001, 'Welfare and Macroeconomic Interdependence', *Quarterly Journal of Economics* 116(2), 421–46.

Cubitt, R. P., 1995, 'Corporativism, Monetary Policy and Macroeconomic Performance: A Simple Game Theoretic Analysis', *Scandinavian Journal of Economics* 97, 245–59.

Cukierman, A. and F. Lippi, 1999, 'Central Bank Independence, Centralisation of Wage Bargaining, Inflation and Unemployment: Theory and Some Evidence', *European Economic Review* 43, 1395–434.

2001, 'Labour Markets and Monetary Union: A Strategic Analysis', *Economic Journal* 111, 541–65.

Dixit, A. and L. Lambertini, 2003, 'Symbiosis of Monetary and Fiscal Policies in a Monetary Union', *Journal of International Economics* 60, 235–47.

Grüner, H. P. and C. Hefeker, 1999, 'How Will EMU Affect Inflation and Unemployment in Europe?', *Scandinavian Journal of Economics* 101(1), 33–47.

Holden, S., 1999, 'Monetary Regimes and the Coordination of Wage Setting', mimeo, University of Oslo.

Jensen, H., 1997, 'Monetary Policy Cooperation May Not Be Counterproductive', *Scandinavian Journal of Economics* 99, 73–80.

Jerger, J., 2002, 'How Strong Is the Case for a Populist Central Banker: A Note', *European Economic Review* 46, 623–32.

Kydland, F. and E. Prescott, 1977, 'Rules Rather than Discretion: The Inconsistency of Optimal Plans', *Journal of Political Economy* 85, 473–92.

Lane, P., 1997, 'Inflation in Open Economics', *Journal of International Economics* 42, 327–47.

Lawler, P., 2000, 'Centralised Wage Setting, Inflation Contracts and the Optimal Choice of Central Banker', *Economic Journal* 110, 559–75.

Lippi, F., 1999, 'Strategic Monetary Policy with Non-atomistic Wage Setters: A Case for Non-neutrality', CEPR Discussion Paper no. 2218.

Obstfeld, M. and K. Rogoff, 1996, *Foundations of International Macroeconomics*, Cambridge, MA: MIT Press.

Oswald, A. J., 1982, 'The Microeconomic Theory of Trade Union', *Economic Journal* 92, 576–95.

Rantala, A., 2001, 'Does Monetary Union Reduce Employment?', mimeo, University of Helsinki.

Rogoff, K., 1985a, 'Can International Monetary Policy Cooperation Be Counterproductive?', *Journal of International Economics* 18, 199–217.

1985b, 'The Optimal Degree of Commitment to a Monetary Target', *Quarterly Journal of Economics* 100, 1169–90.

Romer, D., 1993, 'Openness and Inflation: Theory and Evidence', *Quarterly Journal of Economics* 108(4), 869–903.

Soskice, D. and T. Iversen, 1998, 'Multiple Wage-Bargaining Systems in the Single European Currency Area', *Oxford Review of Economic Policy* 14(3), 110–24.

2000, 'The Non-neutrality of Monetary Policy with Large Price or Wage Setters', *Quarterly Journal of Economics* 115, 265–84.

2001, 'Multiple Wage Bargaining Systems in the Single European Currency Area', *Empirica*, 28(4), 435–56.

Velasco, A. and V. Guzzo, 1999, 'The Case for a Populist Central Banker', *European Economic Review* 43, 1317–44.

Zervoyanni, A., 1997, 'Monetary Policy Games and Coalitions in a Two-Country Model with Unionized Wage-Setting', *Oxford Economic Papers* 49, 57–76.

13 On the enlargement of currency unions: incentives to join and incentives to reform

Andrew Hughes Hallett and Svend E. Hougaard Jensen

1 Introduction

The issue of structural reform is, perhaps, the leading economic policy issue in Europe. But enlargement of the EU and the euro zone must be the other. On one hand, it is widely argued that structural reform is a prerequisite for a successful currency union. Moreover, since the European economies appear less reformed in market flexibility terms than their American counterparts, efforts to restore the value of the euro vis-à-vis the dollar have been associated with the need for higher productivity and more flexible labour markets in Europe. But structural reform also plays a role in the context of EU enlargement. Here the issue has generally been seen as a question of whether, or at what pace, a less reformed candidate country would be able to meet a certain set of entrance criteria before being let into a better reformed union.[1]

While there is little disagreement that monetary unification and structural reform are related, the nature of this relationship is not well understood. For example, the blueprint for EMU (Delors Report 1989) stressed the importance of *parallelism* in the monetary and economic policy spheres towards monetary union. This approach assumes economic structures to be exogenous, and changeable only through economic policy reform. Such reforms are then seen as necessary to ensure that economic structures are similar across member states. But others (e.g. Frankel and Rose 1998) have pointed out that economic structures

The authors thank Helge Berger, Jens Larsen, Jacques Mélitz, Ruud De Mooij, Thomas Moutos, Jean Pisani-Ferry, Hans-Werner Sinn, Roberto Tamborini and several conference/seminar participants at New Orleans, Milan, Munich and Copenhagen for helpful comments and discussion. The usual disclaimer applies. Financial assistance from the Danish Ministry of Economics and Business Affairs and the Danish National Research Foundation is gratefully acknowledged.

[1] See, for example, Hansen (2001, ch. 9) for this point of view. It is based on the analytic and empirical evidence for a negative link between economic performance and (real) wage rigidity across many countries in Bruno (1986). The same kind of link has been examined in both the labour and product markets in Europe (Koedijk and Kremers 1996), and in the transition economies (Kaminski, Wang and Winters 1996), where performance is measured in rates of growth, exports and factor productivities, and where deregulation appears in the labour markets, competition policy, merger codes or employment restrictions.

might be endogenous, at least up to a point. If so, the need for structural reform is less obvious, since it might materialise as a consequence of monetary unification anyway. In that spirit, Andersen, Haldrop and Sørensen (2000) have found that monetary integration in Europe is changing labour market structures and inducing wage convergences and wage interdependences, albeit on a rather small scale.

By contrast, Calmfors (1998, 2001) has argued that although money-wage flexibility is likely to be larger inside the EMU, labour market reforms are less likely to be implemented if they are linked to a time-consistency problem. As monetary union is seen as a vehicle for solving time inconsistencies, the incentive to reform the economy would, therefore, be reduced under monetary unification. Sibert (1999) and Sibert and Sutherland (2000) argue that asymmetric shocks may modify this conclusion, since countries would have an incentive to develop measures against such shocks as a replacement for exchange rate adjustments.[2] But that means that in an enlarged union, where newcomers have above-average distortions, existing members would face strong incentives either to reform or to keep the newcomers out.

Recent research has also focused on the strategic aspects associated with accession to a monetary union, relative to the pressure for reform. Countries outside the union typically have a time-consistency problem, associated with rigid economic structures and a relatively high level of inflation. Thus, in the model of Beetsma and Jensen (1999), it would always pay for the outsider to join the union, so it is up to the insider to decide whether to accept new members. However, while candidates from central and eastern Europe or the Mediterranean area may fit into this category, the UK or the Scandinavian countries do not. They have lower inflation and more flexible markets. And, in any case, reforms may be expensive. Hence, in a paper by Ozkan, Sibert and Sutherland (2000), candidate countries must decide whether they want to meet the criteria for joining; but if the criteria are fulfilled they will be admitted.

The purpose of this chapter is to offer a judgement on which of these alternative scenarios is more likely, and why. We analyse the costs and benefits of joining a monetary union, or of staying outside, using an extended version of an optimal currency area model originally proposed in Bayoumi (1994). In our model, countries are divided into three categories. First, there are 'insiders' which are already members of the EMU. Second, there are 'Northern' countries, being those able but possibly unwilling to join the EMU (e.g., the

---

[2] This conclusion may not carry over to the case where there are asymmetries in structures since there will be a one-way incentive to pass over the burden of adjustment to the economy with the more flexible markets or more effective policy institutions (see Hughes Hallett and Viegi 2003). That supports Calmfors' conjecture that reform is unlikely.

UK, Denmark and Sweden). These 'N-countries' would enjoy relatively small transactions benefits if they join, and output disturbances that are the same or larger than outside. But they have relatively small reform needs, and typically less need for (or gains from) reform, than the 'insiders'. Third, there are 'Eastern' countries, being those willing but potentially unable to join Euroland. These 'E-countries' (here we have the east and central European countries in mind) would enjoy larger transactions gains than average, and smaller output disturbances. But they will typically also have larger reform needs than the 'insiders'.

In modelling these issues we retain the option of staying outside the union. Our model enables us to calculate the gains and losses for the insiders, the N-countries and the E-countries, when the insiders do and do not undertake reforms. This allows us to say something about why some countries are more eager to join the union than others; and about the incentives to undertake reforms of different types. We can also make predictions about which structural reforms are the more important, and whether the pressures for (and gains from) reform are diluted when the candidates represent small or large economies or when the insiders form a large group.

Our analytical framework contains a number of asymmetries which are crucial in this context. There is asymmetric wage adjustment behaviour (up vs. down) which allows us to get a handle on the market flexibility issue. Those asymmetries can then be extended to cover labour mobility or migration. Countries are also distinguished by different costs and benefits depending on whether they choose to be 'in' or 'out'. Finally, while we retain the assumption that countries have identical structures, they can face asymmetric shocks.

Structural reform is defined here to mean increasing the degree of wage and price flexibility, or increasing the degree of labour mobility. Thus, structural reform might be thought of as simply removing or weakening the assumption that real wages or unemployment can go up but not down. But we can also view it as a matter of greater labour mobility, which is of particular importance for the E-country case. Either way, we end up varying the degree of wage rigidity or imperfect competition that is applied to the marginal productivity conditions in the benchmark specification of the model's labour market. This shows the potential gains of *market reforms*.

The rest of the chapter is divided as follows. In section 2 we outline a formal model of the decision to join or enlarge a currency union. In section 3 labour mobility is introduced as an instrument of structural reform. In section 4 we allow wages to be more flexible than in the basic model. Section 5 then provides an empirical analysis of our theoretical results, both for the N-countries and for the E-countries which constitute the first wave of accession countries due to join in 2005. Finally, section 6 offers some suggestions for future research.

2 The model

Consider the case of two arbitrary countries contemplating a common currency. One country will be the candidate and the other a potential partner in the case of creating a union, or the rest of an existing union in the case of enlargement. Each country or region has the same structure of production but produces its own goods with a fixed amount of labour:

$$Y_i = L_i^\alpha e^{\varepsilon_i}, \tag{13.1}$$

where Y_i is the output of region i, L_i the labour input in region i and ε_i is a disturbance with mean zero and independent of the exchange rate regime. The capital stock has been normalised at 1. In logs:

$$y_i = \alpha l_i + \varepsilon_i. \tag{13.2}$$

For simplicity, all goods are treated as potentially tradable. Prices are therefore determined on the world market and may be written in terms of some numeraire and converted into domestic currencies for comparison purposes.

In a competitive market, labour will be employed up to the point where real wages equal the marginal product of labour in the numeraire:

$$w_i - p_i + e_i = \log \alpha - (1 - \alpha) l_i + \varepsilon_i, \tag{13.3}$$

where e_i is the (log of the) bilateral exchange rate with region 1. The level of wages and prices are similarly W_i and P_i, with their log counterparts in (13.3). To incorporate wage stickiness we assume that full employment wages, $\bar{w} = \alpha$, hold when there is full employment ($L_i = 1$) and no shocks ($\varepsilon_i = 0$), when the initial level of prices is normalised at 1 for convenience, and when the exchange rate is at its parity value ($E_i = 1$). If there is excess demand for labour when $W_i = \alpha$, then wages will be raised until the demand falls to $L_i = 1$. But if there is excess supply at $W_i = \alpha$, then wages remain at this level and unemployment results. That is the crucial asymmetry and it completes the supply side.

Each region now has to choose its preferred exchange rate regime. If regions i and j form a currency union then their exchange rate ratio, E_i/E_j, is fixed at unity and they have a common currency. If they choose separate currencies then E_i/E_j may vary, but there is a transactions cost between the two currencies. This cost implies that, in value terms, goods exported from region i 'shrink' by a factor $(1 - T_i)$ when they arrive in region j.[3] For simplicity, let $T_i = T$ for all regions.

Finally, on the *demand* side, if production is owned locally, region i's income will be $P_i Y_i$. Utility levels are given by the Cobb–Douglas function

$$U_j = \sum_{i=1}^{N} \beta_{ji} \log C_{ji} - \phi, \tag{13.4}$$

---

[3] This is the usual 'iceberg' assumption.

where C_{ji} is the consumption of good i in region j, and $\phi = \sum_j \beta_{ji} \log \beta_{ji}$ is a constant. The β_{ji} parameters are subject to the normalisations $\sum_i \beta_{ji} = 1$ and $\sum_j \beta_{ji} = 1$. Since β_{ji} is the proportion of region j's income spent on goods produced in region i – see (13.5) below – these restrictions ensure that total income is spent and that aggregate demand exhausts income spent on each good. Under these conditions the demand for good i from region j is

$$Y_{ji} = (\beta_{ji} P_j Y_j / P_i) e^{v_{ji}}, \tag{13.5}$$

where v_{ji} is another exogenous normally distributed disturbance with zero mean arising on the demand side. Note that production in region i will be expected to equal unity in the absence of shocks ($y_i = 0$ in (13.2) at full employment). Now, given that prices have been normalised with $P_1 = 1$, we have $E(P_1 Y_1) = 1$ in the long run (E denotes expectations). That means all other national incomes are also unity in expectation since, if $P_j Y_j = 1$, then

$$Y_i = \sum_j Y_{ji} = \left(\sum \beta_{ji} e^{v_{ji}} / P_i \right), \tag{13.6}$$

which implies $P_i E Y_i = 1$. But $P_1 Y_1 = 1$, so $P_i E Y_i = 1$ for $i = 2 \dots N$.

Hence, in the long run, output in each region will be independent of the real exchange rate, but in the short term actual output will depend on relative prices. Thus, if region j and region i do *not* form a currency union, the equilibrium consumption of good i in region j will be

$$C_{ji} = (\beta_{ji}(1 - T_j) / P_i) e^{v_{ji}}, \tag{13.7}$$

where the production of good i is given by (13.6) and, for simplicity, $T_j = T$. This implies

$$c_{ji} = \log \beta_{ji} + \log (1 - T) + d_{ji}, \tag{13.8}$$

where $d_{ji} = v_{ji} + \varepsilon_i$ is a composite disturbance term, since full employment with equilibrium wages and exchange rates implies, in deviations from the initial state, $y_i = -p_i = \varepsilon_i$. Each region's utility level is therefore

$$U_j = \sum_i \beta_{ji} d_{ji} - \sum_{i \neq j} \beta_{ji} \tau; \quad \tau = - \log (1 - T). \tag{13.9}$$

Now, suppose region j and region k decide to form a currency union. Equations (13.6) to (13.9) hold with k replacing j and $T_k = 0$. The external exchange rate will be the mean of the free-float exchange rates which, under the normalisation of $E_j = E_k = 1$ vs. region 1, implies $e_{jk} = e_j = e_k = (\varepsilon_j + \varepsilon_k)/2$ with a mean value of $E e_{jk} = 0$. Suppose wages adjust to provide full employment in the high demand region (region j, say) but are sticky downwards in the other region.

Then

$$y_j = \varepsilon_j \quad \text{and} \quad w_j = \log(\bar{w}) + (\varepsilon_j - \varepsilon_k)/2 \tag{13.10}$$

using (13.3) and the results above for e_j and p_j, where $\bar{w}$ is the log equilibrium real wage with no shocks and $E_j = 1$.

Notice that there is no labour mobility here, so the entire adjustment to absorb the shock ε_j has had to be taken by a rise in wages w_j above their equilibrium level. However, region k (the low demand region) will have unemployment, but wages 'stuck' at their full employment level: $\log \bar{w} = \log \alpha + p_k$, where p_k is as yet unchanged. Hence solving (13.3) for ℓ_k, the employment level in region k, we get $e_k = -(1 - \alpha)\ell_k + \varepsilon_k$, or $\ell_k = -(e_k - \varepsilon_k)/(1 - \alpha)$. But the single currency assumption between j and k means $e_k = e_j = (\varepsilon_j + \varepsilon_k)/2$. Substituting that into the expression just obtained for ℓ_k implies, by (13.2),

$$y_k = \varepsilon_k - \alpha(\varepsilon_j - \varepsilon_k)/(2(1 - \alpha)) \quad \text{and} \quad w_k = \log(\bar{w}) \tag{13.11}$$

for the 'low-demand' region k.

Now, evaluating the difference between (13.9) and the utilities generated by (13.10) and (13.11), we find the utilities gained by being in the currency union are

$$\Delta U_j = \beta_{jk}\tau - \beta_{jk}\alpha(\varepsilon_j - \varepsilon_k)/(2(1 - \alpha)) + \sum_i \beta_{ji} \Delta \upsilon_{ji}$$

$$\Delta U_k = \beta_{kj}\tau - \beta_{kk}\alpha(\varepsilon_j - \varepsilon_k)/(2(1 - \alpha)) + \sum_i \beta_{ki} \Delta \upsilon_{ki}, \tag{13.12}$$

while the loss to region 1 (say) staying outside the union is

$$\Delta U_1 = -\beta_{1k}\alpha(\varepsilon_j - \varepsilon_k)/(2(1 - \alpha)) + \sum_i \beta_{1i} \Delta \upsilon_{1i} \tag{13.13}$$

where $\Delta \upsilon_{ji}$ is the increase in region j's demand for goods produced in region i as a result of joining the currency union, i.e. the trade creation and trade diversion effects of the monetary union itself. But, in our case, all countries are already members of the single European market. Hence there is no reason to suppose that there would be any additional systematic shocks to demand in the union countries, as a result of the single currency itself, beyond those already reflected in τ. We can therefore ignore the $\Delta \upsilon_{ji}$ terms, or treat them as only small.

It should be noticed, however, that $\beta_{jk}\tau > 0$ and $\beta_{kj}\tau > 0$. So there are always gains in terms of lower transactions costs within the union. These gains may be small or large. But the crucial question is whether these gains outweigh the costs that arise because adjustment is more difficult without an independent monetary policy. The remaining terms in (13.12) and (13.13) show the particular costs which are at issue in this chapter, namely the losses in welfare due to having sticky real wages in the union which make internal adjustment more difficult and hence more costly.

The cost–benefit ratio therefore depends on the demand elasticities (β_{ji}), the transactions costs (τ), the elasticity of the demand for labour (α), and the degree of similarity of the shocks in different regions. But non-members will be worse off because adjustment difficulties in the union spill over to cause disequilibria outside, without any benefits being created to offset those costs. Thus a core monetary union will always impose costs on the periphery or candidate countries, but the outsiders will impose no such costs on the core. However, since the shocks are symmetrically distributed around zero, there will be times when $\varepsilon_j < \varepsilon_k$, and times when $\varepsilon_k > \varepsilon_j$, with a probability of one-half of either event occurring. That means the ex-ante expected benefit in joining a currency union is

$$E(\Delta U_j) = \beta_{jk}\tau - \beta_{jj}\gamma E(\varepsilon_j - \varepsilon_k \mid \varepsilon_j < \varepsilon_k)P(\varepsilon_j < \varepsilon_k)$$

$$- \beta_{jk}\gamma E(\varepsilon_k - \varepsilon_j \mid \varepsilon_j > \varepsilon_k)P(\varepsilon_j > \varepsilon_k)$$

$$= \beta_{jk}\tau - \gamma(\beta_{jj} + \beta_{jk})\phi(0)\sqrt{\sigma_j^2 - 2\rho\sigma_j\sigma_k + \sigma_k^2}. \quad (13.14)$$

And for the non-members the welfare costs are

$$E(\Delta U_1) = -\gamma(\beta_{1j} + \beta_{1k})\phi(0)\sqrt{\sigma_j^2 - 2\rho\sigma_j\sigma_k + \sigma_k^2}, \quad (13.15)$$

where $\phi(0)$ is the distribution function of a standard jointly normal distribution of random variables and $\gamma = \alpha/(2(1-\alpha))$.

That produces our first result. Irrespective of the degree of flexibility in the labour markets, the expected costs of monetary union are minimised, for members and non-members alike, if $\rho \to 1$; but only if $\sigma_j \approx \sigma_k$. Hence a necessary condition for low costs is a high positive correlation between the shocks in regions j and k. But the necessary and sufficient condition is a high positive correlation and shocks of similar size.

A second implication of these results is that the gains and losses from integration in the union will get stronger over time, since the trade linkage parameters (β_{ji}, β_{jk}) will become stronger as the single market's trade links develop and the domestic expenditure shares (β_{jj}, β_{kk}) fall. Consequently, if the demand elasticities change on joining the currency union, the separation between those who want to join (or be joined), and those who do not, will – if anything – get stronger.[4] So, changing demand elasticities may be another factor in this cost–benefit analysis, but they will not change the underlying conclusions.

---

[4] It is important to contrast this result with the conclusions drawn by Frankel and Rose (1998) or Hughes Hallett and Piscitelli (2002) when market flexibility is *not* an issue.

3   Labour mobility and structural reform

3.1   *One-way mobility*

We now examine how this model would work if there were labour mobility in countries with unemployment or excess demand. We suppose that, whenever there is unemployment in the low demand region k, a proportion of those unemployed (because wages w_k are sticky) can move and take up employment in the high demand economy j.

This implies some flexibility in economy j since its markets are the ones which have to be able to absorb the additional workers from k. In a single market with a common currency, no one can prevent the unemployed trying to leave k if they want to; the question is whether j's markets have sufficient wage and price flexibility to absorb them. But since it is only a proportion, $0 \leq \delta_k \leq 1$, of the unemployed who leave k, there will be no reason for a change in the wages in k – which remain stuck at their full employment equilibrium level, $\log \bar{w}$. There are therefore two effects of this change: first, δ_k of the unemployed move to j; and, second, w_j rises by less than in equation (13.10) because j's labour supply has expanded. That means the degree of excess demand in j's labour market is less.[5] Consequently (13.11) continues to hold unchanged for w_k and y_k. But ℓ_j now rises from its old value of $\bar{\ell}_j$ to

$$\ell_j = \bar{\ell}_j + \delta_k(\ell_k - \bar{\ell}_k) = \frac{-(e_j - \varepsilon_j)}{1 - \alpha}, \tag{13.16}$$

where, by normalisation, $\bar{\ell}_j = \bar{\ell}_k = 0$. That immediately implies

$$y_j = \varepsilon_j + \frac{\delta_k(e_j - \varepsilon_j)}{1 - \alpha} = \varepsilon_j + \gamma \delta_k(\varepsilon_j - \varepsilon_k) \tag{13.17}$$

by (13.2) and the steps following (13.10), where $\gamma = \alpha/(2(1-\alpha))$. We have used the fact that, by (13.3), $w_j = \log(\bar{w}) + \delta_k (\varepsilon_j - \varepsilon_k)/2$ in this case. Thus, inserting (13.17) and (13.11) into (13.9) as before, we now have the changes in welfare if j joins the union – represented by region k – as

$$\Delta U_j = \beta_{jk}\tau + \beta_{jj}\gamma\delta_k(\varepsilon_j - \varepsilon_k) - \beta_{jk}\gamma(\varepsilon_j - \varepsilon_k) \tag{13.18}$$

and

$$\Delta U_k = \beta_{kj}\tau + \beta_{kj}\gamma\delta_k(\varepsilon_j - \varepsilon_k) - \beta_{kk}\gamma(\varepsilon_j - \varepsilon_k). \tag{13.19}$$

That shows that labour mobility, and the flexibility to accept these movements in labour supply, would uniformly *reduce* the costs of forming or joining a

---

[5] The third option, that the unemployed remaining in k will exert some downward pressure on wages there, will be considered in the next section.

monetary union for both parties – both those gaining the extra labour and those losing the unemployed – and the more so, the more flexible are the markets in j (i.e. the higher is δ_k). However, the ability of labour to move would be an appropriate response only if the shocks to country j or country k were perceived as persistent. Because of the costs for those having to move, transitory shocks are better handled through flexible wages. We treat that case separately in section 4.

3.2   Two-way mobility

We now extend our model to allow for migration/labour mobility in either direction. We therefore define δ_j as the proportion of the unemployed in economy j that would migrate to economy k if the occasion demanded it. There is *no* requirement for $\delta_j = \delta_k$.

Repeating the steps which generated (13.16) to (13.19), we get

$$\Delta U_j = \beta_{jk}\tau + [\beta_{jj}\gamma\delta_k(\varepsilon_j - \varepsilon_k) - \beta_{jk}\gamma(\varepsilon_j - \varepsilon_k)]$$
$$+ [\beta_{jk}\gamma\delta_j(\varepsilon_j - \varepsilon_k) - \beta_{jj}\gamma(\varepsilon_j - \varepsilon_k)] \tag{13.20}$$

in place of (13.18); and in place of (13.19) we get

$$\Delta U_k = \beta_{kj}\tau + [\beta_{jj}\gamma\delta_j(\varepsilon_j - \varepsilon_k) - \beta_{kj}\gamma(\varepsilon_j - \varepsilon_k)]$$
$$+ [\beta_{kj}\gamma\delta_k(\varepsilon_j - \varepsilon_k) - \beta_{kk}\gamma(\varepsilon_j - \varepsilon_k)]. \tag{13.21}$$

As a result, we can write the welfare gain from j joining the union as

$$E(\Delta U_j) = \beta_{jk}\tau - \gamma(\beta_{jk} - \delta_k\beta_{jj})E(\varepsilon_j - \varepsilon_k \mid \varepsilon_j > \varepsilon_k)P(\varepsilon_j > \varepsilon_k)$$
$$- \gamma(\beta_{jj} - \delta_j\beta_{jk})E(\varepsilon_j - \varepsilon_k \mid \varepsilon_j < \varepsilon_k)P(\varepsilon_j < \varepsilon_k) \tag{13.22}$$

This replaces (13.14) when there is some market flexibility or mobility in each direction. If both ε_j and ε_k are symmetrically and normally distributed about their mean values, (13.22) may be simplified to

$$E(\Delta U_j) = \beta_{jk}\tau - \gamma[\beta_{jk}(1 - \delta_j) + \beta_{jj}(1 - \delta_k)]$$
$$\times\phi(0)\sqrt{\sigma_j^2 - 2\rho\sigma_j\sigma_k + \sigma_k^2}. \tag{13.23}$$

Likewise, we can write the corresponding expressions for the welfare gain to the existing members of the union, if j does join, as

$$E(\Delta U_k) = \beta_{kj}\tau - \gamma(\beta_{kj} - \delta_j\beta_{kk})E(\varepsilon_j - \varepsilon_k \mid \varepsilon_k > \varepsilon_j)P(\varepsilon_k > \varepsilon_j)$$
$$- \gamma(\beta_{kk} - \delta_k\beta_{kj})E(\varepsilon_k - \varepsilon_j \mid \varepsilon_k < \varepsilon_j)P(\varepsilon_k < \varepsilon_j) \tag{13.24}$$

If ε_j and ε_k are symmetrically and normally distributed, this expression simplifies to

$$E(\Delta U_k) = \beta_{kj}\tau - \gamma[\beta_{kj}(1 - \delta_k) + \beta_{kk}(1 - \delta_j)]$$
$$\times \phi(0)\sqrt{\sigma_j^2 - 2\rho\sigma_j\sigma_k + \sigma_k^2}. \qquad (13.25)$$

3.3   Discussion of results

3.3.1   Incentives of insiders and outsiders   Our model has shown that there is *always* a cost to joining EMU under conditions of imperfect market flexibility, and also to allowing others to join if you are already a member. This holds for both N-countries and E-countries, should they choose to join — but not equally so, as can be seen from (13.22) and (13.23). That is, for a given level of flexibility in the union (δ_j measures the degree of flexibility in the union, k, and hence the ability to absorb excess workers from j), the cost, to j, of joining the union will be lower the larger is δ_k – i.e. the more flexible or reformed is the joining economy. It is reasonable to assume that that varies between N-countries and E-countries. In fact, N-countries typically have larger and more diversified economies, as well as better trained/more highly skilled work forces. They are therefore better placed to absorb additional workers, than are the E-countries, should there be unemployment in the k economies or excess demand in j.

The same result holds for the existing members of the union, by virtue of (13.24) and (13.25). For a given level of δ_j in the union, the cost of having new members join the union is reduced if δ_k is larger; i.e. if the new members come from the relatively reformed and flexible North, rather than from the less reformed East. This easily explains why the existing EMU members have been very keen to encourage the N-countries to join; but also why, when it came to the point, they were less keen to enlarge the EU and its monetary union to include the E-countries.

Conversely, if it is correct to assume that the N-economies are more reformed and flexible than the union, while the union's markets are more flexible and reformed than those in the E-countries, then these results also explain why the N-countries have been reluctant to join EMU (although they easily could) – while the E-countries have been very keen to join even though they were not entirely qualified. The average level of market flexibility faced by the N-countries would fall if they joined, whereas it would rise for the E-countries if they joined. Of course, if wage flexibility is much higher in the E-countries than in the union (which seems likely), or than in the N-economies (which is also possible, but less likely), then the results might look quite different. We will deal with that case in section 4.

It therefore becomes more attractive to join a union that has undertaken a lot of market reform, and it becomes safer to do so if one has undertaken a lot of reform oneself. Similarly, it becomes more attractive to have candidates joining your union if they have already undertaken a lot of market reform, and it will be easier to accept them if you are relatively flexible yourself.

3.3.2   The role of asymmetries   The only exception to that conclusion, where the costs could vanish altogether, is where the random shocks are asymmetrically distributed and the structural dependencies between the candidate and the union are also asymmetrically distributed in the right way. Returning to the more general expression (13.22), and recalling that $0 \le \delta_j$, $\delta_k \le 1$, we could have $\beta_{jk} - \delta_k \beta_{jj} < 0$ if δ_k was large and $\beta_{jj} > \beta_{jk}$ by some margin. If, then, $P(\varepsilon_j > \varepsilon_k)$ was larger than $P(\varepsilon_j < \varepsilon_k)$ by enough, then the net costs of country j joining (country k or an existing union) would be zero or negative. This would be a case where

(i) country j has flexible markets, or had undertaken sufficient reforms;

(ii) country j is a 'large', open part of the union (meaning the share of consumption expenditures spent on domestically produced goods exceeds the share spent on goods produced from elsewhere in the union);[6] and

(iii) the chances of getting country specific shocks favouring country j are greater (or at least no less) than the chances of getting country specific shocks favouring the union.

These conditions represent a special, but entirely possible, set of circumstances – with the exception perhaps of the last. They have two further implications: first, there will always be some costs involved (on both sides) *even* if the optimal currency area criteria between candidate member and union are reasonably well satisfied. And, second, the pattern of those costs will depend on the 'size' of each economy in terms of the relative importance of its trade links with the other party compared to the size of its domestic market. The former includes the optimal currency case where δ_k and δ_j are large because factor mobility is high; and where β_{jk} is large because intra-union trade is important; and where ε_j and ε_k are roughly symmetrically distributed. But it also includes the opposite case; i.e. where there is little flexibility or mobility, where trade links are weak, and where shocks are either symmetric or asymmetric.

3.3.3   Regional origin of market reforms   To enlarge on the last observation, note that (13.22) implies that the costs of EMU, for given levels of flexibility and market reform, may be quite different for a 'large' country joining ($\beta_{jj} > \beta_{jk}$) than for a 'small' one ($\beta_{jj} < \beta_{jk}$). Because δ_j and δ_k are bounded above,

---

[6] In what follows, 'large' means 'having a large impact on the union' and hence can be equated with being 'open' with respect to the rest of the union. But the same economy may not be 'large' or 'open' with respect to the rest of world, which is why the word 'open' is avoided here. Similarly, 'small' means having a small impact on the union, and hence possibly 'closed' with respect to the union, though not necessarily with respect to the rest of the world.

a joining country will always have costs in the third term of (13.22) if it is large –
but it may or may not have costs in the second term. Conversely, a small country
joining a larger one, or joining an existing union (which is large by definition),
will have costs in the second term, but not in the third.

Hence it matters where the flexibility and market reforms are introduced. A
large country joining will find it more important that the reforms and market
flexibility should be at home (i.e. in δ_k, rather than δ_j) so that it is in a position
to profit from the union's relative inflexibility. It can profit in that case because
the costs of having to make larger adjustments on behalf of the rest of the union,
when there are shocks, will be relatively unimportant for country j unless the
shocks are distributed very asymmetrically. This follows from the fact that a unit
increase in δ_k has a larger impact on j's utility than δ_j, if j is a large economy:

$$\frac{\partial E(\Delta U_j)}{\partial \delta_j} = \gamma \beta_{jk} E(.)P(.) < \frac{\partial E(\Delta U_j)}{\partial \delta_k} = \gamma \beta_{jj} E(.)P(.) \qquad (13.26)$$

holds by virtue of (13.22) when $\beta_{jj} > \beta_{jk}$, provided that the joint probability
distribution of ε_j and ε_k is not skewed too far on the downside for ε_j. The latter
will be true provided that $E(\varepsilon_k - \varepsilon_j \mid \varepsilon_j > \varepsilon_k)P(\varepsilon_j > \varepsilon_k)$ is not smaller than
$E(\varepsilon_j - \varepsilon_k \mid \varepsilon_j < \varepsilon_k)P(\varepsilon_j < \varepsilon_k)$, or not smaller by too much.[7]

Thus, a large open economy would prefer to carry out any reforms before
entering, unless the union is largely unreformed or consistently underperforms.
But a small country joining a larger union, k, will have costs in the second term,
not in the third. Such a country would find it more important to join an already
flexible union, rather than carry out those reforms itself (i.e. to increase δ_j rather
than δ_k), since the adjustment burden on its economy if the union is inflexible
would be proportionately much larger, and the ability to profit from the union's
inflexibility that much smaller. A small country would therefore be reluctant to
engage in large-scale market reforms before joining, and will not see its own
lack of reforms as a barrier to entry.

Finally, it is reasonable to assume that an existing union, k, is always large
in this sense – whatever the size of the joining economy. That means $\beta_{kk} > \beta_{kj}$
in (13.24)–(13.25). Hence we replace (13.26) with

$$\frac{\partial E(\Delta U_k)}{\partial \delta_j} = \gamma \beta_{kk} E(.)P(.) > \frac{\partial E(\Delta U_k)}{\partial \delta_k} = \gamma \beta_{kj} E(.)P(.) \qquad (13.27)$$

from (13.24), when considering the union's preferences for where the reforms
should take place. This means an existing union will always prefer the joining
economy to carry out the reforms and provide the market flexibility, rather than

---

[7] If the distribution of shocks were very asymmetric in this sense, then country j would find that
the chances of being able to profit from the union's inflexibility were far smaller than the chances
of having to shoulder the greatest part of the burden of adjustment for the union as a whole. It
would not want to join in those circumstances.

do so itself.[8] Hence an existing union will be reluctant to embark on a large reform programme itself; it would, under our assumptions, prefer N-countries to join rather than E-countries.

4   Wage and price flexibility

Suppose instead of migration, we allow wages to be more flexible, where we have a temporary positive shock to demand in country j similar to that in (13.10). Employment will remain at 1 for country j, and wages will move as before to

$$w_j = \log(\bar{w}) + (\varepsilon_j - \varepsilon_k)/2. \tag{13.28}$$

But suppose wages fall in the low demand country by enough to re-employ a proportion, δ_k say, of those who would have been unemployed had *no* wage adjustments taken place there. Applying the usual marginal productivity conditions we now get

$$w_k = \log(\bar{w}) + \varepsilon_k - (1 - \alpha)\ell_k, \tag{13.29}$$

where $\ell_k = \log(L_k)$; and $L_k = 1 - (1 - \delta_k)X$. In this expression, X denotes the number of unemployed when there are no wage adjustments. Using the results of section 2, we can write (13.3) as

$$w_k + e_k = \log(\bar{w}) - (1 - \alpha)(-x) + \varepsilon_k, \tag{13.30}$$

where $x \cong \log(1 - X)$. And $\delta_k = 0$ implies $w_k = \log(\bar{w})$, so that

$$(1 - \alpha)x = e_k - \varepsilon_k = (e_j - \varepsilon_k)/2, \tag{13.31}$$

because $e_k = (\varepsilon_j + \varepsilon_k)/2$ still holds. From here it follows that

$$\ell_k \cong -(1 - \delta_k)x = -(1 - \delta_k)\frac{\varepsilon_j - \varepsilon_k}{2(1 - \alpha)} \tag{13.32}$$

and hence that

$$w_k = \log(\bar{w}) - (1 - \delta_k)\left(\frac{\varepsilon_j + \varepsilon_k}{2}\right) \tag{13.33}$$

using (13.29) again. That leaves us with

$$y_k = \varepsilon_k - \frac{\alpha(1 - \delta_k)(\varepsilon_j - \varepsilon_k)}{2(1 - \alpha)} \tag{13.34}$$

and (13.33) in place of (13.11). From here we can make the same steps which led us to (13.12) and (13.14), to show that the gains (for j) from joining the

---

[8] Subject, of course, to the (joint) error distribution not being skewed too far on the downside for ε_k.

union are

$$\Delta U_j = \beta_{jk}\tau - \beta_{jk}\gamma \, (1 - \delta_k)(\varepsilon_j - \varepsilon_k) \tag{13.35}$$

if $\varepsilon_j > \varepsilon_k$ and k's wages have to fall; but

$$\Delta U_j = \beta_{jk}\tau - \beta_{jj}\gamma(1 - \delta_j)(\varepsilon_j - \varepsilon_k) \tag{13.36}$$

if $\varepsilon_j < \varepsilon_k$ and it is j's wages which have to fall. Thus, if $\delta_j \neq \delta_k$ is possible or likely, then

$$E(\Delta U_j) = \beta_{jk}\tau - \gamma\beta_{jk}(1 - \delta_k)E(\varepsilon_k - \varepsilon_j \mid \varepsilon_j > \varepsilon_k)P(\varepsilon_j > \varepsilon_k)$$
$$- \gamma\beta_{jj}(1 - \delta_j)E(\varepsilon_j - \varepsilon_k \mid \varepsilon_j < \varepsilon_k)P(\varepsilon_j < \varepsilon_k) \tag{13.37}$$

replaces (13.14) in the base case, and (13.22) in the labour mobility case. If the shocks are symmetrically and normally distributed, this expression becomes

$$E(\Delta U_j) = \beta_{jk}\tau - \gamma[\beta_{jk}(1 - \delta_k) + \beta_{jj}(1 - \delta_j)]$$
$$\times \phi(0)\sqrt{\sigma_j^2 + \sigma_k^2 - 2\rho\sigma_j\sigma_k}. \tag{13.38}$$

The corresponding expression for the members of an existing union if country j is allowed to join is

$$E(\Delta U_k) = \beta_{kj}\tau - \gamma\beta_{kj}(1 - \delta_j)E(\varepsilon_k - \varepsilon_j \mid \varepsilon_k > \varepsilon_j)P(\varepsilon_k > \varepsilon_j)$$
$$- \gamma\beta_{kk}(1 - \delta_k)E(\varepsilon_k - \varepsilon_j \mid \varepsilon_k < \varepsilon_j)P(\varepsilon_k < \varepsilon_j). \tag{13.39}$$

Thus, on the face of it, it appears that we get results which are the exact opposite of those in the migration case, since δ_j and δ_k have swapped positions in (13.37) and (13.38) compared to (13.22) and (13.23). And similarly for (13.39) versus (13.24). That is because $\delta_k \ell_k$ is saved from being lost to γ_k when $\varepsilon_k < \varepsilon_j$ in the former case, and does not have to be added to γ_j. However, δ_j and δ_k also carry a reversed interpretation. In section 3, δ_k represented the ease of migration from k to j, and therefore depended on market flexibility and reform in j. But δ_k here indicates the degree of wage flexibility and the ability to redeploy workers within k; i.e. the degree of market flexibility and reform in country k.

Consequently, the overall interpretation which δ_j and δ_k bring to these expressions is actually the same as before: First, a lack of wage price flexibility or reform brings costs for both new entrants and existing union members alike – and that is true whether the lack of reform is in the entrants or in the existing union. Second, to reduce those costs requires action by the existing members as well as by the new entrants. Third, countries will only want to join a union where markets are more flexible than their own. But existing members will want the same properties of their new partners as well – which raises the prospect of a Groucho Marx problem again. Fourth, in this case, and in contrast to the migration case, a 'large' country would want to ensure as much wage and price flexibility as possible at home (j) before agreeing to join – whereas a 'small' country would want the union (k) to reform before joining.

5   Some empirical implications

At this point it would be useful to have some 'orders of magnitude' calculations to indicate the likely size of the incentives which the N-countries and the E-countries face for joining, or not joining, the EMU. At the same time we can calculate the corresponding incentives for the existing members of the union to accept new members from either group into the EMU.

5.1   Data

Table 13.1 shows the expenditure shares of each of the candidate countries, spent on their own domestically produced goods (β_{jj}) and on imports from the rest of the euro area (β_{jk}). Note that the candidate country is indexed by j, and the existing currency union by k. In line with the earlier analysis, we assume that each country decides whether to join or not to join on a unilateral basis, not as part of a group. The E-countries are here represented by the 'first-wave' of candidate countries from eastern and central Europe. Table 13.1 also shows the existing euro area's expenditure share on its own domestically produced goods, and on goods imported from the various candidate countries.

From these figures we can already see that the E-countries are qualitatively different from the N-countries, as we had surmised in sections 3.3.1 and 3.3.3, and with predictable consequences for the incentives to join or be joined. The β_{jk} parameters are 2 to 4 times larger in the E-countries, while their β_{jj} parameters are 70–100% smaller. Evidently, the E-countries do tend to be the 'smaller' countries and more dependent on the rest of the EU/euro area, while the N-countries, tend to be 'big' countries, economically speaking, and less dependent on euro area trade.[9]

Table 13.2 supplies standard deviations for the demand, supply and monetary shocks in the N-countries,[10] and the correlations of each of those individual country shocks with the corresponding average for the core or periphery group of countries in the EU. These figures are taken from Demertzis, Hughes Hallett

---

[9] Note that the figures are calculated from the IMFs Direction of Trade Statistics for 1998, and the OECDs National Accounts Statistics. They assume that the E-countries would join a euro area consisting of all fifteen EU members, whereas the N-countries would join the twelve existing members of the euro area on an individual basis. But to vary these assumptions makes no effective difference to our numerical results.

[10] Measured as a proportion of GDP in each case.

Table 13.1. *Stylized facts of trade flows*

Country j	Proportion of country j's income spent on goods produced in the EU-15 (EU-12)	Proportion of country j's income spent on domestically produced goods
E-countries		
	β_{jk}	β_{jj}
Czech Republic	0.39	0.37
Hungary	0.36	0.45
Poland	0.21	0.67
Slovenia	0.39	0.43
Estonia	0.44	0.26
N-countries		
Denmark	0.19	0.74
Sweden	0.18	0.71
United Kingdom	0.11	0.78
The euro area		
	β_{kj}	β_{kk}
Denmark	0.004	0.81
Sweden	0.006	0.81
United Kingdom	0.017	0.81
Czech Republic	0.004	0.81
Hungary	0.003	0.81
Poland	0.001	0.81
Slovenia	0.001	0.81
Estonia	0.001	0.81

Source: IMF Direction of Trade Statistics and OECD National Accounts Data.

and Rummel (1998), and are estimated using data for the period 1972–95 inclusive; they use the conventional Blanchard and Quah (1989) decomposition to ensure that each group of calculated shocks (demand, supply and monetary) are orthogonal to one another.

The core countries are defined as Austria, France, Germany, Belgium, the Netherlands and Denmark; the periphery countries as UK, Greece, Ireland, Portugal, Spain, Finland, Sweden and Italy.

From the figures in table 13.2, one can see that, with the exception of the demand shocks, none of the N-countries is well correlated with the other members of the euro area. And as far as the demand shocks are concerned, Denmark is correlated only with the core, and Sweden and the UK only with the periphery. Sweden, meanwhile, appears to suffer rather larger shocks than the other two candidates. Note that the group averages do not include the candidates' own shocks here.

Table 13.2. *Correlation coefficients and standard deviations of demand, supply and monetary shocks for selected members of the EU-15, 1972–95*

	Demand shocks		Supply shocks		Monetary shocks	
	Core	Periphery	Core	Periphery	Core	Periphery
(a) Correlation						
Denmark	0.73*	0.34	0.03	0.04	0.27	0.09
Sweden	−0.12	0.81*	−0.03	−0.07	−0.07	0.22
UK	0.11	0.60*	0.12	0.02	−0.07	−0.24
Greece	0.30	0.90*	0.20	0.46*	−0.30	−0.37
(b) Standard deviations						
Denmark	0.0085		0.0067		0.0068	
Sweden	0.0164		0.0086		0.0172	
UK	0.0091		0.0036		0.0106	
Core	0.0012		0.0051		0.0244	
Periphery	0.0053		0.0061		0.0241	
Greece	0.0246		0.0227		0.0119	

Note: *Denotes statistically significantly different from zero at the 5% level.
Source: Demertzis, Hughes Hallett and Rummel (1998).

Unfortunately, we do not have corresponding figures for the E-countries because, as far as we are aware, there have been no such studies of the patterns of their shocks. This may be because the sample period since the transition of those economies to a market-based system has been too short to make any reliable estimates of the relevant standard deviations or correlation coefficients. The best we can do is to calculate rough orders of magnitude, using the patterns of shocks from Greece or Portugal, as comparably sized economies with convergence problems, as a guide. (We use Greece.)

Table 13.3 shows our assumptions for the remaining parameters. The value of γ is calculated by setting α equal to the labour share in national income, as implied by the Cobb–Douglas production function in equation (13.2). And the figures for δ_j represent the degree of flexibility in the labour market, which allows either 10% (column 2) or 50% (column 4) of the domestically unemployed to migrate to jobs elsewhere in the euro area. The corresponding figures for δ_k (columns 3 and 5) are the degrees of flexibility which allows 10% or 50% of the euro area's unemployed to migrate elsewhere in Europe. But that migration is assumed to be distributed equally across all member countries, so that each of the candidate countries gets only its GDP share of the total migration.

An alternative interpretation of these parameters, as we have shown in section 4, is that they represent the degree of market flexibility that will allow

Table 13.3. *Degrees of market flexibility (assumed)*

	γ	δ_j	δ_k	δ_j	δ_k	$\delta^*_j(=\delta^*_k)$	$\delta^*_k(=\delta^*_j)$
N-countries							
Denmark	0.566	0.1	0.002	0.5	0.010	0.70	0.99
Sweden	0.714	0.1	0.003	0.5	0.015	0.77	0.99
UK	0.592	0.1	0.020	0.5	0.100	0.90	0.98
E-countries							
Czech Republic	0.471	0.1	0.003	0.5	0.015	0.29	0.40
Hungary	0.419	0.1	0.003	0.5	0.015	0.31	0.44
Poland	0.423	0.1	0.010	0.5	0.050	0.63	0.67
Slovenia	0.575	0.1	0.005	0.5	0.010	0.46	0.39
Estonia	0.518	0.1	0.004	0.5	0.020	0.21	0.32

wages (and prices) to adjust so that 10% or 50% of the domestically unemployed are re-employed at home – whether in the candidate country or in the euro area as a whole. Columns (6) and (7) of table 13.3 show our calculation of degrees of market flexibility which, when shared equally between the candidate and the existing union, would overcome the disincentives caused by a lack of structural or market reform and make joining attractive from an economic point of view.

5.2   N-countries

Inserting these parameter values into (13.23) and assuming normally distributed shocks provides the cost–benefit analysis enabling each candidate country to answer the question 'Do we want to join?' Similarly, inserting the relevant values into (13.25) will give the cost–benefit calculated for the existing EU-12 (when the candidates are the N-countries) or EU-15 (when the candidates are the E-countries), to answer the question 'Do we want them to join?'

The results for the N-countries are set out in table 13.4. Note that in each case we have calculated the net benefit of joining or being joined under the 10% market flexibility and 50% market flexibility assumptions (columns 1 and 2, respectively), and also when the candidate joins alone or as one of the group (corresponding to the different β_{jk} and β_{kj} parameters in table 13.1). The value of τ is taken to be 2% throughout. That is the upper bound of the gains from adopting the single currency, as estimated by the European Commission (1990).

The results show that none of the N-countries would benefit from joining the euro area on current data, with either limited market flexibility, or with a stronger degree of labour market reform. Interestingly, greater labour market flexibility does make joining the euro area more attractive in each case. But it

Table 13.4. *Cost–benefit analysis of a northern enlargement without full structural reform (changes in utility units, by percentage)*

N-countries ('Do we want to join?')				
	Joining singly		Joining as a group	
	(1)	(2)	(1)	(2)
Denmark	−0.87	−0.79	−0.94	−0.82
Sweden	−1.23	−1.11	−1.31	−1.15
United Kingdom	−1.87	−1.62	−1.88	−1.63

EU-12 ('Do we want them to join?')				
	Joining singly		Joining as a group	
	(1)	(2)	(1)	(2)
Denmark	−0.97	−0.54	−0.96	−0.54
Sweden	−1.01	−0.55	−1.00	−0.55
United Kingdom	−1.55	−0.89	−1.54	−0.86

does not do so by very much. The degree of rigidity, as captured by our model, is simply too large.

In fact the degree of flexibility needed to reduce these welfare/utility losses to zero, if shared equally between the candidate country and the rest of the EU, runs from about 70% for Denmark to 90% for the UK (table 13.3, column (6)). That means substantial labour market reforms would have to be undertaken in order to reach the point at which wage and price flexibility (or labour mobility) would clear between 70% and 90% of any unemployment or other macroeconomic disequilibria, before it would become worthwhile for these countries to join on economic grounds.

Such a strong liberalisation seems somewhat implausible in the current political environment. However, that said, the expected losses, at 1–2% *net* in utility units, are not huge and imply absolute losses which are roughly double the conventional estimates of the expected gains (EC 1990). And Denmark is clearly the closest to wanting to join, while the UK is furthest away. Similarly, it makes very little difference if these countries join as a group; the net losses are slightly larger if they do so, since they then have to deal with the rigidities of their fellow N-countries as well as the rest of the euro area, but the extra costs are very small.

The net losses reported in the *EU-12* panel also conform to the theory in that, at these levels of market flexibility, the euro area would be made *net* worse off if the N-countries were to join. The effect of the additional rigidities would outweigh the transactions and price stability gains. But the euro-area countries would, as our model predicted, be more willing to have the N-countries join than the N-countries would be to join. Taking them singly, the EU-12's losses are 17% smaller under column 1 for Sweden and the UK than Sweden and the

Table 13.5. *Cost–benefit analysis of an eastern enlargement without full structural reform (changes in utility units, by percentage)*

E-countries ('Do we want to join?')	(1)	(2)
Czech Republic	−0.26	0.03
Hungary	−0.28	−0.08
Poland	−0.69	−0.58
Slovenia	−0.60	−0.35
Estonia	−0.16	0.12
EU-15 ('Do we want them to join?')		
Czech Republic	−1.15	−0.64
Hungary	−1.15	−0.65
Poland	−1.16	−0.64
Slovenia	−1.16	−0.64
Estonia	−1.16	−0.64

Notes: (a) Only 'first wave' countries are considered; (b) joining singly, or as a group, gives the same results for each country, but they should be accumulated to give the overall impact on the EU-15 if they join as a group; (c) we assume the euro area has all 15 members in these calculations.

UKs own net losses. And they are 45–50% smaller under column 2 than the corresponding national net losses.

5.3   E-countries

Repeating the same steps with the data for the E-countries produces the net gains reported in table 13.5.[11] Several points stand out. First, as predicted, the losses for the E-countries due to insufficient flexibility or reform are indeed much smaller: typically one-third to one-tenth the size of the corresponding figure for the N-countries, at the same level of market inflexibility – with net gains starting to appear when the degree of flexibility reaches the level where wage (or migration) adjustments can be relied on to eliminate half the E-countries' unemployment.

Evidently, the Czech Republic, Hungary and Estonia are closer to being able to benefit at low levels of market flexibility/reform than Poland and Slovenia. On the other hand, again as predicted, the existing EU would find accession by the E-countries a good deal less attractive (at any level of market flexibility) than the E-countries would find it to join. Two to four times less attractive, in fact.

---

[11] These figures are strictly for guidance only, as they have been calculated under the heroic assumption that the E-countries have a pattern of shocks similar to Greece in 1995.

That contrasts with the results of table 13.4, which showed the opposite holds for the N-countries: the EU-12 would find it up to 50% more attractive to have the N-countries join than the N-countries would find it advantageous to join. In other words, our theoretical model stands confirmed: those who have the largest incentive to join are the least acceptable, and those who might not wish to join are the most welcome. However, what our theoretical model did not show is the extent to which ordinary market rigidities, or the lack of structural reform, can affect the incentives to join a single currency zone. Net benefits do not appear until the degree of flexibility has gone past the 40% mark (only half of any unemployment problem can be cured by wage flexibility or migration: table 13.3, columns 6 and 7). And for the N-countries, we need this flexibility index to rise above 70–90%. To put these numbers in perspective, the 90% figure for the UK in table 13.3 would mean absorbing roughly twice as many emigrants from the EU as it has actually done in the past two decades; or establishing the wage flexibility to create an equivalent number of jobs (2.7 million) over the same period.

6   Conclusions

This chapter suggests that the interests and incentives for the countries in northern Europe (Sweden, Denmark and the UK), and for the countries in central and eastern Europe (Poland, Hungary, the Czech Republic, the Baltic states etc.), to join the EMU may be very different, as are the incentives for the existing union to admit new members from either camp.

The bottom line is that it all turns on the degree of labour market flexibility, hence labour market reform, both in and out of the union. The existing union will be pleased to have the larger, more flexible N-countries join – but that is unlikely to make the N-countries want to join, or the existing members wish to reform. Conversely, the existing union would be less enthusiastic to have the smaller, less reformed, E-countries join, whereas these E-countries would be keener to join. But the interesting new result here is to see how severely market inflexibilities can affect the incentives to join, and the incentives to reform. That is important information which has not been available before.

In this chapter, we have restricted ourselves to identifying where reforms need to happen, and how far they matter, and whether there are any natural incentives within the system for them to happen. That done, our approach needs to be extended in several directions.

First, the reforms modelled here are imposed exogenously, and a more sophisticated approach would be to define the reforms in terms of the development of the model's endogenous variables. Second, the model is solved for a single period. Within a dynamic setting, however, we would also be able to study when the reforms would happen, and it would be useful to distinguish between the alterations in the scope for short-run stabilisation outcomes resulting from being 'in' or 'out', and the longer run changes in output capacity, wages/prices and trade that would follow. Third, a natural extension of that would be to include costs of reform, in order to see if the short-run costs might outweigh the longerterm (and perhaps more uncertain) benefits of labour market reform.

REFERENCES

Alesina, A. and V. Grilli, 1993, 'On the Feasibility of a One- or Multispeed European Monetary Union', *Economics and Politics* 5, 145–66.

Andersen, T. M., N. Haldrup and J. R. Sørensen, 2000, 'Labour Market Implications of EU Product Market Integration', *Economic Policy* 30, 107–33.

Bayoumi, T., 1994, 'A Formal Model of Optimum Currency Areas', *IMF Staff Papers* 44, 537–54.

Beetsma, R. and H. Jensen, 1999, 'Structural Convergence under Reversible and Irreversible Monetary Unification', CEPR Discussion Paper no. 2292; available at http://www.cepr.org/Pubs/new-dps/dplist.asp?dpno = 2116.

Blanchard, O. and D. Quah, 1989, 'The Dynamic Effects of Aggregate Demand and Aggregate Supply Shocks', *American Economic Review* 79, 655–73.

Bruno, M., 1986, 'Aggregate Supply and Demand Factors in OECD Unemployment: An Update', *Economica* 53, S35–S52.

Calmfors, L., 1998, 'Macroeconomic Policy, Wage Setting and Employment: What Difference Does the EMU Make?', *Oxford Review of Economic Policy* 14, 125–51.

2001, 'Unemployment, Labour-Market Reform and Monetary Union', *Journal of Labor Economics* 19, 265–89.

Delors Report, 1989, 'Report on Economic and Monetary Union', Committee for the Study of Economic and Monetary Union, Luxembourg.

Demertzis, M., A. Hughes Hallett and O. Rummel, 1998, 'Is a 2-Speed System the Answer to the Conflict between the German and Anglo-Saxon Models of Monetary Control?', in S. Black and M. Moersch (eds.), *Competition and Convergence in Financial Markets: The German and Anglo-American Models*, New York: Elsevier.

European Commission, 1990, *One Market – One Money*, European Economy Series, 44, Luxembourg: EC Official Publications.

Frankel, J. A. and A. K. Rose, 1998, 'The Endogeneity of the Optimum Currency Area Criterion', *Economic Journal* 108, 1009–25.

Hansen, J. D., 2001, *European Integration: An Economic Perspective*, Oxford: Oxford University Press.

Hughes Hallett, A. and L. Piscitelli, 2002, 'Does Trade Cause Convergence?', *Economics Letters* 75, 165–70.

Hughes Hallett, A. and N. Viegi, 2003, 'Labour Market Reform and the Effectiveness of Monetary Policy in EMU', forthcoming, *Journal of Economic Integration*.

Kaminski, B., Z. Wang and L. A. Winters, 1996, 'Export Performance in Transition Economies', *Economic Policy* 23, 423–42.

Koedijk, K. and J. Kremers, 1996, 'Market Opening, Regulation and Growth in Europe', *Economic Policy* 23, 445–67.

Ozkan, F. G., A. Sibert and A. Sutherland, 2000, 'Monetary Union, Entry Conditions and Economic Reform', EPRU Working Paper no. 2000–03.

Sibert, A., 1999, 'Monetary Integration and Economic Reform', *Economic Journal* 109, 78–92.

Sibert, A. and A. Sutherland, 2000, 'Monetary Regimes and Labour Market Reform', *Journal of International Economics* 51, 421–35.

Index